PUBLISHED by PARABLES
Earthly Stories with a Heavenly Meaning

Randall J. Brewer

JESUS
A MAN LIKE NO OTHER
BY
RANDALL J. BREWER

PUBLISHED by PARABLES
Earthly Stories with a Heavenly Meaning

Randall J. Brewer

Jesus: A Man Like No Other
Randall J. Brewer

Published By Parables
March, 2019

All Rights Reserved. No part of this book may be reproduced or utilized in any form or by any means, electronic or mechanical, including photocopying, recording, or by any information storage and retrieval system, without permission in writing from the author.

    ISBN 978-1-945698-99-6
    Printed in the United States of America

Readers should be aware that Internet Web sites offered as citations and/or sources for further information may have been changed or disappeared between the time this was written and the time it is read.

JESUS

A Man Like No Other
By
Randall J. Brewer

PUBLISHED by PARABLES
Earthly Stories with a Heavenly Meaning

Randall J. Brewer

"There is no one holy like the LORD; There is no one besides You;
There is no Rock like our God" (1 Samuel 2:2).

Randall J. Brewer

-1-

"A MAN LIKE NO OTHER"

The Bible is a book about salvation for that is its central theme from Genesis to Revelation. The Old Testament law told people how to be saved but Jesus came to fulfill the law (Matt. 5:17) and show people how to be saved. In His own words Jesus said "the Son of Man has come to seek and to save that which was lost" (Luke 19:10). Because all have sinned and fall short of the glory of God (Rom. 3:23), and since sinners cannot save themselves, God in all His mercy came up with a plan by which He could forgive people of all their sins. In order to satisfy His holy justice, a payment for sin had to be made. For that to happen, a substitute had to be found who could pay the price for sin and suffer the penalty reserved for those who willfully turn their backs on God. Because of His deep love for all people, the Father chose His only begotten Son to be this substitute. Jesus then came into the world in human flesh for the purpose of bearing the wrath of God and dying in the place of sinners. This was His mission, to become the One person people turned to that would cause God the Father to open up the fountain of forgiveness to those who believed in Him.

There is no scripture as overwhelming and heartfelt as what Jesus said in Matt. 20:28 (NLT), "For even the Son of Man came not to be served but to serve others and to give His life as a ransom for many." Jesus demonstrated His love by serving others and then gives His followers the command to go do likewise (Luke 10:37). He showed people how to love through His own words and actions and ultimately gave His life out of love for those who were yet sinners. It was this type of love that conquered the power of sin and death. The life of Jesus clearly reveals how much God loves you. 1 John 4:8 says "God is love" which means that when Jesus was born, love became a man. He was a man like no other for He reached out to the lowly and to those trapped in the bondage of sin. He came to meet the physical and spiritual needs of people and to give godly instructions on how to live a sin-free life. He was "the light of the world" (John 8:12) for He came to cast away the darkness of sin and ignorance. In Jesus your life will brighten up for His love brings life in abundance to anyone who will receive it.

Who was Jesus and why did He come to the earth? In Gen. 3:15 He is referred to as the "seed of the woman, He who will bruise the serpent's head." He is the suffering Servant who was wounded for your transgressions and bruised for your iniquities. He is the true Lamb of God who takes away the sins of the world. As the Emmaus road disciples said, Jesus of Nazareth "was a Prophet mighty in deed and word before God and all the people" (Luke 24:19). This is who Jesus was but who better to tell you why He came than the Lord Himself? Jesus had been ministering for almost a year when He traveled north to His hometown of Nazareth. He went into the synagogue as was His custom on the Sabbath and began to read from the book of Isaiah, "The Spirit of the Lord is upon Me, because He has anointed Me to preach the gospel to the poor. He has sent Me to heal the brokenhearted, to preach deliverance to the captives and recovery of sight to the blind, to set at liberty those who are oppressed, to preach the acceptable year of the Lord" (Luke 4:18,19). He then sat down and began to say to them, "Today this Scripture is fulfilled in your hearing" (vs. 21).

This was an unusual Sabbath because on this day the young man known to the gathering crowd as the son of the carpenter now revealed Himself to be the long-awaited Messiah. Jesus said He came to preach "the acceptable year of the Lord" which refers to the day when God's favor and His reign would break forth and the poor would be lifted up, the oppressed set free, forgiveness granted, debts paid off, and slaves released from captivity. The Lord's concern was for the wounded and lonely, the lost and rejected. His heart went out to those living in poverty and those whose hearts were broken beyond repair. It was time for what most deemed acceptable to come to an end. Jesus was saying the time of being complacent is now over. The Messiah is here and it is now time for the devil's reign on earth to end. What Jesus read here framed His entire ministry from beginning to end. When He finished reading He told the crowd of people that the time for which the faithful people of God have waited generations for had finally come.

Jesus is the same yesterday, today, and forever and the same ministry He had back then is the same ministry He has today. Recorded here are the foundational ministries of Jesus. The word "gospel" means 'good news' and Jesus taught His followers that salvation could be theirs by grace through faith. Christianity is different from every other religion in the world in that it is the only religion where you don't have to work to get to heaven. You don't have to become a suicide bomber and you don't have to be on your knees for hours on end with a set of prayer beads in your hand. No, you are saved by grace through faith because Jesus suffered and died on your behalf. Jesus came to preach the good news to the poor. The Greek word for "poor" is "ptochos" and is from a verb that means 'to cringe; to shrink back; to cower.' It is a word that refers to a beggar, someone who cringes in the shadows. It was used to refer to a person in total destitution, a person without hope who crouched somewhere in a corner begging.

The people identified as being poor are those who are spiritually impoverished and living in abject poverty and privation. They have reached the point of utter and total bankruptcy of all resources. On the surface many people may be rich and in good physical health thinking they have the freedom to express themselves any way they may choose. They may think they're on top of the world but no matter how well people appear to be, apart from the salvation that Christ alone brings, they are all poor, they are prisoners, they are blind, and they are oppressed. Ps. 107:4,5 says, "They wandered in the wilderness in a desperate way; They found no city to dwell in. Hungry and thirsty, their soul fainted in them." This is the condition of every sinner. They are morally bankrupt in spite of all their earthly treasures. The good news is that the Messiah is here and in Him is life eternal. He said in Is. 66:2 (NIV), "These are the ones I look on with favor: those who are humble and contrite in spirit, and who tremble at My word."

Jesus came to preach deliverance to the captives, to those held in bondage by the enemy and their own fleshly appetites. There is probably nothing more true of sinners today than that they think they are free to do whatever it is they want to do. These people are not free, they are spiritual prisoners who are in spiritual bondage. Jesus said in John 8:34, "Most assuredly I say to you, whoever commits sin is a slave to sin." Sinners are prisoners by virtue of their sin and they are doomed to die "for the wages of sin is death" (Rom. 6:23). Ps. 107:10-12 says, "Those who sat in darkness and in the shadow of death, bound in affliction and irons. Because they rebelled against the words of God, and despised the counsel of the Most High, therefore He brought down their heart with labor; They fell down, and there was none to help." The only hope, of course, is the Messiah who came to free the captives from the dungeon of sin and death. Ps. 79:11 (NLT) says, "Listen to the moaning of the prisoners. Demonstrate Your great power by saving those condemned to die."

The coming of the Messiah stands as the defining moment by which modern time is measured. His coming is the key event in world history for He ordained and offered a message of forgiveness and salvation. He came "to give knowledge of salvation to His people by the remission of their sins" (Luke 1:77). It is forgiveness that sets the prisoners of sin free and the only reason you can be forgiven is because Jesus took the penalty. He said in John 8:36, "Therefore if the Son makes you free, you shall be freed indeed." Jesus is a man like no other and He came to deliver people from demonic influence. Demons are real and very active in the world today. There are spirits of unforgiveness, bitterness, and resentment that hinder the lives of born again believers each and every day. Jesus has the Name that is above every name (Phil. 2:9) and that includes the names of anger, hate, envy, pride, and lust. There is no power of the enemy that Jesus can't deliver you from. Jesus came to the poor, the oppressed, and the captives to set them free. Eph. 5:8 says, "For you were once darkness, but now you are light in the Lord. Walk as children of light."

Jesus also came to heal people. He opened the eyes of the blind and caused the lame to rise up and walk. Acts 10:38 says God "anointed Jesus of Nazareth with the Holy Spirit and with power, who went about doing good and healing all who were oppressed by the devil, for God was with Him." Jesus came to bring physical healing and He also came to bring inner healing. He heals the brokenhearted, those who have been hurt and bruised emotionally. He is a friend to those who are helpless and in deep despair and He undertakes the cause of the downtrodden. Ps. 10:14 (NIV) says, "But You, God, see the trouble of the afflicted; You consider their grief and take it in hand. The victims commit themselves to You; You are the helper of the fatherless." He came to set free those who are overwhelmed by the pain of life, those in abusive relationships and those engulfed by poverty, sickness, and disease. He came to bring joy to the depressed person who has no hope of ever being happy again. He said in Matt. 11:28,29, "Come to Me, all you who labor and are heavy laden, and I will give you rest. Take My yoke upon you and learn from Me, for I am gentle and lowly in heart, and you will find rest for your souls."

Jesus is the God of all comfort and He doesn't help people cope with their problems, He came to take the problems away. There is a law in the Old Testament that tells people what to do when they went to the temple of God. Ezek. 46:9 says, "Whoever enters by way of the south gate shall go out by way of the north gate. He shall not return by way of the gate through which he came, but shall go out through the opposite gate." This was more than a lesson on logistics or directions of travel. This is God's way of telling you that when you come into His presence, you will never leave the same way you came in. Col. 1:13 says, "He has delivered us from the power of darkness and translated us into the kingdom of the Son of His love." In His presence you will be transformed. You will enter one way and leave a changed person. If you enter His presence in deep depression and anxiety, you will leave in peace and have joy unspeakable. If you enter His presence with your body riddled with sickness and disease, you will leave strong and in divine health. The Lord who spoke the stars into existence will speak into your life and you will never be the same.

Ps. 31:19 (NLT) says, "How great is the goodness You have stored up for those who fear You. You lavish it on those who come to You for protection, blessing them before the watching world." Jesus announcing who He was and what He came to do should have been a day of great celebration but even He said in Luke 4:24, "Assuredly, I say to you, no prophet is accepted in his own country." The people in that synagogue knew that the Messiah would one day come into their midst bringing with Him the kingdom of God and the age of salvation. The Jews had been waiting centuries for the Messiah to come and it was a common occurrence for them to read about this glorious event in their Sabbath gatherings. Then the day came when Jesus stood up and proclaimed that the promised Messiah is here and that salvation has arrived. He said, "No longer do you have to wait for the Messiah to come. He is here now. I who stand before you am your Savior and Messiah. I am the fulfillment of these prophecies." What Jesus said was too much for the crowd to bear and they were filled with great wrath.

Instead of giving their much anticipated Messiah praise and honor, the people in their rage "rose up and thrust Him out of the city; and they led Him to the brow of the hill on which the city was built, that they might throw Him down over the cliff" (Luke 4:29). Now was not the Lord's time to die and He passed through the midst of the people and went His way. The problem that day is the people didn't know Jesus for who He truly was. Standing before them was love manifested in the flesh. He was clothed with honor and majesty (Ps. 104:1) and He wrapped Himself in a cloak of divine passion (Is. 59:17). He was merciful, tender-hearted, and full of compassion. Luke 1:79 says He came "to give light to those who sit in darkness and the shadow of death, to guide our feet into the way of peace." Jesus was a man like no other yet He knew the pain of rejection and the struggles of temptation. He is wonderful and to know Him is to love Him. The question is, how well do you know Jesus? The Bible teaches that He is all things to all people and you need to ask yourself who He is to you.

There are not a lot of Bible verses about Jesus before He began His earthly ministry but one thing that is known for sure is that He was a carpenter (Mark 6:3). The Greek word for this occupation means "builder" and this is precisely what the ministry of Jesus is all about. He framed the worlds with the power of His words (Heb. 11:3) and He framed you when you were in your mother's womb (Ps. 139:15). Jesus was a builder in eternity past, He was a builder when He walked the earth, and He is still a builder today. Like all builders, He has a plan and a blueprint for your life and He is forever endeavoring to mold and shape you into His image. Jer. 29:11 (NLT) says, "'For I know the plans I have for you,' says the Lord. 'They are plans for good and not for disaster, to give you a future and a hope.'" It matters not what your past looks like. Jesus is a master builder and He always sees the end from the beginning. He sees the person you're about to become, not the person you once were. 2 Cor. 5:17 says, "Therefore, if anyone is in Christ, he is a new creature; old things have passed away; behold, all things become new."

Anyone who allows Jesus to be the builder of their life always gets a fresh start. The old life is gone, a new life blossoms. If you have not given your life to Jesus, don't put it off any longer. Do it right now, do it today. Jesus is still a builder and 2 Cor. 6:2 (NLT) says, "For God says, 'At just the right time, I heard you. On the day of salvation, I helped you.' Indeed, the 'right time' is now. Today is the day of salvation." The Message Bible says, "Well, now is the right time to listen, the day to be helped. Don't put it off; don't frustrate God's work by showing up late." Always remember that God is the God of today. He said in Deut. 11:13 that you are to "diligently obey My commandments which I command you today, to love the Lord your God and serve Him with all your heart and with all your soul." Your future, along with all its consequences, is determined by what you do with your life today. Jesus wants to build something special in your life today. Not tomorrow, today. Will you allow Him to do so? Your answer determines what the rest of your life will be like. Just remember that those who wait until tomorrow usually die today.

James 4:8 says, "Draw near to God and He will draw near to you." What this verse is saying is that God responds to the decisions you make. Will you welcome the Messiah with opened arms or will you seek to throw Him off a cliff like they did so many years ago? When you make the right choice, God will respond to you in a special way. Deut. 26:17-19 says, "Today you have proclaimed the Lord to be your God, and that you will walk in His ways and keep His statutes, His commandments, and His judgments, and that you will obey His voice. Also, today the Lord has proclaimed you to be His special people, just as He has promised you, that you should keep all His commandments, and that He will set you high above all nations which He has made, in praise, in name, and in honor, and that you may be a holy people to the Lord your God, just as He has spoken." What these verses are saying is that if you will make a commitment to God today, today He will make a commitment to you. When you say "yes," God says "yes." When you draw near to God, He will draw near to you. There is nothing in life that is as rewarding or as exciting as that.

Is Jesus the builder of your life? If so, are you allowing Him to use you as material in the building of His kingdom? 1 Peter 2:5 says, "You also, as living stones, are being built up a spiritual house, a holy priesthood, to offer up spiritual sacrifices acceptable to God through Jesus Christ." Don't waste your life on the pursuit of financial gain just so you can retire early and play golf every day. Life has more meaning than that. The Message Bible says, "Present yourselves as building stones for the construction of a sanctuary vibrant with life, in which you'll serve as holy priests offering Christ-approved lives up to God." The foundation of God's kingdom is Jesus and the living stones are believers who come to Jesus and place their lives upon this rock solid foundation. You are a living stone and if you don't do what you're told to do today, the building process abruptly stops. Problems arise when people try to build their lives their own way and not God's way. God accepts no person who refuses to become a part of His blueprint. Jesus is a builder and He is the only foundation upon which all living stones can be built.

Heb. 3:1 says you are "partakers of the heavenly calling." This means that all living stones are bound for heaven. They are partakers of the call and are of the household of God. Know for sure that Jesus is also the builder of tomorrow. Not only does He want to build something for you today, He also wants to build something for your children, your grandchildren, and all future generations. But it all starts with you and it all starts today. Ps. 95:7 (NLT) says, "For He is our God. We are the people He watches over, the flock under His care. If only you would listen to His voice today!" Today is the most important day for you to hear God's voice. Today is the day you stop fortune and fame from being the foundation you build your life on. Today is the day you stop trying to be your own god, the day you stop serving your own desires, the day you stop making your own decisions. Jesus is standing beside you as the Messiah, as love manifested in the flesh. He is saying to you, "Come, follow me." He loves you so much that He laid down His life for you. He bled for you and He died for you. Can't you at least live your life for Him?

The biggest desire in the heart of Jesus is that He wants to have a close relationship with you. It is oftentimes easier to relate to another person when they've gone through the same experiences you've gone through. This is what makes Jesus coming to the earth so wonderful. He was born a human and He lived as a human. He knows what it's like to go through the same things you're going through. Why is this so important? Heb. 2:17,18 (NLT) says, "Therefore, it was necessary for Him to be made in every respect like us, His brothers and sisters, so that He could be our merciful and faithful High Priest before God. Then He could offer a sacrifice that would take away the sins of the people. Since He Himself has gone through suffering and testing, He is able to help us when we are being tempted." Jesus has been where you currently are and is therefore able to help you in your dilemma. He can sympathize with your weaknesses and "was in all points tempted as we are, yet without sin. Let us therefore come boldly to the throne of grace, that we may obtain mercy and find grace to help in time of need" (Heb. 4:15,16).

Jesus is sitting on a throne of grace because He was tempted with the same things you are. Because He lived as a human, He knew what it was like to be hungry, thirsty, and tired. He knew what it was like to be mocked, ridiculed, and betrayed by friends. From the start of His ministry to the very end, the devil used all his influence and strategies to get Jesus to sin. Jesus knows what it's like to be you and when you come to the throne of grace He won't belittle you but instead will welcome you as a father welcomes his children to his side to protect them from the dangers of life. In His loving arms you will receive mercy and find grace to help in time of need. What a wonderful promise! You won't be scolded for having a need and you won't be told your need is too trivial. No, Jesus will comfort you and wipe away all your tears. Jesus knows the battle you're in because He was in the same battle. He fought it all the way to the end and defeated the enemy every time. He knows what to do so when you come to the throne of grace He'll take you by the hand and lead you in the way you should go.

There is nothing you're going through that Jesus does not understand. He grew up in a huge family with several brothers and sisters and He knows the problems that come with relationships among siblings. Once, during a time of ministry, Mark 3:20,21 (NLT) says, "One time Jesus entered a house, and the crowds began to gather again. Soon He and His disciples couldn't even find time to eat. When His family heard what was happening, they tried to take Him away. 'He's out of His mind,' they said." Jesus knows what it's like to be single and since the church is His bride, He knows what it's like to have an unfaithful spouse. All believers are children of God and Jesus knows what it's like to have disobedient children. There is no type of relationship that Jesus does not understand. He had friends turn their backs on Him when He needed them most. He even had a close friend deny Him three times and another friend who betrayed Him into the hands of the enemy. Because of all this, there is nothing going on in your life and your relationships that you can't talk to Him about.

Jesus also knows what it's like to work and toil under the sweat of His brow. Jewish history records that the male child usually starts working with their father at age twelve. This means that Jesus travailed under a hot sun as a carpenter for eighteen years. He had calluses on His feet and blisters on His hands. He had skin burned red by the blazing sun and muscles that ached so bad that He couldn't work any longer. He was in the work force longer than He was in the ministry. Are you having trouble on your job? Jesus understands what you're going through. Working as a carpenter prepared Jesus for His ministry for He would spend three years working with people who were broken. He knew how to fix things on His job and He knew how to fix broken people in His ministry. Jesus can fix broken relationships or lost opportunities or the death of a loved one. You can trust Jesus knowing that He can fix your broken life. He is the only One who can put your life back together again. He is standing at the door of your heart waiting to be invited into your disaster zone. Invite Him in today.

As a human there was nothing Jesus understood more than pain and this is why you can go to Him anytime, anywhere. He suffered emotional pain as well as physical pain. Is. 53:3 says, "He is despised and rejected by men, a Man of sorrows and acquainted with grief." The Message Bible says, "He was looked down on and passed over, a man who suffered, who knew pain firsthand. One look at Him and people turned away. We looked down on Him, thought He was scum." Vs. 5 says, "He was wounded for our transgressions, He was bruised for our iniquities." At the cross He was mocked and ridiculed and was tortured until He died. Yes, Jesus understands pain. In His life He even felt the sting of death. History records that in His third year of ministry His step-father Joseph passed away. We know Joseph died before the Lord's crucifixion because on the cross Jesus told John to take care of His mother. He would not have done this if Joseph had been alive. Jesus also could have raised Joseph from the dead but He didn't. Why? Because He needed to experience the death of a loved one so He could be a merciful and sympathetic High Priest. Indeed, He was a man like no other.

Randall J. Brewer

-2-

"A SERVANT TO ALL"

The life of Jesus changed the course of human history. He came to earth as a man but was not what the religious leaders at that time were expecting. Roman law ruled in that day and historians say Rome was the most status conscious society of that time. These people were obsessed with climbing the social ladder and rank-and-file was everything to them. Your status gave you certain rights and privileges that others did not have. You could buy things others couldn't buy and go places other people couldn't go. James and John once asked Jesus, "Grant us that we may sit, one on Your right hand and the other on Your left, in Your glory" (Mark 10:37). They weren't looking to be close to Jesus, they were seeking positions of status and honor. They wanted the glory of sitting on a throne with Jesus. Back then where you sat defined who you were and for this reason the religious leaders were anticipating a warrior king who would rule and reign with great power and authority. Instead, they were introduced to a man with humble beginnings who came to be a servant to all.

In Roman culture everybody wanted to be a celebrity. Everybody wanted to be famous and everybody wanted to be great. Little were they prepared for the message Jesus came to give. He said in Matt. 20:25-28 (MSG), "You've observed how godless rulers throw their weight around, how quickly a little power goes to their heads. It's not going to be that way with you. Whoever wants to be great must become a servant. Whoever wants to be first among you must be your slave. That is what the Son of Man has done. He came to serve, not be served, and then to give away His life in exchange for the many who are held hostage." To be great in God's kingdom you've got to lay aside your rights as a Roman citizen. Paul was from Rome (Acts 16:37) yet he allowed himself to be beaten and thrown into prison for preaching the gospel message. He humbled himself and took the beating that was put upon him. He was criticized and ridiculed because he said Jesus was Lord and not Caesar. As a Roman citizen he could have avoided all that pain yet he chose instead to be identified with Christ rather than the city of Rome.

It was in prison that Paul wrote about the greatest servant of all, the Lord Jesus Christ. Phil. 2:7,8 says Jesus "made Himself of no reputation, taking the form of a servant, and coming in the likeness of men. And being found in appearance as a man, He humbled Himself and became obedient to the point of death, even the death on the cross." The Message Bible says, "It was an incredibly humbling process. He didn't claim special privileges. Instead, He lived a selfless life and then died a selfless, obedient death." Not long before this Jesus was seated at the right hand of the Father, the highest place of honor in all the universe. Now here He was, naked and bleeding on a cross between two thieves. He did this not because He came to be served but that He came to be a servant to all. He left the glorious splendor of heaven and wrapped Himself in humanity so He could know and experience everything you go through. He took on the nature of man so He could become just like you. He laid down His ability to determine His future and put His entire existence in the hands of the Heavenly Father. He then bowed His head and died so that you might have a chance to live.

The message of the cross is the message of the suffering servant. The good news is that Jesus did not have to suffer very long. Three days later He stepped out of that tomb filled with glory and majesty. Still, the message of the servant continues. Jesus came to redefine what status is all about and Paul wrote about this in Phil. 2:3,4, "Let nothing be done through selfish ambition or conceit, but in lowliness of mind let each esteem others better than himself. Let each of you look out not only for his own interests, but also for the interests of others." The Message Bible says, "Put yourself aside, and help others get ahead. Don't be obsessed with getting your own advantage. Forget yourselves long enough to lend a helping hand." This was in stark contrast to the culture that prevailed at that time. Status was everything to the Roman citizen but here was the Son of

God come in the flesh not asserting Himself on these people. No, He humbled Himself and didn't fight for or demand some sense of status and honor. He was a man like no other and He came to the earth to be a servant to all. He didn't climb the ladder of success but instead descended into greatness.

Today the proud and arrogant are looked down upon but during the time of the Romans they were admired and looked up to. Humility was rejected at all costs for to become a servant was an open disgrace. Jesus came and turned the culture of the Romans upside down. The rulers of that day could not fathom and comprehend that the way up is down and the way down is up. James 4:10 says, "Humble yourselves in the sight of the Lord, and He will lift you up." Jesus walked in true humility because He didn't feel the need to impress others and this is what enabled Him to be a servant to all. Jesus knew who He was. John 13:3 (NIV) says, "Jesus knew that the Father had put all things under His power, and that He had come from God and was returning to God." After this verse Jesus then got down on His knees and washed the feet of the disciples. This was humility in action and when finished Jesus said in vs. 15, "For I have given you an example, that you should do as I have done to you." You can do this if you know who you are in Christ. Nothing is beneath you and no one is above you for all people are equal in the eyes of God.

Jesus took the Roman culture and threw it out the window. Phil. 2:7 (NIV) says, "He made Himself nothing by taking the very nature of a servant, being made in human likeness." Jesus left His high status in heaven so He could come to earth as a man and identify with the trials and weaknesses that you deal with on a daily basis. In the eyes of the Romans, Jesus was a slave with no honor and dignity and at the cross their wrath was unleashed on Him. Is. 53:7 (MSG) says, "He was beaten, He was tortured, but He didn't say a word. Like a lamb taken to be slaughtered and like a sheep being sheared, He took it all in silence." As your servant Jesus stood there and took the pain for He knew that "God resists the proud, but gives grace to the humble" (James 4:6). Jesus came to be a servant to all and He wasn't going to let His status as the Son of God stop Him from fulfilling what He came to do. Jesus embraced His submission to the will of the Father and humbled Himself to the point of dying a humiliating death on a cross. To lay down your life for the well-being of another is what being a servant is all about.

The greatest manifestation of strength is to bend your knee to give help to a person in need. The way up is down and this is the lesson Jesus taught by the way He lived His life. He didn't come to be served but to serve and to give His life as a ransom for many. When Jesus was born love became a man and His life was an authentic expression of what love does and says. You were on His mind as He carried that heavy cross up to the hill of Calvary. You were on His mind as the spikes were driven into His hands and His feet. You were on His mind as He breathed His last and said, "It is finished!" And yes, you were on His mind when He walked away from that empty tomb. Because of His humble obedience, the Father "has highly exalted Him and given Him the name which is above every name" (Phil. 2:9). Jesus is once again seated at the right hand of the Father where He is continually interceding on your behalf (Rom. 8:34). He was a servant then and He is still a servant today. Yes, Jesus wants you to serve Him but, more than that, He wants to be a servant to you.

1 Peter 5:7 (NLT) says, "Give all your worries and cares to God, for He cares about you." Jesus is a faithful servant and you can trust Him to take care of all your needs, worries, and concerns. That's what He's there for. Jesus said He would take care of you and it's your responsibility to believe that He will. Peace comes to your heart and mind no other way. Is. 26:3,4 (ESV) says, "You keep him in perfect peace whose mind is stayed on You, because he trusts in You. Trust in the Lord forever, for the Lord God is an everlasting rock." Jesus will bring stability to your life if you will do your part and trust Him to do so. He told you what to do in John 14:1, "Let not your heart be troubled; you believe in God, believe also in Me." Most believers do not have the revelation nor do they believe that it is within their power to determine whether they're troubled or not. The enemy has convinced most Christians that whatever will be, will be. They are troubled because they believe

they are helpless victims to whatever is going on around them. They think the devil is troubling their soul when the truth is they're doing it to themselves.

Believers need mind renewal because they're convinced it can't be helped if they're troubled or not. Apparently Jesus did not know that because He told you specifically to let not your heart be troubled. Therefore, if your heart is troubled and upset, it's because you let it be troubled and upset. There's no other explanation. The question to be asked is how can a person be upset if they truly believe that Jesus came to be a servant to all? Faith in that fact alone gives you the power that will set you free. Take a stand today and refuse to let your heart be troubled. Believe that Jesus is the Good Shepherd who restores your soul and leads you beside the still waters. He said in John 10:11, "I am the good shepherd. The good shepherd gives His life for the sheep." He says again in vs. 14, "I am the good shepherd; and I know My sheep, and am known by My sheep." A good shepherd always gives what the sheep under his care need to live a good life. In the days of Jesus the Jewish people wanted a political leader but they needed a Savior who would be a servant to all.

Every Christian life should be characterized with contentment and peace and it's the Good Shepherd who provides them for you. Ps. 23:2 says, "He makes me to lie down in green pastures; He leads me beside the still waters." Green pastures symbolize contentment and still waters represent peace. The Message Bible says, "You have bedded me down in lush meadows, You find me quiet pools to drink from." God designed you to rest in Him because when you do that your heart will not be troubled. As you lie down in peaceful slumber He will restore your mind, will, and emotions. An anointed calm comes over you and you just know that you know everything is going to be okay. Rom. 8:28 (NLT) says, "And we know that God causes everything to work together for the good of those who love God and are called according to His purpose for them." The thing to learn about shepherds is that they don't drive the sheep by getting behind them and pushing them forward. No, he gets in front of them and leads them in the way they should go.

Jesus said in John 10:27, "My sheep hear My voice, and I know them, and they follow Me."

Here's where life gets interesting. Shepherds don't care for their sheep in the city but rather out in the wilderness which at times can be a place of barrenness, isolation, and despondency. David wrote in Ps. 23:4, "Yea, though I walk through the valley of the shadow of death, I will fear no evil; For You are with me; Your rod and Your staff, they comfort me." If the shepherd is leading the sheep, then this means he led them into this wilderness valley. In the New Testament wasn't it Jesus who got into a boat with His disciples and told them to cross over to the other side of the lake (Luke 8:22)? And wasn't it on this journey that a mighty storm arose and the disciples feared for their lives? These men went where Jesus told them to go yet they found themselves in the midst of a raging tempest. Also, Matt. 4:1 says the Spirit led Jesus into the wilderness to be tempted by the devil. What's going on here? People tend to avoid wilderness experiences at all costs but could it be that this is the very place Jesus wants you to be? After all, He led you there, didn't He?

The wilderness is not a bad place to be if Jesus is there at your side. It can be a place of excitement because encounters with the Lord can happen in very unique ways. It was on the back side of the desert that Moses met God at a burning bush. His wilderness experience changed the course of history forever and possibly yours may also. The good news is that it's in the wilderness of your heart that you'll experience total and complete dependency on God and that's the way it should be. The Lord never promised you an easy life but He did say you could have a victorious life if you would just trust in Him. Prov. 3:5,6 says, "Trust in the Lord with all your heart, and lean not on your own understanding. In all your ways acknowledge Him, and He shall direct your paths." Understand that there will be times when God wants to prepare you to face new challenges or maybe comfort you to face new realities. To do that He's got to take you away from all the noise and activity of city life and take you to a place where it's just you and Him. That place is the wilderness and what happens there can be the defining moment that will change your life forever.

Is. 40:3 (NLT) says, "Listen! It's the voice of someone shouting, 'Clear the way through the wilderness for the Lord! Make a straight highway through the wasteland for our God!'" The NIV says, "In the wilderness prepare the way for the Lord." God will meet you in the wilderness but first you must prepare your heart in order for this to happen. Examine your life and prepare yourself for all the things God is about to say and do. Meeting God is not a casual thing and you show Him reverence by getting ready for this divine encounter. This is not always a joyous thing to do but it must be done anyway. The garden of Gethsemane was where Jesus had His second wilderness experience and it was the most trying moment of His life. It was here that He walked through the valley of the shadow of death. He was in agony over what He was about to go through and in that garden He prepared Himself to be the sacrificial lamb sent to be slaughtered as an offering for all the sin of mankind. He said in Matt. 26:39, "O My Father, if it is possible, let this cup pass from Me; nevertheless, not as I will, but as You will." That was His defining moment.

The wilderness is a place where you bare all your feelings and get honest with God. Jesus came right out and said He didn't want to be separated from the Father because of all the sin He was about to carry. The children of Israel complained about the manna they were forced to eat and in the wilderness Moses got honest and said to God, "I cannot carry all these people by myself; the burden is too heavy for me" (Num. 11:14 NIV). Is this how you sometimes feel? If so, then the wilderness is the place to say it. Get real with God and tell Him your deepest thoughts. Don't pretend everything is okay when it isn't. You may not realize it but what's happening is that you are preparing yourself to hear from Him. Some people just can't listen until they first express that which they want to say. That's okay because Jesus is a good listener. 1 Peter 3:12 says, "For the eyes of the Lord are on the righteous, and His ears are open to their prayers." Ps. 66:19,20 also says, "But certainly God has heard me; He has attended to the voice of my prayer. Blessed be God, who has not turned away my prayer, nor His mercy from me!"

God will listen to you as you prepare your heart to listen to Him. He is a true gentleman and He won't interrupt you with a voice that sounds like thunder and lightning. No, He speaks in a gentle whisper and this is why you must be still and know that He is God (Ps. 46:10). To be still means to be silent. God listened to you, now give Him reverence and listen to Him. Indeed, silence is golden for it's when you stop talking that you will hear His "still small voice" (1 Kings 19:12). He speaks in the silence of your heart and this is why James 1:19 says, "Let every man be swift to hear, slow to speak, slow to wrath." Jesus said in Mark 4:9, "He who has ears to hear, let him hear!" The NLT says, "Anyone with ears to hear should listen and understand." Get rid of all the excess noise in your life. Some people all they want to do is talk, talk, talk and these are the ones who never hear God speak. Walk away from endless chatter and go off into the wilderness where you can be alone with God. It is there that you will hear His silent whisper. It is there that you will know He is God.

Jesus came to the earth to be a servant to all and He is the ultimate servant leader. This means that He leads by serving and serves by leading. He is the Good Shepherd and He leads you in the path you should go. Everybody at one time or another had their own personal plans for their life and, quite frankly, the majority of those plans rarely, if ever, came to fruition. In fact, many times the exact opposite occurs. Nobody plans to lose their job, get cancer, have a broken marriage, or have a loved one pass away at a young age. What does a person do when life doesn't go the way they planned it to go? The answer is simple. You go to the wilderness and get God's plan for your life. Go to Him and say, "Not my will but Your will be done." Allow Jesus to take you by the hand and He will lead you to Jer. 29:11 that says, "For I know the thoughts that I think toward you, says the Lord, thoughts of peace and not of evil, to give you a future and a hope." The NIV says, "For I know the plans I have for you," declares the Lord, "plans to prosper you and not to harm you, plans to give you hope and a future."

To receive God's plan for your life you must step aside from a world that is spinning out of control and get alone with God. The wilderness is a place of isolation so don't be surprised if this is the place Jesus takes you to. In Mark 6 Jesus sent the disciples off on a mission to preach the Word, cast out demons, and heal the sick. It was a busy time filled with much activity and when they came back they "gathered around Jesus and reported to Him all they had done and taught. Then, because so many people were coming that they did not even have a chance to eat, He said to them, 'Come with me by yourselves to a quiet place and get some rest.' So they went away by themselves in a boat to a solitary place" (vs. 30-32 NIV). Shortly after this Jesus fed a great multitude with five loaves of bread and two fish. After everybody was filled and satisfied Jesus sent the people away. Vs. 46 then says, "And when He had sent them away, He departed to the mountain to pray." Jesus is serving you by giving you a pattern on how to live your life. In the course of a busy life you must always take time to be alone with God.

If you're too busy to get alone with God, you're too busy and you need to slow down. One of the greatest threats to your spiritual journey is a fast-paced lifestyle that is out of control. People who don't have time for God are those who are in a relentless struggle to do more and more things in less and less time. Their time of isolation with God is non-existent and they're going to pay a heavy price for the chaotic life they're living. They'll lose their family, their friends, and any chance of having a close, personal relationship with Jesus. And then, before you know it, their life is over and they'll have to stand before the throne of God and give an account for what they did and didn't do with their life. What should be a joyous occasion will instead be a time of regret and sorrow and who knows what after that. The rhythm of life that Jesus lived is His way of telling you to slow down and make sure you spend time alone with God. It is no accident that He said in Matt. 11:28 (MSG), "Are you tired? Worn out? Burned out on religion? Come to Me. Get away with Me and you'll recover your life. I'll show you how to take a real rest."

People are just too tense because they've become addicted to a toxic lifestyle. They don't know if they're coming or going and don't know what to do about it. Jesus does. He continued in Matt. 11:29,30, "Take My yoke upon you and learn from Me, for I am gentle and lowly in heart, and you will find rest for your souls. For My yoke is easy and My burden is light." Jesus said to learn from Him. He knew what to say and do because He was always going off by Himself to spend quality time alone with the Father. To be yoked with Jesus is to act like Jesus. His actions determine your actions. The Message Bible says, "Walk with Me and work with Me - watch how I do it. Learn the unforced rhythms of grace. I won't lay anything heavy or ill-fitting on you. Keep company with Me and you'll learn to live freely and lightly." You can't keep company with Jesus if you're always running around like a chicken with its head cut off. Slow down! Be still and know that He is God. Jesus went into the wilderness to pray and you need to go there as well. Follow Him there freely and willingly and enjoy the presence of the Father with Him.

David wrote in Ps. 4:4, "Meditate within your heart on your bed, and be still." The NIV says, "Search your hearts and be silent." God lives in your heart and to rest spiritually you must be silent and meditate on Him. It is during these times of silence that God will reveal Himself to you and give direction for your life. Go to the wilderness and with faith and patience learn to wait on Him. Understand that you don't have to be doing something all the time. Busybodies get no rest and eventually burn out. Resting is simple but sometimes it takes effort to put your flesh down in order to do it. When you rest you're not putting out, you're taking in. You're being still and you are meditating on Jesus. Ps. 63:6 says, "When I remember You on my bed, I meditate on You in the night watches." Put your mind on Jesus and be quiet. It's just you and the Lord. Nothing is more important than Him so don't let your mind wander. If you can rest then you can receive all that God has for you so purpose in your heart to go into the wilderness and find rest for your soul.

You need a wilderness experience for it is there that you give up control of your life. The truth of the matter is that you really don't know how to control your life because, if you did, it wouldn't be out of control in the first place. Life simply isn't going the way you want it to and in the wilderness God will use your disappointment as an opportunity to point you in the direction you should go. Stop being confrontational with God and other people and begin to confront who you are on the inside. Admit to yourself that your way of doing things isn't working. A change is needed and it's in the wilderness where transformation takes place. Rom. 12:2 (MSG) says, "Don't become so well-adjusted to your culture that you fit into it without even thinking. Instead, fix your attention on God. You'll be changed from the inside out. Readily recognize what He wants from you, and quickly respond to it. Unlike the culture around you, always dragging you down to its level of immaturity, God brings the best out of you, develops well-formed maturity in you."

Change is hard but you can rest knowing God has a better plan for your life. In the wilderness God will have your full attention and it is there that He'll give you the confident assurance "that He who has begun a good work in you will complete it until the day of Jesus Christ" (Phil. 1:6). If danger lurks in the wilderness don't worry about it. Jesus is the Good Shepherd and He'll protect you. He'll prepare a table before you in the presence of your enemies (Ps. 23:5). He's by your side in the battle and if the Servant to all is for you, who can be against you? David said, "I will fear no evil; For You are with me; Your rod and Your staff, they comfort me" (Ps. 23:4). The rod and staff were weapons the shepherd used against the wild animals who tried to get the sheep. Knowing the shepherd had these weapons brought David comfort. Sometimes Jesus calms the storm, other times He'll calm you in the midst of the storm. Just understand that the hungry wolves and lions don't fear the sheep, they fear the shepherd watching over the sheep. This is why you need to stay as close to the Shepherd as you possibly can. He's there to serve you. Allow Him to do it.

Randall J. Brewer

-3-

"THE LION OF JUDAH"

Jesus was a gift given to the world by the Heavenly Father and He needs to be received with opened arms and a willing heart. John 3:16 says, "For God so loved the world that He gave His only begotten Son, that whoever believes in Him should not perish but have everlasting life." At one time God walked side by side with Adam in the cool of the evening and life was good and perfect. That glorious relationship was broken when Adam ate of the forbidden fruit and he and his wife was cast out of the garden never to return. Jesus came to restore man's relationship with the Father and He did that by living a sinless life and then by dying a sinner's death. He paid the penalty for the sin of all mankind and Heb. 10:20-22 (NLT) says, "By His death, Jesus opened a new and life-giving way through the curtain into a Most Holy Place. And since we have a great High Priest who rules over God's house, let us go right into the presence of God with sincere hearts, fully trusting Him." The Message Bible says, "The 'curtain' into God's presence is His body."

In the Old Testament there was a veil that stood in front of the Holy of Holies where the presence of God was manifested at the Ark of the Covenant. The writer of Hebrews says the veil in the tabernacle represented the humanity of Jesus. This veil was held up by four pillars and these represent the four gospels. The gospels are four different portraits of the Messiah and you need to read and study each one. Each are written by different types of people from different backgrounds and this is why each gospel in unique in its own way. These stories were written by a tax collector, a man of unknown occupation, a doctor, and a fisherman. Their names were Matthew, Mark, Luke, and John and it is the plan of God that you be changed from the inside out as you behold each of these stories about the Messiah. 2 Cor. 3:18 (MSG) says, "Nothing between us and God, our faces shining with the brightness of His face. And so we are transfigured much like the Messiah, our lives gradually becoming brighter and more beautiful as God enters our lives and we become like Him."

God has put in your hands four gospels that covers everything you need to live a victorious life. Four is the number of ultimate stability and completeness. There are four seasons in a year, four points on a compass, four personality types, and four legs on a table or chair. Four rivers flowed out of the Garden of Eden and there are four living creatures around the throne of God with four different faces. Rev. 4:7 says, "The first living creature was like a lion, the second living creature like an ox, the third living creature had a face like a man, and the fourth living creature was like a flying eagle." John began the book of revelation by saying, "The Revelation of Jesus Christ" (Rev. 1:1) and this means that the four living creatures around the throne is a revelation of who Jesus is. There are four gospels because each one has an emblem of Christ that is represented by these four living creatures. Each gospel corresponds in order to these creatures which means the gospels of Matthew, Mark, Luke, and John are in fact the gospels of the lion, the ox, the man, and the flying eagle.

The symbolism of these four creatures is found throughout the Bible. Rev. 4:6 says these creatures were "around the throne," one each on the north, south, east, and west. The Old Testament tells how the twelve tribes of Israel were camped around the tabernacle of God. There were three tribes on each of the four sides. In each group of three tribes there was a main tribe with the most people that stood out from among the other tribes. The main tribe to the east of the tabernacle was Judah whose emblem was that of a lion. To the west was Ephraim whose emblem was an ox, to the south was Reuben whose emblem was a man, and to the north was the tribe of Dan whose emblem was that of an eagle. God chose to give the four main tribes that surrounded the tabernacle the same emblem as the four living creatures that surround the throne of God. God's throne is in the middle of heaven and the tabernacle sat in the middle of the camp where the glory of God came down. God patterned what was happening at the tabernacle after what was happening in heaven.

It is revealed throughout the entire Bible that God is a God of patterns. When you understand these patterns you can understand the mysteries of God. The four gospels reveal that Jesus was a man with four faces and His divine character was patterned after the faces of the four living creatures. Matthew's gospel corresponds to the first living creature which is a lion and in Rev. 1:5 Jesus is called "the Lion of the tribe of Judah." The lion represents kingship and authority. Jesus said in Matt. 18:18, "Assuredly, I say to you, whatever you bind on earth will be bound in heaven, and whatever you loose on earth will be loosed in heaven." Matt. 1:1 begins by saying, "The book of the genealogy of Jesus Christ, the Son of David, the son of Abraham." He then traces the lineage of Jesus from Abraham down to David, and on through all the kings of Israel. David was a great king and, as a direct descendant of him, Jesus has royal blood flowing through His veins. He is truly "the King of kings and Lord of lords" (Rev. 19:16).

A lion is the king of the beasts and Matthew is the gospel of the King. Only Matthew records the visit of the wise men who came asking, "Where is He who has been born King of the Jews? For we have seen His star in the East and have come to worship Him" (Matt. 2:2). At the end of Matthew when Jesus gave the great commission He said, "All authority has been given to Me in heaven and on earth" (Matt. 28:18). These are the words of a king. The Lion of Judah is the conquering Savior. He breaks every chain and gives you the victory again and again. In the Old Testament Jacob prophesied in Gen. 49:8-10 (NLT), "Judah, your brothers will praise you. You will grasp your enemies by the neck. All your relatives will bow before you. Judah, my son, is a young lion that has finished eating its prey. Like a lion he crouches and lies down; like a lioness - who dares to rouse him? The scepter shall not depart from Judah, nor the ruler's staff from his descendants, until the coming of the One to whom it belongs, the One whom all nations will honor."

Jesus is a King but still He came to the earth to die for the sins of humanity. In the kingdom of man people serve the king, the king don't serve the people. Not so in God's kingdom. Jesus is a King who serves you. In the words of a king there is power (Eccl. 8:9) and Jesus uses that power to cleanse you from all unrighteousness. After the sermon on the mount, Matthew records how Jesus used His power to cleanse the leper, heal the centurion's servant, cast the fever out of Peter's mother-in-law, and calm the raging storm. In Matt. 13 Jesus tells several parables about the kingdom of heaven. Unlike the ancient kings of old, Jesus exercised His power only for good. Also unlike them He willingly passed His power on to others. In Luke 10:19 He said, "Behold, I give you the authority to trample on serpents and scorpions, and over all the power of the enemy, and nothing shall by any means hurt you." Likewise He said in John 14:12, "Most assuredly, I say to you, he who believes in Me, the works that I do he will do also; and greater works than these he will do, because I go to My Father."

The Bible records in Rev. 4:8 that these four living creatures also have six wings. Four is an earthly number and in scripture six is the number representing mankind for God created man on the sixth day of creation. God has these heavenly creatures around His throne yet He assigned to them earthly numbers. Why is that? Because every one of these faces also represent you and the type of life you've been called upon to live. As a follower of Jesus you also must put on these four faces. 1 John 4:17 says, "Because as He is, so are we in this world." Jesus is a conquering lion and so are you. In Christ you've been changed from a nobody to a somebody, from a zero to a hero. In boldness openly declare that the enemy will never dare touch anything that pertains to your world. Like the children of Israel did in Egypt, you'll mark every entrance to your life with the blood of Jesus which speaks on your behalf at all times. As a lion you let the devil know he picked the wrong person to mess with. In Christ Jesus you are more than a conqueror.

God has commanded you to have the spirit of a lion. In scripture a lion always refers to authority, strength, and power. Prov. 30:30 says, "A lion, which is mighty among beasts and does not turn away from any." A lion has tremendous strength and is rightfully called the king of the beasts. He fears no other creature and like a lion you need to "be strong in the Lord and in the power of His might" (Eph. 6:10). God is strong and He wants you to be strong in Him. They say in Africa that a lion's roar can be heard two hours away. When the lion roars all other animals freeze in their tracks or they quickly run away. With the spirit of a lion you're anointed to consistently win battles. In Christ you have the ability to overcome every test and trial. No weapon formed against you shall prosper and when the battle is over you'll still be standing strong. Jesus is the Lion of Judah and when you put on the whole armor of God you'll "be able to withstand in the evil day, and having done all, to stand" (Eph. 6:13). A lion never caves in under pressure no matter what's going on around him.

A lion backs down from nobody and neither do you. When you wake up in the morning, put on your lion face and don't let the devil push you around. It's time for him to be afraid of you instead of you being afraid of him. A lion has strength of will and strength of character. The spirit of a lion is strong for he possesses great courage and determination. 2 Sam. 17:10 talks about "he who is valiant, whose heart is like the heart of a lion." This same verse says David "is a mighty man, and those who are with him are valiant men." Is. 11:1 speaks about the Spirit of might and this is what came upon Samson and the three Hebrew children in the fiery furnace. Gideon was called a "mighty man of valor" (Judges 6:12) and with the spirit of a lion you will be called the same thing. The Spirit of might is a powerful anointing and is needed to fulfill your destiny and to survive here in the last days. It is important that you become and remain strong in the Lord. You will not survive if you don't because demonic activity is increasing on the earth like never before.

Always remember that Jesus is a lion and so are you. Eph. 4:16 (MSG) says, "We take our lead from Christ, who is the source of everything we do. He keeps us in step with each other. His very breath and blood flow through us, nourishing us so that we will grow up healthy in God, robust in love." A lion is fearless and a lion is bold. Prov. 28:1 says, "The wicked flee when no one pursues, but the righteous are bold as a lion." The Message Bible says, "Honest people are relaxed and confident, bold as lions." In order to survive in this world you must be free from all fear. Commit your life to the Lion of Judah and trust Him to take care of you. He is willing and able to stop the enemy from doing harm to you if you will but trust Him to do so. David wrote in Ps. 27:1, "The Lord is my light and my salvation; Whom shall I fear? The Lord is the strength of my life; Of whom shall I be afraid?" Jesus is coming soon and He needs people who are totally fearless to rise up and get people ready for this glorious event.

Lions know no fear and all lions are bold. In both Greek and Hebrew the word "boldness" refers to a person's speech. Acts 19:8 says, "And he went into the synagogue and spoke boldly for three months, reasoning and persuading concerning the things of the kingdom of God." God speaks through people and He wants you to be a person He can roar through. He roars in power and strength and authority. Amos 1:2 says, "The Lord roars from Zion, and utters His voice from Jerusalem." Amos 3:8 says, "A lion has roared! Who will not fear? The Lord God has spoken!" Yes, God does speak in a still, small voice but there are other times when He roars with power and authority. Never speak softly to the devil but with a commanding roar tell him to leave and never return. Without doubt, the church today needs the roar of a lion in its midst. Change happens when a lion roars. Order is restored and direction is given. Is. 5:29 (NLT) says, "They will roar like lions, like the strongest of lions. Growling, they will pounce on their victims and carry them off, and no one will be there to rescue them."

There are so many non-scriptural things happening in the local church today and God needs fearless believers who will stand up boldly and say, "Thus says the Lord!" The church needs strong and decisive leadership. They need lions who are not afraid of the opinions of other people but are willing to speak the truth in love. A lion knows no fear. Nahum 2:11 (ISV) says, "Where is the lion's den? Where is the place where the young lions fed, where the lion and its mate walked with their young, the place where they feared nothing?" Heb. 13:6 says, "So we may boldly say, 'The Lord is my helper; I will not fear. What can man do to me?'" A lion wears a prophetic mantle. He hears the voice of God and he allows the Lord to roar through him. A lion roars as the result of a direct encounter with God and he declares openly that which he has heard. David had the face of a lion when he faced the giant as did Elijah when he faced the prophets of Baal. Don't let the devil push you around. Roar like a lion and say what God tells you to say. The Lion of Judah has prevailed and so shall you.

A lion is territorial. He will guard and protect his territory and will also seek to enlarge that which belongs to him. Jabez cried out to the Lord, "Oh, that you would bless me indeed, and enlarge my territory" (1 Chron. 4:10). Is. 54:2,3 (NET) says, "Make your tent larger, stretch your tent curtains farther out! Spare no effort, lengthen your ropes, and pound your stakes deep. For you will spread out to the right and to the left; your children will conquer nations and will resettle desolate cities." The Message Bible says, "Make your tents large. Spread out! Think big!" A lion will enlarge his territory and he will maintain it as well. He will not allow an outsider to come in and set up camp in his territory. Num. 23:24 (MSG) says, "Look, a people rising to its feet, stretching like a lion, a king-of-the-beasts, aroused, unsleeping, unresting until the hunt is over and it's eaten and drunk its fill." Your home, your church, your city, your place of business, and your destiny is all a part of your territory. Guard it diligently and when the enemy comes knocking at your door, stand up and roar like a lion.

Jesus is the Lion of Judah but He was also a tireless servant represented by the ox and this is the theme of the gospel of Mark. For the most part, servants are unknown to those of prominence in this dark world and this fits in with the fact that Mark was a man of unknown occupation. There is no genealogy of Jesus in this gospel nor is there any mention of His birth. You would not expect either of these in regards to a servant and, appropriately so, Mark's portrayal of Jesus as a servant is the shortest of the four gospels. As you study and meditate on this gospel message you will notice that Mark does not record much teaching. His gospel is all about action and he tells how Jesus was always moving around and serving people all the time. He was busy, busy, busy being the divine Servant that He was. Throughout his gospel Mark used the word "immediately" to describe things that happened. He told how Jesus spoke to the leper and Mark 1:42 says, "Immediately the leprosy left him, and he was cleansed." The nature of a servant is to do things immediately.

An ox is a strong creature. He is more powerful than man yet he serves man with endless labor. He is submissive and surrenders all that he is and all that he has to its master every minute of its life. Jesus was the perfect servant and He said in John 6:38, "For I have come down from heaven, not to do My own will, but the will of Him who sent Me." Jesus gave every moment of His life to His Heavenly Father whose will totally governed His every thought, word, and action. What is so amazing about Jesus is that He didn't serve the Father by compulsion but by His own choice. He felt the same way David did when he wrote in Ps. 40:8, "I delight to do Your will, O my God, and Your law is within my heart." This service to the Father was the foundation of His service to His fellow man. This was manifested most beautifully when He bowed down and washed the feet of the disciples. He then instructed them to do likewise. His life was the model for all His followers. Jesus came to be a servant to all and when you're yoked to Jesus you also will be a servant to all. He said in Matt. 23:11, "But he who is greatest among you shall be your servant."

You put on the ox face when you take up your cross and follow Jesus. An ox is a humble creature but they are strong and were used in the Old Testament for sacrifices made unto God (Num. 7:17). To you, the ox represents a life of sacrifice. No matter what you do in life, there will come a time when you will have to sacrifice parts of your life for God and other people. There's no way around it. The face of an ox represents a crucified life. Paul said in Gal. 2:20, "I have been crucified with Christ; it is no longer I who live, but Christ lives in me; and the life which I now live in the flesh I live by faith in the Son of God, who loved me and gave Himself for me." As an ox you carry the yoke of Christ which includes the destiny you've been called upon to fulfill. Sad to say, very few people are truly yoked with Jesus for the life of a servant is not always an easy one. Jesus sweat blood fulfilling the will of the Father. Sometimes you will have to go out on a limb but, if you're yoked with Jesus, He'll be out on that limb with you.

In scripture an ox is always portrayed as a beast of burden. An ox was a farmer's tractor before tractors were invented and its function is to work and perform labor for its master. All believers must come to the point where they learn and accept that everybody has been called to work in and for the kingdom of God. Everybody has a call on their life and a destiny to fulfill. Everybody! No matter how relevant or irrelevant the task may be, every person on the planet is called upon to work for God. There are two levels of service unto the Lord and both are necessary and profitable. You can either work "for" God or else you can rise to a higher level and work "with" God. 1 Cor. 3:9 says "we are God's fellow workers" and 2 Cor. 6:1 says God's children are "workers together with Him." There are levels of service for beginners in their walk with the Lord as well as for those who are more spiritually mature. Luke 12:48 says, "For everyone to whom much is given, from him much will be required." The Message Bible says, "Great gifts mean great responsibilities; greater gifts, greater responsibilities!"

The first level of service is when you respond to a command in the Word of God. The Bible tells of many things you can do and the person who wears the face of an ox will set his or her will to do it. An example of this is found in Mark 16:15 where Jesus said, "Go into all the world and preach the gospel to every creature." Many believers have answered this call and have risen up in obedience to it. They are serving God in response to this command in the Bible. Mission programs have been birthed because of these words. Jesus spoke and those who answer the call to go into all the world have become a great and mighty work force in the body of Christ. As an ox they serve and bear the burden of lost souls. Much sacrifice is needed to do what they do which they make freely and willingly, even to the point of giving their lives for the sake of the gospel. Praise God for all the missionaries who have gone to the four corners of this planet. The hand of God is on their lives and thousands have given their hearts to the Lord as a result of their efforts and sacrifice.

Another level of service is to be a co-laborer with God. In the field of service a farmer would bind two oxen together with a wooden yoke that went around their necks and down their shoulders. Together as a team more work could be done than the combined effort of each ox individually. There is always strength in numbers and this is why Deut. 32:30 says, "One can chase a thousand, and two put ten thousand to flight." As a servant of the Lord you will always be yoked together with Jesus. For sure, it is a different way of life to be yoked with the greatest servant of all. A heavy yoke is around your neck and there will be some restrictions on what you can and cannot do. You are, after all, a servant. In Indonesia a large ox is always yoked together with a much smaller ox. This is done to train and develop the smaller ox. The little ox goes everywhere the big ox goes and does what the big ox does. This teaches the smaller ox discipline and how to submit to authority. To do well in this level of service all you have to do is follow the direction of the bigger ox who is Jesus.

As the Lord's ministry partner, your attitude should be the same as His when He said to the Father in the Garden of Gethsemane, "Nevertheless, not My will, but Yours, be done" (Luke 22:42). In other words, when He moves, you move with Him. When He stops, you also stop. Ps. 123:2 says, "Behold, as the eyes of servants look to the hand of their masters, as the eyes of a maid to the hand of her mistress, so our eyes look to the Lord our God." Back when this verse was written the servants were trained to wait by keeping their eyes on the master. They wouldn't move until the master told them to do so. Don't go off and get involved in something you shouldn't be a part of. It may be a good thing you want to do but if God didn't direct you to do it then don't do it. Much harm can be done when people do things they shouldn't be doing. They can be very sincere but they can also be sincerely wrong. There are many believers doing things today they shouldn't be doing. There is no anointing flowing in their lives and mere human effort alone is not enough to get the job done.

Around the world people are working with God and you need to become one of these people. When God is ready to move, He moves and you must move with Him. Remember, you are not working for God now, you are working with God. When the big ox turns, you turn with it. Prov. 21:1 says, "The king's heart is in the hand of the Lord, like the rivers of water; He turns it wherever He wishes." The Message Bible says, "Good leadership is a channel of water controlled by God; He directs it to whatever ends He chooses." When you are yoked with Jesus, the number of your options for service becomes very limited. You can't go off and do whatever you want but only what the Master wants you to do. You won't be very useful to God unless there's a yoke around your neck and when that happens you will lose much of your freedom of choice. You are doing His will now and not your own. When the Lord tells you to do something, respond quickly. When He knocks on the door of your heart, open it with no hesitation.

Song of Solomon 5:2-5 tells how a woman's beloved came knocking on her door in the middle of the night. The woman was in bed sleeping and she began to complain and make excuses why she couldn't open the door. She soon had second thoughts and got up to open the door. Vs. 6 tells what happened next, "I opened for my beloved, but my beloved had turned away and was gone. My heart went out to him when he spoke. I sought him, but I could not find him; I called him. but he gave me no answer." This is a picture of the Lord Jesus Christ. He may knock at a time when it's not convenient for you but when He does knock you must drop everything and respond immediately. If you hesitate and make excuses, the Lord will not be there when you finally get around to opening the door. Being yoked with Jesus is a great honor but it takes utmost dedication and extreme obedience. The end is near and God does not have time for excuses and disobedience. If you won't diligently serve Him then He will walk away from your door and go find somebody who will. Don't let this happen to you.

Randall J. Brewer

-4-

"BOTH GOD AND MAN"

Jesus rules like a lion, serves like an ox, and He came to earth where He lived and walked as a man. The gospel of Luke tells of Jesus being a perfect man and how He was able to relate to people on a human level. This story of Jesus corresponds to the third living creature around the throne which had the face of a man. Luke was the only Gentile among all the New Testament writers and he often shows Jesus interacting with those who were treated as outsiders by the religious establishment of the day. As a man Jesus knew exactly who these people were, what they needed, and how best to meet the need. Luke continually calls Jesus the Son of Man and this terminology is used in this gospel more than all the others. Luke was a doctor and his concern for people makes it appropriate that he should view Jesus in this way. Luke goes into great detail about the birth of Jesus. He tells the story of the angel Gabriel's visit to Mary and her conception and only Luke mentions the inn at Bethlehem and the manger where Jesus first slept.

Like Matthew, Luke gives the genealogy of Jesus but not in the same way. Matthew begins with Abraham and goes down through David and all the past kings of Israel. Luke, on the other hand, begins with Mary and Joseph and goes back to Adam. The final words of Luke's genealogy are "the son of Adam, the son of God" (Luke 3:38). The word "Adam" in Hebrew means 'man' so this verse can be translated "the son of man, the son of God." Luke gives other more personal details of the life of Jesus. He tells of Jesus growing up as a child and how at age twelve He was found in the temple listening and asking questions of the scholars who were there. Only Luke tells how the mob threw Jesus out of His hometown of Nazareth and how Jesus sweat drops of blood in Gethsemane. Luke focused on the manhood of Jesus and how He came to earth in a human body. Luke 2:52 says, "And Jesus increased in wisdom and stature, and in favor with God and man." Jesus grew up and as a man He had emotions just like you do. He wept, He got angry, He showed compassion. He was a man through and through and 1 John 4:3 says that whoever does not believe that has the spirit of Antichrist.

Jesus came to show how important people really are. Man is God's greatest creation because he was made in the image of God. Gen. 1:27 says, "So God created man in His own image; in the image of God He created him; male and female He created them." In Hebrew the word "image" is used referring to physical form, meaning that man was created in the same physical design as God. Man was also made in God's likeness (vs. 26) which means he was "patterned after the original." This is not only a physical likeness but is also an emotional, intellectual, and spiritual likeness as well. Man was made wholly after the complete nature of God, internally and externally. You were created to look like God, think like God, feel like God, and to act and talk like God. To show you how to do that the Father sent Jesus to the earth to live and die as a man made in the likeness of God. He was a man like no other and He patterned His life after the Father in heaven. He said in John 5;19, "Most assuredly, I say to you, the Son can do nothing of Himself, but what He sees the Father do; for whatever He does, the Son also does in like manner."

David asks an interesting question in Ps. 8:4-6 (NLT), "What are mere mortals that You should think about them, human beings that You should care for them? Yet You made them only a little lower than God and crowned them with glory and honor. You gave them charge of everything You made, putting all things under their authority." As vast and as great as the universe may be, it was man who was made in the image of God and a being who can measure the distance of a star is infinitely greater than the stars whose distance he measures. Man was created to be an heir of God and he's been crowned with glory and honor. In Hebrew the word "glory" means to have 'a quantity of wealth, power, and position; possessing all things' and "honor" means 'to be physically attractive and to have high social position.' In other words, man was created to be good looking and to have great rank and position in the universe. He was created to reflect God's glory on the earth and he wears this glory as a crown. He was brought into existence to be a king on the earth and this is how God intended it to be.

Manhood as God intended is the most noble thing in all the universe. The true greatness of man can only be manifested as he is renewed by the Spirit of God to the point that he "may grow up in all things unto Him who is the head, that is, Christ" (Eph. 4:15). The Message Bible says, "We take our lead from Christ, who is the source of everything we do. He keeps us in step with each other. His very breath and blood flow through us, nourishing us so that we will grow up healthy in God, robust in love." You need to thank God and appreciate the fact that He made you to be just like Him. He even went so far as to say in Ps. 82:6, "You are gods, and all of you are children of the Most High." This is earthly greatness at its highest elevation. Jesus quoted this verse in John 10:34 and went on to say in vs. 35 that gods were those "to whom the word of God came." He is talking about the position of man in the universe and if the God of heaven has appointed you to be gods on the earth, then you should walk as gods and work as gods among those around you.

Do not let it surprise you that God says you are gods. Acts 17:28 says you are "His offspring" and in Ps. 82:6 the word "gods" is equated with "children of the Most High." This makes perfect sense when you think about it. When any entity bears offspring, its offspring are the same kind of entity. The offspring of dogs are dogs and the offspring of people are people. In like manner, the offspring of God are gods. Paul prayed in Eph. 3:19 "that you may be filled with all the fullness of God." How can someone be filled with all the fullness of God and be less than a god on the earth? Let's also not forget 1 John 4:17 that says "as He is, so are we in this world." You need to grasp the reality of the fact that God has called you to walk as gods among men. Wherever you go and whatever you do, you need to remember whose image you bear and who you've been called to represent. You are gods on the earth and you need to walk worthy of that calling. This is the ultimate destiny for your life. Indeed, it can't get any higher than that.

The destiny for which God created man is a glorious one. When Adam was created he stood there as God's representative on the earth. He was made in the image and likeness of God and he was perfect in every way. God gave him the entire planet to rule over and Adam's sole responsibility was to establish God's kingdom on the earth. When God formed man out of the dust of the earth "He put all in subjection under him, He left nothing that is not put under him" (Heb. 2:8). To be human is to be God-like so when you miss the mark and sin never use the excuse that you're only human. No, being a human is very godly so never downgrade your humanity. A redeemed human being is an incredible creation for he is God-like in mind, will, and emotion. Creative powers flow through his veins for he is a powerful and noble living representative of God on the earth. God made Adam with God-like abilities and powers and the potential he had to do great things was tremendous. Sin then entered in and changed everything until four thousand years later when the last Adam was born in a tiny stable in Bethlehem.

1 Cor. 15:45-49 says, "And so it is written, 'The first man Adam became a living being.' The last Adam became a life-giving spirit. However, the spiritual is not first, but the natural, and afterward the spiritual. The first man was of the earth, made of dust; the second Man is the Lord from heaven. As was the man of dust, so also are those who are made of dust; and as is the heavenly Man, so also are those who are heavenly. And as we have borne the image of the man of dust, we shall also bear the image of the heavenly Man." The Lord Jesus is the last Adam and the second Man. He is the last man to be born without a sin nature. He was a man like no other and was both God and man. He was human and divine at the same time and for that reason He was able to be the perfect and acceptable sacrifice for the sins of the world. The first Adam lost his crown and gained death whereas the last Adam was crowned because He tasted death for every man. Sin and death entered the world through the sin of one man but because of the obedience of the second Man life abounds to many.

Yes, Jesus is the Lion of the tribe of Judah but He is also the "Lamb of God who takes away the sin of the world!" (John 1:29). In the Old Testament the priests had to offer up two lambs everyday as a sin offering, one lamb in the morning and one lamb in the evening (Ex. 29:38,39). This they did continually, day after day, year after year. The offering made at twilight was for the sins committed during the day and the offering in the morning was for the sins committed during the night. In this sinful world the middle of the night is when most sins happen so the morning offering was deemed necessary. The good news is that no longer does man have to provide for himself a lamb to be offered for his sin, God has provided a lamb for him. His name is Jesus. In Gen. 22:7,8 Abraham was going up the mountain to offer up his son Isaac as an offering unto the Lord. The lad said to his father, "Look, the fire and the wood, but where is the lamb for a burnt offering?' And Abraham said, "My son, God will provide for Himself the lamb for a burnt offering." And the two of them went together up the mountain.

The words "God will provide" is the answer to every problem you'll ever have. Whether it be a health problem, a financial problem, or a relationship problem, in faith you can believe God will provide for you a way of escape from the claws of the enemy. It is interesting to note that on that day God did not provide Abraham with a lamb to offer in place of his son. Gen. 22:13 says a full-grown ram was provided that day and it was not until two thousand years later that the Lamb of God was provided to be offered up as a sacrifice for sin. When Jesus went to the cross He was a man without sin thus fulfilling Ex. 12:5 which says, "Your lamb shall be without blemish." 1 Peter 1:18,19 (MSG) says, "Your life is a journey you must travel with a deep consciousness of God. It cost God plenty to get you out of that dead-end, empty-headed life you grew up in. He paid with Christ's sacred blood, you know. He died like an unblemished, sacrificial lamb." Jesus was a lamb without blemish and without spot and He died so that you could be the same way.

Eph. 5:27 (MSG) says, "Christ's love makes the church whole. His words evoke her beauty. Everything He does and says is designed to bring the best out of her, dressing her in dazzling white silk, radiant with holiness." Jesus lived a pure and holy life and was perfect in every way. He had to be or else He could not have become an offering for sin. Lev. 22:21 says, "And whoever offers a sacrifice of peace offering to the Lord, to fulfill his vow, or a freewill offering from the cattle or the sheep, it must be perfect to be accepted; there shall be no defect in it." Lay hold of what's being said here. You must be perfect in order to be accepted by God. You don't go to heaven because you're perfect, you go to heaven because Jesus is perfect and He's the One you trusted in. Because you accepted Jesus as your personal Savior, the Father now sees you as perfect just like His Son is perfect. And because of that, you will be welcomed into heaven with opened arms. This is why the Bible says you are saved by grave through faith. Eph. 1:6 (NLT) says, "So we praise God for the glorious grace He has poured out on us who belong to His dear Son."

Jesus lived and died as a man and on the third day He arose from the grave and He now rules and reigns forevermore. Dan. 7:14 says, "Then to Him was given dominion and glory and a kingdom, that all peoples, nations, and languages should serve Him. His dominion is an everlasting dominion which shall not pass away, and His kingdom the one which shall not be destroyed." On that third day Jesus was given the glory of royalty and His rule is forever and ever. He is the King of kings and Lord of lords and He's been given the Name that is above every name. Jesus is God and this is how the gospel of John sees Him. John's portrayal of Jesus corresponds to the fourth living creature, the flying eagle. The other three beings are creatures of the earth but an eagle soars high in the heavenlies. An eagle is the king of the air and is the strongest of all birds. As an eagle, Jesus destroyed the prince of the power of the air (Eph. 2:2) and the Father "put all things under His feet, and gave Him to be head over all things to the church, which is His body, the fullness of Him who fills all in all' (Eph. 1:22,23).

John's gospel is very different from those of Matthew, Mark, and Luke. An eagle can fly while the other three creatures cannot. Matthew and Luke both have an earthly birth story and genealogy but John's gospel does not have one for God does not have a beginning nor an ending. Just as an eagle flies in the heavenlies, John records a heavenly birth story. He writes in John 1:1, "In the beginning was the Word, and the Word was with God, and the Word was God." He then wrote in vs. 14, "And the Word became flesh and dwelt among us, and we beheld His glory, the glory as of the only begotten of the Father, full of grace and truth." The Message Bible says, "The Word became flesh and blood, and moved into the neighborhood. We saw the glory with our own eyes, the one-of-a-kind glory, like Father, like Son, generous inside and out, true from start to finish." In Luke the birth story is human; in John it is divine. Put all four gospels together and you will learn that Jesus is King and yet servant, man and yet God. He is the servant-King and the man-God. He is both God and man.

John says that Jesus is the Word made flesh and the miracles recorded in his gospel do not show Jesus laying His hands upon people to heal them as frequently as He does in the other gospels. In Matt. 9:25 Jesus took the dead daughter of Jairus by the hand and raised her up. In Mark 7:33 He put His fingers into the ears and upon the tongue of the deaf and dumb man who immediately was able to speak and hear. The gospel of John is different for it shows Jesus speaking God's Word in power. At the marriage feast when Jesus turned water into wine He didn't fill the water pots Himself but instead told the servants to do it (John 2:7). Jesus did not personally go to the home of a certain nobleman but He sent the Word to heal the man's servant (John 4:50). At the tomb of Lazarus Jesus did not roll the stone away and neither did He lay hands on His dead friend. John 11:43 says that Jesus cried out with a loud voice, "Lazarus, come forth!" He spoke the Word with power and authority and he who had died came alive and walked out of that tomb. The spoken Word brings life and it brings miracles.

Jesus is called "the Word" because He is the One who speaks every Word that the Father has to say. Words clothe thoughts to make them capable of being understood and, as the Word made flesh, Jesus manifested an invisible God. In other words, when you know Jesus, you know the Father. He said in John 14:7, "If you had known Me, you would have known My Father also; and from now on you know Him, and have seen Him." Words also transmit information from one person to another. The words Jesus spoke revealed the Father's perfect and holy character, His love and wisdom. They unveiled the heart of God and His will for all of mankind. Jesus was a divine communicator and as God's spokesman He came to explain the ways of the Father and to bring to the world a message of hope and love. John 1:18 (NLT) says, "No one has ever seen God. But the unique One, who is Himself God, is near to the Father's heart. He has revealed God to us." The Message Bible says, "No one has ever seen God, not so much as a glimpse. This one-of-a-kind God-Expression, who exists at the very heart of the Father, has made Him plain as day."

What makes Jesus so special is that He came to earth and "dwelt among us." The word "dwelt" is the same word as "tabernacle" and just as the Old Testament tabernacle was moved from place to place, so also did Jesus move about in His ministry (Matt. 8:20). The tabernacle was God's dwelling place and the Shekinah glory of God manifested itself there. This same glory manifested itself in Jesus on the Mount of Transfiguration (Matt. 17:1,2). The tabernacle was the place where God met with man and Jesus is the way to the Father. He said in John 14:6, "I am the way, the truth, and the life. No one comes to the Father except through Me." The tabernacle was placed in the center of Israel's camp and so is Jesus to be in the center of the lives of all believers. He said in Matt. 18:20, "For where two or three are gathered together in My name, I am there in the midst of them." The tabernacle was also the place where sacrifices were made. Animals were sacrificed on the brazen altar in the outer court. Jesus was the spotless Lamb of God who was sacrificed on the cross just outside the city (Heb. 13:11,12).

Jesus was both God and man yet in the gospel of John He never directly said He was God. What He did say was, "Most assuredly, I say to you, before Abraham was, I AM" (John 8:58). Centuries before, Moses asked God what His name was to which God replied, "I am who I am" (Ex. 3:14). To the Jews, the name "I am" was part of the divine name of God and they took the words of

Jesus as a blasphemous claim to be God. They took up stones to throw at Him (vs. 59) for death by stoning was the penalty for blasphemy in the law of Moses. Jesus never said He was God but 21 times in John's gospel He spoke the words "I am." Only John records the great claims of Jesus when He said "I am the bread of life" (John 6:35), "I am the light of the world" (John 8:12), "I am the door of the sheep" (John 10:9), "I am the good shepherd" (John 10:11), "I am the resurrection and the life" (John 11:25), "I am the way, the truth, and the life" (John 14:6), and "I am the true vine" (John 15:1). Amazingly, the numeric value of "I am" in Hebrew is 21, the exact number of times Jesus spoke these words. Also, 21 is the product of 3 times 7 and both these numbers are associated with perfection and with God.

The gospel of John reveals Jesus as God, the great flying eagle. In Rom. 8:29 Paul calls Jesus "the firstborn of many brethren." This means that if Jesus wears the face of an eagle, then you are supposed to wear this face also. You are to "mount up with wings as eagles" (Is. 40:31) where you soar into the heavenlies and not be touched or influenced by the world beneath. There are two classes of Christians portrayed in the Bible. There are believers who are eagles and there are those who are chickens. You choose which one of these birds you will be. You need to strive to be like the flying eagle who is the king of the air and rules in heavenly places. He is master, he is king. It is to eagle Christians that Jesus speaks in Luke 10:19, "Behold, I give you the authority to trample on serpents and scorpions, and over all the power of the enemy, and nothing shall by any means hurt you." Chickens, on the other hand, are babes in Christ who haven't been willing to pay the price to grow and mature in the things of God. Chickens always flock together on the ground whereas an eagle soars alone in the heavenlies.

The eagle is one of the most majestic of all God's creatures. It's sharp eyesight allows it to spot its prey from a great distance after which it flies in for the kill. Its eyes represent the eyes of the Holy Spirit in whose sight nothing can be hidden. Its two mighty wings represent a life of prayer and fasting. This gives you the power to rise up and soar far above the sinful reams of the earth. Its sharp claws grab and bind the head of the serpent and render it helpless to harm you in any way. Its double-edged beak represents the "sharp two-edged sword" (Rev. 1:16) that you must quote and declare with your mouth in order to pull down every stronghold and to destroy the enemy. This two-edged sword is the Word of God. The eagle eats the prey it has caught and its intestines represent the winding tunnels that lead to eternal judgment. You must bind and subdue these evil spirits and send them where they belong, to "the everlasting fire prepared for the devil and his angels" (Matt. 25:41).

An eagle was made to soar. It cannot survive in a confined captivity like a chicken coop or barnyard. It must be free and when one is captured it begins to die. He was made to fly in the heavenly realm and to look down on his prey. An eagle doesn't flap its wings but rather soars on the thermal air currents high in the air. They've entered into the rest of the Lord knowing that He has promised to go before them and defeat all their enemies so that they can live securely. They know that Christ alone can provide the eternal rest of salvation through His shed blood on the cross. Chickens hear the same Word eagles hear but they reject it for a lack of faith. Heb. 4:1,2 says, "Therefore, since a promise remains of entering His rest, let us fear lest any of you seem to have come short of it. For indeed the gospel was preached to us as well as to them, but the word which they heard did not profit them, not being mixed with faith in those who heard it." A chicken flaps its wings but doesn't go anywhere. It's relying on self-effort to fly and this is why it never gets off the ground and is stranded in the barnyard all its life.

An eagle lives in a different realm for it has learned to move and flow in heavenly places. Paul writes in Eph. 1:3, "Blessed be the God and Father of our Lord Jesus Christ, who has blessed us with every spiritual blessing in the heavenly places in Christ." These blessings are not for chickens who scratch around in the dirt in the barnyard, they're for believers who mount up with wings as eagles and soar in heavenly places. Eph. 2:6 says God "raised us up together, and made us sit together in the heavenly places in Christ Jesus." You need to spend time alone with God and wait on

Him. Before long the wind currents of the Holy Spirit will begin to blow and this is when you spread your wings and soar like an eagle. Chickens are busy bodies and never take the time to wait on God. This is why they never go up to the high places of God. They never learn to rest in God and flow in that heavenly realm. The first Adam was a man of the earth but the last Adam was a man of the heavenlies. He has the face of a flying eagle and you are called to have one also.

As an eagle, victory is always assured. An eagle has incredible eyesight and even if victory seems afar off he can still see himself wearing the crown of victory. Job 39:27-29 says, "Does the eagle mount up at your command and makes its nest on high? It dwells on the rock and resides on the crag of the rock and the stronghold. From there it spies out the prey; its eyes observe from afar." Faith always sees the end from the beginning no matter how far away it appears to be at the time. A chicken can only see as far as the barnyard but a soaring eagle can see miles and miles in either direction. He has an unbroken view of the entire region over which he flies and the farther up he soars, the farther he can see. Eagle Christians see things others can't see. Where others see doom and gloom, eagles see victory knowing "that all things work together for good to those who love God, to those who are the called according to His purpose" (Rom. 8:28). An eagle is an incredible bird just like Jesus is an incredible Savior. And when you wear the face of a flying eagle, you will be just as incredible.

Randall J. Brewer

-5-

"THE LIGHT OF MEN"

The apostle John lived and walked with Jesus for over three years and it is quite evident he had a more intimate relationship with the Lord than all the other disciples. In his own words, John records what happened at the last supper, "Now there was leaning on Jesus' bosom one of His disciples, whom Jesus loved" (John 13:23). John was writing about himself here and after spending so much time with Jesus he knew that human affection for the Lord is one of the sweetest and most heartfelt emotions a person is capable of having. The love of Jesus flowed from His heart and this was the place John wanted to be. John was a young man when he was called to follow Jesus as evidenced by the long period he lived after Jesus ascended back into heaven. He was sincere in his love for the Lord and was earnest and intensely enthusiastic. He was extremely dedicated and his passionate heart was given wholly and persistently to Jesus. He had a commitment that surpassed all the others and his deep, fervent love for Jesus unconsciously broke forth in many ways.

The love John had for Jesus was described back in Ps. 42:1, "As the deer pants for the water brooks, so pants my soul for You, O God." Desires are the throbbing of the soul and you are in the sight of God what you habitually desire and aim to be. Thirst is the strongest of all desires for it creates love for that which you are thirsty for. John had a living thirst for Jesus and this was caused by his admiration and deep love for his beloved Master. His desire to know Jesus and to become like Him was implanted and cherished deep in his heart. He had a thirst for fuller and deeper discoveries of his Lord and for the glories associated with His life. It was this panting, longing love that caused John to sit nearest to Jesus at the last supper, to follow Him to the judgment hall, and to be the only disciple at the cross when all the others denied Him and ran away. It was John's admiration for Jesus that made him foremost in the race to the empty tomb (John 20:4), the first to believe the story told by the forsaken and orderly grave clothes (John 20:8), and the first to recognize Jesus on the shores of Tiberias (John 21:7).

John seems to have been among men what Mary the sister of Lazarus was among women. Like Mary, John sat at the feet of Jesus and heard every word He said hence his gospel is different from the others. The closeness John felt toward Jesus gave him a deeper insight into the divine glory of the Lord and the spiritual nature of His work. In the book of Genesis, God is presented as speaking the universe into existence. In deliberate parallel to the creation story, John presents God as speaking salvation into existence. The other gospels deal mainly with the manhood of Jesus and all the works He did in regards to the physical needs of people. John, on the other hand, dwells more on the Lord's dealings with the souls of men and their spiritual condition. John's gospel speaks of the glory of grace and truth and how the words of Jesus were spoken with life and power. John had plenty to write about, so much so that he closed his gospel with these glowing words, "Jesus also did many other things. If they were all written down, I suppose the whole world could not contain the books that would be written" (John 21:25 NLT).

John could have started his gospel message a variety of ways but it was no accident that he began it the way he did. Two of the other gospels began with the earthly lineage of Jesus and His birth but John begins with the eternal Godhead. He wrote, "In the beginning was the Word, and the Word was with God, and the Word was God. He was in the beginning with God" (John 1:1,2). John was overwhelmed with things to write about and he chose by the direction of the Holy Spirit to tell how the life of Jesus did not begin at the moment of His birth. John wanted his readers to know that Jesus came into the world from a preexistent state to fulfill a specific mission. He began his gospel by saying "In the beginning." The Bible tells of many beginnings. Gen. 1:1 talks about the beginning of the world and Mark 1:1 records "The beginning of the gospel of Jesus Christ." Mark 13:8 mentions the "beginning of sorrows" and John 2:11 gives reference to the "beginning of miracles." This specific beginning that John gives in the prologue of his gospel precedes all the others. He tells how Jesus was not only "from" the beginning but rather was "in" the beginning for He was the Creator of all things (vs. 3).

John's introduction goes back before the beginning of creation and tells how Jesus was in a continuous state of existence. This he did with the words, "In the beginning was the Word." He next goes on to state that Jesus has a distinct personality from the Father and that they had intimate communion and fellowship with one another. This John articulated with the words, "The Word was with God." And, most important of all, the deity of Jesus is affirmed with the words, "The Word was God." John also tells how Jesus always was and always will be when he wrote, "He was with God in the beginning." John presents to the world the eternal Son of the eternal Father who took upon Himself human flesh so that He might fulfill the special ministry for which He was sent into the world. The purpose of John's gospel is communicated in John 20:30,31 where he wrote, "And truly Jesus did many other signs in the presence of His disciples which are not written in this book; but these are written that you may believe that Jesus is the Christ, the Son of God, and that believing you may have life in His name."

Just as a coin has two sides, so also does Jesus have two natures. Luke presents Christ in His humanity as the Son of Man while John portrays Him in His deity as the Son of God. The gospel of John is a book of love and clearly reveals God's love for man. He tells how the love of God will bring light into your life for it casts away the darkness of sin and ignorance. John tells how this love brings life in abundance to any who will receive it. He knew firsthand the transforming power of this love. At one time Jesus called John and his brother James "Sons of Thunder" (Mark 3:17) and it was a name they rightfully earned. Jesus and His disciples once went into a village of Samaria and, when the people did not receive them, James and John asked, "Lord, do You want us to command fire to come down from heaven and consume them, just as Elijah did?" (Luke 9:54). Jesus turned and rebuked them, rightfully so, and in the course of time John mellowed out and became known as the apostle of love. He was the only one of the original apostles who was not martyred and he outlived them all, living probably until the end of the first century.

Jesus is referred to by John as "the Word" and this is a most revealing name for the Son of God. In the Old Testament the law prohibited a Jew from taking the name of the Lord their God in vain. Out of fear that they may do so, they came up with a substitute name for God. Whenever He revealed Himself or declared a specific truth to them, the people referred to Him as "Memra" which is the Hebrew word for "a word." Because the people feared God, they used this Hebrew word which emphasized what was being said more than on who was saying it. John saw God in a different light. To him "the Word" is a person who came into the world to reveal the person of the Father to men. John fills what was being said with the personality of the person saying it. So real was Jesus to John that the most important truth he could tell people is that "the Word became flesh and dwelt among us" (John 1:14). Not only is what God says important, but here in the flesh was Jesus, a person you could see and hear and touch. He was God in the flesh. He was the Heavenly Man.

The single most important question ever asked came from the lips of Jesus and it was addressed to His disciples. He asked in Matt. 16:15, "But who do you say that I am?" Peter responded by saying, "You are the Christ, the Son of the living God" (vs. 17). John gives his answer when he says Jesus is the Word and the Word became flesh. Everything John wrote about pointed to the person of Jesus. He called the miracles Jesus did "signs" because he wanted to point the people to Jesus and not the miracle itself. John knew that abundant life comes from Jesus (John 10:10) and with that life comes new values, new relationships, and a new sense of destiny. John emphasizes that those who believe in the person of Jesus will receive eternal life in His Name. His gospel has been called God's love letter to the world and it has blessed the hearts of people through the centuries. John 3:16 is the most popular verse in all the Bible and has been the means by which more people have come to know Jesus as their Lord and Savior than any other verse of scripture.

When John said "the Word became flesh" he was saying that Jesus became human but never ceased to be God. Many call Jesus a good man and wise teacher but reject Him as God. John makes it very clear at the beginning of his gospel that Jesus is God come in the flesh, that He is "the only begotten of the Father, full of grace and truth." John opens by immediately presenting Christ not as the Son of David or the Son of Man but rather as the Son of God. He takes his readers back to the beginning and shows them that Jesus had no beginning. He goes behind the scenes of creation and shows that Jesus was Himself the Creator. Mark begins his story of Jesus at the Jordan River and Matthew and Luke start at Bethlehem. John, on the other hand, goes back beyond the beginning of history to reveal Jesus to you in the light of eternity. The message of John is that Jesus always was and always will be. He takes you to the eternal sanctuary of God and tells you that Jesus was always present with the Father and was not bound by time or space. John presents the Word as being fully God who then came to earth and became fully man.

There would be no Christian faith if Jesus did not come to the earth to live among His creation. His birth was foretold in Is. 7:14 and this prophesy was repeated in Matt. 1:23, "Behold, a virgin shall be with child, and bear a Son, and they shall call His name Immanuel, which is translated, 'God with us.'" The angel Gabriel said to Mary, "And behold, you will conceive in your womb and bring forth a Son, and shall call His name Jesus. He will be great, and will be called the Son of the Highest; and the Lord God will give Him the throne of His father David. And He will reign over the house of Jacob forever, and of His kingdom there will be no end" (Luke 1:31-33). The essential truth of the Christian faith is based on the massive reality that the all-knowing, all-powerful God of the universe came to earth to live in the form of a heavenly man. John spends his entire gospel convincing people who Jesus truly is and that in Him, and only Him, can one be saved. Every word he writes points to the fact that Jesus is God came to the earth in human flesh. He explains beyond a shadow of a doubt that Jesus is both the heavenly God and the heavenly man.

Jesus was a man like no other and when He walked the earth He did things that only God could do. He created things when He turned water into wine and multiplied the loaves and fish. He raised the dead, He forgave sin, He overpowered the kingdom of darkness, and He received praise and worship. He also said things that only God could say. Jesus was God's means of communication and this is confirmed in Heb. 1:1-3 (MSG), "Going through a long line of prophets, God has been addressing our ancestors in different ways for centuries. Recently He spoke to us directly through His Son. By His Son, God created the world in the beginning, and it will all belong to the Son at the end. This Son perfectly mirrors God, and is stamped with God's nature. He holds everything together by what He says - powerful words!" John calls Jesus "the Word" for it is through Him that God the Father speaks. As the divine transmitter, Jesus told of the love of the Father and spoke life into people. John 1:4,5 says, "In Him was life, and the life was the light of men. And the light shines in the darkness, and the darkness did not comprehend it."

John begins his gospel message by calling Jesus the Word, the life, and the light. These words in a clear and detailed manner explicitly reveal the deity of Christ. He is the Word because He is the communicator of God, He is life because He is the creator who gives life to everything that lives, and He is the light for He is the illuminator of all spiritual realities. John says in Jesus was the same life that the Father has in Himself (John 5:26) and this life became the light of men. Jesus is called "the Prince of life" (Acts 3:15) and for that reason "whoever believes in Him should not perish but have eternal life" (John 3:15). Jesus said in John 6:35, "I am the bread of life, He who comes to Me shall never hunger, and he who believes in Me shall never thirst." This very life that Jesus has in Himself is the very life you've been given. 1 John 1:2,3 (MSG) says, "The infinite Life of God Himself took shape before us. We saw it, we heard it, and now we're telling you so you can experience it along with us, this experience of communion with the Father and His Son, Jesus Christ."

Jesus is the giver of life and He said in John 10:10, "I have come that they may have life, and that they may have it more abundantly." The Amplified Bible says, "I came that they may have and enjoy life, and have it in abundance to the full, till it overflows." All believers are meant to live life with so much joy and exuberance that their lives will overflow and be a blessing to others. Jesus is the bread of life who satisfies all your hunger and He's the water of life that quenches your deepest thirst. Notice that John does not say that life comes "through" Jesus but that life is "in" Him. Jesus is the fountain of life and is the source of all you need to live a long, victorious life. The life Jesus gives refers to the fullness of who God is. It speaks of His very essence for He is the author of life, the source of life, and the cause of life. Acts 17:28 says, "For in Him we live and move and have our being." This supernatural life includes a fullness of life which alone belongs to God and is available to all His children now and forevermore.

Jesus said, "I am the way, the truth, and the life" (John 14:6). Jesus is life and you can look at Him no other way. He is the fundamental reality of all that exists for all things that are alive get their life from Him. He is the giver of life and Heb. 1:3 says He is "upholding all things by the word of His power." He gives life and He sustains life because He is life. In the same way that John says the Word was God, so also does he say that the life in Jesus is the light of men. Jesus came to shine light in the darkness and He said in John 8:12, "I am the light of the world. He who follows Me shall not walk in darkness, but have the light of life." Jesus is the life and He is the light for they are both the same thing. Light is the revelation of the life that is manifested in Christ Jesus. John 1:9 says Jesus "was the true Light which gives light to every man who comes into the world." The Message Bible says, "The Life-Light was the real thing: Every person entering Life He brings into Light." Light overtakes darkness and the life that is in Christ Jesus is shining forever bright all over the world. Put your trust in Him and let His light shine in you as well.

Jesus is life and light and without Him in their lives people have an inborn fear of both death and darkness. This is why Jesus closed out His public ministry by saying in John 12:35,36, "A little while longer the light is with you. Walk while you have the light, lest darkness overtake you; he who walks in darkness does not know where he is going. While you have the light, believe in the light, that you may become sons of light." Science will tell you that light is radiant energy that travels at a great speed. It is a wave of power that is indescribable and when it hits the retina of the eye it makes things visible. This is a description of who Jesus is and what He does. The divine power of His life had been walking the earth as a light shining into the spiritual darkness of men. Jesus came to show people the error of their ways and to point them to a higher and better way of living. Quite pointedly, Jesus made it clear that He was the light of the world. David said the same thing in Ps. 36:9, "For with You is the fountain of life; In Your light we see light."

John openly declares that Jesus is the light of men meaning that He is the living wave of divine power, moving at infinite speed, shining brightly into the spiritual realm to illuminate all that is otherwise dark. The good news is that when light enters in, all darkness has to flee. By this title, John is saying that Jesus is the One who knows the Father and has come to earth to make Him known. Light is a universal language for the illumination of the mind through understanding. Before Jesus came, the world was in darkness and did not know God personally nor did they understand Him. Without light there is no vision, no view of reality, no growth, no health, and no life. Is. 64:6 says, "But we are all like an unclean thing, and all our righteousness are like filthy rags; We all fade like a leaf, and our iniquities, like the wind, have taken us away." The Message Bible says, "We're all sin-infected, sin-contaminated. Our best efforts are grease-stained rags." This is the world Jesus walked into. His life was the light of men for they now had the knowledge of who the Father was as seen in the person of Jesus.

John makes this very clear in John 14:7-9. Jesus said, "If you had known Me, you would have known My Father also; and from now on you know Him and have seen Him." Philip said to Him, "Lord, show us the father, and it is sufficient for us." Jesus said to him, "Have I been with you so long, and yet you have not known Me, Philip? He who has seen Me has seen the Father." It was hard for those who heard these words to comprehend what Jesus was saying even though He said plainly in John 10:30, "I and My Father are one." These people needed light and this is what Jesus came to give them. The light of men penetrates the unimaginable depths of who God is and goes far beyond the limits of human vision. The only way to understand spiritual truths is in the light of Christ for He came to make the things of God discernible and visible. Jesus is the light of men for apart from Him everything is darkness. 2 Cor. 4:4 (NLT) says, "Satan, who is the god of this world, has blinded the minds of those who don't believe. They are unable to see the glorious light of the Good News."

Like a switch on the wall, God uses John's gospel to turn the light on some very essential truths that pertain to believers and sinners, ministry, and the nature of God and who He is. It is one thing to be alive, it is quite another to know how to live and to know the true purpose of life. Jesus came to provide you with light that illuminates the path on which you've been called upon to travel. The light which Jesus brings is a revealing light for you will never see yourself as you truly are until you see yourself through the eyes of God. The light of men is a guiding light for it will take you to the opened arms of God by revealing you to yourself. When you receive this light that only Jesus can give, and believe in it, no more will you walk in darkness. Jesus said in John 12:45,46, "And he who sees Me sees Him who sent Me. I have come as a light into the world, that whoever believes in Me should not abide in darkness." When Jesus comes into your life the time of doubt and uncertainty is over. The path you're on that was once in darkness has now been illuminated with a bright light from heaven.

Ps. 119:105 says, "Your word is a lamp to my feet and a light to my path." John sheds light on the nature of Christian ministry when he talks about the forerunner of Christ, John the Baptist. John 1:6,7 says, "There was a man sent from God, whose name was John. This man came for a witness, to bear witness of the

Light, that all through him might believe." John the Baptist was a witness sent from God whose ministry was to direct others toward the Messiah when He appeared. His name means "the gift of God" and Is. 40:3 prophesied about his ministry 700 years before he was born. Isaiah says John was "The voice of one crying in the wilderness: Prepare the way of the Lord; make straight in the desert a highway for our God." His birth was due to the direct intervention of God and he was filled with the Holy Spirit from the time he was in his mother's womb. Jesus said in Matt. 11:11 that John the Baptist was the greatest person to have ever lived up until that time. He said that because no man ever had a greater responsibility which was to prepare people for the coming of the Messiah and to introduce Him when He did come.

John the Baptist introduced people to the Messiah and this is to be your ministry as well. You need to dedicate your entire life to being a witness for Jesus Christ. A witness is a person who knows what he says and says what he knows. You don't have to know the entire Bible before you become a witness. All you have to do is tell people what Jesus did for you. Witnessing is not the giving of opinions and speculations but rather of showing how the light of men has shown in your life. In John 5:35 Jesus says John the Baptist "was the burning and shining lamp." John was the lamp but Jesus is the Light burning in the lamp. A lamp has no light of its own but Jesus is the Light that burns forever. The world is filled with people who are walking in darkness and you've been called to be a lamp that will bring the Light of Jesus into their lives. John had a message that the entire world needs to hear and so do you. John was the voice of one crying in the wilderness, you need to be the voice crying in your home, your church, your place of employment, and everywhere the soles of your feet take you.

Angels announced Christ's physical arrival in the world, John the Baptist announced the arrival of His spiritual ministry. The life of Jesus is the light of men and, like John, you need to bear witness of that light. You need to be forever ready to tell people who Jesus is, why He came, and what He has done. You need to share with others how Jesus is the Word, the Life, and the Light. John 1:29

tells how John saw Jesus coming toward him and he said, "Behold! The Lamb of God who takes away the sin of the world!" This is precisely what you need to tell other people for this is the foundation of all Christian ministry. The ministry of John the Baptist was a Christ-centered testimony. In John 1:34 he said, "And I have seen and testified that this is the Son of God." He said again in vs. 36, "Behold the Lamb of God!" Paul built on this in 1 Cor. 2:2 when he said, "For I determined not to know anything among you except Jesus Christ and Him crucified." The Message Bible says, "I deliberately kept it plain and simple: first Jesus and who He is; then Jesus and what He did - Jesus crucified."

Paul also made an interesting statement when he said in 1 Cor. 9:16, "Yes, woe is me if I do not preach the gospel." The Message Bible says, "I'm compelled to do it, and doomed if I don't." Is this how you feel? It should be. Inside of you is a message the sinner must hear in order to be saved. It's a testimony that pertains to life and godliness that comes to all people when the light of Jesus shines in their heart. People need to know that "God is greatly to be feared in the assembly of the saints, and to be held in reverence by all those who are around Him" (Ps. 89:7). The world is in trouble, real trouble, because "there is no fear of God before their eyes" (Rom. 3:18). This is a stinging rebuke to those who think they're good in and of themselves. Even Jesus said, "No one is good but One, that is, God" (Mark 10:18). To fear God means to keep Him and His Word as the focus and center of your attention. If Jesus is not the center of your life then you will not be able to do anything that is pleasing to God. Without the fear of God, no good is to be expected.

Jesus confirms that you have the same ministry as John the Baptist when He said in Acts 1:8, "But you shall receive power when the Holy Spirit has come upon you; and you shall be witnesses to Me in Jerusalem, and in all Judea and Samaria, and to the end of the earth." John came to bear witness of the Light (John 1:8) and the world needs you to do the same thing. Rom. 10:14 (NLT) says, "But how can they call on Him to save them unless they believe in Him? And how can they believe in Him if they have never heard about Him? And how can they hear about Him unless someone tells them?" People get saved when they hear believers giving witness to the fact that the life of Jesus is the light of men. Faith comes to these people when they hear the Word of God being spoken out of your mouth. People give their lives to Jesus because they believe the evidence you present to them. Is. 52:7 says, "How beautiful upon the mountains are the feet of him who brings good news, who proclaim peace, who brings glad tidings of good things, who proclaims salvation, who says to Zion, 'Your God reigns!'" Become a witness for Jesus and your feet will also be beautiful.

-6-

"THE POWER AND THE GLORY"

The gospel of John is a very unique story about the life of Christ for ninety percent of the things he writes about is not found in the other gospels. Whereas Matthew, Mark, and Luke deal primarily with the final year of the Lord's three year ministry, it is in the gospel of John where the happenings of the first two years are recorded. John portrays Jesus in His deity as the Son of God and this he makes crystal clear in the opening prologue of his gospel. He goes no further until he makes known that Jesus is God in human flesh. He tells how Jesus is the Creator of the universe who came to earth to become a part of His own creation. This truth is the most essential doctrine in the Christian faith and John knows that until this is believed, the rest of what he writes will be of little or no value to you. John 1:14 says "the Word became flesh" and this is the central theme of all Christianity. This is the required truth that must be believed in order for you to give your life to Christ and to have your name found written in the Lamb's Book of Life (Rev. 3:5).

John was so obsessed with this truth that he wrote about it often in his first epistle. 1 John 1:2,3 (MSG) says, "The Word of Life appeared right before our eyes; we saw it happen! The infinite Life of God Himself took shape before us. We saw it, we heard it, and now we're telling you so you can experience it along with us, this experience of communion with the Father and His Son, Jesus Christ." The deity of Jesus was so real to John that he could hardly contain himself. He goes on to write in 1 John 2:22,23, "Who is a liar but he who denies that Jesus is the Christ? He is antichrist who denies the Father and the Son. Whoever denies the Son does not have the Father either; he who acknowledges the Son has the Father also." What John is saying here is that if you tamper with who Jesus is, you will alienate yourself from God. 1 John 4:2,3 says, "By this you know the Spirit of God: Every spirit that confesses that Jesus Christ has come in the flesh is of God, and every spirit that does not confess that Jesus Christ has come in the flesh is not of God."

John's not finished. He writes in 1 John 4:15, "Whoever confesses that Jesus is the Son of God, God abides in him, and he in God." 1 John 5:1 says, "Whoever believes that Jesus is the Christ is born of God." Vs. 4,5 (NLT) states, "For every child of God defeats this evil world, and we achieve this victory through our faith. And who can win this battle against the world? Only those who believe that Jesus is the Son of God." He closes this epistle with these words, "And we know that the Son of God has come and has given us an understanding, that we may know Him who is true; and we are in Him who is true, in His Son Jesus Christ. This is the true God and eternal life. Little children, keep yourselves from idols. Amen." (1 John 5:20,21). Everything John writes is about Christ and who He is. It should come as no surprise that this is the one truth the enemy attacks the most. In Matt. 24:24,25 Jesus foretold what would happen here in the last days, "For false christs and false prophets will arise and show great signs and wonders, so as to deceive, if possible, even the elect. See, I have told you beforehand."

In order to be saved you must believe in the Lord's deity as well as His humanity. You can't separate the two because Jesus is both God and man. The two are joined together in the person of Jesus, never to be separated. For all eternity Jesus will be identified with both the Heavenly Father and all of mankind because He is the link that joins the two together. Know that the deity of Christ is not lessened by His humanity and His humanity is not overwhelmed by His deity. Together they form the reality of what Christianity is all about. John and the other disciples knew that Jesus was indeed God come in the flesh for he wrote that "we beheld His glory, the glory as of the only begotten of the Father, full of grace and truth" (John 1:14). The Amplified Bible says, "And the Word (Christ) became flesh, and lived among us; and we actually saw His glory, glory as belongs to the One and only begotten Son of the Father, the Son who is truly unique, the only One of His kind, who is full of grace and truth (absolutely free of deception)." John says he saw the Lord's glory and in Greek this means "to gaze at someone or something until something has been grasped of the significance of that person or thing."

The Greek language signifies that when the disciples saw the Lord's glory that this was not a passing glance but instead was a steadfast searching gaze which sought to discover something of the mystery of Christ. What is the glory of God that the disciples saw? It was the sum total of His divine character and all the elements of who He is. All told, the glory of Jesus was seen in His perfect life and in the fulfillment of why He came to the earth. To physically see the glory of Jesus is to see the visible manifestation of His presence displayed in divine perfection. John personally saw the body of Jesus transfigured into a bright and overpowering light. He wrote in John 2:11 that the miracles Jesus did "manifested His glory." When Judas left to betray Jesus, the Lord said, "Now the Son of Man is glorified, and God is glorified in Him" (John 13:31). The glory of Jesus was revealed on the cross of Calvary for it demonstrated the love of God like no other event in human history. In Jesus, there is glory to be seen in His spotless holiness, His boundless love, and in His fullness of grace and truth.

1 Chron. 29:11 says, "Yours, O Lord, is the greatness, the power and the glory, the victory and the majesty; For all that is in heaven and in earth is Yours; Yours is the kingdom, O Lord, and You are exalted as head over all." When Jesus walked the earth He was confined to a human body but still His glory burst forth and manifested itself in the words He spoke and the works He performed. Jesus came to show people what love is all about for there is more glory in the love of God than in all the universe of material creation. God described His glory to Moses in Ex. 34:6,7 (MSG), "God, God, a God of mercy and grace, endlessly patient - so much love, so deeply true - loyal in love for a thousand generations, forgiving iniquity, rebellion, and sin." When a sinner gets born again and finds peace, he has experienced the glory of God. Jesus was a man like no other for He was a man of love, compassion, justice, and truth. Add to this an existence that has no

beginning nor ending and you will see God in human flesh. Just as the glory was in the Old Testament tabernacle, so did it shine in the life of Jesus.

John said "we beheld His glory" meaning they saw the manifested reality that Jesus came to show the Father to the world as He had never been seen before. The things Jesus said and did showed the Father as being a God of love, gentleness, tenderness, and patience. The disciples saw His mercy, compassion, wisdom, and holiness. They saw the power and the glory displayed in the life of Jesus every single day. John said this glory was "the glory as of the only begotten of the Father, full of grace and truth." This means that Jesus was one of a kind and other translations say He was "the One and Only Son" of the Father. The word "begotten" comes from the Greek word "monogenes" and means 'one of a kind, unique.' It pertains to being the only one of its kind or class, unique in being the only example of its category. John is saying that Jesus is the only unique, one of a kind Son of God. He is a man like no other for He has no equal and this makes Him fully capable of revealing the Father to the world.

Jesus is unique in every aspect of His being because He can do for people what no one else can do. He alone can bring God to men and men to God. 2 Peter 3:9 says the Lord is "not willing that any should perish but that all should come to repentance." God loves you so much that He sent His Son to die for you and, just as wonderful as that is, Jesus was willing to do it. God is love and Jesus is love personified. John 1:18 calls Jesus "the only begotten Son, who is in the bosom of the Father." This term tells of the incredible bond between the Father and the Son and the inexpressible intimacy and love between them. It is the heart of the Father for you to have this same type of relationship with Him and He sent Jesus to the earth to make it happen. The life of Jesus expressed fully the revelation of the Father's character and will, His love and grace, and His desire to also have a unique relationship with you. John says that Jesus was full of grace and truth. Grace corresponds to the love of God and truth is the revelation of God as the light that is revealed in the Word.

Grace and truth must go together for in order to receive grace you must believe the truth. The Lord's grace offers love and compassion to guilty sinners and it is only by believing this truth that you can experience God's grace and forgiveness. Since Jesus is full of grace, you can come to Him and know that He will welcome you with opened arms. And because He is full of truth, you can trust in His promises and believe everything He says to you. These two words explain why Jesus came to the earth for they go to the very heart of the gospel message. Because Jesus was full of grace, He was willing to die on the cross even while people were yet sinners. He paid for your sins completely and He forgives you because He bore the sin Himself. No matter what your past looks like, no matter what sins you've committed, no matter how bad you think you are, Jesus invites you to come to Him just as you are with no preconditions except a sincere desire to be forgiven. Because He is forever truthful, you can come in complete confidence knowing He will keep His promises and that you will be pardoned of any wrong doing. That's the grace of God and the truth of the gospel message.

Once John establishes the truth that Jesus is God in human flesh, he next gives a historical narrative on the testimony of John the Baptist. Not once in this gospel is John the Baptist called by this name. A more precise, descriptive title would be to call him John the Witness for fourteen times in the gospel of John is this word associated with his name. John 1:8 says, "He was not that Light, but was sent to bear witness of that Light." Right away John lays the foundation that human witnesses are needed in the body of Christ. Why is that? One would think that "the light of men" would be a witness in and of itself. John 1:5 answers this question when it says, "And the light shines in the darkness, and the darkness did not comprehend it." John is saying that your witness and testimony is necessary in the world today which is covered with darkness. John the Baptist was sent from God and so are you. As Jesus was about to ascend back into heaven He said in John 20:21, "Peace to you! As the Father has sent Me, I also send you."

Another time Jesus said to His disciples, "The harvest truly is plentiful, but the laborers are few. Therefore pray the Lord of the harvest to send out laborers into His harvest" (Matt. 9:37,38). He later said to Paul in Acts 22:21, "Depart, for I will send you far from here to the Gentiles." Your witness is necessary but God does not leave that calling to human initiative. He saves and then He sends. He saves you from the world and then He sends you back to the world to be a witness for Him. Where you came from many times is an indication of where God will send you. Moses came out of Egypt as a young man and God later sent him back to Egypt to deliver His people from slavery and bondage. If you're a former drug addict and alcoholic, God may send you to minister to those dealing with these same addictions. If you were once homeless, God may send you to the streets to minister to the homeless. If you were once an unwed mother, don't be surprised if God uses you to help single teenagers who are now expecting their first child. You were once in their shoes and you now know that if God can help you, He can also help them in their distress.

Nobody has ever gotten saved without first hearing the witness of another human being. God provided the foundation for your salvation and He provides the means for you to get saved. Rom. 10:14,15 says, "How then shall they call on Him in whom they have not believed? And how shall they believe in Him whom they have not heard? And how shall they hear without a preacher? And how shall they preach unless they are sent?" The Message Bible says, "And how can they hear if nobody tells them? And how is anyone going to tell them, unless someone is sent to do it?" John the Baptist was sent by God so "that all through him might believe" (John 1:7). It was he who announced that Jesus was "the Lamb of God who takes away the sin of the world!"(John 1:29). He called Him by that name because he knew that people must first receive Jesus laying on the altar as a sacrifice before they can receive Him sitting on a throne as King. You must believe that Jesus paid the penalty for your sins on Calvary's tree. As you read the gospel of John you will see that the word "faith" is not mentioned one time but the word "believe" is used 98 times.

John the Baptist brought a sevenfold witness to the world concerning the Lord Jesus Christ. Just as the gospel of John begins with the preexistence of Jesus, John the Baptist begins his testimony the same way. He testified about Jesus when he shouted to the crowds, "This is the one I was talking about when I said, 'Someone is coming after me who is far greater than I am, for He existed long before me" (John 1:15 NLT). This is interesting because John was born six months before Jesus but here he announces that Jesus is from everlasting to everlasting. John next bears witness to the Lordship of Jesus. The priests and Levites asked John who he was and he answered them saying, "I am 'The voice of one crying in the wilderness: "Make straight the way of the Lord,"' as the prophet Isaiah said" (John 1;23). Notice that John did not use words of his own choosing to answer their question. He told them who the scriptures said he was and you must do the same. For example, don't tell people you're a wretched sinner but instead tell them you're the righteousness of God in Christ Jesus based on 2 Cor. 5:21.

John next tells of the Lord's unfathomable superiority when he says, "It is He who, coming after me, is preferred before me, whose sandal straps I am not worthy to loose" (John 1:27). Jesus called John the greatest person who ever lived up to this time but here John places himself below the lowest slave whose job it was to remove his master's sandals and wash his feet. John was the humblest of the humble. He sought no honor or recognition for he considered himself to be nothing more than a voice that pointed people to Jesus. He was so humble that his death is not even recorded in the gospel of John. He just disappears. What is recorded are some of the last words he ever spoke. He said in John 3:29,30, "He who has the bride is the bridegroom; but the friend of the bridegroom, who stands and hears him, rejoices greatly because of the bridegroom's voice. Therefore this joy of mine is fulfilled. He must increase, but I must decrease." These are some of the most beautiful and most humble words ever spoken. The Message Bible says, "That's why my cup is running over. This is the assigned moment for Him to move into the center, while I slip off to the sidelines."

John the Baptist was the center of much attention. He was known in all Judea and people were flocking to him to be baptized (Mark 1:5). He was a bright and shining lamp yet he considered himself unworthy of one's praise and respect. All he wanted to do was point people to Jesus and tell of the sacrificial work He came to do. There was a time when John saw Jesus coming toward him and he boldly announced that this is "the Lamb of God who takes away the sin of the world!" (John 1:29). After Jesus was baptized, John bore witness to the Lord's moral perfection when he said, "I saw the Spirit descending from heaven like a dove and He remained upon Him" (vs. 32). John continued speaking and told of the Lord's divine right to baptize in the Holy Spirit, "I did not know Him, but He who sent me to baptize with water said to me. 'Upon whom you see the Spirit descending, and remaining on Him, this is He who baptizes with the Holy Spirit'" (vs. 33). John closes out his testimony by proclaiming the Sonship of Jesus, "And I have seen and testified that this is the Son of God" (vs. 34). The Message Bible says, "I'm telling you, there's no question about it: This is the Son of God."

As the son of a priest, one would think John the Baptist would have followed in his father's footsteps by having a priestly ministry in the temple. God, however, had other plans for John's life. John lived out in the wilderness where he neither cut his hair nor shaved his beard. He wore clothes made from the skin of animals and he ate locusts and wild honey. John ministered outside the city away from the established religious system of the time. John brought a message of comfort and hope to a distressed people. He promised the coming of the Messiah who would bring redemption from sin and deliverance from Gentile aggressors. John lived in isolation from society and had a bold fearlessness toward it. With reckless abandon John boldly declared, "Repent, for the kingdom of heaven is at hand!" (Matt. 3:2). God was sending the Messiah to bless people but first He sent John to be the Lord's forerunner whose message was the baptism of repentance. As God's spokesman, John required changed lives when he called the people to repent. He asked them to forsake their sin and turn in faith to God and walk in obedience before Him.

John's message to the people is the same as what God said to Solomon in 2 Chron. 7:14, "If My people, who are called by My name will humble themselves, and pray and seek My face, and turn from their wicked ways, then I will hear from heaven, and will forgive their sin and heal their land." God hates sin and this is why Mark 1:4 records that John the Baptist was "preaching a baptism of repentance for the forgiveness of sins." The baptism John preached symbolized a complete moral cleansing. It was a public confession of sin and of the need of a Savior. There was a sense of urgency in John's preaching for he told the people "the kingdom of heaven is near." He came to call the people to submit to the reign of God which was about to be manifested in the arrival of Jesus. What John told the people generated much interest and Mark 1:5 says, "The whole Jordan countryside and all the people of Jerusalem went out to him" where they willingly submitted to his baptism. There people believed what John was telling them and they began to anticipate the coming of the Messiah who would provide them with the forgiveness of sin and bring about a kingdom of peace and righteousness.

John the Baptist, this great prophet sent from God, did not speak and prophesy in vain. The people who heard his voice speaking from the banks of the Jordan River were awed by what he said and moved as they've never been moved before. There were, however, others there who did not accept his message. The Pharises and Sadducees also came to hear John preach but these religious leaders rejected what he said. By virtue of their being descendants of Abraham and by means of their self-righteousness they considered themselves acceptable to God. John wasn't afraid of these people and he called them a "brood of vipers" (Matt. 3:7). According to Old Testament law, a viper was unclean and unacceptable to God and would defile anything it touched. John pointed to some stones on the river bank and told these leaders that God could raise up children to Abraham from these stones (Matt. 3:9). John was saying that mere flesh and blood accounts for nothing in the kingdom of God. These leaders had to learn that one is a son of Abraham only when they have the same spirit that was in the heart of Abraham toward his God.

The outcasts who came to hear John speak were just as acceptable to him as those who deemed themselves already to be sons of the kingdom. These were the people who heard his message and then asked, "What shall we do then?" (Luke 3:10). John answered them and said a concern for the needy was evidence of genuine repentance (vs. 11). John was saying that your outward actions are to be a reflection of the change that's taken place in your heart. This is what true repentance is all about and this change of heart was the requirement for acceptance into God's kingdom. The people who believed John knew his message was messianic and Luke 3:15 says "the people were waiting expectantly." Baptism was an outward sign associated with John's ministry but he told the people the soon coming Messiah will have a new sign by which to identify God's people. John promised that the Messiah would "baptize you with the Holy Spirit and with fire" (Luke 3:16). The Message Bible says the Messiah "will ignite the kingdom life, a fire, the Holy Spirit within you, changing you from the inside out. He's going to clean house - make a clean sweep of your lives."

Then it happened! Matt. 3:13 says, "Then Jesus came from Galilee to John to be baptized by him." It was at this moment that John called out, "Behold! The Lamb of God who takes away the sin of the world!" Jesus stood in front of John to be baptized and immediately John tried to discourage this from happening. He knew that Jesus was not a candidate for his baptism which was a sign of confession and repentance. Jesus was sinless thus the nature of John's baptism eliminated Him as an eligible candidate for such a baptism. John knew that Jesus did not need his baptism and he also recognized that he was unworthy to do the baptizing if it were to happen. In humility he said in Matt. 3:14, "I have need to be baptized by You, and are You coming to me?" Jesus did not dispute what John was saying and replied to him, "Permit it to be so now, for thus it is fitting for us to fulfill all righteousness" (vs. 15). Jesus was submitting to the ministry of John and now John was submitting to the authority of Jesus. The Message Bible says, "But Jesus insisted, 'Do it. God's work, putting things right all these centuries, is coming together right now in this baptism.' So John did it."

The Lord's baptism was a monumental event and it is described in Mark 1:9-11, "It came to pass in those days that Jesus came from Nazareth of Galilee, and was baptized by John in the Jordan. And immediately coming up from the water, He saw the heavens parting and the Spirit descending upon Him like a dove. Then a voice came from heaven, 'You are My beloved Son, in whom I am well pleased.'" Why did Jesus get baptized? You need to understand that baptism is a symbol of identification. When believers get baptized, they publicly identify themselves with Christ. Likewise, when Jesus got baptized, He completely and totally identified Himself with lost humanity. Jesus was beginning a three year journey that led to the cross of Calvary and He began His venture by fulfilling the prophesy of Is. 53:12 which says, "He was numbered with the transgressors." John's baptism was a baptism for sinners and the Message Bible says "He embraced the company of the lowest." Jesus was separate from sinners in that He never sinned yet here He identified Himself with them by His immersion in the Jordan River.

Jesus identified Himself with sinners so that they in turn could be identified with Him when He became their substitute on the cross. Paul writes about this in 2 Cor. 5:21 (NLT), "For God made Christ, who never sinned, to be the offering for our sin, so that we could be made right with God through Christ." The Amplified Bible builds on this when it says "we would be made acceptable to Him and placed in a right relationship with Him by His gracious lovingkindness." Jesus began His public ministry by stepping into the place of sinners and this was in anticipation of what would happen at the cross. It is interesting to note that in Luke 12:50 Jesus used the word "baptism" to refer to His death. Jesus identified Himself with sinful humanity both at His water baptism and at His baptism on the cross. Jesus walked over seventy miles to be baptized by John and by doing so He was accepting His mission to become God's suffering Servant for all of humanity. When He came up out of that water He was already anticipating the baptism of His bloody death.

Jesus told John that He came to "fulfill all righteousness" and this He did when He submitted Himself entirely to the Father's will. The Father voiced His response to the Lord's acceptance of His calling by proclaiming His entire delight in His Son. It was at this moment that the Spirit of God whom Jesus possessed in fullness from His conception came to rest on Him. Luke said in Acts 10:38 that "God anointed Jesus of Nazareth with the Holy Spirit and power." The anointing took place as Jesus was stepping out of the Jordan River after having just been baptized. At His baptism "the heavens were opened," the same heavens that had once been closed because of Adam's sin. As He stepped onto that muddy river bank, He had a fullness abiding in Him that gave Him the power to do what He came to do. Jesus was recognized by the Father as Israel's King and He was anointed by the Spirit for the work He had come to perform. The power and the glory was now His. This was the momentous event that John had prepared the people for. It was at this moment that the work of John began to decrease and the work of the Lord began to increase.

-7-

"PUSHED INTO THE WILD"

Jesus has fulfilled all righteousness by being baptized by John. The Holy Spirit has descended upon Him from heaven and the Father has spoken confirming that Jesus is His Son and that He is well pleased with Him. Jesus is now ready to begin His ministry and His entire life had been lived preparing for this special moment. He is anointed and full of power and is ready to embark on the mission for which He came to the earth to fulfill. What will the Holy Spirit direct Him to do now? Mark 1:12,13 says, "And immediately the Spirit drove Him into the wilderness. And He was there in the wilderness forty days, tempted by Satan, and was with the wild beasts; and the angels ministered to Him." Mark's forceful words are consistent with the character of a servant and the Message Bible says the "Spirit pushed Jesus into the wild." Matthew, on the other hand, tells of Jesus being a King and he says that Jesus "was led up by the Spirit into the wilderness to be tempted by the devil." Other translations say the Spirit "impelled Him" (NASB), "sent Him" (NIV), "compelled Him" (NLT), "put Him forth" (YLT), and "from within drove Him" (AMP).

In Greek the word "drove" means 'to cast out, drive out, or send out' with a notion toward violence. This is the same word used in Mark 1:34 where it says Jesus "cast out many demons." Luke 4:1 says Jesus was "filled with the Holy Spirit" which means this compulsion to go to the wilderness came from within. It was the Spirit within that drove Jesus, compelling Him to go. Divine direction comes from within and Rom. 8:14 even goes so far as to say, "For as many as are led by the Spirit of God, these are the sons of God." This is not the same thing as getting direction from one of the Ten Commandments or a set of rules. The person who is "led by the Spirit" is driven by a strong desire to conform his will to the will of God. A radical change has happened for you are now "being transformed into the same image from glory to glory, just as by the Spirit of the Lord" (2 Cor. 3:18). The Message Bible says, "And so we are transfigured much like the Messiah, our lives gradually becoming brighter and more beautiful as God enters our lives and we become like Him."

If Jesus was driven and compelled by the Holy Spirit, don't think it will be any different for you. Self-help books and a long list of rules and regulations do not bring about the spiritual changes and alterations that only take place through the operation of the Holy Spirit. It's just not possible for a person to be directed from within independently of the Spirit of God. Jeremiah prophesies of this inner leading when he said the new covenant that was coming would involve God putting His law in man's inward parts and writing them on their hearts (Jer. 31:33). The local church today needs to wake up and continually be led by the Spirit within and not their own personal desires and preferences. Most churches are filled with people doing what they want to do and not what the Holy Spirit would have them do. Why is that? Because they refuse to let the Spirit lead them into a wilderness experience. In scripture, the wilderness is a solitary, lonely, and desolate place. When people leave the ways of the world and begin to run the race set before them, they're just not ready or prepared for a trip into the wilderness.

This may come as a surprise to most people, but being led into a wilderness experience is the way things are done in the kingdom of God. When Moses left Egypt he first went into a desert (Ex. 3:1). When Israel was delivered from bondage in Egypt they first went into the wilderness (Ex. 19:2). When John the Baptist came of age he first went into the desert (Luke 1:80) and later became the voice of one crying in the wilderness. When Paul was converted he went into Arabia which was a desert region (Gal. 1:17). God doesn't want anybody coming to Him under false pretenses. This is why Jesus said openly, "In the world, you will have tribulation; but be of good cheer, I have overcome the world" (John 16:33). It's in the wilderness where you get a taste of what the world and the Christian life is all about. You'll also find out who you truly are and what it is you're made of. Jesus said in Luke 9:6, "No one, having put his hand to the plow, and looking back, is fit for the kingdom of God." More times than not, it's in the wilderness where people look back and walk away from a life devoted to God.

Putting your hand to the plow means you've decided to commit your life to God and you must now concentrate on the work at hand. A plowman knows that the only way is forward and he can't be distracted by things left behind. If the plowman were to look back, his plow line would become crooked which means his field would not produce a full harvest. In the Old Testament, God told Elijah to anoint Elisha who would later be his successor. Elijah found Elisha "plowing with twelve yoke of ten oxen before him" (1 Kings 19:19). Elisha immediately let go of his plow and began the journey he'd been called to go on. He slaughtered his oxen, burned his plowing equipment, and forsook everything in order to answer the call of God on his life. Jesus said you must do the same thing. People who are pushed into the wild are already saved and have made the choice of what path they want to be on. If that path leads to the wilderness, then so be it. Remember, it's the Spirit who's leading you there. Jesus was led into the wilderness and you will be also "because as he is, so are we in this world" (1 John 4:17).

With the glow of the Spirit still upon Him and the commending voice of the Father still ringing in His ears, Jesus is pushed into the wild for a time of testing and temptation. These sharp contrasts have a way of happening to those who are spiritually exalted and you must be prepared for them when they do occur. 2 Cor. 12:7 tells how after being in the third heaven Paul had a messenger of Satan buffet him. The same dove-like Holy Spirit who descended on Jesus is now thrusting Him into the wilderness. This doesn't mean Jesus was resisting the Spirit but shows how powerfully God was operating in His life. Jesus was tempted at the start of His public ministry and this shows that sometimes the greatest obstacles you'll face in life often begin with the first steps of a new adventure. This may include a new ministry, a new relationship, a new job, or the start of the Christian life. Facing these obstacles will test the genuine substance of your character and will teach you humility and a total reliance on God. God doesn't want you to run from the battle, He wants you to be like David and run toward your giant. It is a great thing to begin your journey with a victory in the first battle.

Jesus being tempted in the wilderness was the will of the Father and this is why the Spirit led Him there. New responsibilities bring new challenges and dangers and this is why you need to learn early on how to pass through the fire of temptation. The prophet Isaiah says, "When you pass through the waters, I will be there with you, and through the rivers, they shall not overflow you. When you walk through the fire, you shall not be burned, nor shall the flame scorch you" (Is. 43:2). Notice this verse does not say "if" you pass through the fire, it says "when" you pass through the fire. Satan will contest everything God wants to do for you and through you and, for sure, tests and trials will come. You must, however, understand that you are not Satan's punching bag. Trials must be faced and not run away from. Jesus was tempted in a solitary place and this shows you can't escape temptation by fleeing from the world. Isolation from humanity is no security from temptation. Trials will be there whether you're in the city or in the field, out in public or in the quiet sanctuary of your own home.

It was the will of the Father that Jesus go out into that desert place to face the enemy and get prepared for the battle at hand. The path upon which Jesus was to walk, the path that led to the fulfillment of His destiny, led straight through the wilderness. Instead of stepping forth into public ministry right away, the Spirit immediately and without delay thrust Him into the wilderness and right into the face of temptation. Jesus was pushed into the wild by an irresistible impulse and did not go there by His own choosing. No, He was driven there, forced, compelled to go because the confrontation with the powers of darkness is central to the whole work of living the Christian life. The truth be told, people don't volunteer to go to the wilderness nor do they look for opportunities to struggle. Still, the evil giants of this world must be confronted and for this reason the Spirit cast Jesus forth into the most remote and savage part of the desert to face the devil in his own territory.

The wilderness is the barren habitation of snakes, lizards, scorpions, and buzzards and is representative of the world of sin, the devil, deception and death.

It cannot be denied that it was the Holy Spirit who initiates the scene, putting Jesus into the setting where He must contend with Satan. This wilderness where Jesus went has been identified by the voice of tradition as that wild and lonely region between Jerusalem and the Dead Sea. It is a vast plateau elevated high above the plain of Jericho and the west bank of the Jordan River. Travelers have described this place as a barren wasteland shut in on the west by a ridge of grey, limestone hills and on the east by the gigantic wall of Moab mountains. A more desolate and forbidding landscape would be hard to find. The wilderness is symbolic of the dwelling place of demons and all the forces of evil. It's the moral and spiritual dumping grounds of the world of darkness. The wilderness is that God-forsaken place where the children of Israel wandered in punishment for refusing to trust God. It is a place of chaos and abandonment for in the wilderness are all the scapegoats who carried upon their heads all the sin of the world (Lev. 16:10). It would be impossible to imagine a more dreary and lonely place and this is where Jesus went for forty days and nights.

The wilderness where Jesus was driven to was fifteen hundred feet above the Jordan Valley and is between six to eight miles from the traditional place of His baptism. The steep road leading up from Jericho to Jerusalem was called the "Accent of Blood" because it was infested with thieves and robbers. It was along this road that Jesus would travel to reach the desolate mountain and His wilderness experience. It would be safe to say that the wilderness was not the first place Jesus was ever tempted. He had lived thirty years prior to this confrontation with the devil and undoubtedly He faced the same temptations all young people face in their early lives. What can be said with certainty is that in the wilderness came the most dramatic and direct assault by the enemy in an attempt to prevent Jesus from fulfilling the purpose for which He came. The devil tempted Jesus three times and the first temptation is described in Matt. 4:2,3, "And when He had fasted forty days and forty nights, afterward He was hungry. Now when the tempter came to Him, he said, 'If You are the Son of God, command that these stones become bread.'"

Jesus was sent to this wild and uncultivated place in order to prepare Himself for the greatest task ever to be accomplished in the history of the world, either before or since. There He remained for forty days and forty nights fasting and praying so that He might be in complete subjection to the divine influence of the Spirit of God. Mark says He was with the wild beasts who dwelt there. This was an area not inhabited by men and was a remote place occupied by the wild and untamed beasts of the earth. At night prowled the wolf, the boar, the jackal, and the leopard. These beasts are brutal, savage, ferocious, and are always on the hunt for their next meal. This was a place where humans could not survive yet Jesus was protected from these hostile animals just like Daniel was in the lion's den. The most challenging situation Jesus faced was not the threat of wild animals but the craftiness of the wicked one. To be tempted by the devil is far more serious than to face threatening circumstances of a physical nature.

Jesus is the Son of God, the promised King from the bloodline of David, and here He is having a similar experience. After David was anointed by Samuel to be the future king of Israel, he almost immediately faced the giant Goliath. Likewise, Jesus was anointed by the Spirit and now He has an encounter with the devil whose name means 'slanderer.' The devil uses deception to achieve his evil purposes, slandering both God and His Word. There is a battle to be fought and wars to be won and this is why the Spirit pushed Jesus into the wild proving you don't run away from the giant, you run to him. For forty days and nights Jesus had been fasting and was unconscious of His physical need. His thoughts had been on things pertaining to the realm of the Spirit and the demands of His physical body had been unrecognized. At the close of this time alone the sense of need and hunger swept over Him and it was at this moment when He came face to face with the prince of the power of the air, the god of this world, the son of the morning, the devil himself.

During the long weeks of being alone, Jesus was in meditation and prayer and continually had communion with the Heavenly Father. During such times bodily appetites are normally restrained and now, as His journey to the wilderness is drawing to a close, the demands of the flesh are undeniable. Matt. 4:2 says afterward Jesus was hungry and the devil's first temptation was to entice Jesus to satisfy His craving for food. The devil is insinuating that if Jesus is the Son of God, then certainly He has the right to gratify His flesh and satisfy His hunger pains. Satan was suggesting that man's highest good comes from the fulfillment of selfish desires and happiness comes from satisfying one's fleshly appetites. He was not simply tempting Jesus to eat for undoubtedly He intended to eat pretty soon anyway. The temptation came when the devil questioned the deity of Jesus and then challenged Him to use His divine power for selfish purposes. The problem is not in what the devil wanted, but rather in the manner of how he wanted this proof of deity to be given.

Jesus came to earth to live as a man and, if He had fed Himself with a miracle, He would have nullified the very terms of His humanity. Yes, He was equipped with power from on high but it existed not for Himself but for the people He came to save. The devil knew that if Jesus stooped so low as to save Himself then He would be disqualified to save man. To satisfy His own desires would have been to abandon the will of God and this Jesus would not do. He answered and said to the devil, "It is written, 'Man shall not live by bread alone, but by every word that proceeds from the mouth of God'" (Matt. 4:4). The Message Bible says, "It takes more than bread to stay alive. It takes a steady stream of word from God's mouth." These words reveal that obedience to the will of God is far more important than the gratification of fleshly appetites. He was saying that submission to the Word of God is essential to flowing in the will of God. He recognized that the highest good in life is to obey God and then to depend on Him to sustain you in the midst of this obedience.

Matthew calls the devil "the tempter" for he is always seeking to exploit the weaknesses of people in order to deflect them from obeying God. He is the "god of this world" (2 Cor. 4:4) and many have fallen prey to his lies and deceptions. 1 John 2:15,16 says, "Do not love the world or the things in the world. If anyone loves the world, the love of the father is not in him. For all that is in the world - the lust of the flesh, the lust of the eyes, and the pride of life - is not of the Father but is of the world." The Message Bible says, "Don't love the world's ways. Don't love the world's goods. Love of the world squeezes out love for the Father. Practically everything that goes on in the world -wanting your own way, wanting everything for yourself, wanting to appear important - has nothing to do with the Father. It just isolates you from Him." The NLT says, "For the world offers only a craving for physical pleasure, a craving for everything we see, and pride in our achievements and possessions. These are not from the Father, but are from this world." It is because of fleshly appetites that many are on the broad and crooked road that leads to destruction (Matt. 7:13).

It is a sad but true reality that most people in the world are caught "in the snare of the devil" (2 Tim. 2:26) and are "under the control of the evil one" (1 John 5:19). Paul tells why this is so in 2 Cor. 4:3,4 (MSG), "If our Message is obscure to anyone, it's not because we're holding back in any way. No, it's because these other people are looking or going the wrong way and refuse to give it serious attention. All they have eyes for is the fashionable god of darkness. They think he can give them what they want, and that they won't have to bother believing a truth they can't see. They're stoneblind to the dayspring brightness of the Message that shines with Christ, who gives us the best picture of God we'll ever get." The story of Jesus in the wilderness shows that it is a foolish thing for believers to believe they're immune from the temptations of the enemy. Let's face it, temptations are a regular occurrence in life. This is an evil world and the temptation to do wrong is a part of it. However, let's not forget that Adam and Eve also faced temptation and they lived in a perfect world.

Temptations come to everybody regardless of their circumstances and this is why 1 Peter 5:8 says, "Be sober, be vigilant; because your adversary the devil walks about like a roaring lion, seeking whom he may devour." The Message Bible says, "Keep a cool head. Stay alert. The devil is poised to pounce, and would like nothing better than to catch you napping. Keep your guard up." Peter is telling you to always be on guard where the devil is concerned because he knows if the devil can't get into your life one way, he'll back off, regroup, and try to get in another way. This is precisely what he did to Jesus. The temptation to turn stones into bread appealed to "the lust of the flesh" and parallels Eve's temptation to see the forbidden fruit as being "good for food" (Gen. 3:6). The devil tried to get Jesus to use His own power but the Lord chose to trust the Father instead. The devil said, "Very well. You want to trust God, here's an opportunity for You to trust Him." He then invited Jesus to throw Himself off the pinnacle of the temple believing that God would send His angels to rescue Him.

Matt. 4:5,6 says, "Then the devil took Him up into the holy city, set Him on the pinnacle of the temple, and said to Him, 'If You are the Son of God, throw Yourself down.'" He then quoted Ps. 91:11,12 that affirmed God would "give His angels charge over you" and that He would not let Jesus dash His foot against a stone. This was a temptation appealing to "the pride of life" and parallels Eve's temptation to see the forbidden fruit as "desired to make one wise" (Gen. 3:6). Historians say the pinnacle of the temple stood 700 feet above the bottom of the valley which is the same height as a 70-story skyscraper. The devil took Jesus out of the wilderness and brought Him to Jerusalem which was the heart of the Promised Land. This was the holy city where God's kingdom on earth was established. It was where all the kings reigned from and was the place where the temple was built. Inside the temple was the ark of the covenant which served as God's throne on earth. In the first temptation Jesus had shown faith in the Father and here on the pinnacle of the temple came a direct attempt to force Jesus to act on that trust.

The devil wanted Jesus to prove that the Father would take care of Him. This was a test rooted in doubt for you only put a person to the test if you don't have confidence in them. It is when you doubt a person that tests are invented to discover how far that person can be trusted. The devil was telling Jesus to prove God would keep His word by putting Himself in a situation where God would have to act. He wanted Jesus to force the hand of God and this Jesus would not do. For Christ to put God to the test would be for Him to abandon His dependence on the Heavenly Father. If you have full confidence in a person then no test is necessary. If Jesus would have acted on the devil's temptation then He would have removed Himself from the very protection the devil quoted to Him in the first place. It was for this reason that Jesus answered the devil, "It is written again, 'You shall not tempt the Lord your God'" (Matt. 4:7). Jesus is showing that you need to accept God's Word by faith and to manipulate situations in an attempt to get God to move is evil.

God the Father made a special promise to His Son in Ps. 2:7,8, "You are My Son, today I have begotten You. Ask of Me, and I will give You the nations for Your inheritance, and the ends of the earth for Your possessions." It was the will of the Father to give Jesus a throne to sit on which would come by way of the cross. Knowing this, the devil now offers Jesus the ultimate fulfillment of why He came to the earth by saying Jesus could have what the Father promised without having to go to the cross. Only one condition was attached to this offer. "Again, the devil took Him up on an exceeding high mountain, and showed Him all the kingdoms of the world and their glory. And he said to Him, 'All these things I will give You if You will fall down and worship me'" (Matt. 4:8,9). Luke 4:15 says "in a moment of time" Jesus was shown in a vision the great Roman empire and the magnificent kingdoms of Greece, Persia, Syria, Judea, Egypt and all the other known kingdoms of the world, including those unexplored lands with their countless nations and tribes.

This must have been a gorgeous sight Jesus was looking at because this third temptation appeals to "the lust of the eye" and parallel's Eve's temptation to see the forbidden fruit as "desired to make one wise" (Gen. 3:6). Jesus came to bring peace and righteousness to the entire world and here in front of Him is His dream spread out before His very eyes. This is the fulfillment of His call and the devil is saying He can have it all right now without the suffering for which He was appointed to go through. The temptation is to forget the cross and take the easy way out. The devil was saying, "Why suffer if You don't have to? Here, take my power. Just bow down and worship me and all these kingdoms and their glory will be Yours" (see Luke 4:6,7). To receive worship has been Satan's chief ambition ever since he attempted to dethrone God and receive the praise and glory that belongs to God alone (Is. 14:12-14). The devil's power and authority was given to him by Adam in the garden and here he is willing to give it all up in order to receive this great desire of his which is to claim worship that belongs only to God.

Jesus had lived most of His days in the low-life, despised city of Nazareth and here He is being offered all the kingdoms of the world in the blink of an eye. What will He do? How will He respond? What the devil left out of his temptation is that worship and service always go together. To pay homage to a person is to give recognition that service is an obligation to be given to that same person. To worship is always to serve and the devil said nothing about this in his temptation to Jesus. The devil asked for worship knowing full well that if it was given then Jesus would be obligated to serve him for all eternity. What needs to be understood about these three temptations is that Jesus was not brought to this humiliating experience to see if He could be made to sin. No, He was pushed into the wild to prove to all that He would not sin. Jesus recognized that God alone has the right to receive worship and service and He said to the devil, "Away with you, Satan! For it is written, 'You shall worship the Lord your God, and Him only shall you serve'" (Matt. 4:10).

Matt. 4:11 brings the Lord's wilderness experience to a close when he says, "Then the devil left Him, and behold, angels came and ministered to Him." As the devil leaves, the same angels who the devil said would catch Jesus if He fell from the temple now came and ministered to Him. Scripture does not say what these angels did but it is evident that Jesus received food, comfort, and strength from their visit. 1 John 2:16 noted that there are three avenues through which the devil can tempt an individual and he approached

Jesus and tempted Him through these three channels. In the wilderness Jesus faced and defeated the lust of the flesh, the lust of the eyes, and the pride of life. On the basis of this threefold temptation, Heb. 4:15 says Jesus "was in all points tempted as we are, yet without sin." The outcome of this confrontation was far different than the temptation of man in the Garden of Eden. The devil challenged the first Adam, the second Adam challenged the devil. The devil ruined the first man, the Second Man spoiled the devil. Jesus was "well pleased" by the Father and He walked out of that wilderness ready to fulfill His destiny.

"COME AND SEE"

Jesus is able to present Himself before the Father as "a merciful and High Priest" (Heb. 2:17) because He knows through His wilderness experience what it's like to endure temptation. Heb. 2:18 says, "For in that He Himself has suffered, being tempted, He is able to aid those who are being tempted." The force of temptation can be strong if you're not in a close relationship with Jesus. People who have close ties with sinners hardly know they're sinning. It's when you try to resist the temptation to sin that you'll be made aware of the devil's existence and his schemes to bring you down. Understand that God never does anything without there being a purpose behind it. Jesus was driven into the wilderness for the purpose of showing you how to resist temptation when "the tempter" comes knocking on your door. The Father is getting Jesus ready to face the reality of His awesome ministry and He wants you to be prepared as well. Great ministries come with great challenges and the higher up you go in your calling the more you'll have to be prepared to face and overcome the trials of that new level of ministry.

The gospel of John does not tell of the Lord's baptism or His experience in the wilderness but it does tell what happened shortly thereafter. Jesus was ready to begin His ministry but first He needed to find and choose a handful of men who would follow Him and learn from Him, men who would later go into all the world and make disciples of all men. The strength of the Lord has returned to Him after being ministered to by the angels. He now leaves the wilderness and returns to where John was still baptizing in the Jordan River. It was here that John proclaimed that Jesus was the Lamb of God who takes away the sin of the world. The people were looking for a king who would deliver them from Roman bondage but God used John to tell them this was a spiritual deliverance and not a physical one. Jesus did not come to overthrow Rome nor was He going to set up a physical throne in

Jerusalem and make Israel a world superpower. No, He was coming to redeem man from the wages of sin which ultimately lead to death, both physical and spiritual. He came to be a suffering Servant, a Lamb to die in place of all the people.

John 1:35,36 says, "Again, the next day, John stood with two of his disciples. And looking at Jesus as He walked, he said, 'Behold the Lamb of God!'" John gives the same proclamation he gave the day before. He did this because he is confronting a nation of self-righteous people who don't think they need to repent, thus they believe they have no need of a savior. This was the dominant view of the religious establishment of that day but John was telling them they were sinners just like the Gentiles. They needed to repent and be baptized as an outward expression of an inward cleansing. John then pointed to Jesus and said here was the Lamb of God who would die and be the sacrifice for their sins. The disciples of John believed the things he told them and vs. 37 says, "The two disciples heard him speak, and they followed Jesus." One of these disciples was Andrew, the brother of Peter (vs. 40) and the other unnamed disciple is believed by most scholars to be John, the writer of this gospel. "Then Jesus turned, and seeing them following, said to them, 'What do you seek?'" (vs. 38).

These are the first words spoken by Jesus in the gospel of John. Jesus was walking and sensed that two people were following close behind Him. He then turned around and used a searching question to test their motives. He wants to know if they understand their own purpose for following Him. He asks, "What do you seek?" This is a question you also need an answer for because one day Jesus is going to ask you the same thing. In the mind of Jesus, it matters a great deal what it is you're seeking after. The reason this is so important is because the Bible says you will find what you're looking for. Jesus said in Matt. 7:8, "Ask, and it will be given to you; seek, and you will find; knock, and it will be opened to you." This is a spiritual principle many believers have yet to comprehend. You will find what you're looking for so you must be on guard so that you don't seek for the wrong things. Stop looking for bad things because it is a certainty that you will find it. Some people are always looking for faults in other people and, sure enough, they find it. Why? It's what they're looking for. This is why they're called fault-finders.

James 4:8 says, "Draw near to God and He will draw near to you." Here you see this happening. It was time for the ministry of John the Baptist to fall back into the shadows and, when Jesus walked by, John had no other thought than to send people His way. These two disciples left John and began to follow Jesus a short distance behind. Jesus then did something totally amazing. He turned around and spoke to them. This shows that when you make the decision to draw near to God, you don't have to keep drawing near until you get to Him. No, God will turn around and begin to draw near to you. Seek and you will find. Know in your heart that it is not a hard thing to find God. All you have to do is take the first step and begin to seek Him out. God is not hiding Himself from you but is anxiously waiting for you to draw near to Him. The father of the prodigal son stood at the doorway waiting for his wayward son to come home. When he did see him coming off in the distance, the father ran out to his son and met him on the road. He drew near to his son and embraced him with arms of love and compassion. This is what Jesus wants to do with you.

When Jesus spoke to these disciples, He was opening the door for them to come in. He was making things easier and He begins by asking one of the most fundamental questions in life, "What are you looking for?" This is a question that has the power to penetrate the soul and should be asked of yourself every single day. The answer to this question will reveal what your true motives are and what it is that drives you forward in life. Your answer will have an incredible impact on your ability or inability to follow Jesus in a worthy manner. The truth of the matter is, people who don't have a close relationship with Jesus are not seeking Him enough. The same thing can be said about the special blessings God wants to bestow on you, things like prosperity, health, and a sound mind. You prove you love Him by seeking Him every minute of every day. Many people selfishly search for fortune and fame with no regards of serving the Lord and these are all inadequate things for which to direct your life. People who are driven by motives of personal ambition will not go far because their horizons are limited by time and this fleshly world.

These two disciples, Andrew and John, knew about the coming Messiah for they had been disciples of John the Baptist. They hungered for the truth and found it first through the witness of John the Baptist and later in the person of Jesus Christ. They were directed to follow Jesus, the Lamb of God, and they soon made Him the most important person in their life for in Him they found the answers they were looking for. Jesus asked them, "What do you seek?" but they didn't answer this question. Instead they said, "Rabbi, where are You staying?" (vs. 38). The word "Rabbi" comes from the Hebrew word meaning 'my great one' and is a title of respect given by students and seekers of knowledge to their teachers and to wise men. In Greek the word means 'teacher' and this is the word John uses in this passage of scripture. They asked where He was staying because they wanted more than just a passing conversation on the dusty road they were traveling on. They had a thirst that couldn't be quenched with a word or two. No, they wanted to talk to Him all day, not as strangers on the road but as friends in His own house.

By calling Jesus "Rabbi" they are asking if they can become His disciples. They had been disciples of John and knew from experience that a true disciple can never be satisfied with just a passing word. They were giving Jesus respect and honor and were saying they wanted to sit down and have a long conversation with Him. Jesus saw that they had the proper motivation and their heart was in the right place. He answered and said to them, "Come and see" (vs. 39). This answer was better than they could have expected for they are now being invited to accompany Jesus at once. They went seeking for Jesus and they found Him. They drew near to Him and He turned around and drew near to them. Jesus was not inviting them to come and see where He laid His head at night. No, He was inviting them to come and find the things that He alone could open up to them. He is the promised Messiah and in His words are truth that can set the captives free. The words of Jesus are "life to those who find them, and health to all their flesh"

(Prov. 4;22). The Message Bible says, "Those who discover these words live, really live."

Jesus said in Matt. 6:33, "But seek first the kingdom of God and His righteousness, and all these things shall be added to you." This is what Andrew and John were doing. When they started following after Jesus they were seeking the kingdom of God. To "seek" something means you have to pursue it for it will not come to you on it's own. To seek "first" means what you're searching for has top priority in your life and the "kingdom" is the object of your pursuit. People today have not grasped the importance of seeking God and His kingdom. Jesus said in Matt. 13:12 (NLT), "To those who listen to My teaching, more understanding will be given, and they will have an abundance of knowledge. But for those who are not listening, even what little understanding they have will be taken away from them." He is saying, "Those who seek the kingdom and want to know more about the kingdom, I will tell them more. And those who have no interest, I will make sure they never find it." The Message Bible says, "Whenever someone has a ready heart for this, the insights and understandings flow freely. But if there is no readiness, any trace of receptivity soon disappears."

The reason it is so important to seek God is because He will only tell you what you want to know and will only show you what you want to see. In other words, He'll only give you what you're willing to receive. It is no secret that some people want God more than others and the proof of their desire of God is their pursuit of God. They are seeking the kingdom morning, noon, and night. God hides Himself from people who have no interest in Him. He forces Himself on nobody and one of the biggest truths in all the Bible is that God must be sought after to be found. The Lord said in Jer. 29:13, "And you will seek Me and find Me, when you search for Me with all your heart." This is why Jesus said your top priority should be to seek first the kingdom of God and His righteousness. Yes, God is everywhere but you'll only find Him when you seek for Him with passion and persistence. If you'll do that, God will open your mind and tell you things He hasn't told anybody else. He'll reveal things to you that you won't be able to understand until

He reveals its meaning to you. He'll withhold nothing from you and in time you'll have an abundance of knowledge of things concerning God and His kingdom.

Life is a serious thing and this is why Jesus is asking, "What do you seek?" Life is not a game and it's not to be played with. Laws are given to stop people from playing the harmful games they want to play. Laws are needed because people do things without considering the consequences of their actions. People say they make decisions and now they have to live with it. No, you don't live with your decisions, you live with the consequences of your decisions. Adam made the decision to eat of the forbidden fruit and today all of mankind is living with the consequences of that horrendous decision. The Heavenly Father also made a decision when He sent Jesus to the earth to become the Lamb of God who takes away the sin of the world. He offers you the chance to live with the consequences of that glorious decision if you would only choose to seek Him with all your heart and soul. You must decide for yourself if you want to live with the consequences of Adam's decision or with the consequences of God's decision. The choice is yours. Just remember that you will live with the consequences of whatever decision you make.

Andrew and John are looking for something. They're looking for salvation. They're looking for the Messiah, the Lamb of God. They're looking for truth and righteousness and the fulfillment of scripture. What are you looking for? If you are looking for these same things, Jesus will also say to you, "Come and see." He didn't tell the two disciples where He was staying, instead He wanted to show them. There are things that Jesus also wants to show you but He'll only do it when you seek first the kingdom of God. When you start out on your journey of faith, like Abraham you may not always know where the path you're on leads to. This is when Jesus will say, "Come and find out." Lay aside those questions that may rise up in your head. Trust Jesus and follow Him. Come and see what He has planned for your life. Many people miss God because they want answers before they're willing to get out of the boat. No, you must be willing to come and see first and then, once you trust

Him, revelation will come. People say seeing is believing, God says believing is seeing. You show God you believe Him when you follow His command to "Come and see."

This is not optional! Faith is a requirement to please God and to operate in His kingdom. When He says "Come and see" you must stop everything you're doing and go come and see. You may not know where you're going and you may not know how your needs are going to be met. But if you love Jesus and trust Him, you don't have to know. All you need is a willingness to come and see. For sure, this is a wonderful and exciting way to live. Doors will be opened and new opportunities will come your way. You will see things you never imagined you'd ever see. Think about all the things Andrew and John saw for the next three years because they obeyed the Lord's command to "Come and see." They heard the Father speak out of heaven, they saw the glory of God, the dead raised to life, storms calmed, sick people made well, the hungry fed, and teachings that only the Son of God could teach. God is no respecter of persons and Jesus is the same yesterday, today, and forever. What He showed His disciples back then, He will also show you today. But first you must do what they did. You must come and see.

The problem in the church today is that too many people are doing nothing as they sit and wait on God to do something. They don't understand that God didn't say "Wait and see," He said "Come and see." This means you've got to get up and do something. You must "come" before you can "see" but most people don't realize that. They think it's a godly thing to "wait and see" yet the Bible says faith without works is dead. Don't just sit there waiting to see how everything is going to turn out. No! Do something! Come and see! Seek and you will find! Knock and it will be opened to you! A lot of people can tell you what to do but Jesus wants to show you what to do. He'll show you only if you'll come and see. Many talk the talk but only a few walk the walk. The chosen few are the ones who don't sit and wait for something to happen, they're the people who go out and make things happen. They come and see what the Master wants to show them. They say to Him, "Here I am. Send me." They may not know what the future holds but they're willing to go find out.

John 1:39 says Andrew and John followed Jesus and remained with Him that day. They were hungry for the reality of God and found it in the person of Jesus. So real was He to them that when their visit was over they immediately set out to tell others to come and see also. Vs. 41 says Andrew went out and found his brother Simon Peter and said to him, "We have found the Messiah" which is translated "the Christ." The word "Messiah" is Hebrew and "Christ" is Greek and both words are referring to God's anointed King and His anointing. Peter went on to become more famous than his brother and it is clear that Andrew lived under the shadow of Peter. Many times in scripture he is identified as Simon Peter's brother and it seems he was content to stand back and let his brother have the limelight. What Andrew is famous for is that he was always introducing people to Jesus. He brought Peter to Jesus and in John 6:8,9 he brings to Jesus the boy with the five loaves and two small fish. There is also the incident in John 12:22 when he brings some enquiring Greeks into the presence of Jesus. Andrew had the heart of a missionary and he spent all his life introducing people to the same Jesus he had come to love and serve.

Andrew brought his brother to Jesus and vs. 42 says Jesus looked at him. This was not a casual glance but was a concentrated, piercing gaze that looked into the depths of the man's heart. Jesus said to him, "You are Simon the son of Jonah. You shall be called Cephas." This was the Aramaic name for the Greek word "Peter" and both words mean 'rock' or 'a hiding place.' Jesus revealed that He was all-knowing and all-seeing for He knew Simon's name and the lineage from which he came. Jesus also knew that Simon was compulsive and quick to hear yet did not always respond properly to what he heard. The name "Simon" means 'vacillating and unstable' so Jesus changed his name to Peter which meant he would become a rock for Jesus, stable and unmovable. In the Old Testament a name change often marked a new relationship with God. Abram became Abraham (Gen. 17:5) and Jacob became

Israel (Gen. 32:28). Any person who comes to Christ is a new person. Old things have passed away, behold, all things become new (2 Cor. 5:17). Simon would become a new man, thus he needed a new name.

The great thing about this story is that it shows how Jesus looks at people. Not only does Jesus look at the person you are now, He also sees the person you can become. He sees all the possibilities that are inside of you. Peter was compulsive and often uncontrollable but Jesus knew one day he would be filled with the Holy Spirit and entrusted with a great ministry. Jesus sees the person you will one day be and He invites you to follow Him and become that person. One day Michaelangelo was chipping away with his chisel on a huge shapeless piece of rock. Someone walked by and asked what he was doing to which he replied, "I am releasing the angel imprisoned in this marble." This is precisely what Jesus wants to do with you. He sees what's inside your stony exterior and he wants to release out into the open the hidden greatness that is in the heart of every person. Jesus looked at Peter and saw in him not only a Galilaean fisherman but one who had the potential to become a rock for the kingdom of God, a person who would stand up and boldly declare that Jesus was the Christ, the Son of the living God (Matt. 16:16).

Rom. 4:17 says God "gives life to the dead and calls those things which do not exist as though they did." This is what happened when Jesus called Peter a stone. The NLT says God is the one "who brings the dead back to life and who creates new things out of nothing." This was faith in action because Peter was a long way from having a rock-like character when Jesus changed his name. Jesus was operating in the principle of faith described in Joel 3:10 when God told the prophet to proclaim among the nations, "Let the weak say, 'I am strong!'" The NLT says, "Train even your weaklings to be warriors." Jesus knew what He was doing even though in the days ahead Peter would often say things he shouldn't have said and did things he shouldn't have done. One minute he was walking on water by faith and the next he was sinking in doubts. He is best known for denying Jesus three times but in the gospels whenever the disciples are listed Peter's name is always listed first. Peter had many faults yet inside he was a rock and later became a bold evangelist and missionary and one of the greatest leaders in the early church.

John 1:43 says, "The following day Jesus wanted to go to Galilee and He found Philip and said, 'Follow Me.'" Jesus left Judea and traveled north for He needed to break away from the place where John the Baptist was ministering and begin to reach out to people on the basis of who He was and the message He came to give. To Peter He gave a declaration and a promise and to Philip He gave a simple command. He said "Follow Me" and this same command has been issued to people ever since. This is not a command to be taken lightly for with it comes the obligation to leave everything behind and have a willingness to pay any price to become a follower of Jesus. Philip answered the call on his life and, like Andrew, he could not keep the good news about Jesus to himself. A lighted match is often used to light another so Philip went and found his friend Nathaniel and told him they had found the promised Messiah, Jesus of Nazareth (vs. 45). Nazareth was not a notable town and to hear that Jesus came from this undistinguished place was offensive to Nathaniel. Being skeptical he asked, "Can anything good come out of Nazareth?" (vs. 46).

Never is arguing with somebody an effective way in leading a person to Jesus. More times than not, this does more harm than good. People who use offensive words to defend what they believe in have a tendency to push people away rather than draw them in. To his credit, Philip did not argue with Nathaniel nor did he respond to his criticism. He said simply, "Come and see" (vs. 46). These were the same words Jesus spoke to Andrew and John the previous day. Any merchant will tell you that when you've got a good product, it will sell itself. Philip had just met Jesus and right away knew the best argument is to say to people, "Come and see!" So Nathaniel came and as he drew near Jesus could see into his heart. He had a warm word for Nathaniel and this drove away any prejudice he may have had against the residents of Nazareth. Jesus said to him, "Behold, an Israelite indeed, in whom is no guile!" (vs. 47). The NLT says Jesus called him "a man of complete integrity."

Not much is known about Nathaniel since not many of his actions are recorded. But Jesus knew him. He was an Israelite in whom was no deceit.

What Jesus said to Nathaniel was a tribute that any devout Israelite would recognize. David wrote in Ps. 32:2, "Blessed is the man to whom the Lord does not impute iniquity, and in whose spirit there is no guile." Honesty is important to God and He hates all forms of lying and deception. You should hate it also for lying is of the devil "for he is a liar and the father of it" (John 8:44). Jesus never speaks in vain and here He openly declares that Nathaniel is an honest and sincere man. If he told you something, you can believe it. He was also a humble man because honesty and humility always go hand-in-hand. Nathaniel was surprised at what Jesus said and demanded to know how He could possibly know him. Jesus answered and said to him, "Before Philip called you, when you were under the fig tree, I saw you." To the Jew the fig tree always stood for peace for it was their custom to sit and meditate under the shady roof of its branches (1 Kings 4:25). No doubt this is what Nathaniel had been doing and immediately he cried out, "Rabbi, You are the Son of God! You are the King of Israel!" (vs. 49).

Like Nathaniel, the first revelation you need to have of Jesus is that He is the Son of God. He had been meditating under the fig tree and for sure Jesus knew what he was thinking. Ps. 139:1 (MSG) says, "I'm an open book to You; even from a distance You know what I'm thinking." Jesus answered and said to him, "Because I said to you, 'I saw you under the fig tree,' do you believe? You will see greater things than these. Most assuredly, I say to you, hereafter you shall see heaven open and the angels of God ascending and descending upon the Son of God." The Message Bible says, "You haven't seen anything yet!" Jesus was quoting the story of Jacob at Bethel who had seen a golden ladder leading up to heaven (Gen. 28:12). He was saying that it is through Him alone that the hearts of men can mount the ladder that leads to heaven. This revelation of the deity of Jesus drove away any prejudice Nathaniel may have had against the residents of Nazareth. In Jesus he found the one person who could satisfy the longings of a seeking heart. He was now prepared to follow Jesus to the ends of the earth and beyond. He knew the time was now to "come and see."

-9-

"THE FIRST OF MANY"

Jesus now has a handful of men following Him who want to be His disciples and the first thing they do is walk approximately ninety miles to the city of Cana of Galilee which is six miles north of Nazareth. It took three days to make this journey and John 2:1,2 says, "On the third day there was a wedding in Cana of Galilee, and the mother of Jesus was there. Now both Jesus and His disciples were invited to the wedding." Mary was at this joyous occasion and this would indicate that she was related to or was a close friend of those getting married. Historians say that Mary was a sister of the bridegroom's mother which meant she held a special place at this feast and had the authority to tell the servants what to do. Because Jesus was related to Mary, He also was invited. A wedding feast among the Jews was a time of great gladness and joyful festivity and lasted between two to seven days, depending on the resources of the bridegroom. The timeline of John's account of this event seems to suggest that Jesus and His followers arrived together in the midst of all the fun and games.

For reasons unknown, many theologians have a hard time teaching that Jesus went to places where He had a good time. They think all He did was pray from morning to night and fight demons all day. No, Jesus knew how to have fun. This wedding feast was a big party where there was singing and dancing and people drank wine and thoroughly enjoyed themselves. This week of festivity was a joyous occasion with much happiness and celebration. It was an event Jesus willingly and gladly shared with all the people who were there. The sad reality of it all is that religion takes all the fun out of Christianity and is the reason many people don't give their lives to Jesus. Who wants to get saved if you have to be sad and downcast all the time? Why do people ignore 1 Tim. 6:17 that says

God "gives us richly all things to enjoy"? This is why you need to lighten up, have fun, and enjoy your life. Ps. 16:11 says, "You will show me the path of life; In Your presence is fullness of joy; At Your right hand are pleasures forevermore." The NET says, "You always give me sheer delight."

God is not opposed to you having fun, He is only opposed to sin. The fact alone that Jesus accepted this invitation is proof that it's okay for believers to make having fun a regular part of their lives. You can't let yourself get so high-minded thinking you're too good to participate in trivial things like going to a party. After all, there's a world to get saved and you've got to pray and study your Bible. People who feel this way are in danger of falling into spiritual pride and if they're not careful this way of thinking can pull them away from the very gospel they claim to follow and love. Don't get so high-minded that you're no earthly good. Granted, there are many people who need to do a lot more praying and studying of God's Word. Just don't get so spiritual that you think you're better than everybody else. People like this have no joy in their life and have a tendency to be outright mean to those around them. They become judgmental and drive others away from God. Their wrong attitude and actions have the opposite effect of what God intended.

Jesus said in John 10:10 (AMP), "I came that they may have and enjoy life, and have it in abundance to the full, till it overflows." You won't be able to truly enjoy your life until you come to understand that God is the life of every true party. He is the creator of fun and when your life is centered around Him, you'll experience heaven on earth. Yes, there are some temporary pleasures in sin but the life of Jesus shows you don't have to sin to have fun. The devil uses perverted fun to lure people into the deadly snare of sin but afterward comes the bitter consequences of having done wrong. You can't mock God. What you sow is what you'll reap (Gal. 6:7). The aftermath of what some people do for the sake of sensual fun and pleasure can bring hurt and pain that will stay with them for the rest of their lives. Why are people so foolish when they can have even more fun in the presence of God and be blessed forevermore? You need to follow God and let Him show what fun really is. Jesus went to a party and as He is, so are we in this world (1 John 4:17).

There are certain religious people who spread doom and gloom wherever they go. They have the personality of an undertaker where they wear black clothes, speak in hushed tones, and are suspicious of all happiness and joy. Not so with Jesus. He never counted it a crime to be happy and was perfectly at home at this wedding feast. The newly married couple did not go away for their honeymoon but stayed home to be the hosts of this feast given in their honor. They wore crowns on their heads and were dressed in bridal robes. For the duration of this grand celebration they were treated like a king and queen and their word was law. Jesus was here and He shared and participated in all the happy rejoicing that was going on. He laughed. He sang songs. You can even picture Him dancing with the bride along with all the other guests. So here Jesus is having a good time when suddenly the unthinkable happened. The wine ran out. For the bride and groom hospitality is a sacred duty and to run out of any provision would be a terrible humiliation. What were they going to do?

For a Jewish feast wine was essential. Marriage is a feast of joy and wine in scripture was given as an emblem of joy. Ps. 104:14,15 says, "He causes the grass to grow for the cattle, and vegetation for the service of man, that he may bring forth food from the earth, and wine that makes glad the heart of man." In the days of old wine was a common beverage and was a mixture of two parts wine and three parts water. This mixture would correspond to modern day grape juice that was a little spiked. It had the potential to take your sobriety away but only after great quantities were consumed. Drunkenness was in fact a great disgrace and Prov. 20:1 and many other scriptures clearly show there is a distinction between wine and intoxicating alcohol. In ancient times there were not many beverages that were safe to drink. There was a danger in drinking unfiltered water and it was tedious and costly to boil it all day. The safest and easiest method of making water safe to drink was to mix it with wine. The drinking of wine, therefore, served as a safety measure since the water by itself was often not safe to drink.

John 2:3 says, "And when they ran out of wine, the mother of Jesus said to Him, 'They have no wine.'" Why did Mary say this to Jesus? She didn't come right out and ask Him to do something but simply stated that the wine had run out. Her concern suggests that she was involved in the planning and organization of the wedding. This was a family affair and honor was of vital importance. Her family was about to be shamed in the community and she knew her Son could do something about it. As a personal favor to the bride and groom, she turned to Jesus for help. By stating they have no wine, Mary was dropping a hint that she wanted Jesus to do something the servants themselves could not do. She was, in fact, asking for a miracle to be performed. She remembered that her conception of Jesus was in itself a miracle and, even though He had not performed any miracles up until this time, she reasoned that now was as good a time as any to show the world that Jesus was indeed the promised Messiah. Little was she prepared for the response Jesus would give to her.

Jesus said, "Woman, what does your concern have to do with Me? My hour has not yet come" (John 2:4). Jesus was not being rude to His mother and the word "woman" was not said out of disrespect. In fact, it was a term of reverence and affection and is the same word Jesus used on the cross to address Mary as He left her to the care of John (John 19:26). Other translations say Jesus addressed her as "Dear woman" (NLT) and "dear lady" (ISV). What Jesus was doing, however, was calling attention to the fact that He was not speaking as a son to a mother, but as the Son of God to a woman. Jesus is not recognizing her motherly authority over Him and He was saying it was not up to her to determine or suggest how and when He would begin His work as the Messiah. The intentions of Mary were noble but still Jesus said to her, "Is this any of our business, Mother - yours or Mine? This isn't My time. Don't push Me" (MSG). There is great significance in what Jesus said. If He thought this way, then it is appropriate that you think this way also.

What did Jesus mean when He said, "Woman, why do you involve Me?" (NIV). How do these words apply to you and your everyday life? Jesus is saying that there are a lot of things in life and the lives of other people that don't pertain to you. People will try to make you their source of supply, especially if God has used you as a channel to help them in times past. This includes family, friends, and the minister down at the local church. Carnal believers who walk after the flesh tend to look to other people for help more than they look to God. These same people may have seen God move in your life in times past and reason that you should be the person they go to for help. Jesus is speaking to you here at this wedding feast and He is saying to never allow other people to make you their source. Just because you're a believer and have learned to walk by faith, and just because God has blessed you with financial and material resources, does not mean it is your responsibility to meet the needs of every person who comes to you asking for assistance. Don't let anyone make you their source.

If you've got a heart that cares, you can count on the fact that the devil will send people your way. He'll then try to make you feel like it's your fault if you don't help them and something bad happens. What the devil won't tell you is that these same people may have squandered their resources gambling or on the consumption of drugs and alcohol. These people are now in a bind and they'll come to you shedding crocodile tears saying they're going to be kicked out of their house if you don't help them out. Jesus is telling you to say to these people, "What does your concern have to do with me?" This does not mean you don't love these people and that you don't care. What it means is that you are not their source. They have the same Provider you do and He is their source whether they know it or not. This also does not mean that God won't use you to help them. What it does mean is that you are to be led by God and not the sobbing tactics of the devil. If you do something then do it because the Lord told you to do it and not because they pulled on the heart strings of your caring heart.

You need to follow the example of Jesus in everything you say and do. How did Jesus know what to do and when to do it? Many say because He was the Son of God but that is not true. When He came to the earth He lived and operated as a man. Phil. 2:6,7 (MSG) says, "He had equal status with God but didn't think so much of

Himself that He had to cling to the advantages of that status no matter what. Not at all. When the time came, He set aside the privileges of deity and took on the status of a slave, became human! Having become human, He stayed human." Jesus was anointed with power from on high at His baptism and He knew what to do by having a continual dependence on the Holy Spirit. He had a working relationship with the third Person of the Trinity and this is how He received divine direction. Jesus said in John 14:13, "He will guide you into all truth; for He will not speak on His own authority, but whatever He hears He will speak; and He will tell you things to come." Jesus was led by the Holy Spirit and you need to be also. Rom. 8:14 (NIV) says, "For those who are led by the Spirit of God are the children of God."

Jesus knew what to do because the Holy Spirit told Him what to do. If the Holy Spirit didn't move, then neither did He. Jesus said that His hour had not yet come. He knew that He had come to the earth for a specific purpose and each day He moved steadily toward that hour for which He had come into the world. Jesus spoke seven times in the gospel of John of this hour which was to come, the hour of His crucifixion when He would submit to the will of man in order to complete the work of redemption. Jesus was constantly working from a divine timetable and He wasn't going to reveal His power sooner than the Father intended (John 5:30). He had a request for a miracle but as of yet had no leading from the Spirit. One of the points Jesus made clear in the wilderness is that there is such a thing as doing the right thing for the wrong reasons. Jesus is saying to Mary that it would be wrong to perform a miracle if the time and place is not according to the leading and direction of the Holy Spirit. Up until this moment Jesus had not yet been told to intervene in this dilemma. All that was about to change.

Mary appeared to be neither offended or discouraged by what Jesus said to her, that the working of miracles was under the control of the Holy Spirit and not the two of them. Mary said not another word to Jesus about this, proving there is a time when it's best to keep quiet and give God time to move. Job 40:5 (MSG) says, "I've talked too much, way too much. I'm ready to shut up and listen." Ps. 39:9 (MSG) also says, "I'll say no more, I'll shut my mouth, since You, Lord, are behind all this." Mary respectfully understands that she is excluded from all control over when and where miracles are to happen. With submission and faith she surrenders the matter over to Jesus, still hopeful that her request will be granted. She has confidence in His compassion and ability and in admirable submission she backs off and lets Jesus take charge of the situation. As soon as Mary retired to her proper place, no longer making suggestions to the Lord, then, and only then, did the time come for her Son's glory to be manifested. It was then that she said to the servants, "Whatever He says to you, do it" (vs. 5).

In all of scripture, there are no better words of advice than these spoken by Mary. In order to fulfill your destiny and live a victorious life, you must always do what Jesus tells you to do. Mary was telling the servants to get ready to obey because deep in her heart she believed Jesus was about to speak. He is also about to speak to you and this is why you need to take time off from your busy schedule and spend some quality time alone with Him. You need to hourly be listening for His voice and always be training your inner man to recognize His voice when He does speak. Be like the boy Samuel who said, "Speak, Lord, for Your servant hears" (1 Sam. 3:9). God is a God of infinite wisdom and infinite love and you must have a deep determination to trust Him no matter what He tells you to do. God told Abraham to sacrifice his son on the altar and the old patriarch willingly obeyed. It takes courage to step out of the boat in stormy waters but, when you trust God enough to obey Him, you'll soon find that His sustaining power is able to hold you up and pull you through even the worst of circumstances. Obedience prevents hardness of heart and is the only way to true success. It's what draws you to the very heart of God.

In every realm of life, do what Jesus tells you to do. You need to submit to Him with no thought or argument for the matchless will of God is the perfection of all reason. You can trust Him completely even if you don't fully understand what it is He's telling you to do or why He's telling you to do it. The wisdom to overcome the trials in life must be in the Person giving the command, not in the person obeying the command. It made no sense for Jesus to tell the fishermen to launch out into the deep for a catch (Luke 5:4). It was the very spot they had toiled in vain all night and still they caught nothing. They obeyed nonetheless and shortly thereafter they caught so many fish that their nets began to break and their boats began to sink. They learned that it is wise to do whatever Jesus tells you to do. And when you obey God, do it cheerfully. It's the joyful willingness of your heart to obey that is acceptable to God. It is the utmost desire of the Lord's heart that you obey Him so that you can become His friend (John 15:14) and receive all the wonderful blessings He has for your life.

Jesus is perfect and when you obey His voice you are aiming at the perfection that is in Him. He knows what you need more than you do and this is why you need to do what He tells you to do. These words of wisdom were given to the servants by Christ's mother who had lived with Him for an entire generation. A more highly tribute could not be given than to say He was worthy of total and complete obedience. In the heart of Mary was reverence and trust for she carried in her soul the memory of the events that brought about His birth. Moments before, Jesus had placed her on that level of total dependence on the Holy Spirit, a place she must forever remain. As she stood there looking at Him in all her loveliness and beauty, her inability to understand the realm in which her Son lived and her impatience began to diminish and was replaced with a declaration of trusting obedience. She was convinced in her heart that any kind of lack or difficulty is cured by prompt obedience to the words of Jesus. She knew all too well that many of the failures and agonies of life happen somewhere between the hearing of God's command and the obedience of doing it.

Close at hand were six empty stone waterpots each capable of holding between twenty and thirty gallons of water (vs. 6). These vessels were for ceremonial washings for the Jews considered themselves to be unclean if they did not wash their hands before eating (Matt. 15:2). To the Jews, seven is the number of perfection and six is the number of man for it represents the flesh and all that is unfinished and imperfect. These stone waterpots represented the Old Testament law with all its fleshly efforts that had nothing to offer the heart. Judaism had become a religious system that offered no provision for the joy of mankind. At this wedding feast the provisions of man had run out. There was no more wine and the waterpots were empty. This is what religion does to you. This great void happened on the third day (vs. 21) and this speaks of the resurrection. When Jesus comes into a joyless, empty situation, He fills it with resurrection life and power. In His presence is joyful abundance and heavenly bliss that lasts a lifetime. He said to the servants, "Fill the waterpots with water" (vs. 7). And they filled them to the brim.

Many miracles in the Bible began with an instruction that had to be followed. Naaman was told to go wash in the Jordan River seven times (2 Kings 5:10), the man with the withered hand was told to stretch it out (Matt. 12:13), and the impotent man was told to take up his bed and walk (John 5:11). Their obedience to these instructions determined the outcome of their situation and on this day it would be no different. If what Jesus told the servants to do was not acted upon, there would be no miracle. Filling these waterpots with water was not an easy task to perform. The servants had to go outside to the well that could have been a long distance away. Buckets had to be dropped down into this well and carried back to where the waterpots were at. Over and over this had to be done until the vessels were filled to the brim. What Jesus told them to do didn't make any sense but these were instructions that had to be followed no matter how much labor was involved. Fortunately, the servants did not dispute His command but yielded in total and absolute obedience to what His instructions were.

Faith never asks "Why?" Abraham set off on his journey for the Lord not knowing where he was going. He didn't question the Lord's command but willfully obeyed. Neither did the servants ask "Why?" and when they were finished Jesus said to them, "Draw some out now, and take it to the master of the feast" (vs. 8). Once again the servants did what Jesus told them to do and out of their obedience came a miracle, the first of many that Jesus would perform in His ministry. If there is a season of lack in your life, don't be surprised if the Lord asks you to do something that at first appears contrary to sound reasoning. Just do what He tells you to do and then stand back and watch Him fill your life with goodness until it overflows. The quality of the wine He supplied was far superior to anything that had been served thus far. It was so good that the master of the feast was stunned and surprised that the bridegroom had kept his best wine until the last (vs. 10). No, he had already given his best. Man's best can never equal what Jesus wants to give for He is able to do exceedingly, abundantly above all you can ask or think (Eph. 3:20).

A question is often asked if Jesus made real wine or a diluted wine that tasted like grape juice. The Greek word for "wine" in this passage is "oinos" which was the common word for wine that was fermented and alcoholic. This is the same Greek word used in Eph. 5:18 that tells people "do not get drunk on wine." It is obvious that getting drunk from drinking wine requires the presence of alcohol. In other words, Jesus created the real thing and not some watered down version. Those who oppose the drinking of alcohol may argue that Jesus was promoting drunkenness which the Bible clearly identifies as sinful. This is not a valid argument because some scriptures portray alcohol in positive terms. Eccl. 9:7 says, "Drink your wine with a merry heart." Amos 9:14 discusses drinking vine from your own vineyard as a sign of God's blessing. No, Jesus was not promoting drunkenness just like He wasn't promoting gluttony when He multiplied the loaves and fishes beyond what the people needed. Wine is not sinful but the abuse of it is. Creating a substance that can be abused does not make one responsible when another person foolishly chooses to abuse it.

John 2:9 says the master of the feast didn't know where the new wine came from "but the servants knew." The bridegroom also didn't know what happened and not even the disciples were part of this miracle. The revelation of what happened was reserved for the humble servants. Amos 3:7 says, "Surely the Lord God does nothing, unless He reveals His secret to His servants the prophets." Servants of Jesus know things that no one else knows. These servants knew that Jesus is the great Provider, that He sometimes acts quietly with no fanfare, and that His resources are extravagantly greater that what man can produce on his own. If you want to be in on the miracles of Jesus, if you want Him to reveal things to you, then work closely with Him as an obedient servant. Those who serve understand the process because they are part of the process. The miracle of Cana was not about changing water into wine but that some miracles require the cooperation of others. This miracle was the first sign because it teaches you the first lesson. If you want to see miracles, you must serve God with all your heart and soul.

Randall J. Brewer

-10-

"A HOUSE OF PRAYER"

Jesus saved the day when He turned water into wine. The guests at the wedding feast continued to eat, drink, and be merry, and the bride and groom went on to live happily ever after. John 2:11 says, "This beginning of signs Jesus did in Cana of Galilee, and manifested His glory; and His disciples believed in Him." The Message Bible says this miracle was "the first glimpse of His glory" for it showed that He had divine power and was in fact sent by God to the earth. He was a man like no other and Acts 10:38 says Jesus "went about doing good" and this wedding feast was the appropriate place to initiate a life of being a blessing to other people. Religion had become a ritual and the joy of a personal relationship with God was not evident with most of the people. The wine had run out and so had their joy. Jesus came on the scene and said in John 15:11, "These things have I spoken to you, that My joy may be in you, and that your joy may be full." What better place to have fullness of joy than at a wedding feast? Marriage was the first institution ordained by God, and so it was at a wedding feast that Jesus performed His first miracle.

John says the miracle of Cana was the beginning of signs that Jesus would work in His life. It had been centuries since anyone had witnessed a miracle and on this day the glory of God was manifested in a blaze of splendor and majesty. Few people at the time knew what had happened but the disciples knew and believed in Him. Adam's sin turned the paradise of the garden into a wilderness and this miracle turned the wilderness into a paradise. Man's sin brought barrenness, Jesus came and restored spiritual fruitfulness back to the earth. This was also a miracle of luxury. Wine is not needed to maintain life but loaves and fishes are. Man does not live by bread alone and Jesus makes it plain that it is permitted to have and enjoy the finer things in life. The potato may be more needful but that is not to say the rose is unnecessary. God wants your life to overflow with His blessings and all He is saying is that self-restraint should be practiced in the midst of all this abundance. Your earthly life is to be blessed and glorified by the heavenly life of Jesus. He came to turn the common into the uncommon and to enrich and awaken human gladness.

The Lord's glory did not begin with this miracle, the miracle only manifested the power and love that is at work everywhere. All miracles point to Jesus and the manifestation of who He is contains the evidence and essence of all Christianity. Just as the first rays of the morning sun reveal the glorious light which is to come, so did this first miracle reveal the glory of Him who came to bring all things together unto Himself. This miracle was a sign to show people that the worst things in life can be made better, the broken can be made whole. The value of a miracle is in what it signifies, not in what actually took place. It is the glory that allows Jesus to transform sinners into people made in His own likeness, to turn a nobody into a somebody. Glory is the signature of divinity and when it is poured into your life your heart will become a fountain that springs up into life eternal. Ps. 84:6 (NLT) says, "When they walk through the Valley of Weeping, it will become a place of refreshing springs. The autumn rains will clothe it with blessings." It is Jesus who transforms the water of lack and need into the wine of heavenly blessings and abundance.

"After this He went down to Capernaum, He, His mother, His brothers, and His disciples; and they did not stay there many days" (John 2:12). Capernaum was on the northwest coast of the Sea of Galilee and was about twenty miles east of Cana. This was a city of considerable importance. It had a moderate population and much commercial trade happened in this city. It was the home of high ranking government officials and military officers, plus several of the Lord's future disciples had their homes there. In Matt. 9:1 the town is referred to as "His own city" and, according to all four gospels, Jesus selected this town as the center of His public ministry after He left the small mountainous village of

Nazareth. Many of the Lord's most notable deeds were done in this city, among them the raising of the daughter of Jairus from the dead and the healing of the centurion's servant. Sad to say, most of the people there didn't follow Jesus and He cursed the city in Matt. 11:23 (NIV), "And you, Capernaum, will you be lifted up to heaven? No, you will go down to Hades. For if the miracles that were performed in you had been performed in Sodom, it would have remained to this day."

Jesus did not stay many days in Capernaum for the Passover of the Jews was at hand and He wished to be at the celebration of this feast in Jerusalem (vs. 13). This was the first Passover after His baptism, the second one is mentioned in Luke 6:1, the third in John 6:4, and the fourth, which was when He was crucified, in John 11:55. The Passover is one of the most widely celebrated Jewish holidays and takes place in the spring during the Hebrew month of Niran, in early to mid-April. The book of Exodus tells of the origin of this feast. God sent Moses to Egypt to tell Pharaoh to "let My people go" (Ex. 8:1). Pharaoh refused and God brought ten plagues on the land of Egypt. The tenth and last of the plagues was the death of all the firstborn of Egypt. God told the Israelites to sacrifice a spotless lamb and mark their doorposts and lintels with its blood (Ex. 12:21,22). When the Lord passed through the nation, He passed over the households that showed the blood (vs. 23). The Israelites were saved from the plague and their firstborn children stayed alive. God then told the people to "observe this thing as an ordinance for you and your sons forever" (vs. 24).

The Passover was the greatest of all Jewish feasts and, according to Jewish law, it was mandatory that every male Jew who lived within fifteen miles of Jerusalem attend the celebration of this feast. By this time the Jewish people were scattered all over the region but they never forgot their heritage and the faith of their forefathers. It was the dream of every Jew, no matter where they lived, to celebrate at least one Passover in Jerusalem and it was likely that thousands upon thousands of people were assembled in the Holy City at the time of this feast. Jesus made the eighty-five mile journey to Jerusalem and went to the temple which had been dedicated as a place of meeting between God and His people. This temple was to be a house of prayer and worship and Ps. 69:9 tells how the people were consumed with zeal for the house of God. Jesus had great regard for the pure worship of the Father and when He went to the temple this He did not find. Instead, John 2:14 says, "And He found in the temple those who sold oxen and sheep and doves, and the moneychangers doing business."

Until the time when Jesus became the ultimate sacrifice on the cross, people were still required to make animal sacrifices at the temple. Because of the long distance some of these people had to travel they did not bring their own animals with them. It was difficult to bring all the animals from the distant parts of Judea so a lucrative business was set up where the animals were sold up to double of what they were worth. Oxen and doves were needed for sacrificial purposes and a lamb was required for the Passover meal. Historians say that nearly two hundred thousand lambs were needed for this Passover feast which only increased the merchant's opportunity to make a greater profit. Religion was being turned into a money-making scandal. 1 Tim. 6:5 (NLT) says, "These people always cause trouble. Their minds are corrupt, and they have turned their backs on the truth. To them, a show of godliness is just a way to become wealthy." Strong is the love of money and for many it is the ruling passion of their lives. Not even the sacredness of the temple stopped these shrewd businessmen from taking advantage of the situation at hand.

The Jewish law also required every person over the age of nineteen to pay a tribute tax so that the sacrifices and other rituals might be carried out day by day (Ex. 30:11-16). The price of this tribute was half a shekel which was a Jewish coin and worth about two days wages. People arrived from all over the known world with all kinds of coins yet no foreign coins were allowed to pollute the temple. It became a matter of convenience to have a place where the Roman coin could be exchanged for the Jewish half shekel. Those with foreign currency could come and exchange it for the sacred currency and pay their temple tax. The moneychangers provided this service and if done properly they would have been fulfilling an honest and necessary purpose. But honest was the last thing these people were and the interest for their service was fifty percent. The temple had become a place for personal profit at the expense of the poor and the foreign traveler. This was an unbridled and shameless form of social injustice that resulted in fraud and oppression to those who meant well. What's worse, it was all being done in the name of religion.

Evil prevails when good people stand by and do nothing. Such was not the case on this day. It was impossible for Jesus to stand passively by while the true worshippers were treated in such a despicable way. What was being done here was also making it impossible for the seeking person to get into the temple to make contact with God. Jesus was filled with righteous indignation and was moved to flaming anger. God's house had become a place of covetousness, personal gain, and robbery of the poor. John 2:15 says, "When He had made a whip of cords, He drove them all out of the temple, with the sheep and oxen, and poured out the charger's money and overturned the tables." A fiery light shone from His eyes and the majesty of God gleamed on His face. Jesus was one man but He spoke and moved with authority and the whole crowd fled before Him. Even the worst of sinners recognize authority. A whip in the strong hand of an angry carpenter was enough incentive that deterred all from making resistance. As stated in Zech. 14:21 (ESV), "And there shall no longer be a trader in the house of the Lord of hosts on that day."

"And He said to those who sold doves, 'Take these things away! Do not make My Father's house a house of merchandise!'" (vs. 16). Jesus called the temple His "Father's house" which immediately identified Him as the Son of God. No prophet had ever called the temple by that name for, until that time, only Jesus could claim divine Sonship. Jesus had a fervent passion for that which pertained to His Father and He expressed it in what He did. Do things like this bother you? It should. When you love God, it should bother you when people defile that which is sacred. Never should personal business be done at the local church. Don't try to sell your car in the parking lot or beauty products at the woman's Bible study. Don't do it because the Father's house is not a house of merchandise. It is a house of prayer and you are there to worship

Him and not to make a business deal. To turn the house of God into a market place is blasphemous in the eyes of Jesus. It angers Him and you must remember that in order to grasp the full meaning of His love.

Mal. 2:17 asks the question, "Where is the God of justice?" He's right here with a whip in His hand. Mal. 3:1 then says, "And the Lord, whom you seek, will suddenly come to His temple." Without warning the Lord indeed came to the temple. He came unexpectedly, like a thief, like lightning flashing to the east and to the west. With a dramatic explosion of emotional energy He announced that the Messiah was here in their midst. Mal. 3:2 (NLT) says, "But who will be able to endure it when He comes? Who will be able to stand and face Him when He appears? For He will be like a blazing fire that refines metal, or like a strong soap that bleaches clothes." He came to cleanse the temple from its defilement and fill it with His teaching and glory. Scripture records two separate occasions when Jesus cleansed the temple. The first cleansing happened here at the beginning of His public ministry and the second just after His triumphant entry into Jerusalem shortly before He was crucified. Only John records this first cleansing yet he makes no mention of the latter incident.

Three years after this first cleansing the abuse Jesus corrected returned in full force. Mark 11:11 says Jesus went into the temple to look around and didn't like what He saw. He took no action then for the hour was already late and temple activities were shutting down for the night. The next day He once again came suddenly to the temple and, taking vehement action, begins to drive out those selling and buying at this sacred place of worship. He then said in vs. 17, "Is it not written, 'My house shall be called a house of prayer for all nations'? But you have made it a 'den of thieves.'" Jesus takes personal what happens in the temple and so should you. The first time He called the temple "My Father's house" but here He calls it "My house." Later, in Matt. 23:38, He calls it "your house." The house of God is your house also and you need to treat it as such. Don't allow gossip and murmuring to go on in the house of prayer. Say something! Do something! Doing nothing is the same as consenting to what's going on. Don't allow the church to become a place of merchandise and a den of thieves. This is a holy place and it must be honored with reverence and a holy fear of displeasing God.

God's house is a house of prayer which means you are to forever be communicating with Him. This does not mean you always have to pray for an hour at a time. What it does mean is that you should never go an hour without praying. 1 Thess. 5:16-18 says you are to "Rejoice always, pray without ceasing, in everything give thanks; for this is the will of God in Christ Jesus for you." The more you pray, the more rejoicing you will do. When prayer and joy come together they create a spirit of gratitude. It is a privilege to talk with the great God of the universe and this is why you must continually be in a spirit of prayer, day in and day out. Prayer is simply talking with God and you need to maintain a continual, uninterrupted open line of communication with Him. God is speaking to you and you need to be speaking to Him. Listen to Him the same way you want Him to listen to you. Whenever you have a conversation with God, you are giving Him glory and this is why you need to be habitually talking to Him. Jesus called you His friend and friends talk to one another. This should be happening all through the day, wherever you are and wherever you go.

Prayer is the magnet that pulls you in to the presence of God. Speaking to Him should be the greatest longing of your heart and this impulse must be acted upon the moment it arrives. Avoid all unnecessary interruptions and never allow yourself to get too busy to pray. If you're too busy for God, you're too busy. Give God the time He deserves and watch what He'll do with the rest of your day. When it comes to prayer you must avoid laziness, idleness, and passivity. Be aware that the devil will always supply you with an excuse not to pray. Resist that temptation and pray even more. James 4:7,8 says, "Therefore submit to God. Resist the devil and he will flee from you. Draw near to God and He will draw near to you." The Message Bible says, "So let God work His will in you. Yell a loud 'no' to the devil and watch him scamper. Say a quiet 'yes' to God and He'll be there in no time." The "Spirit of life in Christ Jesus" (Rom. 8:2) is inside of you and the persevering spirit of prayer causes this life to spring forth and energize everything that pertains to you and your walk with God. Prayer is the remedy for confusion, comfort in time of sorrow and strength against temptation. It's during times of prayer that your awareness of God is at its fullest.

Daily you should be striving to know God better and better. Job 22:21 says, "Now acquaint yourself with Him, and be at peace; Thereby good will come to you." Friends visit one another and Is. 26:16 says you are visiting with God when you pray. You need to pray without ceasing for prayer is the mold in which all your thoughts, words, and actions are cast. He is to be on your mind every second of every hour of every day and never are you to stop telling Him how much He means to you. Make your time of prayer a heavenly banquet between you and your God, an appointment never to be canceled. Be like David who said in Ps. 16:8, "I have set the Lord always before me; Because He is at my right hand I shall not be moved." Take prayer seriously because you are in a war with an enemy who comes to steal, kill, and destroy (John 10:10). In order for you not to be moved in times of trouble, you've got to take your prayer life to a higher level. Whether by night or by day, always be in the constant, continual presence of God. If you'll do that, nothing will be able to move you away from your purpose and prevent you from fulfilling your destiny.

Jesus is at the right hand of the Father and He is at your right hand as well. In scripture, the right hand is regarded as a place of honor and dignity. It is also mentioned as a position of defense and protection. Ps. 121:5 says, "The Lord is your keeper; The Lord is your shade at your right hand." Jesus is at your side and you shall be protected from your enemies. He is your counselor, companion, guide, and defender. He is your "refuge and strength, a very present help in trouble" (Ps. 46:1). With Jesus by your side you are never alone. He still has a whip in His hand so you never have to fear those who would abuse the temple of your life. Ps. 110:5 says, "The Lord is at your right hand; He shall execute kings in the day of His wrath." David believed that God was always near him and he would frequently have close communion with Him. You need to do the same. Embrace Him morning to night and see Him everywhere. Ps. 16:8 (MSG) says, "Day and night I'll stick with God; I've got a good thing going and I'm not letting go." Vs. 11 (MSG) says, "Now You've got my feet on the life path, all radiant from the shining of Your face. Ever since You took my hand, I'm on the right way."

Your body is the temple of the Holy Spirit (1 Cor. 6:19) which means it needs to become a house of prayer. Daily you need to be talking to God and then be still long enough to allow Him to talk to you. Pitied is the person who does not hear God speak for He is the Good Shepherd and His sheep hear His voice (John 10:3). God wants you to hear Him when He speaks so He has ingrained in you the instinctive ability to hear His voice. It's a natural phenomenon that took place inside of you the moment you gave your life to Christ. Sheep have the ability to hear the Shepherd so, if you're born again, never say you can't hear from God. You can hear from Him if you would only take the time to listen to Him. This is why Ps. 46:10 says, "Be still, and know that I am God." He speaks in the realm of silence and this is why you need to be still and allow a blissful calm to overtake your mind. Some people are so busy that they never take time to get still and these are the people who never hear from God. Without stillness there can be no communication with the great God of the universe. Jesus often went off by Himself to pray and this is an example that must be followed in your life.

It is not easy to be still in this restless world but God says to do it anyway. He said in Is. 30:15, "In returning and rest you shall be saved; In quietness and confidence shall be your strength." People need to be taught how to hear from God and the first lesson is to be still before Him. Indeed, silence is golden. Do not allow the devil of haste to possess your life to the point that you have no time to spend with God. Be still for it is in silence that the power of life grows. It is in silence that the moon passes through the night sky. It is in silence that a mighty oak tree grows and gains the strength to defeat the fury of a raging storm. And it is in silence that you hear the voice of God. In times of trial people are quick to talk to God but leave and go about their business without giving Him a chance to speak. They don't realize that they were about to be told the solution to all their problems but they were too busy to listen. God deserves more honor than that. He deserves to be heard. He takes the time to listen to you and you need to slow down and take the time to listen to Him. In other words, be still and know He is God.

Not only do shepherds hear the voice of God, the sheep do as well. This can and will happen but first you must value His voice and those times when He does speak to you. 1 Sam. 3:1 says, "And the word of the Lord was rare in those days." Yes, because of sin "there was no widespread revelation" in those days but the primary definition for the Hebrew word "rare" means 'valuable.' Rarely did He speak but, when He did, it was valuable and precious to those who heard Him. On purpose you need to set a time during the day when you can get alone with God. Jesus did. Mark 1:35 says, "Now in the morning, having risen a long while before daylight, He went out and departed to a solitary place; and there He prayed." Make an appointment with God and don't cancel it. What does it say about God's value to you if you miss a planned meeting with Him? People say they want to hear God but never set up a time to meet with Him. You need to understand that God only speaks to people who are prepared to hear from Him. Prepare your heart and mind to be open to whatever He has to say and then be committed to put His guidance into action.

Ask God to put a hunger in your heart to hear His voice for there is no greater experience in life. To hear Him speak is the greatest joy you'll ever have. But first, you must put a high value on having this happen. God is constantly speaking but most people aren't listening. Don't be one of these people. Daily set an appointment to meet with Him for by doing so you'll develop the kind of relationship with Him that will enable you to hear Him speak on a regular basis. The closer you get to God, both listening and hearing from one another, the more those conversations will transform you into the person He wants you to become. Value your time alone with Him and allow the temple of your body to become a house of prayer. Have the confidence that God is willing to speak to you just as powerfully as He did to the people in the Bible. The Bible begins with God talking to Adam in the Garden of Eden and ends with Him talking to John on the island of Patmos. Throughout the Bible God is talking to His people. He never changes and He values you just as much as He values them. Those He values, He speaks to. The question is, how much do you value Him?

After Jesus cleansed the temple at the start of His ministry, the Jews who were there demanded from Him a sign that showed He had the right to do what He did (John 2:18). They must have remembered how when Moses came to deliver the children of Israel he performed signs and wonders to prove he was acting under the direction of God. It was always expected that the coming Messiah would also do some amazing things so they asked Jesus to show them some wondrous sign that proved His claim to be the Son of God. His deity was on display at this moment for He just did something a normal person would not do. The temple at Jerusalem was the dwelling place of God and His visible presence was often manifested there. The manner in which Jesus had cleansed the house of God was of itself a sign, if only the people had eyes to see it. Jesus is angry over religious corruption and zealous for the proper worship of His father. His answer to their request was not what they expected. He vehemently said to them, "Destroy this temple, and in three days I will raise it up" (vs. 19).

John does not leave his readers wondering what Jesus meant by this statement for he immediately says that Jesus was referring to the temple of His body (vs. 21). Paul said in Col. 2:9, "For in Him dwells all the fullness of the Godhead bodily" making it appropriate that the body of Jesus be called a temple. It needs to be remembered that John's interpretation of what Jesus said was written many years after this event took place. It has been written by Biblical scholars that no prophecy is fully understood until after the fulfillment of it. The Jews who heard these words did not understand their full meaning so they became indignant and mockingly said, "It has taken forty-six years to build this temple, and will You raise it up in three says?" (vs. 20). Jesus did not respond to this question but three years later when He had risen from the dead His disciples remembered what was spoken that day "and they believed the Scripture and the word which Jesus had said" (vs. 22). Jesus did perform signs here at Jerusalem but John does not record what they were for the people were not yet ready to embrace Him as their Messiah. That would soon begin to change.

-11-

"THE NEW BIRTH"

It would take little persuasion to convince most believers that John 3 is the most important and essential chapter in all the Bible, with John 3:16 being the champion of all Biblical scripture. There can be no debate that the message of transformation contained in this chapter is relevant for the eternal well-being of all mankind. The message of this chapter teaches you that life doesn't work unless Jesus is Lord of your life. It answers the questions, "Who's in charge of your life?" and "Whose side are you on?" Are you on God's side or the devil's side? Hopefully, by chapter's end, you will be prompted, once and for all, to allow the will of God to be the determining factor in every decision you make. You must put Him in charge of your life, your ministry, your marriage, and your finances. He needs to be Lord over everything that pertains to your life. This chapter begins when Nicodemus, a leader of the Jews, comes to Jesus by night for he recognized that He was "a teacher come down from God; for no one can do these signs that You do unless God is with him" (John 3:2). The conversation that followed reveals the essence of life.

The name "Nicodemus" means 'innocent blood' in Hebrew and 'victor over the people' in Greek. He was a Pharisee, a man of prominence and dignity. When the body of Jesus was being prepared for burial it was Nicodemus who brought nearly a hundred pounds of spices to anoint Jesus, which indicates he was a man of considerable wealth. He was not a common man for in many ways the Pharisees were the best people in the whole country. They were zealous for God and completely committed to what they believed in. They excelled in all things spiritual and were masters of the Biblical text. You couldn't get more religious than the Pharisees and it was a badge of honor to be one. There were never more than six thousand of them at one time and together they formed a sacred brotherhood vowing to obey and observe every detail of the first five books of the Old Testament. They embraced spiritual discipline and believed their sometimes harsh and arrogant behavior was justified because they were paying a price no one else was willing to pay. It is astonishing that a man in his position would wish to talk to Jesus at all.

Being a ruler of the Jews meant that Nicodemus was also a member of the Sanhedrin who were the most powerful men in all Israel. The term "Sanhedrin" comes from a Greek word that means 'assembly' or 'council' and their history dates back to Deut. 16:18 where God said to Moses, "You shall appoint judges and officers in all your gates, which the Lord your God gives you, according to your tribes, and they shall judge the people with just judgment." The Great Sanhedrin was the supreme court of ancient Israel and was made up of seventy men and the High Priest (Num. 11:16). They had religious jurisdiction over every Jew in the world and they met in the temple in Jerusalem every day except for festivals and on the Sabbath. They had the power to try the king if necessary and were the ones to whom all questions of the law were brought. Another one of their duties was to examine and deal with anyone suspected of being a false prophet. Although Nicodemus later spoke up on behalf of Jesus, it was the Sanhedrin who made the decision to turn Jesus over to the Roman authorities to be tried and crucified.

It is not mentioned why Nicodemus came to Jesus by night but it did show a desire to not have his actions seen by the other rulers. He did not want to encounter the hostility of the priests who were still filled with rage over the cleansing of the temple. The interest of Nicodemus was real and genuine and yet he wished to be cautious. By avoiding the wrath of his colleagues he was also obtaining a more personal and uninterrupted audience with Jesus. Nicodemus was a man of great importance and significance yet deep inside there was something lacking in his life. He came to Jesus in the darkness of the night in hopes that he might find the true light. Right away he gave recognition that there was something special about Jesus for he addressed Him as "Rabbi" (vs. 2). This was a title of respect given to distinguished Jewish teachers and, by saying this, Nicodemus was acknowledging the divine mission of Jesus. He said openly that no one could help being impressed with the signs and wonders that He did. Little was he prepared for what Jesus would say to him next.

Jesus was a master with the words He spoke. They flowed with the wind of the Spirit and He always said the right thing at the right time whether His listeners wanted to hear it or not. Jesus answered Nicodemus and said to him, "Most assuredly, I say to you, unless one is born again, he cannot see the kingdom of God" (vs. 3). Nicodemus was the best of the best and it is stunning that Jesus would say something like this to a person of his character. There was nobody more religious than Nicodemus but still Jesus told him that he had to be born again. Jesus didn't say this to a wretched sinner off the street, He said it to a man who practically lived inside the four walls of the church. The Lord's response was saying that outward signs is not what's important but rather the inner change of a person's heart that can only be described as a new birth. Even if your self-righteousness puts you at the top of the class, Jesus is saying that you still must be born again. When the rule applies to the greatest among you, it applies to everyone else. If Nicodemus has to be born again, then so do you.

Jesus is saying that being religious does not mean you're going to heaven. When Jesus walked the earth there were no people more religious than the Pharisees. They believed in the God of Abraham, Isaac, and Jacob. They worshiped God, they prayed, they tithed, they fasted twice a week, and they were all required to memorize the first five books of the Old Testament. They were very religious but still 2 Tim. 3:5 says there are people who have a form of godliness but deny its power. Paul is saying that a lot of people have religion in their words and actions but not in their hearts. Their names are on the roster at church but they're like chickens who have wings but never fly. They're like a hollow tree that may be tall but inside they're sapless and unstable. They put on a vain and empty show of piety and religion but renounce its power over their hearts and the life they live. They wear a mask but underneath there is no substance or spiritual reality. These people think they're saved and going to heaven, but are they really?

Many people are caught in the crosshairs of deception when it comes to their salvation. They know they're not good enough to go to heaven but think they're not bad enough to go to hell. They're caught somewhere in the middle not knowing if they're coming or going. This was the mindset of the rich, young ruler who came running up to Jesus, knelt before Him, and asked, "Good Teacher, what good thing shall I do that I may have eternal life?" (Matt. 19:16). Who was this young man? Luke 18:23 says "he was a man of great wealth." The Jewish historian Josephus said he had so much wealth that he could support all the inhabitants of Jerusalem for ten years. Matt. 19:22 says he was a "young man" somewhere between the age of twenty-four and forty. Luke 18:18 says he was a "ruler" which meant he was in charge of a synagogue and a member of the Sanhedrin just like Nicodemus. Josephus said he was the richest and youngest member of the Sanhedrin ever. Here this young man is, dressed in fine robes, not a hair out of place, kneeling in the dirt in front of Jesus with a question burning in his heart.

Mark 10:17 says the young man asked Jesus, "Good Teacher, what shall I do that I may inherit eternal life?" This man was different from the other religious leaders who questioned Jesus in public. They asked questions pertaining to taxes, sin, and the Sabbath in hopes of tricking Him into making a rash and imprudent statement. Such was not the case with this young man for it was a sincere question to which he needed to know the answer. Jesus answered his question with a question of His own, "Why do you call Me good? No one is good but One, that is, God" (vs. 18). Jesus is saying that to be good is to be God. Rom. 3:12 says, "There is none who does good, no, not one." The Bible says if you've broken one commandment, you've broken them all. Jesus said this because He knows the young ruler won't be able to understand anything else he's told until he understands there is a difference between man's goodness and God's standards of righteousness. The primary focus of his life is that he did more good things than bad, and still this wasn't enough to give him eternal life. This is why Jesus said there is no one good but God.

After pointing out the young man's inadequate understanding of what it means to be good, Jesus then listed six of the ten commandments that God gave to Moses. Immediately the man responded, "Teacher, all these I have observed from my youth" (Mark 11:20). This answer came as no surprise because the religious leaders of that time believed that the law could indeed be kept in its entirety. This young ruler had observed and kept all the commandments Jesus listed but still he sensed an incompleteness inside of him otherwise he wouldn't have come to Jesus in the first place. Jesus knew what was missing in his life and this is why He only quoted six commandments and not all ten. The first four commandments have to do with man's relationships with God, the last six, the one's Jesus quoted, have to do with man's relationship to man. Jesus didn't mention the first four commandments because this rich young ruler had already broken the first one. God said "you shall have no other gods before Me" (Deut. 5:7) and yet the man had already made his great possessions his god.

God requires total commitment and for this reason Jesus said in Mark 10:21, "One thing you lack: Go your way, sell whatever you have and give to the poor and you will have treasure in heaven; and come, take up your cross and follow Me." These words upset the young man and he went away grieved for he had great possessions (vs. 22). The truth be told, these words from Jesus would upset most believers in the world today. People value their possessions too much and inwardly fear that one day Jesus may require them to give it all up for the sake of the kingdom. Why are they even worried about this? What are they afraid of? What Jesus said to the rich young ruler is consistent with what He said throughout His journeys. He said in Luke 14:33, "In the same way, any of you who does not give up everything he has cannot be My disciple." Luke 9:24 says, "For whoever wants to save his life will lose it, but whoever loses his life for Me will save it." Jesus said the kingdom of heaven is like treasure hidden in a field and a man sold all he had and bought the field (Matt. 13:44). Why do people fear? They fear because inwardly they also are not fully surrendered to the will of God.

Before Jesus told this young man what to do, vs. 21 says He looked at him and loved him. Jesus loved him enough to tell him the truth, to confront him right where he was in his walk with God. What most people don't realize is that nowhere in scripture does God ask anyone else to do this. Only him. Jesus did not say he had to sell his possessions in order to go to heaven. Jesus was telling him that to inherit eternal life he had to take up his cross and follow Him. Another time Jesus said, "If anyone desires to come after Me, let him deny himself, and take up his cross, and follow Me" (Matt. 16:24). In order to do this the young man had to first deny himself and the love he had for all his possessions. This was the one thing stopping him from giving Jesus control of his life. Giving his possessions away would give him treasure in heaven but dying to self and following Jesus is what would give him salvation and eternal life. Following Jesus demands sacrifice and Jesus never hid that cost. You must put to death your own plans and desires and exchange them for His. The sacrifice may be hard but the reward is matchless.

The lesson from the story of the rich young ruler is that being good and doing good is not enough to get you into heaven. Jesus is saying that it's impossible for you to save yourself. You can't buy your way into heaven and you can never be good enough to earn passage through the pearly gates. The only way you can be saved is through a Savior and for this reason Jesus told Nicodemus that a person must be born again. Jesus spoke of spiritual things yet Nicodemus could not get past his natural way of thinking. He was seeking answers and he asked, "How can a man be born when he is old? Can he enter a second time into his mother's womb and be born?" (John 3:4). Nicodemus is hungry to see and understand the kingdom and Jesus is very intent on teaching him that he needed to be made alive spiritually. He is saying that without the born again experience you cannot enter or see the kingdom of God. The people were expecting a physical kingdom to be set up by a Messiah who was a military leader. Jesus is saying the kingdom is spiritually discerned and you can't see it or grasp it unless you've been born from above.

Jesus answered, "Most assuredly, I say to you, unless one is born of water and the Spirit, he cannot enter the kingdom of God. That which is born of the flesh is flesh, and that which is born of the Spirit is spirit. Do not marvel that I said to you, 'You must be born again'" (vs. 5-7). The ancient Jew knew all about rebirth and regeneration. When a man from another faith became a Jew and had been accepted into Judaism by prayer and sacrifice and baptism, he was regarded as being reborn. The teaching of a new birth from God should not have been a strange thing to Nicodemus. He knew the Old Testament inside out and surely he knew the words of Ezek. 18:31, "Cast away from you all the transgressions which you have committed, and get yourselves a new heart and a new spirit. For why should you die, O house of Israel?" Then there's Ezek. 36:26,27, "I will give you a new heart and put a new spirit within you; I will take the heart of stone out of your flesh and give you a heart of flesh. I will put My Spirit within you and cause you to walk in My statutes, and you will keep My judgments and do them."

Nicodemus was an expert in scripture and over and over again the prophets had spoken of the very experience Jesus was talking to him about. He knew about the concept of being reborn but clearly he didn't understand how it works. To help remove his confusion, Jesus said in vs. 8, "The wind blows where it wishes, and you hear the sound of it, but cannot tell where it comes from and where it goes. So is everyone who is born of the Spirit." Jesus is saying that the blowing wind is an example of the Spirit. Man cannot control the wind for it comes and goes at will. The wind blows in a variety of directions. You can hear its sound and perceive its operation in the movement of the trees. While no one can see the wind, one knows of its existence by the effects which it produces. Jesus was saying that even though you can't see the Spirit, you can know of its existence by what the Spirit does. The wind is a powerful force and so is the Holy Spirit when He comes into a person's life. He removes prejudices, changes stubborn wills, and turns rebellion into repentance. Just as a strong wind can change any landscape, so can the Holy Spirit change any life.

The proof of salvation is a changed life and not the fact that way back when somebody mumbled the sinner's prayer with no conviction in their heart. Nearly every person who goes to church believes they're born again yet it is scriptural to "Examine yourselves to see whether you are in the faith" (2 Cor. 13:5 NIV). The reason Paul says this is because the stark reality of life is that there are many who think they're going to heaven when in fact they're heading in the opposite direction. The Message Bible says, "Test yourselves to make sure you are solid in the faith. Don't drift along taking everything for granted. Give yourselves regular checkups. You need firsthand evidence, not mere hearsay, that Jesus Christ is in you. Test it out. If you fail the test, do something about it." You must examine yourself because Jesus said in Matt. 7:21, "Not everyone who says to Me, 'Lord, Lord,' shall enter the kingdom of heaven, but he who does the will of My Father in heaven." This was said about people who are actively involved in the work of God (vs. 22). How much more does this apply to people who only attend church yet do nothing for God?

Matt. 7:14 (MSG) says, "The way to life - to God! - is vigorous and requires total attention." There are many people who mentally believe in Jesus and yet have never been born again. They think they're saved even though they've not submitted to Jesus nor surrendered their lives to Him. At the sermon on the mount Jesus said, "Enter by the narrow gate; for wide is the gate and broad is the way that leads to destruction, and there are many who go in by it. Because narrow is the gate which leads to life, and there are few who find it" (Matt. 7:13,14). Jesus is saying here that more people are going to hell than are going to heaven. People refuse to believe this because at every funeral they go to they're told that the worst sinner on the planet is now in a better place. Nobody preaches hell and damnation at funerals and, because of that, people think if this wretched sinner who lived like the devil can go to heaven then so can they. This is a deception of the highest order for people walk away from funerals without the conviction that they need to be born again.

For the second time, Nicodemus said he did not understand what Jesus was saying (John 3:9) to which the Lord responded, "Are you the teacher of Israel, and do not know these things?" (vs. 10). Nicodemus had a religious mind and had to learn that the things of God was not just to be discussed but was to be experienced as well. He was to bring light to the nation of Israel but still he was in the dark regarding the born again experience. He was like the people described in Eph. 4:18 (NLT), "Their minds are full of darkness, they wander far from the life God gives because they have closed their minds and hardened their hearts against Him." The Message Bible says, "They've refused for so long to deal with God that they've lost touch not only with God but with reality itself. They can't think straight anymore." Nicodemus did not mean to be hard but that was the condition he was in. He could not see what Jesus was trying to show him even though He used simple human examples taken from everyday life. Jesus was asking how Nicodemus could understand the deep things of God if even the simple things were beyond his realm of understanding (vs. 12).

What Nicodemus had to learn is that you must believe and receive what God says even if you don't understand it in your mind. When you receive it by faith you can have the confidence that God will give you the enlightenment concerning it. Heb. 11:3 says, "By faith we understand." Jesus switched gears and then told of a story found in Num. 21:4-9. He said, "And as Moses lifted up the serpent in the wilderness, even so must the Son of Man be lifted up, that whoever believes in Him should not perish but have eternal life." The children of Israel murmured against God and many of them were bitten by poisonous snakes that came into the camp. Moses asked God what he should do and soon a bronze snake was lifted up on a pole for the people to look at in faith, and in looking they were healed. Jesus was showing Nicodemus what had to be done in order for the new birth to be made available to mankind. He was saying that He also had to be lifted up as a sacrifice on the cross just as Moses lifted up a bronze serpent made in the likeness of one of the deadly serpents. In like manner, Jesus was made "in the likeness of sinful flesh" (Rom. 8:3) and was nailed to a cross and lifted up for all to see.

2 Cor. 5:21 says, "For He made Him who knew no sin to be sin for us, that we might become the righteousness of God in Him." The serpent that was lifted up in the wilderness was a reminder of the curse that had come upon mankind. On the cross, Jesus became the curse. Gal. 3:13 (NLT) says, "But Christ has rescued us from the curse pronounced by the law. When He was hung on the cross, He took upon Himself the curse for our wrongdoing. For it is written in the scriptures, 'Cursed is everyone who is hung on a tree.'" Jesus then said to Nicodemus the most powerful words ever spoken on the face of this planet, "For God so loved the world that He gave His only begotten Son, that whoever believes in Him should not perish but have everlasting life. For God did not send His Son into the world to condemn the world, but that the world through Him might be saved" (John 3:16,17). Sin had to be dealt with and Jesus on the cross demonstrated the righteousness of God. It also revealed the love God has for all people. It was love that held Jesus to that cross for love is the foundation for everything God does.

Jesus, a man like no other, was sent on a rescue mission to a doomed and dying planet. Rom. 3:23 says, "For all have sinned and fall short of the glory of God." He came to make a way for sinful man to come back to Him so that fellowship could be restored. The problem with most people is when they sin they have a tendency to try to hide from God just like Adam and Eve did in the garden. The good news is that sin does not stop God from seeking after you. Jesus said in Luke 19:10, "For the Son of Man has come to seek and to save that which is lost." All men and women are lost and need rescuing and it's your responsibility to look upon Jesus on the cross just like the Israelites looked upon the bronze serpent in the wilderness. Your eternal destiny is determined by where you choose to spend it for it would be unjust for God to violate your free will. God is just and He wouldn't be that way if He sent somebody to hell without first giving them a chance to get saved. Rest assured, God reveals Himself to everybody in one way or another.

The Lord wants everybody to be saved so He reveals Himself to all people so that no person can say they've never heard of God. Ps. 98:2 says, "The Lord has made known His salvation; His righteousness He has openly shown in the sight of the nations." To see the glory of God all you have to do is go outside and look around you. The sun rising in the east and a tree growing in the field are all signs that point to the existence of God. Rom. 1:19,20 (MSG) says, "But the basic reality of God is plain enough. Open your eyes and there it is! By taking a long and thoughtful look at what God has created, people have always been able to see what their eyes as such can't see: eternal power, for instance, and the mystery of His divine being. So nobody has a good excuse." You never have to worry about finding God for He is always there. He reveals Himself to anybody who wants to know Him. Jer. 29:12-14 says, "Then you will call upon Me and go and pray to Me, and I will listen to you. And you will seek Me and find Me, when you search for Me with all your heart. I will be found by you, says the Lord."

God is always there but He must be sought after to be found. Acts 17:27,28 (MSG) says, "Starting from scratch, He made the entire human race and made the earth hospitable, with plenty of time and space for living so we could seek after God, and not just grope around in the dark but actually find Him. He doesn't play hide-and-seek with us. He's not remote; He's near. We live and move in Him, can't get away from Him!" It you're tired of what this crazy world has to offer and want to begin a new and exciting life, then give your heart to Jesus today. Rom. 10:13 promises that "whoever calls upon the name of the Lord shall be saved." Jesus is the only way to experience the new birth for He said in John 14:6, "I am the way, the truth, and the life. No one comes to the Father except through Me." Peter reaffirms this in Acts 4:12 when he said to the Sanhedrin, "Nor is there salvation in any other, for there is no other name under heaven given among men by which we must be saved." The Message Bible says, "Salvation comes no other way; no other name has been or will be given to us by which we can be saved, only this one."

God doesn't play games and if you're serious about making Jesus the Lord of your life, then Rom. 10:9,10 tells you what to do, "If you confess with your mouth the Lord Jesus Christ and believe in your heart that God raised Him from the dead, you will be saved. For with the heart one believes to righteousness, and with the mouth confession is made to salvation." Say out loud, "Heavenly Father, I ask you to forgive me of all my sin. I believe Jesus died for my sins and arose the third day. I receive Jesus as my Lord and Savior. I give You my life. Thank You, Jesus, for saving me today." If you prayed that prayer and meant it, congratulations, you are now born again. Do not allow doubt to enter in. You are now saved so don't let the devil or anybody else tell you differently. 1 John 5:13 says, "These things I have written to you who believe in the name of the Son of God, that you may know that you have eternal life." The Message Bible says, "My purpose in writing is simply this: that you who believe in God's Son will know beyond the shadow of a doubt that you have eternal life, the reality and not the illusion."

When you've truly been saved there will be no doubt because your life will be radically changed. What confuses most people is they think it's their responsibility to bring about this change. It's not. This is God's responsibility. It is, however, your responsibility to give Him complete control of your life. Your life will not change unless you do this. You don't change yourself but you give God control and then He changes you. You then start to learn and grow and develop into the image of Christ. This only happens after the inward change takes place. 2 Cor. 3:18 (MSG) says, "And so we are transfigured much like the Messiah, our lives gradually becoming brighter and more beautiful as God enters our lives and we become like Him." Salvation becomes a reality when you stop making the decisions on the direction your life will go. Your eternal destiny is determined by who's in control of your life. People who say the sinner's prayer but maintain control of their lives are not truly born again. They think they are but they're being deceived. These people say they have Jesus but Jesus doesn't have them.

-12-

"A DIVINE ENCOUNTER"

John 4 tells the story of Jesus going out of His way to go to a sinful city to confront a sinful woman. He had just been talking to Nicodemus who was a Pharisee with a good reputation. Soon He would be talking to an unnamed woman with a bad reputation showing that God's love reaches out to both ends of society. This meeting didn't happen by chance but was a divine encounter orchestrated by the hand of God. Jesus and His disciples had been ministering in Judea and was baptizing more people than John the Baptist. The Pharisees in Jerusalem heard about this and a spirit of rivalry and jealousy rose up (John 4:1,2). Jesus did not wish to be involved in such a controversy at this stage of His ministry so He decided to leave Judea for the time being and transfer His operations to Galilee. Vs. 3,4 says, "He left Judea and departed again to Galilee. But He needed to go through Samaria." This must have shocked those traveling with Jesus for the Samaritans were a people despised by the Jews and were looked upon as being religiously unacceptable.

Palestine is only 120 miles long from north to south. In the north was the territory of Galilee, in the south was Judea, and in between lay Samaria. The quickest route from Judea to Galilee was through Samaria which was a three day journey. However, there was a centuries old feud between the Jews and the Samaritans so most Jews crossed over the Jordan River and traveled north through Perea and then crossed back over north of Samaria. This alternate route was more than twice as long as the shorter route through Samaria. It was a seven day trip that most Jews were willing to take because of their intense hatred for the people who lived there. So great was this hatred that when the enemies of Jesus wanted to insult Him they called Him a Samaritan with a demon (John 8:48).

Still He needed to go through Samaria because there was a woman there who needed an encounter with God. Jesus said in John 10:16, "And other sheep I have which are not of this fold; them also I must bring, and they will hear My voice; and there will be one flock and one shepherd."

1 Kings 16:24 tells how the wicked King Omri had purchased the hill on which he built the city of Samaria as the new capital of the northern kingdom of Israel. The name Samaria eventually came to describe the entire district in which the city stood and this included the entire northern kingdom. After the Assyrians captured the city in 722 B.C. they imported foreigners who intermarried with the remaining Israelites who lived there. Most of these foreigners continued to worship their pagan gods (2 Kings 17,18) and the Jews in Jerusalem regarded the residents of Samaria as racial half-breeds and religious compromisers. Samaria was part of the Roman province and during the days of Jesus their civil affairs were governed by Pontius Pilate. It was here, at the start of His ministry and in the midst of this despicable land, that Jesus demonstrated that there are no barriers of race or past morals to prevent anyone from coming to God. His journey through Samaria was taken as the result of His knowledge of His Father's will. He needed to go there because He had an appointment that He was going to keep.

John 4:5 says, "So He came to a city of Samaria which is called Sychar, near the plot of ground that Jacob gave to his son Joseph." This city stood about eight miles southeast of the city called Samaria and was between Mount Ebal and Mount Gerzim. It was one of the oldest cities of Palestine and was anciently called Shechem. It was located forty miles north of Jerusalem and was an area that had many Jewish memories attached to it. It was the place where God first appeared to Abraham and promised to give the land to his descendants. It was where Abraham built an altar to the Lord and called upon His name (Gen. 12:7). There was a piece of ground there purchased by Jacob from Hamor for one hundred pieces of silver (Gen. 33:18,19) which was later given to his son Joseph (Gen. 48:22). It was also the place where he dug a well a mile and a half east of the city. Shechem was the burial place of Joseph when the children of Israel brought his bones out of Egypt (Josh. 24:32). It was also the place where Joshua assembled the people before his death and here they renewed their covenant with the Lord (Josh. 24:1).

A lot of Biblical history is associated with the city of Shechem which was located on a portion of the land inherited by Ephraim, the son of Joseph. It's name was later changed to Sychar because of the drunkenness of its inhabitants. This new name means "town of drunkards" and in Is. 28:1 the prophet rebukes the Ephraimites for their excess drinking, "Woe to the crown of pride, to the drunkards of Ephraim, whose glorious beauty is a fading flower which is at the head of the verdant valleys, to those who are overcome with wine!" The prophet goes on to say in vs. 7,8, "But they also have erred through wine, and through intoxicating drink are out of the way; The priest and the prophet have erred through intoxicating drink, they are swallowed up by wine, they are out of the way through intoxicating drink; They err in vision, they stumble in judgment. For all their tables are full of vomit and filthiness, so that no place is clean." Sychar was the lowest of the low of all Samaritan cities and the Jews despised all who lived there. This was also the place Jesus said He had to go.

John 4:6 says, "Now Jacob's well was there. Jesus, therefore, being wearied from His journey, sat thus by the well. It was about the sixth hour." The Jewish day runs from 6 a.m. to 6 p.m. and the sixth hour is twelve o'clock noon. At this time of day the heat was at its greatest and Jesus was weary from three days of travel. He was the Son of God but still He was very human. In the wilderness He was hungry and on the cross He was thirsty. Here, at Jacob's well, He was weary. What does this say about His love for you? He was the Lord of the universe and yet He voluntarily allowed Himself to be subject to hunger, thirst, weariness, rejection, and hatred. He was truly a man like no other. He was very much human but still His divinity was present wherever He went. He was a helpless baby lying in a manger yet the angels of heaven announced His arrival. He was asleep in the bottom of a boat but still He rose up and calmed the storm. He wept because of all the unbelief when His friend Lazarus died but then He called him back to life. Now here He was at the well, weary and resting, ready to fulfill the assignment He was now on.

"A woman of Samaria came to draw water. Jesus said to her, 'Give Me a drink.' For His disciples had gone away into the city to buy food" (vs. 7,8). Had it not been for Jesus it is highly unlikely that these disciples would have even thought of buying food in any Samaritan town. Jesus sent them off anyway because He wanted to be alone at this well at the very moment this woman came to draw water. Jesus understands timing for with God nothing happens by chance. Prov. 16:33 (NLT) says, "We may throw the dice, but the Lord determines how they fall." In God's kingdom there is nothing that ought to be attributed to fortune or chance for all things are directed and determined by God's counsel and providence. Jesus is operating on a divine timeline and not a human timeline. Is. 46:10 says God declares the end from the beginning. The NLT says, "Only I can tell you the future before it even happens. Everything I plan will come to pass, for I do whatever I wish." Most people give up in life because God isn't following their own personal timeline yet Eccl. 3:11 says, "He has made everything beautiful in its time."

The Amplified Bible says, "He has made everything beautiful and appropriate in its time. He has also planned eternity, a sense of divine purpose, in the human heart, a mysterious longing which nothing under the sun can satisfy, except God." God doesn't have a general plan for your life, He has a detailed minute-by-minute plan for your life. With that plan He also created a divine timeline for your life. He sees things years in advance, things you can't see or even imagine, and then He sets in motion divine encounters that will take you to the place you need to be. Eph. 1:9,10 (MSG) says, "He thought of everything, provided for everything we could possibly need, letting us in on the plan He took such delight in making. He set it all out before us in Christ, a long-range plan in which everything would be brought together and summed up in Him, everything in deepest heaven, everything on planet earth." God has a plan and a purpose for your life and it doesn't matter what your past has been like. With God on your side, those with the greatest mess have the greatest potential.

Jesus went to the well and waited for this woman to arrive. What does it say about a busy God who's willing to take time to wait on people to get to where He wants them to be? He was looking for a woman who was not even aware of who He was. Is. 65:1 (NIV) says, "I revealed Myself to those who did not seek me. To a nation that did not call on My name, I said, 'Here am I, here am I.'" Paul testified of the same experience in Phil. 3:12 (MSG), "I'm not saying that I have this all together, that I have it made. But I am well on my way, reaching out for Christ, who has so wondrously reached out for me." God always takes the initiative. He is love and love reaches out in hopes of drawing people in to a personal relationship with the one, true God. Jesus is knocking on the door of every heart hoping that He will be invited into the lives of all those who open the door. This woman of Samaria had an appointment with destiny and didn't even know it. It is amazing how you can sometimes stumble into a divine encounter with God. Most of the things God did in your life you had little to do with it. He just orchestrated your affairs to fit in with His divine purpose.

Only poor women came to this well for it was reserved for those who didn't have servants. They came twice a day to draw water, normally early in the morning and late in the afternoon. It was located outside of town away from the normal crowds of people and was a place where women could socialize among themselves. The woman Jesus was waiting for came to the well at noontime when the sun was the highest, the ground parched, and the well deserted. She came at this hour so she could escape the condemning glares and the spiteful whispers of her neighbors. She was the subject of all the rumors and gossip of town and was considered an outcast among her fellow citizens. Her life was in a state of hopelessness and she had nothing to live for. She was insecure and felt worthless until one day a stranger showed up at the well. Jesus was waiting for her and it was no accident that she came at that particular hour. In a matter of minutes her life would be changed for she was about to have a divine encounter with Jesus.

The truth is, this woman was no different from anybody else. There are those who drop their buckets in the well of fortune and fame and each time they bring their bucket up it is empty. God has purposely planned that nothing satisfies a person's need for fulfillment other than a personal relationship with Himself. Every person needs a purpose, something they can give their passion to. People need a reason to get up in the morning, something to get excited about today and not ten years into the future. People need enthusiasm for right now because purpose is found in the details of daily living. It has been said that life is not a journey to the grave with the intention of arriving safely in a pretty, well preserved body but rather to skid in broadside, thoroughly used up, totally worn out and loudly proclaiming, "Wow, Lord, what a ride!" God understands a person's need for purpose and apparently this woman never found what she was looking for, thus the reason for this divine encounter. When all hope is gone, there is always Jesus. An encounter with Him can radically change a life that seems hopeless.

Inside of Jesus was a well of life. He was a well sitting by a well. He was spiritually what the well was naturally. He was filled with the glorious waters for the soul and He was waiting for a thirsty woman to come and get filled. The woman came and Jesus spoke to her in broad daylight. It was forbidden for rabbis to greet a woman in public, especially one with her background and definitely not a Samaritan. So strict were they that a rabbi could not even speak to his own wife or daughter or sister in public. Some were even of the "bruised and bleeding" sect because they would shut their eyes when they saw a woman on the street and would walk into walls and houses. For a rabbi to be seen speaking to a woman in public was the end of his reputation but here was Jesus talking to a sinful Samaritan woman at midday. No decent man, let alone a rabbi, would have been seen in her company. God knew that nobody else could help this woman so He planned for her to have a divine encounter with Jesus. The people of the city thought she was a tramp but Jesus thought she was important enough to wait for.

Jesus came to offer this woman an alternate lifestyle unlike anything she thought possible. People remain in bondage because they think they're trapped in a certain situation and there's no way out. In Jesus there is always another alternative and this is what this woman is about to find out. She's about to learn that people can change and their situation can change if they truly want them to. The sad thing is, a lot of people don't want help for they subconsciously cling to the familiarity of hard times. A person who is drowning oftentimes fights and resists the lifeguard who is there to rescue them. Hard times make some people so bitter that they don't even know how to receive help when it's offered to them. They become hateful and their hearts turn to stone because they have no shoulder to cry on in the midst of their trial and misery. Jesus knew there was a special place for her in the kingdom and this is why the devil had her bound for so many years. If this woman was important to the Master, never doubt that you are likewise important. Jesus waited for her and He'll also wait for you.

Jesus asked for the simplest gift a person could give to another. He asked for a drink of water. "Then the woman of Samaria said to Him, 'How is it that You, being a Jew, ask a drink from me, a Samaritan woman?' For Jews have no dealings with Samaria" (vs. 9). It was beyond comprehension that a Jew would talk to a Samaritan let alone ask them for a favor. In a single moment Jesus swept away many prejudices that people have. It cannot be denied that evil preconceptions of people is alive and well on planet earth and it goes way beyond the color of a person's skin. Young people are prejudice against older people and older people think younger people don't know much. Poor people think all rich people are crooks and rich people think all poor people are ignorant and lazy. Some men are chauvinistic toward women and some women think all men are creeps. This evil atrocity has even made its way into the local church. Denominational people are prejudice against non-denominational people and non-denominational people are against any type of denomination. Jesus was sitting in front of this woman and all she could think of was the prejudice of the Jews.

This woman was asking "How can this conversation be happening?" Nicodemus also asked, "How can it be?" Both were so preoccupied with human reasoning that they didn't realize who was talking to them. Jesus is tactful and diplomatic for He did not respond to what she said. Instead, He says something provocative to her, something designed to provoke a response, "If you knew the gift of God, and who it is who says to you, 'Give Me a drink,' you would have asked Him, and He would have given you living water" (vs. 10). The phrase "living water" is referring to flowing water from a river or stream as opposed to standing water from a pond or well. To the Jew, running water was always better. Jesus is saying that the sinner has the responsibility to ask for this living water which is a figure of salvation. "Ask and you shall receive" (John 16:24). God is offering everybody the gift of living water. It's not something you can buy or work for and earn. It's a free gift but you must ask for it. You must admit how thirsty you are and go to the One who is offering you this living water. This is spiritual water, the forgiveness of your sins because of the cross and resurrection. When you ask for this water, God will give it to you.

Is. 55:1 (NLT) says, "Is anyone thirsty? Come and drink even if you have no money! Come, take your choice of wine or milk, it's all free!" Water is a gift from God. Man cannot create water and one must forever depend on God for it. So also is salvation a gift from God. In Jer. 2:13 God calls Himself "the fountain of living water." David says in Ps. 36:8,9, "They are abundantly satisfied with the fullness of Your house, and You give them drink from the river of Your pleasures. For with You is the fountain of life; In Your light we see light." Water is indispensable. It is not a luxury but is a basic necessity in life. So is salvation. This is why Jesus said, "You must be born again." Spiritual water comes from above and it refreshes your soul and satisfies your thirst. Rev. 22:17 says, "And let him who thirsts come. And whoever desires, let him take the water of life freely." As great as this woman's need for natural water may have been, her need for living water from heaven was far greater. The water that the woman had came to draw was Jacob's gift to his children. This water brought temporary satisfaction but the living water Jesus offered would quench her thirst forever.

The woman did not understand the kind of water Jesus was talking about so she said to Him, "Sir, You have nothing to draw with, and the well is deep. Where then do You get that living water? Are you greater than our father Jacob, who gave us the well, and drank from it himself, as well as his sons and his livestock?" (vs. 11,12). The Jews would vehemently deny that Jacob was the father of the Samaritans even though they were descendants of Ephraim, the son of Joseph. This woman was saying it was blasphemous for a person to claim to be greater and more powerful than Jacob. Like Nicodemus, she could not grasp the meaning of what Jesus was saying. 1 Cor. 2:14 says, "But the natural man does not receive the things of the Spirit of God, for they are foolishness to him; nor can he know them, because they are spiritually discerned." There is a supernatural power that blinds people to the truth of the gospel. 2 Cor. 3:14 says "their minds were blinded" and 2 Cor. 4:4 says "whose minds the god of this age has blinded, who do not believe lest the light of the gospel of the glory of Christ, who is the image of God, should shine on them."

Jesus answered her, "Whoever drinks of this water will thirst again, but whoever drinks of the water that I shall give him will never thirst. But the water that I shall give him will become in him a fountain of water springing up into everlasting life" (vs. 13,14). Jesus is offering this living water to you right now. Are you thirsty for something more in life that you haven't yet found? For many there is something lacking deep inside of them. They don't have the fulfillment or the satisfaction or the peace that their heart is crying out for. The well of their heart is dry and inwardly they are craving for this living water. What should these people do? They should say to Jesus what this woman said to Him, "Sir, give me this water, that I may not thirst, nor come here to draw" (vs. 15). The woman saw His offer as a provision that would release her from a physical burden and this was the water she asked for. Even though she still didn't fully understand what Jesus was saying, a desire for the gift of eternal life was taking root deep in her heart.

Like the rich young ruler, little was she prepared for what Jesus would say next.

Jesus said to her, "Go, call your husband, and come here" (vs. 16). Jesus was addressing her conscience for she had to face the truth of her life before she could accept His truth for her. An overwhelming flood of guilt and remorse overtook this woman. She shrinks back for the dirty secret of her life was now exposed openly. Suddenly she was forced to face the immorality and looseness of her life. Jesus said this to show that no person can come to Him until there is conviction in your heart that you have sinned against God followed by repentance and a willingness to change. Jesus wanted her to admit her sinful lifestyle. He wanted her to come to Him so He could change her life. She partly covered up her sin and said to Him, "I have no husband" (vs. 17). Prov. 28:13 says, "He who covers his sin will not prosper, but whoever confesses and forsakes them will have mercy." Jesus said to her, "You have well said, 'I have no husband,' for you have had five husbands, and the one whom you now have is not your husband; in that you spoke truly" (vs. 17,18).

This woman wasn't a prostitute but was a loose woman who went from man to man looking for something that only God can give. This woman was predestined to be used by God so the devil set out to give her such a bad reputation that nobody would dare believe anything she says. She abused other people because she was abused and this is how she learned it was done. Almost all abusers were victims in times past and hurting people always hurt other people. This woman had a need and needs left unattended are dangerous. A need will make you desperate and desperate people do desperate things. A need unmet will leave you weak and faint and frail. Your life will be out of balance and you won't know which way to turn. People who are desperate do things they'll later be ashamed of not knowing that down inside their heart they're better than that. They know better but do wrong things anyway because they're desperate and don't see any way out of their present situation. They don't realize that over at the well there is somebody waiting to talk to them. His message to all desperate people is found in Phil. 4:13, "I can do all things through Christ who strengthens me."

Helping desperate people is a job for Jesus for in Him you can overcome any adversity or circumstance. There is nothing wrong with you and deep inside is the potential to make a positive difference in this crazy, upside down world. All you have to do is go to the well and talk to the person waiting for you there. His name is Jesus and He wants you to have a divine encounter with Him. He wants to turn your life around and point it in another direction. Ps. 30:5 says, "Weeping may endure for a night, but joy comes in the morning." It comes in the morning but it's found at the well of living water. It's found in the person of Jesus. And what happens when you find Him? You want to go out and tell the whole world about it. Jesus revealed Himself to this woman as the Messiah (vs. 26) and her eyes were opened and she became a changed woman. She came with a waterpot and left with a well of living water inside her. She had came to the well to avoid people but now she was seeking them out so she could bring them to Jesus. They came because of her word and then they believed on Jesus because of His word. The whole city got saved and it happened because this one woman had a divine encounter with Jesus.

In John 3 Nicodemus, a ruler of the Jews, came to Jesus by night and learned about the plan of salvation. He was a secret disciple and you don't read about anybody coming to the Lord through his testimony. Compare him with this woman at the well. She was probably uneducated and had made a mess of her life. She had a bad reputation but here she is talking about Jesus in the middle of the day so all can hear. She didn't know much theology and all she did was invite people to come and see Jesus. She probably doesn't even like her neighbors because they've been so mean to her but she can't help herself. She rushes to tell them anyway. She overcomes her past and God uses her to turn her whole city over to the Lord. Now it's your turn. You may not have a college degree or stand behind a pulpit in front of thousands of people but, if you'll be bold about Jesus and not be ashamed of the gospel, God can and will use you far beyond what those who are ashamed will ever see.

You can't be timid to the point of hiding what you believe. No, you've got to boldly declare who Jesus is and how He's touched your life.

If God can use the woman at the well, He can use you and don't ever forget that. God will take your mess and turn it into a message for all to hear. He'll turn your test into a testimony. He'll use your past to bless somebody else's future. You've got more potential to change this world than you realize. Just take your life and turn it over to the Man at the well. With Jesus on your side you can do anything. You can be anybody you want to be and do whatever you need to do. You can overcome any obstacle and live to tell others how they can overcome any test and trial. 1 Cor. 1:27 says, "But God has chosen the foolish things of this world to put to shame the wise, and God has chosen the weak things of the world to put to shame the things that are mighty." The Message Bible says, "Isn't it obvious that God deliberately chose men and women that the culture overlooks and exploits and abuses, chose these 'nobodies' to expose the hollow pretensions of the 'somebodies'?" This is you so rise up and do what Joel 3:10 says, "Let the weak say, I am strong." If you'll do that, the devil doesn't stand a chance.

-13-

"A SNAPSHOT OF PERFECTION"

Every person needs a face-to-face encounter with Jesus for this is what qualifies you to be a witness for Him. Christianity is not about religion or following a set of rules, it's about relationship. God longs to have friends He can share things with, people who will trust Him and not muddy the waters with unbelief. Ps. 42:7 says, "Deep calls unto deep." There is something deep inside of you that wants to reach out and touch the heart of God. He is looking for a person after His own heart, a person who thinks how He thinks, a person who knows how big He is and how good He is and how righteous He is. If you've had a divine encounter with Jesus, then do what the woman at the well did and go out and tell the world about it. Don't be fooled by the outward appearance of those around you. They may be cheerful on the outside but hurting and miserable on the inside. They're looking for something and you have inside of you the answer they're looking for. Inside of you is the spring of living water. It quenched your thirst and now God wants to use you to help quench the thirst of others.

Jesus said to His disciples in John 4:35, "Do you not say, 'There are still four months and then comes the harvest'? Behold, I say to you, lift up your eyes and look at the fields, for they are already white for harvest!" Jesus is comparing an agricultural harvest to a spiritual harvest. It could very well be that just at this moment the people of Samaria started to flock out to see Jesus in response to the woman's testimony. Jesus is telling the disciples to open their eyes and look around them, to become alert to the readiness of harvest. On another occasion Jesus talked about the vastness of the task at hand. "But when He saw the multitudes, He was moved with compassion for them, because they were weary and scattered, like sheep having no shepherd. Then He said to His disciples, 'The harvest truly is plentiful, but the laborers are few. Therefore pray the Lord of the harvest to send out laborers into His harvest'" (Matt. 9:36-38). The Samaritans were introduced to Jesus by the woman at the well. It is also your privilege and responsibility to bring people to Jesus, to a place where they can listen to Him for themselves.

God cannot deliver His message of salvation to a lost world unless there is someone to deliver it. Paul asked, "How then shall they call on Him in whom they have not believed? And how shall they believe in Him of whom they have not heard? And how shall they hear without a preacher?" (Rom. 10:14). The Word of God is spread throughout the world person to person. He has no hands but your hands, no feet but your feet, and no voice but your voice. The story of the woman at the well teaches you how to draw someone into a divine encounter with God. Jesus could have easily gotten His own drink of water. He didn't come to be served but rather to serve. The only reason He started talking to this woman was so that He could help her. To be a good witness you need to initiate conversations with people so you can eventually share Jesus with them. The favorite subject everybody likes to talk about is themselves. This means you can have a conversation with anyone, anywhere, at any time. All you have to do is ask them something that pertains to their life and for sure you will have a captive audience.

You can never lead any person into a personal encounter with Jesus if you don't first talk to them. Don't cram religion down their throat and never argue with them for this is the enemy's way of preventing the gospel message from going forth. Titus 3:9 says, "But avoid foolish disputes, genealogies, contentions, and strivings about the law; for they are unprofitable and useless." When you talk to people show an interest in who they are and the things they're interested in. Ask them questions about their background, their family, their job, and their hobbies. The result of doing this is they'll start to like you and, when people like you, they'll listen to you. Once you have their attention you can tell them about Jesus and the peace and joy that go with having a relationship with Him.

Tell these people about your prior condition before you came to Christ and how His love and goodness turned your situation around. Everybody's got a story to tell. You don't need to know the Bible from cover to cover, just tell people what Jesus did for you. This is what the woman at the well did and the whole city came out to meet Jesus.

This woman needed living water but she also needed someone to talk to her about her sin. This Jesus did but not in a condemning way. Don't avoid the subject of sin but talk about it in the right way. Talk about it without pointing your finger at them and telling them what a wretched sinner they are. No, Jesus loves sinners and sinners love Jesus because He don't condemn people for their sin. The devil gets people to wrongly believe that Christians think they're better than anyone else. If you tell people that you've made some of the same mistakes they've made, their guard will come down and they'll be more open to hear what you have to say. The world today tells people that they have the freedom to do whatever their heart desires in spite of what God says about it. No, sin needs to be confronted and talked about. The key is not what you say but how you say it. You may have a zeal for what you're talking about but don't force God on anybody. Do your best to share the good news with people and leave the outcome of your conversation in the hands of God.

Jesus went into the land of darkness to bring light to all those who lived there. Once the Samaritans had been introduced to Jesus, they asked Him to stay with them so that they could come to know Him better. It is needful after you've been born again that you go on to live in the presence of Jesus daily. This no person can do for you. Others may lead you to Jesus but you must claim and enjoy a personal relationship with Him yourself. It is quite remarkable that Jesus stayed in this Samaritan town for two days (vs. 40) during which time the people came to "know that this is indeed the Christ, the Savior of the world" (vs. 42). This story isn't recorded in the other gospel accounts and it is only here in John's gospel that Jesus is called by this title. John also used this title in 1 John 4:14 for to him this was the preeminent title for Jesus who came to rescue people from the bondage of sin and the hopeless situation in which they find themselves. He breaks the chains that bind people to the past and enables them to experience a better future. Indeed, there is no title adequate to describe Jesus except Savior of the world.

"Now after the two days He departed from there and went to Galilee. For Jesus Himself testified that a prophet has no honor in his home country" (John 4:43,44). Other translations record that Jesus testified "that a prophet is not honored in his own hometown" (NLT, ESV, BLB) and this is a more accurate translation. The term "His own country" is used in Matt. 13:5 and refers to the city of Nazareth where Jesus was brought up. They say familiarity breeds contempt and this is why Jesus said what He did. He had been cast out of Nazareth when He began His ministry and the people there tried to throw Him off a cliff and kill Him (Luke 4:29). This rejection was foretold by Isaiah who said the Messiah would be "despised and rejected of men" (Is. 53:3). It is sad but true that many servants of God receive little or no honor and respect from those closest to them. Their nearest relatives and closest neighbors and acquaintances oftentimes are the last people to give them the honor that is rightfully due them.

If a prophet is without honor in his own hometown, then he must earn it elsewhere. Jesus had done this in Jerusalem and Samaria and now He set His sights on the other people of Galilee. "So when He came to Galilee, the Galileans received Him, having seen all the things He did in Jerusalem at the feast; for they also had gone to the feast" (vs. 46). In Samaria, Jesus had been honored as a prophet because of the words He spoke but here the Galilean's belief in Him was largely based on the miraculous signs which He performed and not in who He was. No doubt they hoped to see a repetition of the signs in their territory that had been given in Jerusalem. "So Jesus came again to Cana of Galilee where He had made the water wine. And there was a certain nobleman whose son was sick at Capernaum" (vs. 46). Nathaniel lived in Cana (John 21:2) and it's possible that it was he who provided lodging for Jesus and His disciples. During the course of His stay, word had reached Capernaum that Jesus was back in Galilee. A royal official who lived there had a son with a high fever and he rushed to Jesus to plead for the well-being of his son.

This nobleman was a royal official of high standing in the court of Herod Antipas. He was very wealthy, had many servants, and was very desperate. Why else would an important court official travel seventeen miles in haste to seek help from a village carpenter? The rich have troubles just like the poor and money definitely does not insure happiness or health. Royal officials don't walk on these long journeys so with the best horses and chariots made available to him, he set off on a pilgrimage took approximately four hours to make. "When he heard that Jesus has come out of Judea into Galilee, he went to Him and implored Him to come down and heal his son, for he was at the point of death" (vs. 47). The nobleman wanted to see Jesus do something. He wanted Jesus to come to his house and physically be there so He could heal his son. On the surface this may not appear to be a wrongful request. In Mark 5:23 Jairus asked Jesus to do the same thing for his daughter and Jesus went with him and raised her up. Likewise, the woman with the issue of blood said, "If only I may touch His clothes, I shall be made well" (Mark 5:28). There is nothing wrong with this level of faith for it brought results. Still, Jesus was about to teach this nobleman a higher way.

Jesus said to him, "Unless you people see signs and wonders, you will by no means believe" (vs. 48). The Message Bible says, "Unless you people are dazzled by a miracle, you refuse to believe." Jesus is leading this man away from all his preconceived ideas of what had to be done and directed him onto the path of simple faith in His Word. The man wanted to see something happen before he was willing to believe. He wanted to see Jesus come to his house. Too many people want to see something before they'll believe but this is not what the Bible teaches about faith. Faith is not based on what you can see or hear or feel. It's based on the Word of God. If you wait until you see something before you believe, you'll miss your miracle. Martin Luther King Jr. once said, "Faith is taking the first step when you don't see the whole staircase." It's your faith in God's Word that delivers the death blow to sickness and disease. You can't go around demanding signs before you trust God. Mark 16:17,18 says that the signs will follow those that believe. When you're in faith you can expect signs to follow when you believe but never are you to ask for signs in order to believe.

The nobleman said to Jesus, "Sir, come down before my child dies!" (vs. 49). The man is persistent. A second time he asks Jesus to come to his house. He's desperate for he believes his son is about to die. Jesus responds with a command and a statement, "Go your way; your son lives" (vs. 50). Jesus was not going to go to the man's house and so now the nobleman has a choice to make. Is he going to stay and plead some more with Jesus or is he going to do what Jesus told him to do? He's already asked Him twice to come down to his house. What's he going to do? Mary told you how to receive your miracle back in John 2:5, "Whatever He says to you, do it." If you believe something, you'll act on it. Jesus told this man what to do. "So the man believed the word that Jesus spoke to him, and he went his way" (vs. 50). It is the very essence of faith that a person believe that what Jesus says is true. The nobleman went his way for he believed that the words of Jesus was truth and that distance is no barrier to them. Ps. 107:20 says, "He sent His word and healed them, and delivered them from their destruction."

This story of the healing of the nobleman's son is in sharp contrast to the healing of the centurion's servant as recorded in Matt. 8:5-10. This centurion was a Gentile but also lived in Capernaum. He came to Jesus and told Him what his need was and did not dictate what needed to be done. Jesus offered to go and heal the servant in person but this centurion had great faith. He said, "Lord, I am not worthy that You should come under my roof. But only speak a word and my servant will be healed" (vs. 8). Jesus marveled at this and said, "Assuredly, I say to you, I have not found such great faith, not even in Israel" (vs. 10). What the scriptures say next about the nobleman indicate that he also became a man of great faith. Ordinarily it would have taken the nobleman a few short hours to get home but John 4:52 says he didn't get home until the next day. The man now believed that his son was healed so he stayed overnight before beginning his journey back home. His faith was rewarded and his servants met him and told him the good news. They said the fever left his son at the same hour when Jesus pronounced him well (vs. 53). That day the nobleman's faith took a giant leap.

John 4:54 says, "This again is the second sign that Jesus did when He had come out of Judea into Galilee." Miracles are wonderful. Miracles are grand. Why wouldn't they be? God is a miracle-working God. Ps. 136:4 says, "To Him who alone does great wonders, for His mercy endures forever." The problem with miracles is that a lot of people are seeking after signs and wonders because they want confirmation that God exists and that His word is truth. These people are deceived because their hearts are hardened toward the truth and they won't believe even if they witnessed a miracle every day of their lives. Ps. 78:32 says, "In spite of this they still sinned, and did not believe in His wondrous works." The Pharisees were like this and Jesus called them "an evil and adulterous generation" (Matt. 12:38,39). It is far better in the eyes of God to believe without needing a miracle. The Samaritans believed Jesus because of His words but the people of Galilee required signs and wonders before they were willing to believe. Getting you to believe in God is not what miracles are for. A miracle is to be a beacon of light, a sign intended for someone who is looking in the right direction.

Yes, God still performs miracles today. Just understand that a faith based on miracles is not a mature faith. There is nothing wrong with miracles and it is not wrong to desire them if the need is there. Just don't base your faith on them. Put your trust in God and God alone. Believe His Word, act on His Word, and leave the miracles in His very capable hands. It will also help if you understand the purpose of miracles. Jesus came to the earth to restore back to man the way things were in the Garden of Eden before the fall of man. The miracles of Jesus were a snapshot of perfection, a picture of how life is supposed to be. Back in the beginning man existed with God in perfect peace and harmony. There was no sickness and disease, no hunger and lack, no sin and death. Jesus came to change things back to the way they were. He came to bring man back to the perfection of Eden. The miracles Jesus performed was the restoration of the way things were originally planned by God to be. Miracles happen so that people can experience a touch of heaven on earth so that the will of the Father can be done on earth just as it is in heaven.

The healing of the nobleman's son was the first of many healing miracles Jesus performed in His earthly ministry. Sickness is one of the deadliest tools of the enemy. He uses it to steal, kill, and destroy. There was no sickness in the Garden of Eden and Jesus came to fix that problem. It began long ago when God said in Ex. 15:27, "For I am the Lord who heals you." The Message Bible says, "I am God, your healer." The Lord will mend you when you are torn and fix you up when you are broken. He is the great "fixer upper" of whatever needs fixing. Jer. 17:14 says, "Heal me, O Lord, and I shall be healed; Save me, and I shall be saved, for You are my praise." The prophet says this because salvation and healing are directly connected to one another. Never separate the two. God will heal your inner man and He'll heal your outer man. Ps. 103:2,3 says, "Bless the Lord, O my soul, and forget not all His benefits: Who forgives all your iniquities, Who heals all your diseases." Sin and sickness are connected to the same source just like they're connected to the same solution.

James 5:15,16 says, "And the prayer of faith will save the sick, and the Lord will raise him up. And if he has committed sins, he will be forgiven. Confess your trespasses to one another, and pray for one another, that you may be healed. The effective, fervent prayer of a righteous man avails much." Sin and sickness are of the devil and forgiveness and healing comes from God. The problem is most people think it's easy to be forgiven but rarely, if ever, can they be healed. They don't realize that the two go together. If you can be forgiven, you can be healed. How do you know you're forgiven? Do you always feel inside of you that you're the righteousness of God in Christ Jesus? You believe that you have received your forgiveness and, the more you believe it and stop focusing on how you feel, the more confidence you'll have and the more free you'll live. This is also how you receive your healing. It's not based on how you feel or on what the doctor tells you. It's based on the word of God and your willingness to believe it and act on it. Jesus told the nobleman to go home and he did.

The first year of the Lord's ministry was coming to a close and John 5:1 continues the story of Jesus several months after the healing of the nobleman's son, "After this there was a feast of the Jews, and Jesus went up to Jerusalem." Of all the feasts that Jesus attended, this is the only one not mentioned by name. Most Bible scholars do believe, however, that this was the feast of Passover. In the time of the Lord's public ministry, which was three and a half years long, there were four Passover feasts. The other three gospels only mention the last one whereas John mentions by name Jesus going to three of them. If this unnamed feast was not the Passover then John skipped over this one and this seems unlikely. Others say that if this was the Passover feast then John passed over a long interval of time in the Lord's ministry. John does this elsewhere and God uses the other gospel accounts to fill in the blanks. A close observation of all four gospels will show that until the time of the cross John primarily focused on what was omitted by the other gospel writers.

Another observation to be made is that in John 4:46 the Passover celebration is called "the feast" so it is not unusual for John to once again use the term "a feast of the Jews" here in his presentation. Also, if this feast was not the Passover, then the timing of all the other events in the Lord's ministry would add up to a total of two and a half years that He ministered. A close look at the chronological data revealed in the gospels does allow for an accurate timeline for how long His ministry actually lasted. Therefore, if this feast was indeed the feast of Passover, making four in all, then the duration of the Lord's public ministry would have been three and a half years, starting from the time He was baptized in the Jordan River. This timeline collaborates with all the recorded documents written in reference to the Lord Jesus Christ, both scriptural and historical. Although John for some reason does not say specifically what feast this was, the circumstances all point to the Passover feast. A great gathering was at Jerusalem and another miracle would soon happen.

"Now there is in Jerusalem by the Sheep Gate a pool, which is called in Hebrew, Bethesda, having five porches" (vs. 2). This Sheep Gate is mentioned in Neh. 3:1 and was the gate the sheep traveled through on their way to be sacrificed in the temple. The word "Bethesda" means 'House of Mercy' and the pool itself had five covered porches. In scripture the number five always stands for grace and favor. Gen. 43:34 says "Benjamin's portion was five times as much as any of theirs." The five loaves fed five thousand men and the fifth commandment is the only one with a promise. "In these lay a great multitude of sick people, blind, lame, paralyzed, waiting for the moving of the water. For an angel went down at a certain time into the pool and stirred up the water; then whoever stepped in first, after the stirring of the water, was made well of whatever disease he had" (vs. 3,4). Ancient historical documents tell how these stirrings started happening after Jesus was born and only happened during the feast of Passover. Was it a coincidence that Jesus was always in town during these feasts? No, in the kingdom of God there is no such thing.

The stirring of these waters was an unusual phenomenon and one is reminded of the time when Namaan dipped seven times in the Jordan River and was healed of his leprosy (2 Kings 5). The only reasonable explanation for this rather unique miraculous occurrence is to say that God is a merciful God who wants people to be whole and complete in every way. They say birds of a feather flock together. At church services all depressed people sit together as do all the gossipers. They just find a way to associate with their own kind of people. They have their own porch for they prefer the security of being accepted over being changed. This was the case here on the porches of Bethesda for all the sick people were gathered together with other sick people. Misery loves company proving that nothing good happens when you associate with people who are as limited as you are. It creates a culture that can be harmful as any disease. The blind can't help the blind and poor people can't help other poor people. Stagnant water that isn't moving becomes contaminated and this was the condition of the people who were gathered around the pool.

You can deny your condition all you want but your associations define your situation. Don't associate with people who aren't moving and not going anywhere with God. Many people today are also sitting around waiting for doctors to prescribe a new medicine or for their boss to increase their pay at work. People say they want a miracle but aren't willing to believe God and act on His promises. And then, suddenly, in the midst of all this stagnation, the water moves. It's when the water stirs that you'll find out who your true friends really are. To get healed at the pool of Bethesda you had to be at the right place at the right time, hoping to be the right person to step into the pool first. If, by chance, you're the first person into the pool, those around you won't be happy for your success but instead will begin to despise you. Single people are friends with one another until one of them gets engaged. Be careful who you hang around with. People will step over you to be the first into the pool but they won't help you into the pool. People you thought were your friends are not your friends at all.

Thankfully there is a friend who sticks closer than a brother. His name is Jesus and one day He came to the pool. He was in Jerusalem but He didn't go to the temple but to where there was a multitude of hurting people. You don't catch fish until you go to where the fish are. He looked around and saw sick people who had become comfortable in their sickness. You will never change if you're comfortable where you're now at. It's easy to become comfortable when you associate with people who are as limited as you are. If you don't want change to come to your life then hang around people just like you. By doing so you'll be part of a fraternity of people not living up to the standards of life that God has set before them. They're sick, you're sick, everything's cool. They've got a limp, you've got a limp. They gossip, you gossip. They murmur and complain, you murmur and complain. They're comfortable where they're at and so are you. If that be the case, then you have nothing to believe for. If what's wrong with you has become normal, then all hope becomes neutralized. Miracles happen when you stop being stagnant and start moving.

"Now a certain man was there who had an infirmity thirty-eight years" (vs. 5). This man had been sick since before Jesus was born and here he was staring at the water, waiting for it to move. As bad as his infirmity was, there is even more torture when you stare at something you can't have or can't reach. It hurts when other people have what you don't have, when they step into the pool without helping you into the pool. Jesus knew this man had been in this condition a long time and He asked him, "Do you want to be made well?" (vs. 6). Jesus is asking you the same question. It's sad but true that many people don't want to be healed because their infirmity brings them attention and they don't want to give that up. They'd rather stay sick than give up all that attention. The man didn't answer the question but instead said there was nobody to put him into the pool (vs. 7). He was saying it wasn't his fault that he was not healed. Most people think their problems are always somebody else's fault and never their own. The burden of blame is transferred to another person so they won't have to take on the responsibility of their present condition.

The lives of people who make excuses are like tires spinning in the mud. They're going nowhere and if this describes you then look up. Jesus is standing in front of you and He is asking, "Do you want to be made well?" Do you want the old way of living or do you want something new? Jesus ignored this man's excuse and said to him, "Rise, take up your bed and walk" (vs. 8). Some action will almost always be necessary in order for a miracle to be released into your life and, more times than not, He'll tell you to do something that seems humanly impossible. Jesus didn't say "Be healed" because He wanted the man to stop making excuses and put some effort into getting his miracle. It's easy to get comfortable in your weakness and Jesus wanted this lame man to change his thinking. You need to understand that no person can hinder your destiny besides you. There is no situation too difficult that you and Jesus can't overcome. Stop making excuses and put some effort into it. Faith without works is dead (James 2:17). "And immediately the man was made well, took up his bed, and walked. And that day was the Sabbath" (vs. 9).

With Jesus comes transformation. He is saying to you, "Behold, I stand at the door of your life and I'm knocking. Won't you open the door and let Me in?" Stop being a face in the crowd of spiritual misfits. Get off that porch and run into the arms of the God of living water. There is nothing stagnant about Jesus. Hook up with Him and get unstuck. Stop stumbling around and go somewhere with Jesus. He challenged the man to do something. He told him to "Rise, take up your bed and walk." What is God telling you to do? Whatever it is, do it. If He is telling you to break up with that person you're going out with, do it. If He says to leave that dead church, do it. If He is telling you to throw away those cigarettes and dirty magazines, don't hesitate a single moment. Do it and do it now! God will always challenge you to do the very thing you think you can't do but do it anyway for this is how miracles happen and transformation comes. Mary got it right. Whatever He says to you, do it. Then step back and watch the miracles come.

Randall J. Brewer

-14-

"LORD OF THE SABBATH"

There are times when God wants to be God. The healing of the lame man at the pool of Bethesda was a grand display of the love of God reaching out and meeting the needs of man. This man did not ask to be healed but through him Jesus was showing the world the nature of God and what was being made available to them. God wants to pour His blessings into your life, so much so that 2 Chron. 16:9 says, "For the eyes of the Lord run to and fro throughout the whole earth, to show Himself strong on behalf of those whose heart is loyal to Him." This healing should have brought about a time of great celebration and of giving praise and glory to God. Such was not the case. It just so happened that this miracle happened on the Sabbath and this brought criticism and condemnation from the Jewish leaders. At this time Jesus was not yet as popular in Jerusalem as He was in Galilee so the Pharisees considered Him an open target for their growing hostility and antagonism. John 5:15,16 says, "The man departed and told the Jews that it was Jesus who had made him well. For this reason the Jews persecuted Jesus, and sought to kill Him, because He had done these things on the Sabbath.

The Sabbath was established in Gen. 2:1-3 when God rested on the seventh day. "Thus the heavens and the earth, and all the host of them, were finished. And on the seventh day God ended His work which He had done. Then God blessed the seventh day and sanctified it, because in it He rested from all His work which God had created and made." Of course, God is God and He doesn't need rest but this was done as a pattern for all people to follow. Before the fall of man work was ordained by God as an honorable activity. It soon became corrupted by sin. God told Adam, "The ground will be under a curse and you will have to work hard all your life to make it produce enough food for you. It will produce weeds and thorns and you'll have to work hard and sweat to make the soil produce anything" (Gen. 3:17-19 TEV). No longer was work fun and it quickly became troublesome and compulsive. People became workaholics and sacrificed their families and even their own souls on the altar of professional achievement.

Because of sin man now had to work in order to survive. It wasn't until Ex. 16:29,30 that the seventh day was set apart as a day of resting from going out and picking up the manna that had fallen. The people were told to pick up a double portion on the sixth day and to rest on the seventh day. Rest is one of nature's primal and universal laws. Without rest neither plants or animals can reach their full potential. In the months of fall and winter trees drop their leaves and rest until the springtime when once again they come alive and sprout new leaves of glorious splendor. Lev. 25:4 says farmers should not plant in the seventh year so the soil can rest and be revitalized. The soil must be left unsown for a season in order to restore its fertility or else its ability to reproduce properly will ultimately become exhausted. People who never rest bring on themselves prematurely the infirmities and decay of old age. They grow old before their time and many die an early death. So important was this need for rest that the Sabbath day was consecrated and ordained by God's own example.

God doesn't need a day of rest, you do. Jesus said in Mark 2:27,28, "The Sabbath was made for man, and not man for the Sabbath. Therefore the Son of Man is also Lord of the Sabbath." The NLT says, "The Sabbath was made to meet the needs of people, and not people to meet the requirements of the Sabbath." The appointment of the Sabbath day did not take place until the work of creation was completed. Man could not have been created for the Sabbath because the Sabbath wasn't created yet. Man was created on the sixth day and then came the Sabbath showing that the Sabbath was created for the benefit of man. It is not a small thing that God would create an entire day all for the purpose of giving man a chance to cease from the cares and labors of this world. The good of man requires a day of rest for it provides a beneficial provision for one's welfare. Without proper rest one's body begins to break down and before long a person won't be able to function on the level that is required to accomplish the purpose for which work was intended. This is why the Message Bible says, "The Sabbath was made to serve us; we weren't made to serve the Sabbath."

People who work and never rest are drawn away from God and are hindered from the pursuit of spiritual matters. Work is all they think about not realizing that they are being pulled into the quicksand of heathen darkness. Without God in their lives they become corrupt and sinful and get immersed in the cares and pleasures of an ensnaring world. This is why God in His infinite love and mercy made this day on purpose for your benefit. The Sabbath is a means to an end and is one of the best gifts God gave to man. It sustains the physical, social, spiritual, intellectual, and eternal well-being of all those who observe it. The Sabbath was made for your good so welcome it for the blessing that it is. If the Sabbath was made for man, it must have been because man needed it. It is also not important what day you rest, just so you do it. Many people are required to work on weekends for society would shut down if they didn't. If that's the case, then rest during the middle of the week. Just understand that the need for rest is permanent and universal. It's the rule and not the exception.

Due to the misunderstanding and misinterpretation of scripture by some religious groups, the meaning of the Sabbath has been confused. Many view the Sabbath as a day when believers are to attend church services. The concept of going to church is emphasized more than having a day of rest. Obviously a day when nobody works would be an ideal day to go to church. However, nowhere in scripture is there a command that the Sabbath be the day of worship. Acts 20:7 and 1 Cor. 16:2 both mention Christians meeting on the first day of the week. There is no evidence in the New Testament that the early church observed the Sabbath day as the prescribed day of worship. It is a tradition that most Christians go to church on Sunday, the first day of the week, in celebration of the Lord's resurrection that occurred on this day (John 20:1). It is important to understand, however, that there is no explicit biblical proclamation or command that sets aside a specific day of the week to be the distinct day of corporate worship. Scriptures such as Rom. 14:5,6 and Col. 2:16 give Christians the freedom to observe a special day to worship or to observe every day as special.

It is the desire of God that His people worship and serve Him continually and not just once a week. It is also important that you understand that going to church is not what the Sabbath command is all about. It was a command to do no work one day a week and nowhere in scripture is the Sabbath day commanded to be the day of worship. When God gave Moses the Ten Commandments on Mount Sinai the fourth command was, "Remember the Sabbath day, to keep it holy. Six days you shall labor and do all your work, but the seventh day is the Sabbath of the Lord your God. In it you shall do no work. For in six days the Lord made the heavens and the earth, the sea, and all that is in them, and rested the seventh day. Therefore the Lord blessed the Sabbath day and hallowed it" (Ex. 20:8-11). The Sabbath is not just a certain day of the week but is a lifestyle. It's how life works. Ex. 31:12-17 goes on to say that the keeping of the Sabbath was declared to be a sign of the Mosaic Covenant, with the death penalty prescribed for anyone who worked on this holy day.

The observance of the Sabbath underwent a dramatic transformation in the centuries leading up to the time of Christ. Throughout the Old Testament God repeatedly warned Israel not to forget His mighty works and laws. The people did not heed His warning and later disintegrated as a nation before being taken away captive by Assyrian and Babylonian invaders. One of their most flagrant sins leading up to their captivity was the violation of the Sabbath law. They knew from the messages of Jeremiah (Jer. 17:21-27) and Ezekiel (Ezek. 20:12-16) that their nation had been destroyed for breaking God's law, and violating the Sabbath was one of their chief sins. Later, when many of the Jews returned to their homeland, they determined among themselves never to make the same mistake again. They went from one ditch to another and over the centuries created several meticulous rules and regulations detailing what could and could not be done on the Sabbath. They went from ignoring the Sabbath to abusing it by imposing an oppressive and legalistic observance of the day.

There were four hundred years between the Old and New Testament and during this time Jewish scholars gave great attention to the interpretation of the Sabbath law. No work was to be done on the Sabbath so these scholars set out to come up with their own definition of what work was. These rabbis spent endless hours arguing whether a man could or could not carry a lamp from one place to another on the Sabbath or if a torn garment could be sown back together with a needle and thread. Over time the religious leaders came up with new definitions of the words "work" and "labor" and changed the spirit of the Sabbath command and nullified what God was saying. Lengthy rules were written that turned the Sabbath into a law of extreme bondage. For example, there were certain knots that couldn't be tied or loosed on the Sabbath day. Knots that were allowed were those that could be untied with one hand. Also, two letters of the alphabet couldn't be written together and one was forbidden to pluck a gray hair out of one's own head. It was forbidden to carry a burden on the Sabbath day so if a person wore false teeth or a wooden leg or put on excess clothing they were in danger of being stoned to death.

The definition of work defined by these religious authorities was vastly different from any ordinary definition. It was accepted that one could not plow their fields on the Sabbath day. These scholars, however, said it was forbidden to drag a chair along the ground because of the possibility that it would make a rut in the dirt. You also couldn't spit on the ground for it would disturb the soil and in the eyes of the rabbis this was a form of plowing. Walking through grass also was not allowed because some of the grass might be bent and broken. The rabbis said this was the same as threshing grain which was one of the forbidden categories of work that one couldn't do on the Sabbath. Instead of being a blessing that the Sabbath was intended to be, it became a grievous burden because of the thousands of restrictions too numerous to mention. So petty were these rules and regulations that a century before Jesus was born a thousand Jews had been slaughtered because they were attacked on the Sabbath day and refused to break the Sabbath by picking up a sword in order to defend themselves.

This was the religious atmosphere Jesus encountered when He began His public ministry. This was the mindset of those Jews who sought to kill Jesus because He healed the lame man on the Sabbath and told him to take up his bed and walk. These leaders could not deny that a miracle had occurred. Instead of rejoicing over this divine intervention they chose instead to accuse Jesus of healing this person on the wrong day. So strange were their list of laws that it was acceptable to carry a man on a bed to the pool on the Sabbath but it was not acceptable to carry a bed without a man on it. With laws like this it was hardly a surprise that the gospel writers recorded numerous occasions when the Jewish leaders clashed with Jesus over the interpretation of the Sabbath law. His many healing miracles done on the Sabbath day and His teaching on how one should observe this holy day stirred frequent controversy, probably none more so than what is recorded in Mark 2:23,24, "Now it happened that He went through the grainfields on the Sabbath; and as they went His disciples began to pluck the heads of grain. And the Pharisees said to Him, 'Look, why do they do what is not lawful on the Sabbath?'"

The disciples were walking through the field with Jesus, they were hungry, and as they walked they picked heads of grain, rubbed them in their hands to remove the chaff, and then ate the kernels. This action required very little effort and could hardly be regarded as work. What the disciples were doing was acceptable according to the laws of harmony God had given the nation of Israel (Deut. 23:25). Even so, the Pharisees were very strict concerning the Sabbath and they viewed the actions of the disciples to be a form of threshing and reaping which were forbidden on this day. Although the disciples did not violate the God's Sabbath commandment, they did violate the man-made regulations of the Pharisees and were harshly criticized for it. Jesus was not intimidated by the challenge of the Jewish leaders and He caught them off guard by referring to an Old Testament story that paralleled this current situation. He pointed out that David and his followers were hungry as they fled from King Saul and were given bread in the house of God that was normally to be eaten only by priests, yet they were guiltless in the eyes of God (Mark 2:25,26).

Jesus turned the table on those who would accuse Him by pointing out that God's law allowed for mercy on the Sabbath. The law said the showbread was holy and was to be eaten only by priests and yet David and his men ate it and were not condemned for doing so. It was not lawful according to the letter of the law but was permitted in the spirit of the law. Jesus is telling the Pharisees that God's love for people is more important than the observance of spiritual rituals. Bread that is holy can be given to ordinary people when they are hungry. Jesus is telling these religious leaders that they are wrong in putting their strict and harsh rules and regulations above the mercy of God. It was here that Jesus said, "The Sabbath was made for man, and not man for the Sabbath. Therefore the Son of Man is also Lord of the Sabbath" (Mark 2:27,28). It was God's will at creation that the Sabbath be a day of rest from normal works of labor, a blessing and benefit to all humanity. It was a time to be enjoyed, not endured. By saying this Jesus was pointing out that it was not He who was being unbiblical, it was the Pharisees who were out of line with the scriptures.

By calling Himself the Lord of the Sabbath, Jesus is openly proclaiming that He has the ultimate authority over the rules and regulations that govern the Sabbath day. The Pharisees had set up strict laws regarding the Sabbath that were oppressive and legalistic, and by doing so these religious leaders had made themselves lords of the Sabbath, thus making themselves lords over the people. Jesus had the authority to overrule these harsh regulations because it was He who created the Sabbath in the first place (John 1:3). Jesus was the original Lord of the Sabbath and here He is saying the Creator is always greater than the creation. And because He is the Lord of the Sabbath, He is free to do on it whatever He pleases. Jesus performed so many miracles during His ministry that the Bible doesn't record them all. It is interesting that the Bible does record seven miracles Jesus did on the Sabbath. The number "seven" denotes perfection and completeness. Just as there are seven colors in the rainbow and seven notes in a musical scale, so is there perfection in everything the Lord of the Sabbath does.

The Sabbath was made for people. It was given to serve their needs and to be a benefit to them. The Sabbath was a servant and not the master the Pharisees made it out to be. Jesus preached on the Sabbath day and performed miracles to deliver people from satanic bondage. He told the crowds of people that the favor of God was on their lives. He gave sight to the blind, healed the sick, drove out evil spirits, and restored physical deformities. All this He did on a day that was made for the benefit of man. When rebuked for what He did Jesus said, "Hypocrite! Does not each one of you on the Sabbath loose his ox or his donkey from the stall, and lead it away to water it?" (Luke 13:15). Jesus also said in Luke 14:5, "Which of you, having a donkey or an ox that has fallen into a pit, will not immediately pull him out on the Sabbath day?" Jesus was saying that the Sabbath was supposed to make life better, not more difficult. The Pharisees had no answer for what Jesus said. They could not prove that what He said was wrong and was one reason they tried to kill Him (Matt. 12:14). How much more would their wrath be enraged when Jesus proclaimed that He was equal with God?

Jesus is the Lord of the Sabbath and He didn't concern Himself with "the tradition of the elders" (Matt. 15:2). He sought to fulfill the spirit of the law and went about giving life to dying people. The Jewish leaders were obsessed that no work of any kind be done on the Sabbath day. To them it was a matter of life and death. How shocked they must have been when Jesus answered their accusations, "My Father has been working until now, and I have been working" (John 4:17). They had just been talking about the Sabbath, a day of rest, and Jesus answered them by talking about work. The Lord's statement was very strong and clear and it shattered everything the Pharisees believed in. God did not stop working on the Sabbath day and neither did Jesus. Yes, God rested on the seventh day from His work of creation but He didn't stop being God. He never ceased from governing that which He created. The sun still rises and the grass and trees still grow. God is a God of love and even on the Sabbath His love and compassion never cease. Jesus is saying that the Father's rest was not one of idleness and that there is no greater work than to relieve someone's pain and distress even if it's on the Sabbath day.

Jesus openly declared that He was doing what His Father was doing. The Father has never ceased in His love for people and what Jesus did was in full character with who the Father is. Heb. 1:3 (MSG) says, "This Son perfectly mirrors God, and is stamped with God's nature." The NLT says, "The Son radiates God's own glory and expresses the very character of God, and He sustains everything by the mighty power of His command." Other work may be laid aside but the work of compassion never ceases. While the Jews are resting on this day the Father and the Son are forever working to give people life and life more abundantly (John 10:10). Jesus also did something that was totally unheard of. He referred to God as His very own Father and this gave the Jews another reason to kill Him. As serious as they considered the breaking of the Sabbath to be, they thought blasphemy was much more serious. Since Jesus claimed God was His Father, they saw Him guilty of blasphemy. "Therefore the Jews sought all the more to kill Him, because He not only broke the Sabbath, but also said that God was His Father, making Himself equal with God" (vs. 18).

According to Mosaic law, the penalty for both blasphemy and violation of the Sabbath was death by stoning. The Jews now had two accusations against Jesus and they increased their efforts to end His life. In no way could anybody be equal with God, or so they claimed. In Greek the word "equal" means 'being equivalent in number, size, quality, equal.' Still they refused to acknowledge that the very miracle that had healed the lame man was a sign that Jesus was indeed the Messiah. The prophet Isaiah foretold of this time in human history, "Then the eyes of the blind shall be opened, and the ears of the deaf shall be unstopped. Then the lame shall leap like a deer, and the tongue of the dumb sing" (Is. 35:5,6). It took great courage for Jesus to say the things He did for He must have known what their reaction would be. He answered the charge against Him by saying, "Most assuredly, I say to you, the Son can do nothing of Himself, but what He sees the Father do; for whatever He does, the Son also does in like manner." The Greek word for "see" means 'to contemplate, to perceive, to know.' Whatever Jesus does is always with the conscious knowledge that He is doing the Father's will.

Jesus is saying that His actions are in full harmony with God's actions. It brings back to memory the words of Nicodemus who said in John 3:2, "No man can do the signs You do unless God is with him." Jesus is claiming absolute equality with God and to see Him is to see the Father. Together they work in perfect unison. Jesus continued, "For the Father loves the Son, and shows Him all things that He Himself does, and He will show Him greater works than these, that you may marvel" (vs. 20). The unity between Jesus and the Father is a unity of love. The Father loves the Son and shows Him everything He is doing. There is no holding back on the part of the Father for their hearts beat as one. For this reason Jesus has the capacity to understand what the Father is telling Him and is able to comprehend all the things He sees the Father doing. Jesus was fearless as He made this claim before the Jewish rulers. He knew it would ignite their wrath and inflame the minds and intentions of those who heard Him. He also knew that His life and future were in the hands of the Father and that these rulers could not stop what God had sent Him to do.

Jesus then declares His supreme power and authority in vs. 21, "For as the Father raises the dead and gives life to them, even so the Son gives life to whom He will." Jesus is the giver of life as seen in Job 12:10 (NIV), "In His hand is the life of every creature and the breath of all mankind." Greater than this is the eternal life one receives when Jesus is made Lord of their lives. Yes, Jesus is the giver of life both in this world and in the world to come. "For the Father judges no one, but has committed all judgment to the Son, that all should honor the Son just as they honor the Father. He who does not honor the Son does not honor the Father who sent Him" (vs. 22,23). The Father gave Jesus total dominion over His kingdom for the purpose that people will honor the Son the same way they honor the Father. The Messiah's right to judge was prophesied in Is. 11:1-4 and if people don't honor the Son they insult the Father who sent Him. When Jesus sent the seventy out two by two He said to them, "He who hears you hears Me, he who rejects you rejects Me, and he who rejects Me rejects Him who sent Me" (Luke 10:16).

Jesus is still talking to the Jewish leaders and He's not giving them a chance to get a word in edgewise. They must have been beside themselves with anger. He says in vs. 24, "Most assuredly, I say to you, he who hears My word and believes in Him who sent Me has everlasting life, and shall not come into judgment, but has passed from death into life." Once again Jesus links Himself to the Father. They are inseparable. He said that whoever believes Him believes the Father also. Doing this results in receiving eternal life now in this present world. It don't begin in the future when you go to heaven, it begins now when you enter into a personal relationship with Jesus. Going to heaven if just a continuation of what's happening in the here in now although it will be much more glorious. Those who are born again have crossed over from death to life and will not be condemned both now and in the world to come. Paul celebrates this truth in Rom. 8:1,2, "There is therefore now no condemnation to those who are in Christ Jesus, who do not walk according to the flesh, but according to the Spirit. For the law of the Spirit of life in Christ Jesus has made me free from the law of sin and death."

Jesus is equal with the Father and He has the power to give eternal life. That is divine power and through it hatred turns into love and bitterness becomes forgiveness. With this power you're able to enter into a new relationship with God, with your fellow man, and with yourself. Jesus is the giver of life and 1 John 5:11,12 says, "God has given us eternal life, and this life is in His Son. He who has the Son has life; he who does not have the Son of God does not have life." Jesus goes on to say that the hour is coming when the dead will rise from their graves and He will be their judge. Those who have done good will be blessed with the resurrection of life and those who have done evil will be given the resurrection of condemnation (vs. 28,29). Even after saying all this, Jesus once again states His complete dependence on the Father, "I can of Myself do nothing. As I hear, I judge; and My judgment is righteous, because I do not seek My own will but the will of the Father who sent Me" (vs. 30). The Message Bible says, "I can't do a solitary thing on My own: I listen, then I decide." Jesus makes Himself One with the Father and so should you.

-15-

"THE BREAKING PROCESS"

When Jesus walked the earth He was a man like no other. He was raised as the son of a carpenter and in His early years He was neither famous or significant. The Roman empire had taken over Jerusalem and all of Israel and the Jews were subordinate and secondary in prominence and power. Not only that but Jesus was brought up in a city whose citizens were not appreciated by the surrounding communities. He was not recognized for who He was and yet here is the Son of God on a mission that He was sent to fulfill. Zech. 4:10 (NLT) says, "Do not despise these small beginnings, for the Lord rejoices to see the work begin." At the age of thirty Jesus sets out on a journey to be about His Father's business and to fulfill the divine assignment He had been given. For that to happen He had to maintain a close, personal relationship with the Heavenly Father and no other gospel gives deeper insight into this relationship then the gospel of John. Jesus had just explained His relationship with the Father to those Jewish rulers who were there to accuse Him of healing on the Sabbath. However, one's own testimony was considered invalid. It needed to be confirmed by another witness.

Jesus said, "If I were to testify on My own behalf, My testimony would not be valid. But someone else is also testifying about Me, and I assure you that everything he says about Me is true" (John 5:31,32 NLT). According to the Jewish legal system based on Deut. 17:6, the unsupported evidence of one person cannot be taken as proof. They believed that a man is not worthy of belief when he is speaking about himself. Everything had to be established on the basis of two or three witnesses and Paul confirms this in 2 Cor. 13:1 and 1 Tim. 5:19. The Jewish authorities needed other witnesses and Jesus had plenty to give them. His first witness was the testimony of John the Baptist, "He was the burning and shining lamp, and you were willing for a time to rejoice in his light" (vs. 35). Many Jews accepted the witness of John the Baptist yet they did not accept Jesus. They saw the miracles Jesus performed and reaped the benefits of all His teachings but still did not believe that He was the Son of God. As great as John the Baptist was, he was still a man and Jesus knew the evidence presented by any human would not support His claim to be the Son of God.

Jesus then presented a greater witness as proof of His deity. John 5:36 (NLT) says, "But I have a greater witness than John - My teachings and My miracles. The Father gave Me these works to accomplish, and they prove that He sent Me." The Message Bible says, "But the witness that really confirms Me far exceeds John's witness. It's the work the Father gave Me to complete. These very tasks, as I go about completing them, confirm that the Father, in fact, sent Me." Jesus did many mighty works wherever He went. They were great and extraordinary works that pointed to the power of God working in Him and through Him. They were done openly for all to see and were a reflection of His character. Jesus was full of love, mercy, and compassion and so were His works. He ministered to people in need and the miracles He performed were the result of who He is. They also bore witness to His deity. Later in John 10:24,25 the Jews said to Him, "How long do You keep us in doubt? If You are the Christ, tell us plainly." Jesus responded, "I told you, and you do not believe. The works that I do in My Father's name, they bear witness of Me."

The third witness Jesus gives is the Father Himself, "And the Father Himself, who sent Me, has testified of Me" (vs. 37). When Jesus was baptized the Father spoke for all to hear, "This is My beloved Son, in whom I am well pleased" (Matt. 3:17). The Father's witness had also come through the prophets of old. A fourth collaborating witness is found in the scriptures themselves (vs. 39-47). These Jewish leaders were masters at memorizing scripture but they read it with a closed mind. They read it not because they loved God but to find arguments to support their twisted way of thinking. They loved their own ideas about God more than they loved Him. Jesus condemned them saying that if they read the scriptures properly they would have seen that they all pointed to Him. They did not have the love of God in their hearts and for that reason they could not receive Jesus. They were self-seeking and sought the glory of man more than the glory that comes from God. Ever since the days of Moses these people had a history of unbelief. It was now directed at the Son of God who was standing in their midst.

It was now time to move on. After the Lord's confrontation with the Jewish rulers He departed from Jerusalem and went into Galilee. He preached in several cities and towns and performed many miracles. John's gospel narrative now finds Jesus a year later in Capernaum seeking a much needed rest with His disciples. There were times when Jesus desired to draw away from the crowds and four separate withdrawals are recorded in scripture. The reason for these departures were to escape the hostility of the Jewish leaders, rest and recreation, prayer, and to give His disciples special instructions and training and to lead them into a deeper understanding of Himself. A lot of activity had recently been going on. Jesus had sent the twelve disciples out two by two and gave them power to cast out many demons and to heal the sick (Mark 6:7-13). They had also been told of the death of John the Baptist and this brought about a turning point in the life of Jesus. No longer did He actively pursue a public ministry but rather devoted Himself to teaching His disciples how to continue the ministry that the Father had entrusted to Him.

John 6:1,2 says, "After these things Jesus went over the Sea of Galilee, which is the Sea of Tiberias. Then a great multitude followed Him, because they saw His signs which He performed on those who were diseased." The miracles Jesus performed grabbed the people's attention and they followed Him not realizing that signs are given to point a person to something greater than the sign. A sign may point you to a majestic waterfall but what's more important, the sign or the waterfall? Mal. 4:2 says, "The Sun of Righteousness shall arise with healing in His wings." In other words, the Person performing the miracle is greater than the miracle itself. Jesus wanted to be alone but the people saw the direction the boat was going and hastened over to the other side and arrived there before them. "And Jesus went up on a mountain, and there He sat with His disciples. Now the Passover, a feast of the Jews, was near. Then Jesus lifted up His eyes, and seeing a great multitude coming toward Him, He said to Philip, 'Where shall we buy bread, that these may eat?' But this He said to test Him, for He Himself knew what He would do"(vs. 3-6).

Luke 9:10 says this gathering occurred on a mountainside above the city of Bethsaida, known today as the Golan Heights. The Lord's departure took place from the city of Capernaum and this four mile journey took Jesus to a region where fewer Jews and more Gentiles lived. The name "Bethsaida" means 'house of fishermen' and the city is located on the northeast side of the Sea of Galilee on a hill where the Jordan River enters the lake. Coming from its source in the Mount Hermon area, the Jordan River flowed through the Sea of Galilee maintaining its freshness so that it was abundantly supplied with fish. Two miles north of the sea were the fords of the Jordan River where one could easily cross over to the other side. Near these fords was the village of Bethsaida which was the home of Andrew and Peter as well as the home of Philip. Since Philip was well acquainted with the town, Jesus asked him where they might buy some food to feed the people. Philip answered Him, "Two hundred denarii worth of bread is not sufficient for them, that every one of them may have a little" (vs. 7).

There were five thousand men on this mountain with Jesus and this number does not include the women and children. There could easily have been over twenty thousand people at this gathering. This was a crowd beyond human imagination for they came from a society that didn't have a huge population when compared to the world as it is today. Jesus was moved with compassion when He saw this great multitude of people "because they were like sheep not having a shepherd" (Mark 6:34). He healed their sick and began to teach them the Word of God. He spoke with so much power and authority that the time slipped away from them. The hour was late and the people were hungry yet they wouldn't allow themselves to pull away from Jesus for the sake of food. So mesmerized were these people that they'd rather faint from hunger than miss a word that came out of His mouth. Jesus, however, was moved to satisfy their hunger and Philip said that the wages from several months of work would not be enough to feed this massive crowd. He was saying the situation was hopeless and nothing could be done about it. Or so he thought.

The other three gospel accounts tell how the disciples urged Jesus to send the crowd away to buy their own food. They were in a desolate place and sending them to the surrounding villages was the only sensible thing to do. Jesus countered this by saying, "You give them something to eat" (Mark 6:37). He commanded the disciples to meet this need but still they were unable to believe that they had among themselves the means to supply what was needed. Jesus was standing by their side and still they were occupied with the enormity of what they were being told to do. It was a task beyond human comprehension. Philip made his unbelieving observation and soon after Andrew followed suit proving that unbelief is contagious. He said to Jesus, "There is a lad here who has five barley loaves and two small fish, but what are they among so many?" (John 6:9). Both Philip and Andrew spoke the language of unbelief. Instead of counting on the Lord, they focused on their limited, temporal resources. Their reply to Jesus was an admission of their inability to fulfill the responsibility Jesus put on them.

Barley loaves was the bread poor people ate whereas those who were better off would eat bread made from wheat. This bread was also held in contempt for ancient Jewish law said a woman who had committed adultery must bring a trespass offering of bread made from barley flour. Barley is the food of beasts and the woman's sin was the sin of a beast. The two fish were no bigger than sardines. Fresh fish was a luxury unheard of in those days for there was no means of transporting it any long distance and keeping it in an eatable condition. These small fish swarmed in the Sea of Galilee. They were caught and pickled and made into a snack or appetizer. John is the only gospel writer who says this bread and fish came from a young lad. The others say they found some bread and fish without mentioning where it came from. It is ironic that this lad was not even counted as being one who was there yet he was the one who had the means for the miracle that was about to take place. It is amazing that God uses those who other people don't count or consider to be important and significant.

The people on this mountain had walked nine miles to be with Jesus. They had been with Him all day and now the day was well spent and the people were hungry. The task at hand was huge yet the resources were scarce. One is reminded of the story in Judges 7 when God used Gideon and only three hundred men to defeat the entire Midianite army. God used this small number of people because He didn't want Israel to claim glory for itself by proclaiming their own might and ability saved them. The victory is the Lord's when the need is huge but the resources are small. Instead of sending the people away, Jesus commanded the people to sit down in groups of hundreds and fifties. There was much grass on this mountainside so the Lord even provided cushioned seats for them to sit on. This had to take a considerable amount of time to do this proving that the best miracles in your life may take some time to implement. Sometimes you've got to get your life organized and in order so that you'll be in a position to receive the magnitude of what's about to take place.

God is a God of order. 1 Cor. 14:33 says, "For God is not the author of confusion but of peace." The Message Bible says, "God doesn't stir us up into confusion; He brings us into harmony." Just because you have a need does not mean you're ready to hold the weight of what God is about to do. Here on this mountain Jesus took the time to get the people ready to receive the miracle He would soon perform. When you're resting you cease from self-effort and vain activity. Out there in the wilderness the people could do nothing to provide for their own needs so they sat down and allowed the Lord to provide. John 6:11 says, "And Jesus took the loaves." Sometimes Jesus takes things without asking. One time He took a fisherman's boat and used it to preach from. Before His triumphant entry into Jerusalem He told the disciples to go take a donkey that had never been ridden before. If Jesus is Lord of your life then everything He has is yours and everything you have is His. You need to submit your life to Jesus and give Him the right to take from you whatever He wants, whenever He wants.

When you surrender your life to Jesus, He'll take what is yours and replace it with what is His. He'll take your dreams and goals and replace them with His plan for your life. He'll take your sin and give you His eternal salvation. He'll take your sickness and disease and give you His divine health. He'll take your poverty and give you His riches in glory forevermore. Why wouldn't you want to have Jesus take what belongs to you? Jesus will take those bad things that will destroy your life and He'll even take that which is good and return it back to you multiplied many times over. Jesus took the fishermen's boat and afterward gave them so much fish that their nets began to break and their boats started to sink. If Jesus wants to take your loaves then give them to Him. Don't hang on to them with a death grip thinking you'll never survive without your loaves and don't tell Him to take the loaves of some other person who has more loaves than you do. Trust Jesus with your loaves and give Him your fish also. When you give Him everything you have, He'll give you everything He has.

There is more to life than the worldly pleasures that you so desperately want to hang on to. These things are temporary and they'll all pass away like the blowing of the wind. What seems to be important today will not be important tomorrow. Jesus asks in Mark 8:36, "For what will it profit a man if he gains the whole world, and loses his own soul?" What good is fortune and fame if you die unsaved and spend eternity in the lake of fire? Rejecting a relationship with God might mean temporary gains in this world system but it comes at a terrible price. The rich young ruler walked away from Jesus because he didn't want to give up his great possessions. Eventually all young people will grow old and they'll then realize that all the wealth and prestige of this world is worthless to the dying man. It is brutally foolish to become so attached to this world that you forget about the world to come. Jesus is forever trying to take you out of a temporal world that doesn't matter into a life that has eternal value and benefits. This temporal life is what He's trying to take out of your hands. Give it to Him and watch the blessings of eternal life flow.

Jesus then took the loaves and blessed it and gave thanks for it. He is blessing something and thanking the Father for something that in itself is not enough to meet the need. Until you can be thankful for something that is not enough, then what you have cannot be multiplied into that which is more than enough. Your marriage, your job, and your house may not live up to your expectations but thank God for them anyway. If you can't be thankful for what you now have, you won't be thankful for the things you'll have in the future. If you can't be thankful for the small things, you'll never be thankful for the big things. Thank God today for that alcoholic spouse and for your prodigal son. Thank God for that low-paying job and for that leaking roof on top of your house. Thank God you've got a job to go to and a house to live in. Thank God for that neighbor who plays loud music into the middle of the night and for that mother-in-law who thinks your spouse could have found somebody better to marry. Thank God with a sincere heart and then step back and watch Him perform a miracle in your life.

Matt. 14:19,20 says, "Then He commanded the multitudes to sit down on the grass. And He took the five loaves and the two fish, and looking up to heaven, He blessed and broke and gave the loaves to the disciples; and the disciples gave to the multitudes. So they all ate and were filled, and they took up twelve baskets full of the fragments that remained." Jesus broke the bread and gave it to His disciples proving that the blessing is in the breaking. Those who refuse to be broken are also refusing to be blessed. It is the breaking of life that produces the blessing of life. Those who are the most blessed are those who have found something that broke them. The more the loaves were broken, the more they were multiplied. Have you come from a broken home? Has your heart been broken because someone you love deeply no longer wants anything to do with you? Have your dreams been broken and shattered? If so, then get ready for a miracle. Jesus fed the multitude that day through the breaking process. Hosea 10:12 says, "Sow for yourself righteousness; Reap in mercy; Break up your fallow ground, for it is time to seek the Lord, till He comes and rains righteousness on you."

Fallow ground is ground that has rested for a year between planting seasons. While resting it can become hard and overgrown with weeds and thorns so it must be broken and prepared before seeds can be planted. If you can be broken, if God can take you through the breaking process, He can plant something new in your life. Hosea is saying to break off your evil ways and repent of your sins. Cease to do evil so that the good seed of the Word of God will have room to grow and bear fruit. Joshua said to the people, "Sanctify yourselves, for tomorrow the Lord will do wonders among you" (Josh. 3:5). Fallow ground is ground that is not plowed. It is ground that can be productive but needs to first be broken up, tilled, plowed, and prepared for planting. The Lord said in Jer. 4:3, "Break up your fallow ground, and do not sow among thorns." God is saying that you need to plow your hearts. Breaking up the fallow ground cleans the heart, renews the inner man, and strengthens your walk with the Lord. Ezra 7:10 says, "For Ezra had prepared his heart to seek the Law of the Lord, and to do it."

Like the children of Israel, sometimes you have to go through the wilderness before you reach your Promised Land. At times life can be filled with obstacles and barriers that will cause you to go through many tests and trials. Some people endure these trials, most do not. The people in the wilderness were then pruned by God for He had to cut away and remove those who didn't have the faith to go all the way through to the other side. In fact, God delayed their gaining access to the Promised Land until all the unbelievers died off in the wilderness, those who were too carnal to complete the journey. He then commanded all the young men who were born in the wilderness to be circumcised. God can not and will not allow carnality into the Promised Land. You must be broken before God can take you to this higher level of blessing. If you've got a tenacious, relentless commitment to break up the fallow ground of your heart, God will personally escort you into the land flowing with milk and honey. Allowing yourself to be broken is a sign that you belong to God. It's a sign of your sincerity and God will honor that by performing a miracle in your life.

Most people don't understand this but you've got to initiate the miracle you want to take place. Too many people are waiting on God to move while He's sitting back waiting for them to move. He is waiting for them to break up the fallow ground in their life. People are just too passive. They're not radical enough to do what needs to be done. They're unwilling to go get that shovel and start breaking up the hard soil that's preventing the seeds of life from taking root. They want God to do what they're supposed to be doing themselves. You need to enter into a realm of aggressiveness that provokes the release of a miracle. You've got to stop feeling sorry for yourself and accepting as the norm whatever it is you're going through. Get aggressive and make something happen. Be a person of action and go after your blessing. Phil. 3:14 (MSG) says, "I'm off and running, and I'm not turning back." In front of you is the Jordan River which is the gateway to your Promised Land. Rejoice because you've only got one more river to cross before you receive your miracle. God has moved in your life in times past, for sure He'll move again.

Being broken is a sign that you're close to your miracle. This is why James 1:2 tells you to "count it all joy when you fall into various trials." Ps. 30:5 says, "Weeping may endure for a night, but joy comes in the morning." Your broken life needs to be plowed up so you can begin a new life. God will pull the plow and you need to allow Him to break up those resentments you've had from past hurts. 1 Cor. 13:11 says, "When I was a child, I spoke as a child, I understood as a child, I thought as a child; but when I became a man, I put away childish things." Paul was broken and when it happened he put away childish things. The proof that your fallow ground is broken up is revealed by those things you put away. Stop being angry at what your spouse said to you twenty years ago and stop being bitter at your co-worker who got that prized promotion instead of you. Heartfelt repentance and confession allows God to plant something new and fruitful in your heart. Allow Him to heal those wounds and to give you a heart of flesh that is currently hard because of unbelief. Trust Him and you'll be changed from a nobody into a somebody.

1 Peter 3:18 says Jesus was "put to death in the flesh but made alive in the Spirit." This is what happens when you go through the breaking process. You now respond and react to things differently than you did before. No longer do you get angry when you don't get your own way. No longer do you want to use foul language when another driver cuts in front of you. No longer do you want to slap those people who think they're better than you are. No more! The fallow ground has been broken up and seeds of life are now growing. God is moving and miracles are happening. 1 Peter 5:10 (NLT) says, "In His kindness God called you to share in His eternal glory by means of Christ Jesus. So after you have suffered a little while, He will restore, support, and strengthen you, and He will place you on a firm foundation." The Message Bible says He "will have you put together and on your feet for good. He gets the last word; yes He does." You're pressing forward and God is taking you to a higher level in your relationship with Him. It is now that He'll give you exceedingly, abundantly above all that you ask or think.

Signs and wonders are not to be limited to only the healing of one's physical body. Miracles that brought about supernatural provision was also a vital part of the ministry of Jesus. He had turned water into wine and here on the mountainside near Bethsaida He fed the multitude with a few loaves and some small fish. At this gathering He healed their bodies, taught them the Word of God, and provided for them food supernaturally. God can bring provision for your needs just as easily as He can heal your body. Phil. 4:19 (MSG) says, "You can be sure that God will take care of everything you need, His generosity exceeding even yours in the glory that pours from Jesus." These people were filled to the point where they couldn't eat any more, and still there were twelve baskets of bread left over. Job 5:9 (NLT) says, "He does great things too marvelous to understand. He performs countless miracles." God has no limits to how He can supply a need in your life. The Message Bible says, "He's famous for great and unexpected acts; there's no end to His surprises." Wake up in the morning expecting God to surprise you with His goodness. Put a smile on your face and a bounce in your step. Then go out and face the world head on.

-16-

"THE BREAD OF LIFE"

Except for the resurrection, the feeding of the multitude near Bethsaida is the only miracle recorded by all four gospel writers. Preceding this glorious event was the Lord's command to the disciples to feed the people and their admission that they were unable to complete the task. While this miracle was performed to satisfy the hunger of the crowd, Jesus multiplied the loaves and the fish mainly for the benefit of the disciples. He was instructing them concerning the nature of the ministry for which they were being prepared. In time they would encounter sheep not having a shepherd to guide them, people who are starved spiritually. Jesus is saying that it would be their responsibility to "give them something to eat." They may not have the ability within themselves to meet the need but when they make available to the Lord what they do have, He'll take it and multiply it and use them to minister to the multitudes. God often works through people. 1 Cor. 3:9 says "we are God's fellow workers." Jesus fed the multitude through His disciples for it was their work also. The ministry belongs to the Lord but it's carried out through human instruments.

The glory of this miracle is not that the people were filled but rather in the twelve baskets of bread that was left over. The disciples were very tired by now but Jesus gave them one more task to do. He told them to pick up the broken pieces of bread that were scattered over the hillside "so that nothing is lost" (John 6:12). The crowd had eaten until they were thoroughly satisfied and still there was plenty left over. This overflow was on purpose. This is how Jesus planned it. God is El Shaddai, the God of more than enough. This is why David said in Ps. 23:5, "My cup runs over." It was a custom that when people ate together they would leave something to those who served. Prov. 11:25 says, "The generous soul will be made rich, and he who waters will also be watered himself." The Message Bible says, "The one who blesses others is abundantly blessed; those who help others are helped." There were twelve baskets left over, one for each disciple. They had helped in the work and now they were being rewarded. It is also a certainty that the young lad who provided the five loaves and two fish also shared in this bountiful harvest.

Surprisingly, this miracle caused trouble for Jesus. The people had followed Him because of the signs He performed and here on this mountainside they witnessed another miraculous sign. John 6:14 says, "Then those men, when they had seen the sign that Jesus did, said, 'This is truly the Prophet who is to come into the world.'" The Jews had been waiting for the prophet promised to them by Moses in Deut. 18:15, "The Lord your God will raise up for you a Prophet like me from among your own brothers. You must listen to him." These people weren't interested in who Jesus was but rather in what He could do for them. In their eyes this Prophet was to be the king of Israel and the head of God's kingdom on earth. They wanted Him to lead a rebellion against the Romans and drive them from their land. They were looking for a Messiah who would be a king and a conqueror, a person they could use for their own purposes. He had already healed them and fed them so they were now ready to carry Him to power on a wave of glory. The problem here is they wanted a king on their own terms. They wanted to use Him instead of allowing Him to use them.

"Therefore when Jesus perceived that they were about to come and take Him by force to make Him king, He departed again to a mountain by Himself alone" (vs. 15). Jesus often said that His kingdom was not of this world but here the people wanted to seize Him in a violent manner and force Him to be their king. In Greek the term "take by force" means 'to take suddenly and vehemently; to grab or seize suddenly so as to remove or gain control; to snatch and take away.' Just as Moses had provided military leadership to deliver the people from the oppression of the Egyptians, the people now wanted Jesus to do the same thing against the Romans even if He had to be forced to do it. If Jesus had intended to become a political king then now was the opportunity to do so. It didn't happen because an earthly kingdom was never in God's plans from the very beginning. Besides, Jesus didn't need to be made a king, He was born one. He then sent the disciples off to the other side of the lake while He dismissed the crowd. Afterward He went and found a place of refuge on one of the mountains in the region where He spent time alone in prayer (Matt. 14:23).

"And when evening came, His disciples went down to the sea, got into the boat, and went over the sea toward Capernaum" (vs. 16,17). For what reason did Jesus tell the disciples to do this? Mark 6:45 makes it clear they didn't wish to leave. Scripture doesn't say why Jesus gave them this command but there is more than a slight possibility that they had begun to be influenced by the crowd and their desire to take Jesus by force and make Him a king then and there. Like an infectious virus that overtakes the body, the disciples may have become sympathetic with the impulses of the crowd who were about to rebel against the plan of God. This crowd of people were fellow citizens of some of these disciples and many may have been their friends and neighbors. With little or no persuasion it is quite conceivable that the disciples were about to grasp onto the same thoughts and demands of this vast assembly of delusional humanity. Trouble was brewing and Jesus wanted the disciples to have nothing to do with it. To counteract the uncontrolled excitement and wild behavior of this mob of people, Jesus compelled the disciples to get into the boat and go back to the other side of the lake.

"And it was now dark, and Jesus had not come to them. Then the sea arose because a great wind was blowing" (vs. 17,18). The Sea of Galilee is seven hundred feet below the Mediterranean Sea and lies in the lower portion of the Jordan Valley in a mountain range that rises up to four thousand feet above sea level. In addition to the constant wind blowing in from the Mediterranean, cold air is always rushing down from the surrounding mountains and plows into the warm air rising off the surface of the water. This causes the lake to be greatly vulnerable to sudden and extremely violent storms. The disciples left the shore and in the midst of their journey a fierce storm engulfed the boat and threatened their lives.

The waves swelled up and the raging of the sea tossed the boat to and fro (Matt. 14:24). They only had a short distance to travel but still they battled the storm through the long hours of the night. The disciples exerted themselves strenuously, "straining at the oars" (Mark 6:48). Jesus had told them to go to the other side but the storm was preventing them from once again fulfilling what the Lord told them to do.

Has this ever happened to you? Has God ever told you to do something but some unexpected circumstance prevented you from doing what He told you to do? It has probably happened more times than you care to admit. Don't feel bad, there are many others in the same boat you are. Notice that this storm happened on their way to where Jesus told them to go. It happened on the way to their destiny. In truth, this storm should not have come as a surprise. If your dream doesn't stir up the devil's wrath then more than likely the dream didn't come from God. The validity of one's dream is measured by the opposition that comes against it. Big dreams bring big trials. As a teenager David was anointed to be king over all Israel and before you know it he was standing toe to toe with the biggest, most feared enemy warrior in all the land. Understand that God always has a purpose when He sends you to a certain place. Jonah was caught in a storm because of his disobedience but here the disciples were in a storm because they obeyed and did what Jesus told them to do.

Don't fall for the illusion that if you're walking in the perfect will of God for your life that you'll never have any more problems. This is not true. Far from it. The storm these disciples were now in was on the exact path Jesus told them to take. It's not as if they stepped out of the will of God and went off to do their own thing. No, they were right where Jesus told them to be. This is why you need to see your trials as steppingstones that will take you to your destiny. Do not allow yourself to get into fear and doubt because of a temporary setback. You've been to the top of the mountain too many times to allow some stormy trial to cause you to doubt the Person who told you to go to the other side in the first place. It's important that you not allow the circumstances of life to overwhelm you because it's the things you go through that reveal the person you truly are on the inside. Make a commitment to keep pressing forward no matter what it is you're going through believing that this too shall pass. Believe that where a crisis is, Christ is there also.

People are always asking, "Where is God when I'm hurting? Where is God in the storm?" Job wondered the same thing. "Look, I go forward, but He is not there, and backward, but I cannot perceive Him; When He works on the left hand, I cannot behold Him; When He turns to the right hand, I cannot see Him" (Job 23:8,9). Don't allow the storm you're now facing to cause you to think God isn't there by your side. He is there. He's always there. In fact, God does His best work when you're in a storm. Ps. 46:1-3 says, "God is our refuge and strength, a very present help in trouble. Therefore we will not fear, though the earth be removed, and though the mountains be carried into the midst of the sea; Though its waters roar and are troubled, though the mountains shake with its swelling." If you're looking for Jesus, then look no further than the storm you're currently in. He may be asleep in the bottom of the boat but He's still there. Deut. 31:6 says, "Be strong and of good courage, do not fear nor be afraid of them; for the Lord your God, He is the One who goes with you. He will not leave you nor forsake you."

Throw yourself into the work God has given you to do believing that He will take you to the other side. Rom. 8:28 says, "And we know that all things work together for good to those who love God, to those who are the called according to His purpose." When you see a problem, God sees an opportunity for Him to take you to a higher level. Job 23:10 says, "But He knows the way that I take; When He has tested me, I shall come forth as gold." Believing that God will deliver you and bless you even when you can't sense His presence is faith at its highest level. Ps. 119:71 says, "It is good for me that I have been afflicted, that I may learn your statutes." God is always on the scene and you must trust Him even when you can't see Him. Trust that He will be there in the midst of your storm. He said in Is. 43:2 (NLT), "When you go through deep waters, I will be with you. When you go through rivers of difficulty, you will not drown. When you walk through the fire of oppression, you will not be burned up; the flames will not consume you." The disciples are about to learn that stormy trials are not a problem when Jesus is on board your ship.

Anytime God promises you something or tells you to do something, get ready for trouble. At the same time, believe that God is always by your side. David said, "Yea, though I walk through the valley of the shadow of death, I will fear no evil; For You are with me" (Ps. 23:4). The problem with storms is that they limit your visibility and this is why God is always telling you to walk by faith and not by sight. You seek for comfort during hard times not realizing that God moves in the spiritual realm and not in the sensual realm. Don't be so focused on the storm that you lose sight of the God in the storm. You may not see Him or sense His presence but He is always there. When storms come, when it's dark and dreary, many people strain to find the solution by their own effort and strength. The disciples were straining at the oars and this is what happens when you try to live life on your own terms. You work and you struggle and yet you get no where. Your life is going in circles and no progress is being made because faith and fear cannot travel in the same boat. Faith brings God on the scene while fear blinds the eyes to the presence of the Lord.

Back behind the disciples Jesus was doing something they could not see. He was walking on the water coming straight toward them. Job 9:8 says, "He alone spreads out the heavens, and treads on the waves of the sea." Moses divided the sea, Jesus walked on it. Why didn't Jesus walk along the shoreline to get to where the disciples were supposed to be waiting for Him? Because the disciples were still on the water and Jesus wanted to be where they were. Jesus never once performed a miracle for His own convenience. Everything He ever did was for the benefit of other people. He did not walk on the water because it was a shorter distance to travel. No, His friends needed Him and He went to them taking the most direct route possible. For this reason He took command of the elements and walked on the water. John 6:19 says, "So when they had rowed about three or four miles, they saw Jesus walking on the sea and drawing near the boat; and they were afraid." Mark 6:48 says "He would have passed them by" showing that Jesus will pass you by unless He is called upon. Vs. 49 goes on to say that the disciples thought Jesus was a ghost and this was the reason for their fear.

The disciples' response to seeing Jesus was fear. They were not looking for Jesus in this storm nor were they expecting to be delivered. They had just witnessed the great miracle of the feeding of the five thousand so seeing Jesus now at their time of need should have been a thing to be expected. Their faith was paralyzed because that was then and this was now. How many times has God delivered you from a trial one day only to have a different circumstance the next day fill you with doubt and fear? The disciples problem is found in Mark 6:52, "For they had not understood about the loaves, because their heart was hardened." The spiritual condition of a hardened heart renders a person with the inability to see, hear, understand, and remember. The Amplified Bible says "they had not understood the miracles of the loaves and how it revealed the power and deity of Jesus; but in fact their heart was hardened being oblivious and indifferent to His amazing works." The hearts of the disciples dulled their ability to perceive what had happened just a few hours before. If they had remembered what Jesus had done they would have stayed in faith knowing everything would be okay.

All too often people forget how God has blessed them in the past and this is why they have little or no faith that He will provide for them today. The disciples showed the hardness of their hearts in that the working of one miracle did not prepare them to expect another miracle. They had not been sufficiently affected by the miracle they just witnessed because of the insensibility of their hearts. The result of their dullness to receive and understand the nature of Jesus is that fear entered in and gripped their hearts. Jesus dispelled their fear by saying, "It is I; do not be afraid" (John 6:20). Notice that He told them who He was before He told them what to do. The act of turning their attention from the waves to Jesus is what drove their fear away. As soon as Jesus got into the boat the wind ceased and the sea got calm. "Then those who were in the boat came and worshiped Him, saying, 'Truly You are the Son of God'" (Matt. 14:33). This was the first time Jesus was called the Son of God by the disciples and the first time they are said to have worshiped Him. They acknowledged who He is and praised Him for what He had done. Their faith in Jesus was definitely growing.

The next day the same crowd who had been with Jesus came looking for Him. They found Him at Capernaum and asked how He got there since He had not gotten into the boat with the other disciples (vs. 25). To this question Jesus replied, "Most assuredly, I say to you, you seek Me, not because you saw the signs, but because you ate of the loaves and were filled" (vs. 26). Jesus did not answer their question but brought to light what their true motives were for coming to Him. God fed the people in the wilderness for forty years with manna from heaven and the day before Jesus multiplied the five loaves and two fish. The crowd had received a free and lavish meal and now they wanted more. The reason they were coming to Jesus is they wanted Him to give them free food for the rest of their lives. They didn't have to work for the manna that fell out of the sky and they didn't have to work for the meal they ate the day before. They were looking for a way to eliminate their grocery bill forever. They were more concerned with what they put in their stomach while Jesus was concerned about what they put in their heart.

Jesus is at the height of His popularity and He is speaking to a group of people who are searching for the meaning of life. They want their lives to matter to the point of making a lasting impact on other people. They realize that the older a person gets, the more precious life becomes. The fear of squandering the one life they'd been given is what drove them to this young miracle-working teacher named Jesus. These people have already left their homes and jobs to follow Him and are now ready to wrap their lives around this man and make Him king. Thousands of wide-eyed people are standing before Him, ready and eager to hear what He has to say. They're looking for a definition of life and Jesus gives them one they can't understand or accept. He exposes the emptiness of the life they're after by saying you can't solve a spiritual need with a physical solution. Jesus is saying that the need for eternal life transcends the need for physical food. By the time this conversation is over there will be a major shift in the hearts of this massive crowd. The majority of these people will soon walk away from Jesus never again to return.

Jesus continued, "Do not labor for the food which perishes, but for the food which endures to everlasting life, which the Son of Man will give you, because God the Father has set His seal on Him" (vs. 27). Jesus is saying that all these things the people are working for will one day perish and because of that they will never be permanently filled. They'll forever be walking around with a hunger and a thirst that will never be quenched. People know they're not perfect and they've got issues to deal with. The problem is they tend to minimize what those issues are and then turn around and look for solutions that they can control and manage. It is at this time when people turn to alcohol and drugs and other fleshly lusts and desires to find the life they're so desperately looking for. They leave God out of all this and don't allow Him to tell them what the real problem truly is. In other words, they want to face life on their terms and not on God's terms. Jesus had read their motives and the people now wanted to do something to earn God's favor. They asked Him, "What shall we do, that we may work the works of God?" (vs. 28).

The natural man always wants to work to receive from God. The rich young ruler asked, "What shall I do to inherit eternal life?" (Luke 18:18), the Jews on the day of Pentecost said, "What shall we do?" (Acts 2:32), and the Philippian jailer asked, "What must I do to be saved?" (Acts 16:30). The people talking here with Jesus still don't get it. They think He's going to give them some special bread that's loaded down with spiritual steroids. They are looking for a type of bread they can hold in their hands and eat with their mouths. They're looking at the physical realm and not the spiritual realm. They're asking Jesus what works can they do to get this special bread. They have no interest in having a personal relationship with Him and this is why they're willing to work in order to get this bread. They're seeking the benefits of Christianity but not the Christ of Christianity. Jesus answered them and said,

"This is the work of God, that you believe in Him whom He sent" (vs. 29). The one thing that God requires of all people is faith in Him. Belief in Jesus as the Son of God is the one work that pleases God (Heb. 11:6).

The people are startled to hear that to please God the first requirement is faith in Jesus. Instead of bowing down before Him right then, they instead asked for a sign of His divinity (vs. 30). Imagine asking Jesus this the day after they were all fed miraculously. Jesus had performed many signs in their presence but now they want Jesus to perform another sign before they'll put their faith in Him. They then reminded Jesus of how their forefathers ate manna in the wilderness. In response to this Jesus reminded the people that this manna was the provision of God and that the true bread from heaven is the Person they're talking to. He said, "For the bread of God is He who comes down from heaven and gives life to the world" (vs. 33). He was saying that the manna their forefathers ate was a type of Himself. It was small and this speaks of the Lord's humility. He wasn't born in a palace but in a stable. The manna was round and this refers to the eternal nature of Jesus. It was white and points to the holy, sinless nature of Jesus. The manna only fell at night pointing to the fact that Jesus came to a world lost in spiritual darkness.

The people asked Jesus to give them this bread always and He lays it all on the line in vs. 35, "I am the bread of life. He who comes to me shall never hunger, and he who believes in me shall never thirst." This is the turning point in this whole conversation. This is the definition of life the crowd can't bring themselves to accept. Jesus said He didn't come to bring bread; He came to be the bread. He didn't come to improve their life, He came to be their life. Jesus is telling the people that He is all they'll ever need. To have Him and nobody but Him is to have everything. Bread is the one food that is a necessity just as Jesus is a necessity. There is no life without Him. Bread is a daily food and so also must you feed on Jesus daily. Grain was crushed to make bread and so was Jesus bruised for your iniquities. Bread must be eaten in order for it to do you any good. Likewise, David writes in Ps. 34:8, "Oh, taste and see that the Lord is good." The people were hungry and Jesus is telling them to feast on grace and drink cups of forgiveness. He is the bread of life come down from heaven. He is enough to fill them each and every day.

Jesus had drawn a line in the sand by telling the crowd the life they were seeking after only comes by pledging a life of obedience and faithfulness to Him and Him alone. This the people could not accept and vs. 41 says they murmured against Him. They wanted Jesus to conform to their own image and expectations of what a king should be like. Just moments before they were impressed by Him and affected by the things He did and said. All the life they would ever need was standing right there in front of them but they failed to grasp who Jesus truly was. He was the life they so desperately craved and needed. Jesus gives life, He sustains life, and He satisfies life. God arranged it so that nothing this life offers will give you full and complete satisfaction. Jesus challenged the people by telling them the truth that He was the Son of God, the bread of life come down from heaven. He then said something that shook the people to the core, "Whoever eats My flesh and drinks My blood has eternal life, and I will raise him up on the last day. For My flesh is food indeed, and My blood is drink indeed" (vs. 54,55).

The words of Jesus shifted from eating bread to eating flesh and drinking blood and this brought about an immediate reaction from the crowd. They were disgusted by what He said, so repulsed were they that they began to quarrel among themselves (vs. 52). They wrongfully believed that He was speaking literally of His own flesh and blood and refused to consider the deeper and more true meaning of what He was saying. Jesus didn't back down but continued to say, "He who eats My flesh and drinks My blood abides in Me, and I in him. As the living Father sent Me, and I live because of the Father, so he who feeds on Me will live because of Me" (vs. 56,57). Jesus was talking in a figurative language and the metaphor was so vivid and extreme that it caused an uproar among the people. They said, "This is a hard saying; who can understand it?" (vs. 60). These sayings the people did not want to hear. They wanted to hear about a conquering king who would usher in a new kingdom where all their needs were met. They trusted in Moses and followed John the Baptist yet could not find the faith to believe in Jesus.

Jesus was a man like no other and He told the people not what they wanted to hear but what they needed to hear. The people didn't receive what they came looking for and vs. 66 says, "From that time many of His disciples went back and walked with Him no more." These same people who wanted to make Him king after He fed them now want nothing more to do with Him. Jesus told them the truth and they couldn't handle it. He then turned to the twelve disciples and asked, "Do you also want to go away?" (vs. 67). Peter answered and said, "Lord, to whom shall we go? You have the words of eternal life. Also we have come to believe and know that You are the Christ, the Son of the living God" (vs. 68,69). Peter pledged their allegiance to Jesus even though they were just as bewildered and puzzled as everyone else. Still, there was something different about Jesus for which he would willingly die. Peter knew his life had already been changed and in his heart was a conviction that Jesus was who He claimed to be. Faith is proven to be genuine and true when a person stays committed to Jesus even when there are many things they don't understand.

-17-

"LIVING WATER"

Jesus was a masterful and skilled communicator and the words He spoke were said with so much boldness that they shocked the crowds who heard Him. To them, the claims of Jesus were revolting and outrageous and beyond comprehension. He claimed to be the Lord of the Sabbath and the bread of life. He said He was greater than all the forefathers of the Old Testament and even went so far as to say He was alive before Abraham was even born. He declared Himself to be without sin and had been given all authority in heaven and on earth. He was the supreme, righteous Judge and He alone would one day determine the eternal destiny of every human being. Indeed, Jesus was a man like no other for He claimed openly to be the Son of God come down from heaven to be the Savior of the world. He claimed to be the Messiah and the only source of eternal life. In order to be saved, He said, you had to eat His flesh and drink His blood. Nowhere had anybody heard anything as disgraceful and barbaric as this. For this reason many of His followers walked away from Him while others increased their efforts to kill Him.

The words of Jesus, the people said, were words of blasphemy and went beyond what any person could say or do. Certainly He was possessed by a demon and deserved, rightfully so, to be put to death. The Jewish leaders also thought He was a threat to their legalistic form of Judaism, as well as their binding authority over the people. They had more than enough reason to want Him dead and so they plotted how they might kill Him. Because of this threat, John 7:1 says, "After these things Jesus walked in Galilee; for He did not want to walk in Judea, because the Jews sought to kill Him." Jesus wasn't afraid to die but He knew there were still things to do before He gave up His life for the sins of all mankind.

He was still training His disciples to carry on His work after He was gone so He stays in Galilee away from all His enemies, teaching and working with His disciples. Six months has passed since Jesus fed the multitude and the rising storm of hatred against Him has been smoldering and growing more intense by the day. The desire to kill Him is stronger than ever.

Jesus had been ministering in Galilee for over a year and in His absence the fury of the Jewish leaders in Judea continued to grow. Many may say He was a good man but, they reasoned, good people don't say they're God, liars and crazy people do. Their hostility raged on and this caused their hatred toward Him to roar like never before. It was a time of progressive rejection but soon an event would take place that would bring Jesus once again into their midst. John 7:2 says, "Now the Jews' Feast of Tabernacles was at hand." There were seven feasts appointed and ordained by God to be kept in honor of His name. It was on Mt. Sinai that God gave Moses the names and dates of these feasts. Lev. 23 tells what all these feasts are and gives instructions on the observance of each one. These times of celebration were called the "feasts of the Lord" (vs. 2) which meant He was to be the main focus of all the activities that went along with these feasts. They're important to the overall plan of the Bible for each feast foreshadows and symbolizes an aspect of the life, death, and resurrection of the Lord Jesus Christ.

God is a God of order and His divine plan for man is drawn out in these seven feasts. These were feasts of remembrance and they all centered around Jesus. These were feasts and not funerals showing that God wants the Christian life to be a life of feasting where every day is a joyous occasion. All believers are to enjoy the privileges and blessings that come from having a personal relationship with God. Christians today are under no obligation to observe these feasts (Col. 2:16) but an in-depth knowledge and understanding of them will certainly enhance your faith. The Hebrew calendar is based on the phases of the moon. Each month in a lunar calendar begins with a new moon. Lev. 23:5 specifies that the festival year begins with the Passover on "the fourteenth day of the first month" of the year in the Jewish calendar which is the month if Nissan. This month is referred to as the "month of happiness" and the "month of flowers." Passover is the Feast of Salvation and falls on the first full moon of spring and occurs sometime in March or April.

The Jewish feasts are closely related to Israel's spring and fall harvests and their agricultural seasons. Each year these feasts were to remind the people of God's ongoing protection and provision. The Feast of Passover is a reminder how the blood of a lamb was put on the doorpost of every Jewish home in Egypt (Ex. 12:7). The angel of death then passed over those homes while the firstborn were killed in the Egyptian homes where no blood was sprinkled. It is no coincidence that Jesus was sacrificed on Passover where His blood was shed for the salvation of all who will believe. On the cross Jesus was the sacrificial lamb and 1 Cor. 5:7 says Christ is "our Passover." Those whose sins are covered by the blood of the Lamb will escape the eternal judgment that God will put on all those who reject Him. In both the Old and New Testaments the blood of the Lamb delivers from slavery. The Jews were delivered from bondage in Egypt and the Christian who believes is delivered from the shackles of sin. The born again believer is marked with the blood of Jesus thus making Passover a symbol of salvation.

The Feast of Unleavened Bread began the day after Passover and lasted one week (Lev. 23:6-8). In the Bible, leaven represents sin and the people eating unleavened bread for seven days represented a holy walk with the Lord. After you've been saved by the blood of the Lamb you then must purge yourself from all manner of sin and evil and go on to live a new life of godliness and righteousness. Jesus called Himself the "bread of life" and He was born in Bethlehem which in Hebrew means "House of Bread." The Feast of Firstfruits took place at the beginning of the harvest and started the day after the beginning of the Feast of Unleavened Bread (Lev. 23:9-14). An offering from the harvest was given to the priest proclaiming that the entire harvest came from God. This took place on the first day of the week. Jesus also rose from the dead on the first day of the week and this feast represents the Lord's glorious resurrection. 1 Cor. 15:20 says Jesus is "the firstfruits of those who have fallen asleep." Just as Jesus arose and received a new glorified body, so shall all those who are born again inherit an incorruptible body (1 Cor. 15:35-49).

The Feast of Pentecost occurred fifty days after the Firstfruits festival (Lev. 23:15-22) and it celebrated the end of the grain harvest. It was fifty days after the original Passover that God gave Moses the Ten Commandments on Mt. Sinai. It was also fifty days after the Lord's resurrection that on the Day of Pentecost the Holy Spirit was poured out on those who were in the upper room. It was required during the Feast of Pentecost that an offering be made of two loaves of bread baked with leaven. These loaves symbolize that the church would be comprised of both Jew and Gentile and the fulfillment of this happened when Jesus triumphantly walked out of that empty tomb. These four springtime feasts symbolizes historic events in both the Old and New Testament. Passover remembers the sacrifice of the first Passover lamb, Unleavened Bread brings to mind the exodus from Egypt, Firstfruits conjures up the crossing of the Red Sea, and Pentecost recalls the giving of the Ten Commandments. In the New Testament Jesus was crucified on Passover, buried on Unleavened Bread, raised on Firstfruits, and sent the Holy Spirit on Pentecost.

The Feast of Trumpets (Lev. 23:23-25) was held on the first day of the seventh month on the Hebrew calendar. It is a day when trumpets are blown (Num. 29:1) to celebrate the end of the agricultural year. It was also used to announce that Israel was entering a sacred season. In Lev. 25:8-10 trumpets were used to "proclaim liberty throughout all the land unto all the inhabitants thereof." This feast occurs in September and the jump in time from the Feast of Pentecost in May or June represents the church age. To the modern day believer the Feast of Trumpets represents the rapture of the church that happens when a trumpet blast sounds from heaven (1 Thess. 4:16). The Day of Atonement (Lev. 23:26-32) happened on the tenth day of the seventh month and was the day the high priest went into the Holy of Holies each year to make an offering for the sins of Israel. It is the holiest day of the Jewish year and this feast symbolizes the cleansing of Israel that will be fulfilled when the Lord returns at His second coming (Rom. 11:26,27). Regardless of Israel's current state of unbelief, a future remnant will in fact repent and fulfill their calling by accepting their Messiah by faith in the end times (Zech. 12:10).

The Feast of Tabernacles is the seventh and final feast of the Lord and took place five days after the Day of Atonement (Lev. 23:33-44). It is a feast of thanksgiving, a time of rejoicing when the people looked back and celebrated the Lord's goodness toward them even when they weren't faithful to Him. Each year the Jews built little shelters or booths made of tree branches outside their houses and worshiped in them for seven days. This was the most joyous of all the feasts for God wanted to celebrate the fact that He provided shelter for the Israelites as they wandered in the wilderness for many years. There was rest waiting for them in the Promised Land and this feast also symbolized that future time when Christ rules and reigns on the earth. For all eternity people from every tribe, tongue, and nation will celebrate this feast in the New Jerusalem (Rev. 21:9-27). Man's journey in temporary dwellings will be over and he will now be in an eternal state of rest. The four spring feasts look back to what Jesus accomplished at His first coming, the three fall feasts point to the glory of His second coming.

John 7:2 says, "Now the Jews' Feast of Tabernacles was at hand." This is the only specific time this feast is mentioned in the New Testament. It was a time when there would be a great gathering in Jerusalem and the Lord's half-brothers suggested this would be a good time for Him to do some miracles there and get a little publicity (vs. 3,4). They were telling Him how to run His ministry and were in essence daring Him to go. His hard sayings had caused many of His disciples to walk away and a new effort to rebuild His popularity was now necessary. His brothers were urging Him to come out into the open and make a public demonstration of His powers. In other words, stop working in secret. For the past several months Jesus had been focusing mainly on mentoring the twelve disciples, often traveling to the outer borders of Galilee. This is how God does things. He draws a crowd and then teaches them the Word of God. He then separates the true disciples from the false ones, the lambs from the goats, and then spends a considerable amount of time training these true disciples. These were the ones Jesus poured Himself into.

The brothers said in vs. 4, "If You do these things, show Yourself to the world." At this point in time His brothers did not believe in Him (vs. 5) and their comments are full of sarcasm and ridicule. They were taunting Jesus the same way Satan tempted Him three times with the word "if." In John 6:15 the people wanted to make Jesus king and Satan offered Him all the kingdoms of the world. In John 6:31 the people asked for bread miraculously and Satan invited Jesus to turn stones into bread. Here in vs. 3,4 the brothers want Jesus to show His power by performing signs in Jerusalem just like Satan challenged Jesus to jump from the pinnacle of the temple in Jerusalem to show His power. The Lord's brothers believe there's something special about Jesus otherwise they wouldn't have offered Him their advice. The problem is they don't believe He was who He said He is. They don't believe He's God. Ps. 69:8 says, "I have become a stranger to my brothers, and an alien to my mother's children."

There was human logic in what the brothers said but performing miracles in order to gain public acclaim was not how Jesus did things. Yes, the Feast of Tabernacles would be an ideal time to perform great miracles and assert His Messianic status but Jesus knew that this was not the time for such a display. Jesus answered His brothers and said, "My time has not yet come, but your time is always ready. The world cannot hate you, but it hates Me because I testify that its works are evil. You go up to this feast. I am not yet going up to this feast, for My time has not yet fully come" (vs. 6-8). The Lord's brothers tried to force Him into going to Jerusalem not realizing that man's time and God's time is almost always different. People want things now but God's time is always connected to His plan (Gal. 4:4). Jesus was on a divine mission and He was following a divine timetable. Time is precious and valuable and Jesus was a faithful steward of the time the Father gave Him. Nothing in His life is random and nothing is unplanned.

The hand of Jesus is not to be forced for He does things not in man's time but in God's.

Earlier the people had been drawn to Jesus by the signs He performed but the words He spoke were hard and unacceptable to them. It was His words that caused many of His disciples to turn away and walk with Him no more. It was His words that drove people to want to kill Him. This is why His brothers wanted Him to give a nice message and do things that pleased the crowd. The gospel message, however, is not always a nice message. 1 Cor. 15:3,4 says "Christ died for our sins according to the Scriptures" and this is not a message the world wants to hear. The cross is a horrible emblem of pain and suffering. It's where the Father turned His back on Jesus and allowed Him to die for your sins and the sins of the world. Jesus had confronted the rulers because of their evil ways and publicly called them hypocrites, blind guides, and a brood of vipers (Matt. 23). He said their works were evil because they were deceived into thinking good works made them right with God. People foolishly believe they can live a life of sin but if they do a good deed now and then everything is fine between them and God. People who think this way are lying to themselves and Jesus calls this evil.

"But when His brothers had gone up, then He also went up to the feast, not openly, but as it were in secret" (vs. 10). Jesus chose to travel to Jerusalem by Himself, quietly and privately. Even though the people don't yet know He is there, everybody is talking about Him. Some say He's good, others say He's not. Back and forth they went speaking in hushed tones out of fear of the Jews (vs. 13). The Jewish leaders had great power in Jerusalem and the people know they can be punished and even put to death for disagreeing with them. "Now about the middle of the feast Jesus went up into the temple and taught" (vs. 14). The people marveled because they knew He had never studied with the other rabbis yet what He said was beyond anything they had ever heard before. Jesus had a level of knowledge and wisdom that was without equal. The people are dumb-founded and shocked by His flawless in-depth teaching. He quotes scripture to support what He's saying so the people can't contradict His words. Instead, they attack Him and His lack of training.

The Jews were shattered by all the claims He made so they said He was a nobody who was uneducated and was expressing His own opinion of the meaning of the scriptures. This happened before in Matt. 13:54,55 when the people of Nazareth asked, "Where did this Man get this wisdom and these mighty works? Is this not the carpenter's son?" Jesus answered them and said, "My doctrine is not Mine, but His who sent Me" (vs. 16). Jesus is the ultimate truth teller because He only speaks what the Father tells Him to say. He goes on to say in vs. 17 that only the person who does God's will can truly understand His teaching. Truth is not decided by debating with other people. You come to know the truth when God reveals it to you. He does that only when you seek to do His will. Ps. 119:2 says, "Blessed are those who keep His testimonies, who seek Him with the whole heart!" Jesus went on to say in vs. 18 that false teachers and hypocrites seek personal gain for the things they do, things such as power, fortune, and fame. They are self-seeking shepherds who seek their own glory whereas a true teacher only seeks the glory of God.

Jesus has been speaking of doing the Father's will when He suddenly turns the tables on those who were against Him. He reminded them that Moses had given them the law which contained the will of God. The sixth commandment was "Thou shall not kill" so Jesus asked them, "Why do you seek to kill Me?" (vs. 19). He is accusing them of not keeping the law themselves to which they said, "You have a demon. Who is seeking to kill you?" (vs. 20). The response of the people is to describe Jesus as being crazy. Back then insanity was often attributed to one who was possessed by a demon. Jesus then returns to the issue of healing the man at the Pool of Bethesda. He defends what He did as being part of the will of God. The people claimed to keep the Sabbath yet they circumcised on the Sabbath thus making the person whole and complete. Jesus argued that if making a person whole by circumcision is allowable on the Sabbath, then healing and making a crippled man whole is also allowable. What Jesus did was an even greater example of fulfilling the will of God even if it was done on the Sabbath.

Many people in the crowd are now in a state of confusion. They know the rulers want to kill Jesus but still they're letting Him speak publicly. Prov. 28:1 says, "The righteous are bold as a lion" and this is how Jesus spoke. He was making such strong statements about His identity that the people asked if the rulers actually believed that this was the Christ. If they did believe or didn't believe, the authorities still couldn't do anything yet because His hour had not yet come. The invisible hand of God controls all situations for His glory and for the good of all people. The main objection of the crowd is they knew where Jesus came from. They thought the Messiah would come on the scene unexpectedly from a place no one knew about (vs. 27). Jesus said He was the bread come down from heaven but the people thought He was the son of a carpenter from Nazareth. "That provoked Jesus, who was teaching in the Temple, to cry out, 'Yes, you think you know Me and where I'm from, but that's not where I'm from. I didn't set myself up in business. My true origin is in the One who sent Me, and you don't know Him at all. I come from Him - that's how I know Him. He sent Me here" (John 7:28,29 MSG).

Jesus is yelling at the top of His voice as He says this. He's not purring like a kitten, He's roaring like a lion. He was saying the people didn't know who He was, where He came from, and who sent Him. The very idea that the people in their state of confusion would know His true identity is foolhardy and ridiculous. The people of Israel prided themselves as being the people of God and here Jesus is saying they don't know Him at all. The dominating reality in today's world is that most people don't know God. Daily they take His name in vain and yearly they celebrate Christian holidays. Still, their hearts are far from Him. The situation is getting very intense and, in the midst of all this confusion, the people are starting to lean on the fact that Jesus might be the Christ. The Jewish rulers are aware of the Lord's growing popularity and decide to do something about it. They send temple guards in a futile effort to arrest Him but it won't happen for His time had not yet come. Jesus then says He won't be with them much longer (vs. 33,34). In six months He would be hung on a cross to die for sins He did not commit. Jesus loved a nation that hated Him and now He was counting down the time to the moment He will no longer be with them.

Jesus said He was going away and many mocked Him by asking if He was going to go preach to the Greeks (vs. 35). The Greeks were Gentiles and were the last people Jews wanted to hear about God. These Jews were faithless fools who mocked Jesus with sarcasm based on ignorance and a willful rejection of everything He said and the person He claimed to be. Jesus is speaking to a very divided crowd. Some want Him arrested for blasphemy while at the same time many are impressed with His signs and are not ready to reject Him just yet. The Feast of Tabernacles is almost over and the situation is very tense. What will Jesus say in response to all this? On the last day of the feast He stood and cried out, "If anyone thirsts, let him come to Me and drink. He who believes in Me, as the scriptures has said, out of his heart will flow rivers of living water" (vs. 37,38). What did Jesus mean by this? Vs. 39 says, "But this He spoke concerning the Spirit, whom those believing in Him would receive; for the Holy Spirit was not yet given, because Jesus was not yet glorified."

This invitation is magnificent beyond description. It's an invitation that when accepted will give your life eternal significance. These words were spoken "on the last day, that great day of the feast." This was the eighth day of the feast and, being a Sabbath day, was a day of rest and special worship. The crowd was very large and Jesus waited for a maximum audience for His most important message. What is so amazing about this invitation is that Jesus is talking to His enemies, the very people who will cry out for His crucifixion six months later. He is giving an open invitation to everyone within the sound of His voice and His only requirement is that they be thirsty for the things of God. Jesus loves these people and He's inviting them to walk with Him forever. If the people still doubted this was the Son of God then this invitation of love should have changed their minds. It didn't and this is why Jesus mourned over the city of Jerusalem in Matt. 23:37, "O

Jerusalem, Jerusalem, the one who kills the prophets and stones those who are sent to her! How often I wanted to gather your children together, as a hen gathers her chicks under her wings, but you were not willing!"

It is the ultimate desire of Jesus that down inside of you thirst would be awakened and your soul would drink. The water is free, it's a gift. The only condition is need. You don't have to work for this water but you are to need this water to the point that you're thirsty for it. Everything Jesus ever said and did was done so you could drink and be satisfied forever. It's Jesus who satisfies the soul. People waste years of their lives looking for satisfaction and the meaning of life not realizing that it's only found in Jesus. The rich young ruler had everything and did everything yet he was not satisfied. The reason he didn't follow Jesus is because he wasn't thirsty enough. People search for fortune and fame their entire life but there's a shallowness to all of that if Jesus is not the center of their life. Without Jesus they'll never be satisfied so they keep searching and searching until suddenly their life ends with nothing to show for it. The offer Jesus is making is different from any other offer. It's an invitation to have that thirst in your soul to be quenched forever. Nothing that is created can satisfy like the Creator.

Until you pursue Jesus you will be empty and unsatisfied and without purpose and vision. This invitation from Jesus is the most amazing offer from God you'll ever get. If you'll come and believe, you'll be satisfied. Your body was made to live on water, your soul was made to live on God. The reason you read your Bible and listen to anointed preaching is so you can have a heavenly banquet in your soul. Drinking from God's well makes you happy forever for it will give you joy unspeakable (Is. 12:3). Come to Jesus and drink. He's the water you thirst for. He's the water you drink. He is the bread of life and He is the living water. Always remember that He is as close to you as your thirst. Coming to Him and drinking is what it means to believe in Jesus. When you go to Jesus you don't get a single cup of water, you get a river that flows and flows and flows. You get a fountain that springs up to eternal life. When you have Jesus, you have everything. Never again will you have to look anywhere else for whatever it is you need. It's all found in Him. There is no satisfaction for the thirst of the human soul other than Jesus.

Water flows and so does the Holy Spirit. Is. 58:11 says, "The Lord will guide you continually, and satisfy your soul in drought, and strengthen your bones; You shall be like a watered garden, and like a spring of water, whose waters do not fail." The Holy Spirit will move you and lead you in the direction you should go. God created you to be His servant and you need to allow Him to direct your steps so you'll know what to do. You are not to be a stagnant pond but a gushing river that overflows abundantly into a thirsty world. The water that comes to you doesn't stay in you but flows out to others. Your inner man is a fountain that becomes a river. Inside of you is soul-refreshing, soul-cleansing spiritual water and it is thrilling to know that God can and will use you to impact this world. All you have to do is let the rivers flow. Jesus was telling the crowd what would later happen on the Day of Pentecost in Acts 2:1-4. On that day the Holy Spirit opened the gates and the river began to flow. Allow Him to use you today. Be a reflection of the glory of God for out of you flows a brilliant, never ending stream of eternal life.

-18-

"THE CALL OF OBEDIENCE"

God is a God who must be sought after to be found. You can't go through life and think maybe one day you'll stumble upon Him. It won't happen. Jer. 29:13 says, "And you will seek Me and find Me, when you search for Me with all your heart." Notice the intense thirst of the apostle Paul as he wrote in Phil. 3:10 (NLT), "I want to know Christ and experience the mighty power that raised Him from the dead." It's those who thirst who go to heaven. Rev. 2:2 talks about the city of heaven and the wonder of it all. Vs. 14 says, "Blessed are those who do His commandments, that they may have the right to the tree of life, and may enter through the gates into the city." Vs. 17 then says, "And let him who thirsts come. And whoever desires, let him take the water of life freely." The people who go to heaven are the ones who respond to the Lord's call to "come to Me and drink" (John 7:37). Thirsty people are the ones who will spend eternity in God's glorious kingdom, those whom Jesus is satisfied with. On the sermon on the mount Jesus said, "Blessed are those who hunger and thirst for righteousness, for they shall be filled" (Matt. 5:6).

Thirst is a conscious craving. The more thirsty a person is, the more anxious they become. If not quenched, a sense of madness can set in to those who are seriously thirsty. Jesus told the woman at the well, "Whoever drinks of this water will thirst again, but whoever drinks of the water that I shall give him will never thirst" (John 4:14). You must see Jesus as the only source of living water. Come to Him with all your heart and soul and He will satisfy and nourish your inner man. He is the only source of eternal salvation. He is the way, the truth, and the life (John 14:6). His invitation to come to Him and drink is open to all, including His enemies. There were different responses from those who heard this invitation on the last day of the Feast of Tabernacles. John 7:40 tells how there were those who seem convinced that Jesus is the Prophet prophesied by Moses in Deut. 18:15. Much intensity was in the air and these people were risking their lives to make such a confession. This is what happens when rivers of life are flowing out of you. You confess your faith with no regard to what people may say or think.

There were many skeptics in the crowd who openly rejected the truth of who Jesus was. They argued that the Christ would come from the seed of David and would come from the town of Bethlehem (vs. 42). These doubters rejected Jesus without investigating His background. Both Mary and Joseph were from the lineage of David and Jesus was indeed born in Bethlehem. It is very clear that these skeptics don't know what they're talking about. By their own words they affirmed the facts that proved Jesus was the Messiah while at the same time they denied it. This is the nature of willful ignorance. John 7:43 says, "So there was a division among the people because of Him." A division means that both groups stood their ground. In truth, a division is a good thing in the fact that it reveals the genuineness of the faith of those who believed. They didn't walk in fear over what the leaders would say about them or that they may be put out of the synagogue forever. These people held their ground and didn't depart from what they believed in. This division caused the people to once again want to seize Jesus and take Him away but, like before, no one laid hands on Him (vs. 44).

Some people believed, some didn't, and others were so confused they didn't know what to believe. The temple guards who were sent to arrest Jesus in John 7:32 now came back empty-handed. Their explanation to the Jewish rulers was that "No man ever spoke like this Man!" (vs. 46). These officers were under the authority of the temple leaders and they knew the harsh consequences of disobeying the orders given to them. They also recognized the authority of the words of Jesus. It was an authority far beyond their ability to respond. These words were the most powerful, overwhelming words they has ever heard (Matt.

7:28,29). These officers are bewildered and confused. They don't know what to think or do. They're caught in the middle of two extremes. Jesus said to "come to Me and drink" and the Pharisees said to seize and arrest Him. Their knees buckled under the authoritative power of His words so they returned back to the Pharisees empty-handed not realizing they couldn't have taken Jesus even if they wanted to. In the midst of this confusion the Pharisees asked, "Are you also deceived?" (vs. 47).

The Message Bible says, "Are you carried away like the rest of the rabble? You don't see any of the leaders believing in Him, do you? Or any of the Pharisees? It's only this crowd, ignorant of God's Law, that is taken in by Him" (vs. 47-49). The Pharisees have a low opinion of common people not realizing that one of their own is slowly but surely becoming a believer. Nicodemus, who went to Jesus secretly at night two years prior to this, spoke up and asks in vs. 51, "Does our law judge a man before it hears him and knows what he is doing?" He speaks not boldly but in a subtle manner. He wants to make a point but at the same time he doesn't want to rock the boat. For two years he'd been contemplating what Jesus told him that dark night so long ago. No doubt he's been going through a relentless search for the truth. He wants to defend Jesus for he knows enough about Him to know that killing Him would not be the right thing to do. He doesn't openly declare himself to be a believer but he is holding the other rulers accountable for the integrity of their own laws.

What Nicodemus is saying is that you can't condemn and sentence a man until he has first had a trial (Ex. 23:1,2). These are timid words but by saying this he is defending Jesus in a legal way. The law laid it down that every man has a right to state his case and not be condemned by the hearsay words of another person (Deut. 1:16). The Pharisees were ready to break this law but Nicodemus is reminding them that their own laws need to be upheld. It is interesting to note that the question of Nicodemus reflects what Jesus said in John 7:24, "Do not judge according to appearance, but judge with righteous judgment." The Pharisees reasoned that whoever was not for them was against them so they mocked Nicodemus and scorned him. They said, "Are you also from

Galilee? Search and look, for no prophet has arisen out of Galilee" (vs. 52). Being called a Galilean was a major insult for a person from Judea. These rulers, however, don't know their history. Jonah came from Galilee as did Nahum and Hosea. In spite of their ignorance, to the Pharisees nothing more needs to be said. "And everyone went to his own house" (vs. 53).

While everybody went home, John 8:1 says Jesus went to the Mount of Olives. This was a mountain ridge east of Jerusalem and is named for the olive groves that covered its slopes at that time. The Lord's home was up north in Capernaum so He walked about two miles and rested under an olive tree on this cold October night. As He spent time communing with His heavenly Father, behind the scenes the scribes and Pharisees were communing on how they might test Him and discredit His claim to be the Son of God. These Jewish rulers hated Jesus because He was more popular than they were. They were overwhelmed with jealousy, so much so that Matt. 27:18 says it was because of envy that they delivered Him up to be crucified. Not only were the people drawn to His miracles, they were also drawn to His message. "But early in the morning He came again into the temple, and all the people came to Him, and He sat down and taught them" (vs. 2). The Feast of Tabernacles was now over but the multitudes delayed their departure to their home towns and readjusted their schedule in order to hear Him speak.

The words of Jesus were powerful and they drew people to Him. After the sermon on the mount "the people were astonished at His teaching, for He taught them as one having authority, and not as the scribes" (Matt. 7:28,29). The Message Bible says, "When Jesus concluded His address, the crowd burst into applause. They had never heard teaching like this. It was apparent that He was living everything He was saying - quite a contrast to their religion teachers! This was the best teaching they had ever heard." So forceful and authoritative were His words that Luke 12:1 says thousands of people "trampled one another" in order to hear Him speak. Notice also that it was early in the morning that Jesus went to the temple. He put God first and fulfilled the command He gave in Matt. 6:33, "Seek first the kingdom of God and His righteousness." Allow Jesus to be your example and seek God early. Spend time with Him at the beginning of each day. Be like David who wrote in Ps. 63:1, "O God, You are my God; Early will I seek You; My soul thirsts for You; My flesh longs for You in a dry and thirsty land where there is no water."

As Jesus was teaching, a commotion was taking place in the back of the crowd. The people turned and saw the Jewish rulers rudely dragging a woman to the front where Jesus sat. They had failed in their attempt to have Jesus arrested the day before so now they were trying a new approach. They set the woman in their midst and said, "Teacher, this woman was caught in adultery, in the very act" (vs. 4). Why did these scribes and Pharisees address Jesus in such a way? Surely they didn't recognize Him for who He is. In John 1:36-38 the disciples called Jesus the "Lamb of God" before they called Him "Teacher." They first believe He is the Savior of their souls and then afterward they call Him "Teacher" so He can now renew their minds. These verses are saying that Jesus can't be your teacher until He is first your Savior. In John 3 Nicodemus called Jesus a teacher when he is not saved. He was putting the cart before the horse, so to speak, and this is why Jesus right away begins to talk to him about being born again.

After mocking Jesus by calling Him "Teacher" they then begin to question and interrogate Him concerning the Old Testament law. They said in vs. 5, "Now Moses, in the law, commanded us that such should be stoned. But what do You say?" The shame this woman must have felt is unbelievable. The Greek word for "adultery" shows that the man and woman who committed this act were both married to other people. This was a married woman committing adultery with a married man. According to Hebrew law, Lev. 20:10 and Deut. 22:22, both the man and woman were to be brought to the temple along with any witnesses to this horrendous deed. The scribes and Pharisees only brought the woman to Jesus and by doing so were breaking the law themselves. It may have been that the man who also committed this act was part of the scheme to test Jesus so he was allowed to slip away. Nevertheless, this woman was guilty and deserved to die. These rulers are not asking Jesus if this woman is guilty. Everybody knows she is because she was caught in the very act. They're asking what penalty should this woman receive for what she did.

These rulers are asking Jesus about the doctrine of the law which they are the masters of. They are trying to find a way to accuse Jesus and find fault with Him when all along Rev. 12:10 says it's the devil who's the accuser of the brethren. Later on in John 8:44 Jesus openly tells them, "You are of your father the devil." These Pharisees were very legalistic when it came to things pertaining to the law and the spirit of legalism is alive and well today. The problem with legalistic people is they will shame you in public by revealing your spiritual immaturity or your disobedience and they'll do it in a holier-than-thou manner. Legalism is when people pass judgment on other people while not considering their own faults, sins, and shortcomings. It lacks a Christlike attitude while forgetting that all have sinned and fall short of the glory of God (Rom. 3:23). Nobody likes legalistic people while at the same time they're intimidated by them thinking that maybe some of the things they say are true. This is why people avoid them, but not Jesus. In fact, they become His primary target because He can see their heart and the type of people they really are.

The Lord's view of legalism is found in Matt. 7:3-5 when He said, "And why do you look at the speck in your brother's eye, but do not consider the plank in your own eye? Or how can you say to your brother, 'Let me remove the speck out of your eye'; and look, a plank is in your own eye? Hypocrite! First remove the plank from your own eye, and then you will see clearly to remove the speck out of your brother's eye." Instead of using this woman as a means to their shameful ends, these religious leaders should have been looking for ways to help her, ways to offer her a new life. This they did not do. Vs. 6 says, "This they said, testing Him, that they might have something of which to accuse Him." These authorities of religion are using this woman to trap Jesus. They're testing Him. They're trying to put Him between a rock and a hard place. This wasn't anything new, for those who opposed Him were always looking for ways to accuse Him (Mark 3:2). They previously questioned Him as to whether it was lawful for a man to divorce his wife (Mark 10:2) or if a Jew is required to pay taxes to Caesar (Matt. 22:17,18), all for the purpose of finding something to hold against Him.

It is wrong to regard people as things and it is highly unlikely that these scribes and Pharisees even knew this woman's name. To them, she was a piece of worthless flesh who they were using in their attempt to put Jesus in what they thought was a no-win situation. If He says not to stone her, then He'll be going against the law of Moses and undermining the social order. How could He be a prophet in Israel or the Messiah if He doesn't believe in the law of Moses? Didn't He say in Matt. 5:17, "Do not think that I came to destroy the Law or the Prophets. I did not come to destroy but to fulfill"? On the other hand, if He were to say the woman should be stoned, then He'd be going against His claim to be the friend of sinners and one who shows mercy to the broken and those who society rejects. Not only that, but to say she should be stoned would have been in conflict with the Romans for death sentences were only carried out through them (John 18:21). Either way, they had Him trapped. Any answer Jesus gave would discredit His claim to be the Son of God, or so they thought.

His accusers demanded a response from Him but He did not give one right away. Instead, He did something very unusual. "But Jesus stooped down and wrote on the ground with His finger, as though He did not hear" (vs. 6). Scripture does not say what He wrote but one is reminded of another time when the finger of God wrote something. In the days of Moses, Ex. 19:20 says "the Lord came down upon Mount Sinai." In other words, God stooped down and descended upon the mountain. When God stoops down, He gets people's attention. Ex. 31:18 says, "And when He had made an end of speaking with him on Mount Sinai, He gave Moses two tablets of the Testimony, tablets of stone, written with the finger of God." God stooped down and wrote with His finger the Ten Commandments, the very law this woman was accused of breaking. The Pharisees had called Jesus "Teacher" but didn't realize they were talking to God. Stooped down before them was the Savior of their souls but still they persisted in their attempt to test Him. To their chagrin, Jesus was about to speak.

"So when they continued asking Him, He raised Himself up and said to them, 'He who is without sin among you, let him throw a stone at her first.' And again He stooped down and wrote on the ground" (vs. 7,8). There is a lot of speculation about what Jesus wrote in the sand covering the bricks that paved the temple courtyard. Many believe that Jesus was writing in the dust the sins of the very men who were there accusing this woman. Again the Bible doesn't say what Jesus wrote but there could be some validity in this assessment. The Greek word used here for "write" is "katagraphein" and means 'to write down a record against someone.' Job 13:26 says, "For You write bitter things against me, and make me inherit the iniquities of my youth." Jesus wrote what the Holy Spirit was writing on the hearts of those who stood there trying to test Him. Whatever it was, it brought conviction to all of them. Perhaps they remembered what God said in Jer. 17:13, "Those who depart from Me shall be written in the earth, because they have forsaken the Lord, the fountain of living water."

This was the second time Jesus stooped down and wrote on the ground with His finger. Back in Ex. 32:19 Moses had gotten mad at the people for worshiping the golden calf and in his anger he cast the stone tablets down and broke them in pieces. What did God do? Ex. 34:1-5 says He again descended down and with His finger wrote the Ten Commandments on two new tablets of stone. A second time He stooped down and wrote with His finger just like Jesus did right here. "Then those who heard it, being convicted by their conscience, went out one by one, beginning with the oldest even to the last. And Jesus was left alone, and the woman standing in the midst" (vs. 9). The finger of God was writing on the hearts of all those who came to test Jesus causing them to be smitten in their own consciences. They knew they were just as guilty of sin as this woman so they all left. Only one person standing there was without sin. His name is Jesus. He had the right to throw the first stone but He didn't do it. He was the spotless Lamb of God who takes away the sin of the world.

"When Jesus had raised Himself up and saw no one but the woman, He said to her, 'Woman, where are those accusers of yours? Has no one condemned you?' She said, 'No one, Lord.' And Jesus said to her, 'Neither do I condemn you; go and sin no more'" (vs. 10,11). This woman called Him "Lord" and not "Teacher" believing there was something different about Him. She was right because Jesus did not condemn her like the others. The law came through Moses but grace and truth came through Jesus (John 1:14). Grace says "go" and truth says "sin no more." After God wrote with His finger the Ten Commandments a second time, He proclaimed before Moses the type of God He was, "The Lord, the Lord God, merciful and gracious, longsuffering, and abounding in goodness and truth, keeping mercy for thousands, forgiving iniquity and transgressions and sin" (Ex. 34:6,7). This woman was brought to the temple in darkness and shame and was surrounded by hatred. There she met a Man filled with love and compassion. She left forgiven knowing that somebody loved her.

Jesus was not disputing this woman's guilt but He was extending His mercy and giving her another chance. He did, however, challenge her to change her lifestyle for with grace comes a call to obey God (Rom. 6:1,2). Those who call Jesus "Lord" are called to be Christlike in their words and actions. It is unimaginable that Jesus would say, "Go and sin less than you used to." No, He didn't die so you'll sin at an acceptable minimum. He died to give you a new life so you will be a living testimony of His mercy and grace. This woman had been a prisoner to her own lusts and evil desires. Eph. 2:1,2 (MSG) says, "It wasn't so long ago that you were mired in that old stagnant life of sin. You let the world, which doesn't know the first thing about living, tell you how to live. You filled your lungs with polluted unbelief, and then exhaled disobedience." She then reached a place in her life where it was just her and Jesus. It always comes down to that. Eventually all people have to face Jesus. When this woman faced Him, she was facing the Lamb of God who came to unlock the shackles of sin and set people free.

This story is a reflection of what the New Testament is all about. Jesus exalts Himself over the law of Moses, He changes an appointed punishment in the law, and then He reestablishes righteousness on the foundation of grace. There's an order here that took place. This woman came face to face with Jesus, she believed and with that belief came no condemnation, and out of that is the call of obedience, the call to go and sin no more. Change always begins with a faith transformation followed by a call to live according to the scriptures. Change comes because you've met Jesus, not so you can meet Him. Meeting Jesus comes first and then the change happens. Jesus is telling this woman to go and act like a person who's been forgiven. Scripture does not give this woman's name but it does say Jesus called her "Woman" (vs. 10). This was a title of honor and was the same word Jesus called His mother in John 19:26. This woman standing before Him was anything but a woman of honor but Jesus has a way of seeing things that are not as though they were (Rom. 4:17).

This story is not about you cleaning up your life so God will love you. It's a story about you seeing the mercy of the Lord. He sees the unlovable and loves them anyway. He loved the woman at the well, He loved the rich young ruler, and He loved this woman caught in adultery. He also loves you, so much so that He was willing to go to the cross and die for your sins. All you have to do is come face to face with Jesus. When He looks at a lost sinner He sees the potential of their lives, He sees them as who they can become through Him. As you face Jesus and look into His eyes, you will hear Him say, "Neither do I condemn you. Go and sin no more." He's not asking you to get your life together before you come to Him. He's asking you to trust Him and to believe in Him. Regardless of your past, know with certainty that Jesus loves you and accepts you just as you are. The good news is that He won't leave you the same way He found you. He'll change you from the inside out. Along with His salvation comes a new life and liberty from sin's dominion (Rom. 6:14).

What could have been the worst day of this woman's life turned out to be the best day of her life. On this day she learned that she could be forgiven, her sins could be forgotten, and she could be set free. Jesus said, "For God did not send His Son into the world to condemn the world, but that the world through Him might be saved" (John 3:17). Jesus is not surprised when sinners sin because that is what they do. The truth is, people who do not believe are condemned already (John 3:18). On the cross God took all of your sins and put them on Jesus. He was pronounced guilty of all your sin and was condemned and executed for the sins He carried. On that day God removed your sins as far as the east is from the west and for that reason Rom. 8:1 says, "There is therefore now no condemnation to those who are in Christ Jesus." Understand that no means no! God has declared His people not guilty for they "no longer have to live under a continuous, low-lying black cloud" (MSG). In Jesus there is the gospel of the second chance. He took your guilt and shame and because of that you can now live a life free from the condemnation of sin.

Randall J. Brewer

-19-

"RADIANCE OF THE FATHER"

Jesus is still in the temple talking to the people and another confrontation with the Pharisees is about to take place. He is speaking in the temple treasury (John 8:20) where there is a continual flow of people coming and going. In the massive courtyard were thirteen trumpet-shaped treasure chests placed at various locations where the people could come and give their financial offerings. This was the same place where the widow woman came and gave two small coins into the treasury (Luke 21:1-4). The Feast of Tabernacles has just ended and fresh in the minds of all the people were the various ceremonies that took place during this feast. One such ceremony was called the "Illumination of the Temple" which involved the ritual lighting of four huge golden lamps. These lamps were seventy-five feet high and were fed by oil. These burning lamps reminded the people of the pillar of fire that guided Israel in their wilderness journey and their brilliance was said to have illuminated the entire city. All through the night the people danced before the Lord and sang songs of joy and praise to the great God of Israel.

It was in this setting that Jesus spoke to the people again saying, "I am the light of the world. He who follows Me shall not walk in darkness, but have the light of life" (John 8:12). Previously Jesus said He was the bread of life at the Feast of Passover and He proclaimed Himself to be the water of life at the well of Jacob. Here at the temple treasury He is talking about light because it is a central theme of the Old Testament which many of His listeners were familiar with. Gen. 1:2 says, "The earth was without form, and void; and darkness was on the face of the deep." Then God said "Let there be light" and there was light (vs. 3). From that moment on, what was void and empty began to be filled with life.

Light forms the formless and pushes back the darkness, so much so that Is.9:2 prophecies about the coming Messiah, "The people who walked in darkness have seen a great light; Those who dwelt in the land of the shadow of death, upon them a light has shined." Without Jesus, your life will also be formless, dark, and void. Fortune and fame can't fill this void and neither can fast cars or a yacht on a lake. Only Jesus can fill the great void in your heart.

Jesus is the light of the world but is He the light of your world? John 1:4,5 says, "In Him was life, and the life was the light of men. And the light shines in the darkness, and the darkness did not comprehend it." Walking in darkness is when a person tries to live their life without knowing what is ultimate reality. People go about their daily business not knowing if they're going in the right direction. Jesus came to illuminate your world. He came to be the light that shines in a dark place. Col. 1:13 says, "He has delivered us from the power of darkness and translated us into the kingdom of the Son of His love." The Message Bible says, "God rescued us from dead-end alleys and dark dungeons." Jesus came to push back the darkness and bring form to your formless life. 2 Cor. 4:6 (NLT) says, "For God, who said 'Let there be light in the darkness,' had made this light shine in our hearts so we could know the glory of God that is seen in the face of Jesus Christ." The Message Bible says, "Our lives filled up with light as we saw and understood God in the face of Christ, all bright and beautiful."

There is only one light that is powerful enough to penetrate the human heart. His name is Jesus, the light of the world. He didn't say He was "a" light, He said He was "the" light. This statement is all encompassing for He said He was the light of the entire world. The light of Jesus is not a light to be admired or simply looked at. It's a light to be followed the same way a soldier follows his commanding officer. Jesus is the only source of spiritual light because He knows the way out of sin and ignorance, sadness and sorrow, and the darkness of death. Those who walk in the light and perceive its brilliance will never walk in spiritual darkness. Until you have Jesus, you are spiritually dead and dead people don't see anything. They're blind to the things of God. You can't see the kingdom of God until you're born again. Dead people need the life of God which yields the ability to see Jesus as light. Paul said in Eph. 1:18 (NIV), "I pray that the eyes of your heart may be enlightened in order that you may know the hope to which He has called you, the riches of His glorious inheritance in His holy people."

Following Jesus means you'll never walk alone. He walks beside you and His light illuminates the path you are on. This is a continuous light that never fades and never goes out. Jesus is the radiance of the Father and He will fill your life with the light of His glory. You'll see everything as it was originally intended to be. His light illuminates everything in its proper beauty. It reveals the world as seen in the eyes of God. Nothing in your life will be the same for Jesus alone possesses the map of life. 2 Cor. 5:17 says, "Therefore, if anyone is in Christ, he is a new creation; old things are passed away; behold, all things become new." To follow Jesus is to walk in His light. The world belongs to God and one day, when man's lease on the planet is expired, it will be filled with the light of Jesus and nothing else. This light will one day banish all darkness and the sons of darkness from out of the world. In Matt. 22:13 Jesus calls hell a place of outer darkness where there will be weeping and gnashing of teeth. In hell there is no light and there are more horrors there than one could possibly imagine. Without Jesus there is only darkness.

Everything in life takes on a whole new meaning because of its relationship to the light. Jesus said in John 12:36, "While you have the light, believe in the light, that you may become sons of light." Jesus is the light of the world and so are you. Your words, actions, and attitude should reflect the light of Jesus no matter what situation you may be in. Luke 11:36 (NLT) says, "If you are filled with light, with no dark corners, then your whole life will be radiant, as though a floodlight is shining on you." Light is always a witness to a dark world. Jesus said in Matt. 5:14, "You are the light of the world. A city that is set on a hill cannot be hidden." The NLT says you are "like a city on a mountain, glowing in the night for all to see. Don't hide your light under a basket! Instead, put it on a stand and let it shine for all. In the same way, let your good deeds shine out for all to see, so that everyone will praise your heavenly Father" (vs. 14-16). Live in such a way that your life will point people to the light of Jesus, that same light that is forever shining in your heart. 1 John 4:17 says, "As He is, so are we in this world."

Ps. 119:18 says, "Open my eyes, that I may see wondrous things from Your law." The Pharisees knew through Old Testament scripture that someday the Messiah was going to show up and be the light of the world. David said in Ps. 27:1, "The Lord is my light and my salvation; Whom shall I fear?" The Light was God and the rabbis understood that the name of the Messiah was Light. Is. 9:6 says, "The people who walked in darkness have seen a great light." The prophet also writes in Is. 49:6, "I will also give You as a light to the nations, that You should be My salvation to the ends of the earth." Again he writes in Is. 60:1, "Arise, shine; For your light has come! And the glory of the Lord is risen upon you." In the last book of the Old Testament, before God goes silent for four hundred years, is a prophecy that a light was coming. Mal. 4:2 (NLT) says, "But for you who fear My name, the Sun of Righteousness will rise with healing in His wings. And you will go free, leaping with joy like calves let out to pasture." When Jesus said He was the light of the world, He was declaring openly that He was the Messiah.

The Pharisees responded to this claim with great hostility. They said, "You bear witness of Yourself; Your witness is not true" (John 8:13). These rulers are, in fact, repeating what Jesus said in John 5:31, "If I bear witness of Myself, My witness is not true." This was a calculated attack for they think they caught Him testifying about Himself so He therefore can't be the light of the world. What these Pharisees are doing is totally foolish and absurd. They're standing in front of the living God and they want to debate over a play on words. Their hearts and minds are blind to the brightness of the glory of God. Have these Pharisees forgotten the prophecies of Old Testament scripture? Job 29:3 says, "By His light I walked through darkness." Micah 7:8 goes on to say, "When I sit in darkness the Lord shall be a light to me." The Pharisees are making an invalid claim about Jesus because He is talking about Himself. They said He was boasting and had no witness to confirm what He said. The light of the world is shining bright in front of them but in their minds they are plotting His death.

People who don't believe always want proof before they'll believe. The problem is, when they get the proof they want, it's never enough. John 7:17 says if you're willing to know the truth, you'll know the truth. These Pharisees were not willing and their unbelief caused them to be ignorant of what was happening right before their very eyes. They were talking to God Himself and didn't see the light that was shining before them. Unbelief locks you into willful ignorance. They weren't unbelievers because of their ignorance, they were ignorant because of unbelief. This is a terminal condition to be in. Knowing God personally was the last thing on their minds. All they wanted to do was find a way to trap Jesus and kill Him. Jesus then responds to these accusations and corresponds with them as He bears witness to the relationship He has with the Father. He answered and said that His own witness should have been all the proof they needed (vs. 14) but, if a second witness was needed, He had that also. Vs. 18 says, "I am One who bears witness of Myself, and the Father who sent Me bears witness of Me."

The need for two or more witnesses was a law written for a world full of lies and deception (Deut. 19:15). Things had to be confirmed through the witness of several people hoping that maybe the truth will come out. This law doesn't apply to Jesus for He is not subject to a law that was intended for a world of liars. The law was made for man, not for God. The Pharisees wanted two witnesses so Jesus played along and gave them what they wanted. He and the Father are the two witnesses. They then asked Him, "Where is Your Father?" (vs. 19). This was said with scorn, ridicule, and mockery. Jesus responded bluntly by saying they had no real knowledge of who God is, "You know neither Me nor My Father. If you had known Me, you would have known My Father also" (vs. 19). This was the ultimate insult because the Pharisees prided themselves in thinking they knew God better than anyone else. They didn't. Ignorance is cheap, it is common, and it is deadly. Hosea 4:6 (MSG) says, "My people are ruined because they don't know what's right or true. Because you've turned your back on knowledge, I've turned My back on your priests."

Jesus is no stranger to these people. By this time everybody in Israel has heard about Him. He ministered from the north to the south and His miracles were a common conversation among the people. These rulers could not deny the evidence that proved the deity of Jesus. Amazing, unheard of miracles were consistently happening and unparalleled teaching penetrated the hearts of those who dared to believe. There was more than enough evidence to prove that Jesus was who He claimed to be. Even those who have never heard the gospel are without excuse. Rom. 1:20 says the creation of the world itself clearly reveals God and His glory and is proof enough that He exists. How much more inexcusable are those who have heard the gospel and still willfully refuse to believe? Heb. 10:26 says, "For if we sin willfully after we have received the knowledge of the truth, there no longer remains a sacrifice for sins." The Pharisees have no one to blame but themselves for their ignorance. Their unbelief is inexcusable and now Jesus boldly confronts them and says they'll die in their sins.

He said to them, "I am going away, and you will seek Me, and will die in your sin. Where I go you cannot come" (vs. 21). This is as blunt as you can get with unbelievers. This is a matter of life and death and every person is responsible for what they will or will not believe. In the face of all this evidence which God so graciously gives, unbelief is totally inexcusable. John 1:11 says, "He came to His own, and His own did not receive Him." These people were still responsible for what they heard and saw. The offer of salvation was clear and the evidence was compelling. Still, many refused to believe and their escalating hostility toward Him is what prompted Him to say they would die in their sin. He didn't sugarcoat anything but told them truthfully how it was going to be. He told them in John 7:34, "You will seek Me and not find Me, and where I am you cannot come." Jesus is saying they will die unforgiven. Dead people have no light which means they have no life. When it comes to following Jesus, there is no middle ground. You either follow Him or you don't.

Hell is a horrendous place because it is there where people will seek Him and not find Him. For them there is only weeping and gnashing of teeth. In the story of the rich man and Lazarus are the words of one who is in hell (Luke 16:19-31). The rich man requested that Lazarus be sent to him "that he may dip the tip of his finger in water and cool my tongue: for I am tormented in this flame" (vs. 24). To this rich man, all seeking is useless and so it is with these Pharisees to whom Jesus is speaking and to those today who don't believe. To every person is given the opportunity to accept Jesus as Lord and Savior. The time a person has to make this decision is limited and no one knows what their personal time limit is. There are people who wake up this morning who will breath their last breath of air before the day is over. This is why Paul said in 2 Cor. 6:2, "Behold, now is the accepted time; behold, now is the day of salvation." Just because the opportunity to receive Jesus is here now does not mean it will always be here. The clock is ticking and death causes the opportunity to get saved to leave and never return.

Heb. 9:27 says, "And as it is appointed for men to die once, but after this the judgment." There is no second chance to get saved after death. The problem with death is that everybody knows they're one day going to die, they just don't think it will be today. The truth be told, those who wait until tomorrow to give their life to Jesus are the ones who usually die today. Tragically, these people have reached a point of no return. They woke up this morning forgetting that there is never a guarantee that tomorrow will ever get here. They died in their sins just like Jesus told the Pharisees three times that they would die in their sins. Jesus said He was going away and "Where I go you cannot come." The Pharisees thought for sure they were going to heaven so, if they couldn't go where Jesus was going, then apparently Jesus was going to hell. They then asked if He was going to kill Himself (vs.22) believing that the depths of hell was reserved for those who took their own lives. Surely they weren't going to follow Him there. This was said in scorn and mockery thus revealing their self-righteous attitude.

There are four realities that guarantee a person will die in their sins, the first being self-righteousness. These Pharisees followed the religion of self-achievement and in their eyes that didn't need a Savior. People like this reject the truth that you're saved by faith and faith alone (Eph. 2:8,9). Surely these Pharisees were familiar with Is. 64:6 (NLT), "We are all infected and impure with sin. When we display our righteous deeds, they are nothing but filthy rags. Like autumn leaves, we wither and fall, and our sins sweep us away like the wind." These Jews resented the Lord's attacks on their hypocrisy and His indictment on them as sinners. They failed to recognize their true spiritual condition and they mocked Jesus with a grim kind of blasphemy. They laughed when they should have cried. These same people are crying today and nobody hears their painful wailing and howling screams. They are seeking Jesus and are unable to find Him. In their torment they now realize that Jesus did not come to call the righteous, but sinners to repentance (Luke 5:32).

Jesus said in John 8:23, "You are from beneath; I am from above. You are of this world; I am not of this world." If you are worldly, you will die in your sins. 1 John 2:15 says, "Do not love the world or the things in the world. If anyone loves the world, the love of the father is not in Him." Worldliness promotes carnal ambitions and selfish desires and pleasures. It is an invisible, spiritual system of evil that rejects God and is hostile to all that is godly. "Therefore I say to you that you will die in your sins; for if you do not believe that I am He, you will die in your sins" (vs. 24). Being faithless will also cause you to die in your sins. You must believe that Jesus is who He claims to be for faith is the only thing that will prevent you from going to hell forevermore. The Jews asked "Who are You? and Jesus answered, "Just what I have been saying to you from the beginning" (vs. 25). These Jews refused to change their opinion of Jesus despite several attempts to persuade them to do so. They were asking, "Who do You think You are?" Jesus answered, "Haven't you been listening?" The obstinance of these Jews caused them to die in their sins.

As always, Jesus acknowledges that the Father's presence and power is with Him (vs. 28,29). "As He spoke these words, many believed in Him" (vs. 30). These people believed some things about Jesus and what He said but the context of this passage indicates they weren't yet ready to put their complete trust in Him. This is the common condition of the hearts of many people today. They believe there is a higher power somewhere but there's no change in their lives. They say they're Christians but the Christ of their Christianity is no where to be found in their lives. Paul says these people are "lovers of pleasure rather than lovers of God, having a form of godliness but denying its power" (2 Tim. 3:4,5). Most people say they're followers of Christ but are they really? What should they do to find out? They need to look inside their heart and be honest about what's there. 2 Cor. 13:5 (MSG) says, "Test yourselves to make sure you are solid in the faith. Don't drift along taking everything for granted. Give yourself regular checkups. You need firsthand evidence, not mere hearsay, that Jesus Christ is in you. Test it out. If you fail the test, do something about it."

False faith is everywhere. It is very common and very dangerous. Mental assent is not enough for even demons believe and tremble (James 2:19). Jesus is unconvinced about their faith so He says in vs. 31, "If you abide in My word, you are My disciples indeed." Why did Jesus say this? Because many said they believed in Him before and walked away (John 6:66). They didn't remain with Him but were much like Demas who would later forsake Paul and the work of the ministry because he "loved this present world" and the darkness therein (2 Tim. 4:10). The result of people not having a true and sincere faith is they walk away (1 John 2:19). Jesus said in Matt. 7:21-23 that it is a common thing for people to think they're walking with God when they're not walking with Him at all. This is the greatest deception there is. These people Jesus was talking about were going to church and doing good works but were void of a relationship with Jesus. They had a form of Christianity because

Christ was not in it and for them their future is doom and gloom. The solution to all this is to continually abide in the Word of God.

The word "abide" means 'to remain' in a state of being spiritually unchanged. It means 'to live, stay, dwell, lodge.' Continually devoting yourself to the reading of God's Word is the mark of a true disciple. God will speak to you when you read your Bible. Read the Word continually and allow it to speak to your inner man. Study the Word and take time to understand what it means. In the parable of the sower, the enemy was able to take the Word from those who didn't understand it (Matt. 13:19). After you've read the Word and understand it, then go out and do what it tells you to do. Be a doer of the Word and not a hearer only (James 1:22). The Message Bible says, "Act on what you hear!" Doing this puts you in the hands of the Father and nothing can remove you from His care and protection as long as you abide in Him (John 10:28,29). Abiding is the evidence that you've been transformed from darkness into light. 2 John 9 (NLT) says, "Anyone who wanders away from this teaching has no relationship with God. But anyone who remains in the teaching of Christ has a relationship with both the Father and the Son."

Jesus says when you abide in His Word "you shall know the truth, and the truth will make you free" (vs. 32). A lot of people think this verse is talking about getting a good education and this is the key to freedom. Having a college degree is a wonderful thing but it doesn't make you a better human being. At the same time, not having one doesn't make you an evil person. What Jesus is talking about is having a personal relationship with Him for that is the truth that makes you free. He said, "I am the way, the truth, and the life" (John 14:6). It's knowing Jesus that transforms your life and sets you free from fear and all the works of the evil one. Having Jesus as your Lord and Savior is the only true freedom you're ever going to know. When you get saved there is a connection between you and God that can never be broken. This doesn't mean you'll never sin again. To abide in God's Word means that when you do fall, you get right back up. Freedom in a Biblical sense is not about doing what you want or that you'll be king of your own castle. It's about dependence on God and God alone and doing what He intended for you to do.

When Jesus spoke of making the people free the Jews were enraged because they think He is saying they're slaves. "They answered Him, 'We are Abraham's descendants, and have never been in bondage to anyone. How can you say, 'You will be made free'?" (vs. 33). They're saying, "Don't You know who we are? We're God's chosen people. We've never been enslaved to anybody." These people were proud of their heritage and they should have been. However, they must have forgotten their history because throughout the Old Testament the children of Israel were continually enslaved to enemy nations all because of their sin and rebellion against God. The children of Abraham spent years doing hard labor as slaves in Egypt. During the time of the judges the people of Israel were under bondage to surrounding nations seven times. The whole nation was carried off to Babylon for seventy years. Even as they now spoke to Jesus the nation was under the rule of the Romans. They claimed to be free on the basis of their heritage but there's a big difference between worldly freedom and a Biblical view of freedom.

Jesus then said something the people didn't want to hear, "Most assuredly, I say to you, whoever commits sin is a slave of sin. And a slave does not abide in the house forever, but a son abides forever" (vs. 34,35). Jesus is saying they're slaves because of sin and they have no inheritance because they're not a child of God. In other words, lineage without conviction is pointless. Yes, the children of Israel are God's chosen people as a nation but not as individuals. Long ago, in a world full of sin and false idols, God chose to show His goodness to one group of people so through them the world could see His power, His glory, and His righteousness. When the people didn't respond to God's plan, He gave them the law and sent prophets to point them in the way they should go. What did the people do? They broke the law and killed the prophets. Centuries went by until the day came when God sent His Son into the world, the very person these people were now talking to. He said to them, "Therefore if the Son makes you free, you shall be free indeed" (vs. 36). This is one of the most important statements you will hear in your entire life. How you respond to these words is what determines your eternal destiny.

-20-

"THE BURDEN OF CONTINUANCE"

Life is a process. To the chagrin of many, things in life rarely, if ever, happen as quickly as one would like. There is almost always an element of time involved when it comes to getting the things you so adamantly need and desire. After all, Heb. 6:12 says it's through faith and patience that you inherit the promises of God. You may not like it but times of waiting is the stark reality of life. What you need to understand is that the best things in life are worth waiting for. Weeds grow overnight but a mighty oak tree takes decades to grow to full splendor. Paul talks about this in 2 Cor. 5:17 when he says "old things have passed away, behold, all things become new." The changes in your life that you so desperately crave won't happen instantly. It takes time for old things to become new. The good news is that Jesus is by your side, leading and guiding you every step of the way. Freedom also is a process and it's in this same spirit of old things becoming new that Jesus says, "Therefore if the Son makes you free, you shall be free indeed" (John 8:36).

There is a difference between being free and being free indeed. Getting born again makes you free, continuing in His Word and abiding in it will make you free indeed (John 8:31). To continue in His Word is a test of time but is also proof of how authentic your desire is to make Jesus the Lord of your life. Freedom is amazing but people don't understand there is always a struggle to get it. There is a price to pay for freedom and most people don't want to pay that price. These Jews to whom Jesus is talking to think they're already free when the truth is they aren't as free as they think they are. Yes, they may be people who believe but still they continue to walk in the flesh and are, in truth, slaves of sin (vs. 34). The Message Bible says they're "trapped in a dead-end life." Jesus is saying if you'll read your Bible and continue in it, He will take you from free to free indeed. To be free indeed you must bear the burden of continuance. Any commitment not worth pursuing is flawed and gives a person no solid ground to stand on.

Jesus said in Mark 8:34, "Whoever desires to come after Me, let him deny himself and take up his cross, and follow me." Jesus is calling people to walk the same road He walked and that is a very hard road. Still, He says in the Message Bible, "Don't run from suffering; embrace it. Follow Me and I'll show you how." Jesus is asking you to follow in His footsteps and it takes a deep-rooted commitment to do that. For this to happen you must be in the Word and meditate on it morning, noon, and night. Turn off that television and cancel those plans to play golf. Seek first the kingdom of God and His righteousness (Matt. 6:33). Yes, trials will come but they'll show you what you're made of. Are you bound or are you free? Are you free or are you free indeed? People who are not free indeed talk the talk but never walk the walk. At the first sign of trouble they turn and run away from the commitment they made. They take the road of least resistance unlike Paul who said in Acts 21:13, "I am ready not only to be bound, but also to die at Jerusalem for the name of the Lord Jesus."

People say they love God today but how will they feel next week when trouble comes knocking on their door? People praise God when they're living in the honeymoon of life but what happens when reality sets in? Will the chains of doubt and fear grip their heart or will they break off the shackles of bondage and soar free like a mighty eagle? Will they praise God if their house burns to the ground or if they lose their job? They will if they've been abiding in the Word. Anybody can praise God during good times but it's those who are free indeed who praise Him no matter what life brings their way. For sure, freedom comes with a price. It will cost you something to reach the point where you can "count it all joy when you fall into various trials" (James 1:2). It will cost you to love that spouse who just asked you for a divorce. It will cost you to remain joyful and trust God when the doctor says you've only got six months to live. It will cost you to stand strong after you've done everything you know to do and the results you're looking for still have not come to pass.

People like the idea of being free but walk away from the commitment it takes to be free indeed. Freedom is a struggle and it takes time to become free indeed. You must fight for your freedom and you do that by abiding in God's Word continually. The burden of continuance is clearly on your shoulders. Jesus said you must "stick with this, living out what I tell you" (John 8:31 MSG). Jesus will make you free but you must abide in His Word so He can do it. Life is what you make it. It's about you living in the realm of the Spirit and abiding in God's Word as you strive to allow God to make you free indeed. When that happens you'll rise up in the midst of a fiery trial and boldly proclaim, "This too shall pass!" God never changes but He brings change wherever He goes. He is forever seeking to do a new thing in your life. He wants to take you from free to free indeed. That is exciting news. That gives you a reason to get up in the morning. Being free indeed gives you the motivation to keep going forward down the highway of life knowing that good and glorious things are waiting for you at every turn in the road.

When you abide in the Word you'll be able to endure hard times with your mouth closed and your head held high. You don't wear your problems on your sleeves and the world will never know what you're going through. You're a child of the living God and in faith you talk and act like everything is okay. Freedom comes with a price and you've got to be strong enough to endure long enough so that "after you have suffered a while" God will "perfect, establish, strengthen, and settle you" (1 Peter 5:10). The NIV says God "will Himself restore you and make you strong, firm, and steadfast." The NLT says God "will place you on a firm foundation." Don't give up during hard times because God says if you'll abide in Him and continue in His Word, if you'll bear the burden of continuance, you will be made free indeed. Wars have been fought so people could be made free. Freedom comes by the shedding of innocent blood and this is what happened on the cross of Calvary. Jesus shed His blood so you could be set free from the bondage and consequences of sin. Jesus paid the price so you could be free indeed. Never forget that and never take it for granted.

If things are going good for you right now, don't forget that a heavy price was paid for that to happen. If things aren't going so good, then abide in His Word and Jesus will make you free indeed. This means that "old things have passed away, behold, all things become new." Jesus set you free from your past but being free indeed means you never have to look back over your shoulder fearing that maybe your past will catch up to you. Paul said in Rom. 8:1, "There is therefore no condemnation to those who are in Christ Jesus." The children of Israel were set free from bondage in Egypt but soon after they left the Egyptian army rose up and came after them. It wasn't until they crossed over the Red Sea that they were made free indeed. The water came back together and drowned the Egyptian army and no longer did the people of God have to look over their shoulder. They were now free indeed and you will be also when you no longer have to run and hide from your past. You don't look back when you're free indeed so put the past behind you and move on. Your future is waiting for you.

It is a blessing to know that nothing stays the same for very long. The sun rises in the east and, before you know it, it's setting in the west. Change happens. No matter what's going on in your life, whether good or bad, things can always get better. Get up every morning believing that today will be better than yesterday and tomorrow will be better than today. Don't look back and get discouraged believing your situation will never change. Don't let the enemy convince you that things will be the way they've always been. No, you've been made free indeed and have entered a new season in your life. God said in Is. 43:18,19, "Do not remember the former things, nor consider the things of old. Behold, I will do a new thing, now it shall spring forth, shall you not know it? I will even make a road in the wilderness and rivers in the desert." The Message Bible says, "Forget about what's happened; don't keep going over old history. Be alert, be present. I'm about to do something brand new. It's bursting out! Don't you see it? There it is! I'm making a road through the desert, rivers in the badlands."

If you want your life to get better, then go to Jesus and abide in His Word. 2 Cor. 1:20 says, "For all the promises of God in Him are Yes and in Him Amen, to the glory of God through us." When you are free indeed, you can travel on the highway of life knowing that good and glorious things are waiting for you at every turn in the road. Believe that your best days are ahead of you. Job had some struggles but Job 42:12 says, "Now the Lord blessed the latter days of Job more than his beginning." Vs. 17 then says, "So Job died, old and full of days." Abide in the Word of God and see yourself succeeding in whatever you put your hand to do. Believe that today will be the beginning of a fresh, supernatural flow of God's divine power and favor into your life. Don't look back but keep pressing forward. God is a God who forgets the past and so should you. People who keep looking back have no hope for the future and the loss of hope is the peak of spiritual bankruptcy. When you lose hope you doubt your beliefs and believe your doubts. Roads are to be traveled on so keep going forward no matter what.

Let's face it, problems do come and they can't be ignored. The worst thing a person can do is sit back and do nothing for this gives the enemy free reign to wreak havoc in your life. No, to win the battle of life you must forever be moving forward. The trials of life are often compared to storms. There will be times when you may encounter hurricane-type conditions such as what was described by the apostle Paul in 2 Cor. 1:8 when he said he was "burdened beyond measure, above strength, so that we despaired even of life." One thing to learn in the midst of any trial is that life goes on. The clock is always ticking and any meteorologist will tell you that all storms move forward as well. In the center of all hurricanes is a peaceful, calm harbor of rest known as the eye of the hurricane and this is where you will find the throne room of God. You will always find Jesus in the center of your storm. Just understand that the storm you are now in is always moving and with it so is its peaceful center. If you don't move forward as well, then the eye of the hurricane will pass over you and the turbulent winds will hit you from behind when you least expect it.

This is where the burden of continuance comes in. To remain in the peaceful eye of the hurricane, you must continue to abide in

God's Word and keep going forward. Shortly after Paul wrote of his hardships at the beginning of his second letter to the Corinthian church, he went on to write these encouraging words, "Now thanks be to God who always leads us in triumph in Christ" (2 Cor. 2:14). The Message Bible says, "God leads us from place to place in one perpetual victory parade." The reason you must keep going forward is because that is where your victory is. It's out there in front of you. Even while Jesus was hanging on the cross He was looking forward to the victory that would come at His resurrection. Heb. 12:2 (NIV) says, "For the joy set before Him, He endured the cross, scorning the shame, and sat down at the right hand of the throne of God." The Message Bible says, "Because He never lost sight of where He was headed, He could put up with anything along the way." When you are free indeed you'll focus on where you're going to and not on what you're going through. Don't look at what is, look at what is to become.

David wrote in Ps. 27:13, "I would have lost heart, unless I had believed that I would see the goodness of the Lord in the land of the living." Hope deferred makes the heart sick (Prov. 13:12) and causes nothing but fear and sorrow. Every life has a purpose to fulfill and a destination to arrive at. Those who run their race successfully and finish their course are the ones who don't look back but keep their eyes looking forward at all times. There is a reason the front windshield of your car is larger than the rear-view mirror. Those who are free indeed put their hand to the plow and never look back. Trust God and allow your expectations to be more powerful than any negative thing the devil can put before you. In the midst of your storm "do not cast away your confidence which has great reward. For you have need of endurance, so that after you have done the will of God, you may receive the promise" (Heb. 10:35,36). The Message Bible says, "But you need to stick it out, staying with God's plan so you'll be there for the promised completion."

Sometimes you may feel like you're on a rugged obstacle course going through a maze of difficulties and the end to your problem is nowhere in sight. Once again, the only thing you can do is abide in the Word and trust the One who is leading you. This may seem confusing at times but thankfully you don't have to understand it in your mind in order to believe it in your heart. Prov. 20:24 says, "A man's steps are of the Lord; how then can a man understand his own way?" Nobody said this journey was easy. It's not. You are in the midst of a spiritual war and even Jesus said to "count the cost" before you enlist in the army of the Lord. The good news is that He also said He would never leave or forsake you. A valley is not a bad place to be if you and Jesus are going through it together. Ps. 37:23,24 says, "The steps of a good man are ordered by the Lord and He delights in his way. Though he fall, he shall not be utterly cast down for the Lord upholds him with His hand." At all times you must believe that you are on the road to victory and Jesus is leading you every step of the way. Always remember that the only way out of the valley is to march forward and go through the valley.

It has been said that great people are ordinary people with extraordinary amounts of determination. Never allow that trial to keep you idle. Doing nothing only increases the opportunity for you to feel sorry for yourself. Keep going forward and take hold of that victory that rightfully belongs to you. When you've had a setback, don't take a step back, get ready for a comeback. Though the wind may blow and the rain will fall, you can find comfort in the eye of the hurricane by putting your confidence in the words spoken in Nahum 1:3, "But the Lord has His way in the whirlwind and in the storm." Rest assured, the victory is there but you must march forward to get it. Shout aloud the battle cry of the overcomer and put one foot in front of the other and go after it. Who you are and what you become in life is determined by you and you alone. Will you carry the burden of continuance or won't you? Will you continue going forward even when a feeling of helplessness swarms over you and at times you feel like a puppet on a string being controlled by some diabolical force? You can if you'll continue to abide in His Word daily.

Jesus said that God's holy Word must abide in your heart. As a born again believer you must develop a huge appetite for the Word of God. You must crave spiritual food to the point that your craving will be so great that it will be impossible to satisfy. You need to become so addicted to the Word of God that it seems like you can't get enough of it. The more you get, the more you want. Jer. 15:16 says, "Your words were found, and I ate them, and Your word was to me the joy and rejoicing of my heart; For I am called by Your Name, O Lord of hosts." Ezekiel says the same thing, "Moreover He said to me, 'Son of man, eat what you find, eat this scroll, and go, speak to the house of Israel.' So I opened my mouth and He caused me to eat that scroll. And He said to me, 'Son of man, feed your belly, and fill your stomach with this scroll that I give you.' So I ate it, and it was in my mouth like honey in sweetness" (Ezek. 3;1-3).

God says to "fill your stomach" with His Word. Don't nibble on it a little bit. Don't be content reading one verse on some "promise card" you have stored on some dusty shelf in the back bedroom. To become addicted to the Word of God you must abide in it morning, noon, and night. God said in Josh. 1:8, "This Book of the Law shall not depart from your mouth, but you shall meditate in it day and night, that you may observe to do according to all that is written in it. For then you will make your way prosperous, and then you will have good success." Make a quality decision to give yourself completely to the Word of God. Carry a pocket Bible with you in your back pocket or in your purse. Be sure to put one in the glove compartment of your car. Have one on the coffee table in your living room and on the night stand in your bedroom. The more you give yourself to God's Word, the more your desire for it will grow. Job said, "I have treasured the words of His mouth more than my necessary food" (Job 23:12). David wrote, "Oh, taste and see that the Lord is good" (Ps. 34:8).

Being free indeed will cause you to seek God like never before. Everybody, it seems, is searching for something. The devil is roaming about seeking whom he may devour (1 Peter 5:8) and God is searching throughout the whole earth to show Himself strong on behalf of those whose heart is loyal to Him (2 Chron. 16:9). It is interesting to note that both God and the devil are searching for the same thing. They are looking for people who happen to be God's ultimate creation. One wants to destroy them while the other wants to bless them abundantly (John 10:10). In the same mode, sinners and believers are also searching for something in their lives. Sinners are looking for the same thing as believers but they're looking in all the wrong places. They dive headfirst into the world of sex, drugs, and money in hopes of finding the same fulfillment and self-worth that can only come in a personal relationship with the Lord Jesus Christ. Believers, on the other hand, know that true fulfillment comes not in things but can be found by obeying the words of Is. 55:6 which says to "Seek the Lord while He may be found."

Most people don't realize this but there will come a time when He won't be able to be found. More than once Jesus said this to those unbelieving Pharisees. This is why you must take all the more heed to seek Him out while you still have the opportunity to do so. People need to realize that God is never a convenience in life. He must be sought after to be found. Inside of your heart needs to be a strong, intense desire that propels you to search out, crave, and strive after a relationship with the one, true God. Ps. 42:1,2 says, "As the deer pants for the water brooks so pants my soul for You, O God. You are my God, early will I seek You; my soul thirsts for You; my flesh longs for You in a dry and thirsty land where there is no water." The Message Bible says, "I want to drink God." The stronger your desire for the things of God, the greater your effort will be in finding them. Ask yourself, when was the last time you turned off the television set and sought the face of God? Do you refuse overtime on Sundays so you can go to church with your family instead?

The key word here is "desire." 1 Peter 2:2 says, "as newborn babes desire the pure milk of the Word that you may grow thereby" and 1 Cor. 12:31 tells us to "earnestly desire the best gifts." This intense craving will draw you closer to God and cause you to overcome the hindrances of ignorance, carnality, instability, and dullness of hearing. An accurate description of such a search can be found in Ps. 119:15,16, "I will meditate on Your precepts and contemplate Your ways. I will delight myself in Your statutes and I will not forget Your Word." When the promise of finding God is brought into full manifestation, you must forever cling to Him and never let go. Jesus said in John 15:4, "Abide in Me, and I in you." Abiding in Jesus means to live in total unison with God. It also means to take up permanent residence. If you're abiding somewhere you're not just staying there temporarily as in a short stay at a motel or a two week vacation with family and friends. Abiding means you're living there continually. You get to know Jesus by spending time with Him every day.

When you abide in Jesus you think about Him all the time. You think about Him at work and you think about Him at the shopping mall. You think about Him when you're doing the dishes and you think about Him when you're mowing the lawn. When you abide in Jesus, He becomes the Lord of your life twenty-four hours a day, seven days a week. Col. 3:11 says "Christ is all and in all." The Message Bible says, "From now on everyone is defined by Christ, everyone is included in Christ." If Jesus is your "all in all" then you need to allow Him to be involved in your life every moment of every day. Col. 3:2 says. "Set your mind on things above, not on things on the earth." The Message Bible says, "Look up, and be alert to what is going on around Christ - that's where the action is. See things from His perspective." You need to make Jesus the Lord of your life so "that in all things He may have the preeminence" (Col. 1:18). It is in Jesus that you have redemption and the forgiveness of all your sins (Col. 1:14). In Him you are complete (Col. 2:10) and have all the treasures of wisdom and knowledge (Col. 2:3). In Him is the hope of glory (Col. 1:27).

God wants a close relationship with you so much that in His infinite wisdom He created a void in your heart that only He can fill. It is His desire that this void would drive you to the point of searching Him out so that He can fill that emptiness with love, joy, peace, and a sense of fulfillment so deep and meaningful that it can only be described as heaven on earth. As if seeking God and finding Him was not enough of a blessing in and of itself, God rewards all those who seriously seek Him with an endless supply of unspeakable blessings. Heb. 11:6 calls God "a rewarder of those who diligently seek Him." The Message Bible says "He cares enough to respond to those who seek Him." When you seek His face and not His hand, never again will you have to worry or concern yourself with whether or not your needs get met. Jesus said in John 6:35, "I am the bread of life. He who comes to Me shall never hunger, and He who believes in Me shall never thirst." Ps. 107:9 says, "For He satisfies the longing soul and fills the hungry soul with goodness."

Matt. 13:44 says, "Again, the kingdom of heaven is like treasure hidden in a field, which a man found and hid; and for joy over it he goes and sells all that he has and buys the field." If you don't love and treasure Jesus like this man, if you don't truly seek Him out, then you really don't know Him. But if you are enraptured with His love for you and your love for Him, then when you seek Him with all your heart you can have the assurance that He will be found by you (1 Chron. 28:9). In His presence is fullness of joy (Ps. 16:11), He will not forsake you (Ps. 9:10), and His favor (Lam. 3:25) and His protection (Ezra 8:22) will be ever present in your life. Hosea 10:12 says gifts of righteousness will be yours and God will give you understanding in all things (Prov. 28:5). Never again will you walk in fear (Ps. 34:4) and the absolute, all powerful life of God will flow through your veins. The Lord said in Amos 5:4, "Seek Me and live." The gift of life is truly the greatest blessing of all and it comes as a result of seeking the Lord. The end of the age is near and it's time for the church to get on its face and seek God like never before.

Remember, God must be sought after to be found. To show how important seeking God truly is, there is one story in the Bible that describes the consequences for not seeking God. 2 Chron. 15:12,13 says, "Then they entered into a covenant to seek the Lord God of their fathers with all their soul; and whoever would not seek the Lord God of Israel was put to death, whether small or great, whether man or woman." Always remember that if the work done at the cross did not change the message of the old covenant, then the same principles still apply today. No, you will not be taken out and killed for not seeking God but there is an adversary out there seeking a way to destroy your life. Your only hope in avoiding this dreadful calamity is in the arms of a loving Savior. 2 Sam. 22:31

says, "He is a shield to all who trust in Him." He is ready, willing, and more than able to deliver you from life's difficulties and bless you abundantly, but He must be sought after to be found. You must, therefore, be careful not to brush off into nonexistence the importance of seeking God. It truly is a matter of life and death.

-21-

"PROVOKING THE ENEMY"

The conversation Jesus is having with these Jews is not a soft and tender moment. This is a harsh and uncomfortable confrontation between Jesus and the religious leaders and when the conversation is over the people took up stones to try to kill Him. Why did they do this? Jesus said in John 8:37,38, "You seek to kill Me, because My word has no place in you. I speak what I have seen with My Father, and you do what you have seen with your father." These Jews had brought up the fact that they were descendants of Abraham (vs. 33) but Jesus confronts them and says they weren't doing the works of faith and obedience that Abraham did (vs. 39). It is important for some people to know that somewhere in their ancestral background is somebody important, someone who made an impact on their society. Knowing this appeals to the need of human significance. People need a reason to think the best about themselves and for the Jew there was no greater figure in religious history than Abraham. The Jew considered himself safe and secure in the favor of God simply because he was a descendant of Abraham.

The admiration which the Jews gave to Abraham was perfectly legitimate. And yes, being a descendant of his put them in a place of great honor. Even the psalmist said, "O seed of Abraham His servant, You children of Jacob, His chosen ones!" (Ps. 105:6). Jesus is saying to the Pharisees that earthly heritage is not enough to make them right with God. Jesus was very blunt about this as was John the Baptist who said to the Pharisees and Sadducees in Matt. 3:7-9, "Brood of vipers! Who has warned you to flee from the wrath to come? Therefore bear fruits worthy of repentance, and do not think to say to yourselves, 'We have Abraham as our father.' For I say to you that God is able to raise up children to Abraham from these stones." Paul used the same argument when he said in Rom. 3:20, "Therefore by the deeds of the law no flesh is justified in His sight." It's not flesh and blood that makes a person a descendant of Abraham but rather the moral quality of their life and spiritual fidelity. These Jews think they're righteous but don't see their spiritual condition as it truly is.

Jesus came to tell these people that there is no security in religion, good works, or ancestral background. Only in Jesus can sins be forgiven and it is only through Him that one escapes the fiery torment of eternal judgment. This is what Jesus has been saying since His ministry began but still the Pharisees mocked Him to scorn. Jesus knows the hearts of these Jewish leaders have hardened to the point where they firmly reject the words He is saying to them. They resent Him, they hate Him, they want Him dead. As their vehement outrage toward Him increases, so also does the direct severity of the Lord's statements toward them escalate. There is an upsurge in the piercing blows Jesus directs toward their hypocrisy. The stakes are high and Jesus doesn't back down. He is purposely provoking the enemy because their false beliefs have to be confronted and dealt with. Love does not leave people alone when they're on their way to judgment. Jesus came to shatter their false securities and to press the reality of their current situation. This is why they sought to kill Him.

Jesus puts an exclamation point on all of this by saying, "You do the deeds of your father" (vs. 41). The Pharisees then said something very unusual, "We were not born of fornication, we have one Father - God" (vs. 41). Nobody said they were born of sexual immorality so why would they say such a thing? They had heard that Mary had gotten pregnant without coming together with Joseph and they were accusing Jesus of being born through the act of fornication. What a despicable thing to say. These leaders were accusing Jesus of being an illegitimate child to which the Lord responded, "If God were your Father, you would love Me, for I proceeded forth and come from God; nor have I come of Myself, but He sent Me. Why do you not understand My speech? because you are not able to listen to My word. You are of your father the devil, and the desires of your father you want to do. He was a murderer from the beginning, and does not stand in the truth, because there is no truth in him. When he speaks a lie, he speaks from his own resources, for he is a liar and the father of it. But because I tell you the truth, you do not believe Me" (vs. 42-45).

The devil is a murderer for he kills all things that make life lovely. He loves falsehood and every lie is inspired by the devil. Jesus was saying that these Jews may be the physical offspring of Abraham but spiritually their father was the devil. Murder was in their hearts and they were being deceived by the father of lies. They were trying to murder Jesus and were lying about His mother. Their intentions were set on destroying what was good and the maintaining of the false. They were acting precisely like the devil. Like father, like son. This was the most unsettling thing Jesus could have said to these self-righteous Pharisees who prided themselves on being descendants of Abraham and children of God. Another time He boldly said to them, "Serpents, brood of vipers! How can you escape the condemnation of hell?" (Matt. 23:33). The Message Bible says, "Snakes! Reptilian sneaks! Do you think you can worm your way out of this? Never have to pay the piper?" There is great drama here and Jesus then challenges them with this question, "Which of you convicts Me of sin?" (vs. 46).

Jesus is saying, "Is there something I've done that causes you not to believe Me? Is there anyone among you who can testify that I am anything but holy?" A deathly silence engulfed the crowd. These same Pharisees couldn't cast the first stone at the woman caught in adultery proving they had sin in their own lives. Jesus is now challenging them to tell Him what sin He has committed. You can picture Jesus standing there looking each one of them in the eye waiting for anyone to accept the challenge He has given them. "Tell me what I've done wrong." The silence continued. Search as they like, they could not accuse Him but, for some reason, they still refused to believe Him. Jesus continues, "And if I tell the truth, why do you not believe Me? He who is of God hears God's words; therefore you do not hear, because you are not of God" (vs. 46,47). Jesus is not pulling any punches here. These Jews are saying they're of God, Jesus is saying they're not of God. A verbal showdown of epic proportions is taking place with neither side willing to give an inch. Back and forth they go. It's one barrage after another.

These rulers cannot contain their rage and fury because of the hardness of their heart. They aren't ready to throw in the towel just yet so they counter by asking, "Do we not say rightly that You are a Samaritan and have a demon?" (vs. 48). The Aramaic word for "Samaritan" is "Shomeroni" and this was the title for the prince of the devils. They also heard that Jesus passed through Samaria and ministered to those half-breed Jews who were considered unclean. To the Jew, Samaritans were heretics and worse than Gentiles. Rumors were also started saying that Mary had been unfaithful to Joseph and had an affair with a Roman soldier named Panthers. They said Jesus was born as the result of this adulterous union. These Pharisees were now calling Jesus a low-life, half-breed, unclean Jew who was born illegitimately and was possessed by a demon. They called Him an enemy to their Jewish religion and one who was possessed by a demonic spirit. Little do they realize that one day they will bow down before this Man they're accusing and will have to give an account for the actions they are now taking.

Jesus continues, "I do not have a demon; but I honor My Father, and you dishonor Me. And I do not seek My own glory; there is One who seeks and judges. Most assuredly, I say to you, if anyone keeps My word he shall never taste death" (vs. 49-51). These Pharisees now think they have Jesus right where they want Him. They answered and said, "Now we know that You have a demon! Abraham is dead, and the prophets; and You say, 'If anyone keeps My word he shall never taste death?' Are you greater than our father Abraham, who is dead? And the prophets are dead. Whom do You make Yourself out to be? (vs. 52,53). Over and over again Jesus is saying things that are shocking these Jews to the core. The problem is they're thinking in the natural realm and not the spiritual realm. They can't comprehend what Jesus is saying because they're not of God. 1 Cor. 2:14 says, "But the natural man does not receive the things of the Spirit of God, for they are foolishness to him; nor can he know them because they are spiritually discerned." Paul is saying that unbelief leads to ignorance, but once you believe, understanding will come.

Spiritual things are folly to the natural man and these Pharisees are dumbfounded by what Jesus is saying to them. Perhaps the words of Zech. 11:5 are ringing in their ears, "Your fathers, where are they? And the prophets, do they live forever?" They ask Jesus two questions and He answers them by making two claims that are the foundation of His life. He boldly states that He has an exclusive knowledge of God and a unique and uncommon obedience that goes along with that knowledge. He says in vs. 54-56, "If I honor Myself, My honor is nothing. It's My Father who honors Me, of whom you say that He is your God. Yet you have not known Him, but I know Him. And if I say, 'I do not know Him,' I shall be a liar like you; but I do know Him and keep His word. Your father Abraham rejoiced to see My day, and he saw it and was glad." Are these Jews hearing Jesus correctly? Did He just say He once had a personal encounter with Abraham? They can't believe what they're hearing so they ask, "You are not yet fifty years old, and have you seen Abraham?" Jesus responded, "Most assuredly, I say to you, before Abraham was, I AM" (vs. 57,58).

Many times Jesus claimed to have existed as a divine being before His birth. Other scriptures back this up as well. Col. 1:16 says the pre-incarnate Christ was the Creator of all things and 1 Cor. 10:1-4 says it was He who led Israel through the wilderness. In Luke 10:18 Jesus told the disciples, "I saw Satan fall like lightning from heaven," referring to an event that occurred before man was created. In reference to Abraham, Gen. 17:1 and Gen. 18:1 both say the Lord appeared to Abraham and these chapters tell of two lengthy conversations the two of them had together. This was the pre-incarnate Christ and Abraham received Him into his house and believed everything He said. This the Pharisees did not do with Jesus. They didn't embrace the heavenly messenger who came into their midst. They didn't welcome Him and they certainly didn't love Him. 1 Cor. 16:22 says, "If anyone does not love the Lord Jesus Christ, let him be accursed." Their faith in Jesus was non-existent thus proving they were not Abraham's spiritual children. Gal. 3:6,7 says "just as Abraham 'believed God, and it was accounted to him for righteousness.' Therefore know that only those who are of faith are sons of Abraham."

Jesus said Abraham rejoiced to see His day coming. He was speaking in a spiritual language that the Jews could not understand although they had great knowledge of Old Testament scripture. In Gen. 22:1-3 Abraham was permitted to have a vision of the death of the Messiah as a sacrifice for sin represented by the command given by God to sacrifice his son Isaac on the altar. Heb. 11:19 says Abraham was "accounting that God was able to raise him up, even from the dead, from which he also received him in a figurative sense." Abraham saw the resurrection of Jesus in what he believed would happen to his son if he died upon that altar. He also saw the Lord's day in the promise that in his seed all the families (Gen. 12:3) and all the nations (Gen. 22:18) of the earth should be blessed and kings would be born of him (Gen. 17:6). Heb. 11:13 says many of the patriarchs of old, Abraham included, "all died in faith, not having received the promises, but having seen them afar off were assured of them, embraced them, and confessed that they were strangers and pilgrims on the earth."

Jesus said, "Before Abraham was, I AM." This statement appears to have been the goal of this entire conversation. It pulls together everything Jesus has been saying up to this point, that His eternal existence is timeless. He always was and always will be. This was the same name God gave Himself when He talked to Moses at the burning bush (Ex. 3:14). The Pharisees thought it was blasphemy for Jesus to say this, thus He deserved to die. They refused to grasp the greatness of the person standing in front of them. This was the very person Abraham and Moses bowed down to and here they are wanting to kill Him. They don't realize they're talking to God in a human body. They're staring into the eyes of God Himself yet they insult Him and refuse to give Him the honor He so richly deserves. What Jesus said is a statement that cannot be ignored. One must either believe in Jesus and follow Him, or else reject Him and walk away. The choice these Jews made is found in vs. 59, "Then they took up stones to throw at Him, but Jesus hid Himself and went out of the temple, going through the midst of them, and so passed by."

"Now as Jesus passed, He saw a man who was blind from birth" (John 9:1). Blindness was a common and dominating reality in the ancient world and is mentioned many times in the Old Testament. It was so common, in fact, that Is. 42:7 specifically points out that the coming Messiah would "open blind eyes." This blind man is symbolic of the sin-blinded man who has no capacity to see Jesus. Blindness illustrates the spiritual darkness of man and how he is lost without Jesus in their life. Jesus is at high risk here for He is escaping from those who wanted to stone Him. Still, He stops so He can demonstrate grace and compassion to this blind man who was begging at the gates of the temple. But first, His disciples had a question they wanted to ask Him, "Rabbi, who sinned, this man or his parents, that he was born blind?" (vs. 2). This was a theological question that was asked a lot at that time, and still is today. People ask, "Lord, what did I do to deserve this? What is the cause of the calamity I'm going through?"

The disciples didn't show any desire to see this man healed for they were more interested in the reason why this man was born blind. This question was a reflection of how people are always looking for someone to blame for their current condition. They play the blame game because they're disappointed in the outcome of their lives. They don't like where they're at in life so they spend the majority of their time blaming others for it. It's much easier to blame others than it is to take responsibility yourself. People who play this game need to shake it off and learn how to take back what the enemy has stolen. It is only then that they'll move into their destiny. The disciples were more occupied with the cause of this sickness than ministering to him so they introduced the topic of sin. Who sinned, this man or his parents? They believed that where there is sin, there is suffering and where there is suffering, there is sin. The friends of Job said he must have done something wrong to go through the trials he was experiencing. They even wanted him to confess to something he didn't do.

It seems at first that the disciples asked Jesus a ludicrous and irrational question. How could this man have sinned if he wasn't yet born? As foolish as it may sound, some theologians at that time thought a person could sin while in their mother's womb. Sermons were preached from the text of Gen. 25:22 that describes Jacob and Esau fighting with each other in Rebecca's womb, thus proving that a person could sin before they were even born. If not his own sin, could the sin of his parents have caused this blindness? God did say in Ex. 20:5, "For I, the Lord your God, am a jealous God, visiting the iniquity of the fathers on the children to the third and fourth generation of those who hate Me." First of all, this verse is not saying you'll be punished for the sins committed by your great-grandparents. These fathers were the leaders and heads of their generation and their sins were so influential that those under their leadership did the same things they did. Sin penetrates deeply into the souls of men and God is saying it takes three or four generations to turn it around.

God dealt with this very thing in Ezek. 18:19,20 when He said, "Yet you say, 'Why should the son not bear the guilt of the father?' Because the son has done what is lawful and right, and has kept all My statutes and done them, he shall surely live. The soul who sins shall die. The son shall not bear the guilt of the father, nor the father bear the guilt of the son. The righteousness of the righteous shall be upon himself, and the wickedness of the wicked shall be upon himself." God is basically saying here "to each his own." Every individual is responsible for what happens in their own personal lives. So the question remains, is there a connection between a person's sickness and the sins they have committed? Great caution needs to be taken here because the answer is always twofold. Sometimes there is a connection, sometimes there isn't. Sickness can come as the result of sin but it doesn't always happen for that reason. Look around you and you'll see many healthy sinners in the world. The bottom line is that sin is nothing to play with "for the wages of sin is death" (Rom. 6:23).

In a world tainted by sin, sickness and disease will be here and like the devil it is roaming the earth seeking whom it may devour. All sickness and human deformity is of the devil and Jesus testifies of this in Matt. 17:18 and Luke 13:16. The Message Bible says in Acts 10:38, "He went through the country helping people and healing everyone who was beaten down by the devil." The NIV says He was "healing all who were under the power of the devil." Sickness is due to the fall of man and is a part of a fallen world where its inhabitants have rebelled and turned away from God. Willful, habitual sin does open the door to the devil and sickness and disease is one of the biggest weapons in his arsenal. The HIV virus and AIDS is definitely the result of sinful behavior. Ps. 107:17 says, "Fools, because of their transgression, and because of their iniquities, were afflicted." The Message Bible says, "Some of you were sick because you'd lived a bad life, your bodies feeling the effects of your sin." The same thing is said in Ps. 38:3. In other words, you can't play with fire and not be burned (Prov. 6:27).

Sickness is of the devil and yes, there are a few occasions in the Bible where sickness results from sin. There is a "sin unto death" (1 John 5:16) and Paul talks about how those with willful, continuous, unrepentant sin are turned over to Satan for "the destruction of the flesh" (1 Cor. 5:5). God has called His people to holiness (1 Peter 1:16) and when a person who knows better continues to walk in habitual sin it does open the door to the devil who is a thief who comes to steal, kill, and destroy (John 10:10). One cannot forget what happened to Ananias and Sapphira when they willfully lied about their offering (Acts 5:1-11). Miriam received leprosy because of her sin (Num. 12:10) and the children of Israel were bitten by poisonous snakes when they murmured against God (Num. 21:6). 1 Cor. 11:28-32 says "many are weak and sick and some even died" because they partook of the Lord's Supper in an unworthy manner. Jesus warned the healed invalid to "sin no more, lest a worse thing come upon you" (John 5:14) and James 5:16 says, "Confess your trespasses to one another and pray for one another, that you may be healed."

The disciples asked who sinned, this man or his parents, and Jesus answered, "Neither this man nor his parents sinned" (John 9:3). Yes, sin can sometimes cause sickness but Jesus is saying here that this man's blindness was not the result of sin. Here is Biblical proof that not all sickness comes as the result of personal sin. If it did, the whole world would be sick and there would be no healthy person walking the earth today. If you know of someone who is sick, don't point your finger at them and assume it's all because of sin. This is what Job's friends did to him. Whether or not they have sinned is between them and God. You can only be responsible for yourself. If you're sick, be sure to examine yourself and see if you're living a life worthy of God. If you are obedient to Him and His Word, Is. 33:24 says you can enjoy perfect health in an earthly paradise. Jesus said, "You're asking the wrong question. You're looking for someone to blame. There is no cause-effect here. Look instead for what God can do" (John 9:3 MSG).

Jesus said to not blame this man or his parents. It's not important why he is blind, what is important is that Jesus will use this situation for His glory. Because of an error by the translators, it has often been taught that this man was born blind on purpose just so Jesus could one day heal him. This is a gross misunderstanding of the nature of a loving God. A God filled with love, mercy, and compassion would never do such a thing. The problem stems from the wording of vs. 3. Jesus said, "Neither this man nor his parents sinned, but that the works of God should be revealed in him." Vs. 4 then says, "I must work the works of Him who sent Me while it is day; the night is coming when no one can work." The original text had no periods, commas, or verse and chapter numbers. Whoever originally translated this story put the comma and period in the wrong place, thus changing the true meaning of what Jesus is saying. Here is what He actually said, "Neither this man nor his parents sinned." Period. End of sentence. Then, starting a new sentence, He said, "So that the works of God should be revealed in him, I must work the works of Him who sent Me while it is day."

Another thing to take note of is that if God did make this man blind and Jesus healed him, then Jesus would be going against the work of the Father and this He would never do. In fact, Jesus testified in Matt. 12:25, "Every kingdom divided against itself is brought to desolation, and every city or house divided against itself will not stand." Also, if God makes people sick, then why do they take medicine and go see doctors in an effort to get better? Isn't a visit to the doctor going against the will of God? Why don't they sit in pain and wait for God to take the pain away? No, God is not against doctors and these questions reveal the foolishness of the doctrine that says God makes people sick. You can have the assurance that God did not make this man blind so that one day His works could be revealed in him. He does, however, want to be glorified in whatever situation you are in. Jesus is the light that shines beyond physical blindness. This man had an appointment with destiny and so do you. God is searching the earth for a people who will trust Him in every test and trial. Are you one of those He is searching for?

Randall J. Brewer

-22-

"THE DOOR OF SALVATION"

The miracles Jesus performed in the gospel of John were always a sign of the glory and power of God, whereas the other gospel writers regarded them as a demonstration of His love and compassion. Jesus was a man like no other and He was both all loving and all powerful. Everywhere He went, His glory was found in His compassion. Standing in front of this blind man, Jesus said to His disciples, "I must work the works of Him who sent Me while it is day; the night is coming when no one can work" (John 9:4). The cross of Calvary loomed just over the horizon and in a mist of time your life will also be over. Jesus is saying that He and all His followers must do God's work while there is still time to do it. Eph. 5:15-17 (NLT) says, "So be careful how you live. Don't live like fools, but like those who are alive. Make the most of every opportunity in these evil days. Don't act thoughtlessly, but understand what the Lord wants you to do." Never put off until tomorrow what you can do today because tomorrow may never get here. Engraved on a sundial in Glasgow are these insightful words, "Take thought of time before time is ended."

It is of the utmost importance that you spend what little time you have on this earth doing the things God tells you to do. These are desperate times and you need to make the most of the opportunities God gives you. What you do with your life and time is so important. Don't waste your life on trivial things that have little or no value. Pursue the things of God and stop flirting with the sins of this world. Be like Jesus and let your light shine in the darkness. Jesus then said, "As long as I am in the world, I am the light of the world" (vs. 5). The world needs Jesus for all life comes from Him. In Jesus men no longer stumble in darkness, men represented by this blind man who is begging near the gates of the temple. This man said nothing and did nothing. He didn't have to do anything but be there when Jesus walked by. Moses told the people, "Stand still, and see the salvation of the Lord" (Ex. 14:13). Standing still does not mean you're being passive. It's an act of faith, an act of resting on the promises of God. It's a determination to cease from all questions, doubts, and fears.

God promised in Is. 41:10, "Fear not, for I am with you; Be not dismayed, for I am your God. I will strengthen you, yes, I will help you, I will uphold you with My righteous right hand." If you'll stand where you're supposed to stand, and do what you're supposed to do, the miracle will come. Jesus then did something very unusual. He spit on the ground, made some mud with the saliva, and put it on the man's eyes (vs. 6). The man is now worse off than he was before. Even if he was healed he still wouldn't be able to see because of all the mud in his eyes. This man got touched by Jesus but still he was blind. Sometimes things may appear to get worse before they get better. Trust God anyway and do what He tells you to do. Jesus told the man, "Go, wash in the pool of Siloam" (vs. 7). This man's healing didn't come instantly and he now has a bigger burden on him than he had before Jesus passed by. He is still blind but now he has mud in his eyes. Blindness is all this man knows. It can't be compared to anything else. In order to get his miracle, he's going to have to walk to the pool in the dark.

Why did Jesus put mud on this man's eyes and send him away to wash it off? Because it would take some work to do this and James 2:26 says "faith without works is dead." The command to go wash in the pool of Siloam is a call to obedience, a call to submit to the words of Jesus. The man was blind but he wasn't deaf. Jesus told him to "Go" and he went. A spark of faith ignited in his heart and he walked by faith and not by sight. He could see no better with the mud in his eyes than he could before. He was walking by faith and he didn't need his eyes to get to the pool just like you don't need a happy past to have a glorious future. All you need is to hear from Jesus. Stop crying because you don't have a college degree or you came from a broken home or a failed marriage. Be like Paul who said in Phil. 3:13,14, "One thing I do, forgetting those things which are behind and reaching forward to those things which are ahead, I press toward the goal for the prize of the upward call of God in Christ Jesus." The Message Bible says, "I'm off and running, and I'm not turning back."

If you could see clearly it wouldn't require any faith. Walk it out even if you can't see what's in front of you. Go blind if you have to but, by all means, go! Keep going forward and believe that every step you take is a blessing from God. Praise Him continually because every step you take is a step closer to the finish line, a step closer to the blessing you are about to receive. Your miracle is in the going. Believe that He who began a good work in you will complete it in Christ (Phil. 1:6). Abraham obeyed the Lord's command to leave his kinfolks and Heb. 11:8 says, "By faith Abraham obeyed when he was called to go out to the place which he would afterward receive as an inheritance. And he went out, not knowing where he was going." You need to understand that there is a certain amount of blindness that goes along with walking by faith. This is why you must put your faith in the living God who is all knowing and all seeing. Don't be discouraged if you don't see immediate results. Keep on walking out the process. You go from faith to faith and glory to glory. Eventually you'll reach the pool of your miracle.

"So he went and washed, and came back seeing" (vs. 7). The man obeyed Jesus and received his miracle. You, also, must respond to what God tells you to do for it's when you obey that you truly begin to see. You can't sit in a rocking chair all day and ask God to give you a new job. No, you must go out and look for it and believe that God will direct your steps as you go. God works in different ways. How He blessed one person does not mean He'll bless you the same way. This is why you need to obey and do what He tells you to do. Not obeying hinders you from seeing what God wants you to see. This miracle was so great that some of his neighbors didn't believe he was the same man they saw begging (vs. 8). When Jesus touches your life, it's possible that others might not recognize you. He turned water into wine and He'll turn your darkness into light (Ps. 18:28). He'll forgive your sins and heal all your diseases. He'll take you from one victory to another victory. You'll be changed from the inside out and people will say about you what they said about Paul, "He who formerly persecuted us now preaches the faith which he once tried to destroy" (Gal. 1:23).

What happens next shows the step-by-step revelation by which this man came to progressively know who Jesus truly was. The neighbors asked how his eyes were opened and he told them what "a Man called Jesus" instructed him to do (vs. 11). This was all the man knew about Jesus at this time. He was a good man, a Man called Jesus. The neighbors then brought the man to the Pharisees and they also wanted to know how he received his sight. The man said, "He put clay on my eyes, and I washed, and I see" (vs 15). It goes without saying that while others saw a miracle, the self-righteous Pharisees saw the breaking of a Sabbath law. This miracle happened on the Sabbath and making clay was considered work. Medical attention could only be given if a person's life was in danger. Some of the Pharisees said, "This Man is not from God, because He does not keep the Sabbath" (vs. 16). This is a picture of stubborn and willful unbelief. They can't even mention His name. Unbelievers reject the gospel message and are often hostile toward those who do believe. Not all unbelievers are hostile but by nature unbelief is hostile to the truth.

Surprisingly, there is a division among the Pharisees. While some reject who Jesus is, others said, "How can a man who is a sinner do such signs?" (vs. 16). Sadly, you don't hear from these people again until the next chapter. They just fade out of the picture of what's being said here. Those who don't believe then ask the man who received his sight what he thought about Jesus. With no hesitation the man boldly declared, "He is a prophet" (vs. 17). There is an unfolding here of this man's understanding of who Jesus is. First He was just a good Man called Jesus and now He is being called a prophet. In the Old Testament prophets were the mouthpiece of God and what they said was often tested by the signs they performed. This man knew a miracle had happened to him and when asked his opinion of Jesus he gave it without hesitation. He was a brave man to say this for he knew full well what the Pharisees thought about Jesus. Still, he took a stand for Jesus and wouldn't back down. Unbelief cannot be convinced of the truth so the Pharisees called his parents to come forth and testify as to whether or not this was their son (vs. 18). They're not searching for the truth but for a way to justify their own false conclusions.

While this man did not fear the Pharisees, his parents did. These are not loving parents, for if they were their son would not have been a beggar. They said he was their son and he indeed was born blind. They then claimed to have no knowledge about how he could now see. They're lying out of fear knowing that whoever confessed Jesus as the Christ would be put out of the synagogue (vs. 22). They are fearing man more than they're fearing God. They then said, "He is of age; ask him" (vs. 23). Their son didn't have to fear being put out of the synagogue, because he already is because of the sin issue related to his blindness. The Pharisees talk to the man a second time and say, "Give God the glory! We know that this Man is a sinner" (vs. 24). Joshua said the same thing to Achan in Josh. 7:19 when he confronted him about his sin, "Give God the glory and tell me what you have done." The Pharisees are saying the same thing. They're saying God is glorified when you tell the truth. They're telling the man to tell them the truth. The problem is, they can't handle the truth.

The man answered and said, "Whether He is a sinner or not I do not know. One thing I know: that though I was blind, now I see" (vs. 25). You do not have to know all the answers to be a witness for Jesus. The most powerful tool you'll ever have is your own personal testimony. Just tell people what Jesus did for you. It's not always about facts and knowledge, it's about the goodness of God at work in your life. Say, "I once was lost but now am found. I once was sick but now I'm healed. I once was weak but now I'm strong. I once was poor but now all my needs are met. I once was blind but now I see." This man knew a miracle had taken place and nobody was going to take that from him. The Pharisees asked him a second time how he was made to see. The man said, "I told you already, and you did not listen. Why do you want to hear it again?

Do you also want to become His disciple?" (vs. 27). He also is provoking the enemy and the Pharisees don't like it. This man is saying he has chosen to become a disciple of Jesus and was asking if the Pharisees wanted to join him. Once again the Pharisees burned with rage.

Here is an outcast talking to the religious leaders of his time. He has the freedom to provoke these Pharisees because he has the truth on his side. He is moving forward on his journey to salvation. First he says the person who healed him was a Man called Jesus, then he said He was a prophet, and here he says he's going to become one of His disciples. Because of this the Pharisees reviled him and hurled insults at him. They said they didn't even know where Jesus came from. This man had no religious training but he was bold as a lion. In vs. 30 he said the obvious conclusion was simple, "He opened my eyes, therefore He must be from heaven." He continued in vs. 32,33, "Since the world began it has been unheard of that anyone opened the eyes of one who was born blind. If this Man were not from God, He could do nothing." This man's understanding continues to progress for he confessed that Jesus is from God. The more you know Jesus, the greater He becomes. The Pharisees are blinded by their own pride so they insult the man saying he is a sinner and unlearned. They then cast him out of their presence.

This man has been thrown out of the synagogue because he had been given the great revelation that Jesus is the Son of God. Jesus is always true to those who are true to Him and vs. 35 says, "Jesus heard that they had cast him out; and when He found him, He said to him, 'Do you believe in the Son of God?'" Jesus sought this man out proving that when you stand up for Jesus, it always brings Him closer to you. Jesus opened this man's physical eyes and now this man's spiritual eyes are about to open so that he might believe. This is the first time he has seen Jesus with his natural eyes and he answered Him, "Who is He, sir? I want to believe in Him" (vs. 36 NLT). This man wants to believe, he just needs to know who to believe in. For sure, this man's heart is ready to believe. Jesus said to him, "You have both seen Him and it is He who is talking with you." Then the man said, "Lord, I believe!" And he worshiped Him (vs. 37,38). The man goes from calling Jesus "sir" to "Lord." He has elevated Jesus to being Lord of his life and he worships Him. Spiritual sight confesses Jesus as Lord and worship is proof that spiritual sight has come.

This poor beggar has seen nothing his entire life. Now he sees physically but, more importantly, he sees clearly the Son of God. He is gazing upon the glory of God in the face of Jesus and he worships Him. Jesus then said, "I came into the world to bring everything into the clear light of day, making all the distinctions clear, so that those who have never seen will see, and those who have made a great pretense of seeing will be exposed as blind" (vs. 39 MSG). Jesus is the light of the world and those who turn away from that light are truly blind. Jesus came into this world for judgment and like a sharp two-edged sword He separates those who are willing to believe from those who are unwilling to do so. The Pharisees who were there rightly perceived that the words of Jesus were directed at them so they ask, "Are we blind also?" Jesus said, "If you were really blind, you would be blameless, but since you claim to see everything so well, you're accountable for every fault and failure" (vs. 40,41). Jesus is saying that all people are responsible for the knowledge they do have. It is a serious thing to turn a blind eye to the truth that has been revealed to you.

Spiritual blindness is a curse of the devil. Paul said in 2 Cor. 4;4, "The god of this age has blinded the minds of unbelievers, so that they cannot see the light of the gospel of the glory of Christ, who is the image of God." The Lord asked in Jer. 6:10, "To whom can I speak and give warning? Who will listen to me? Their ears are closed so they cannot hear. The word of the Lord is offensive to them; they find no pleasure in it." These Pharisees were supposed to be the shepherds of the people of Israel but as a result of their spiritual blindness the people suffered much harm. Many were led astray by these false shepherds who are not sincere and honest. They are deceptive and have hidden agendas. They use people for their own benefit and care not about the destruction they cause in the lives of others. Ezek. 34:4,5 says, "The weak you have not strengthened, nor have you healed those who were sick, nor bound up the broken, nor brought back what was driven away, nor sought what was lost; but with force and cruelty you have ruled them. So they were scattered because there was no shepherd; and they became food for all the beasts of the field when they were scattered."

In the Bible the leaders of the church are described as shepherds and the people are the flock. It is the duty of these shepherds to feed and protect the flock and not use their position as a means to exercise controlling power over them. God takes this seriously and He said in Jer. 23:1, "Woe to the shepherds who destroy and scatter the sheep of My pasture!" Sheep need a shepherd because they are the most helpless of all animals. If left to themselves they'd get lost for they are incapable of finding their way back to the flock even if it is in plain sight. They are feeble and utterly powerless against savage predators. They don't defend themselves nor do they run away. They just stand still and become an easy target for those wild beasts who wish to have them for their next meal. They fear moving water and will only drink from a stream or a lake that is perfectly still. Sheep are totally dependent upon their shepherd who would lead them to still waters and lush pastures to graze in. In the heat of the day they'd be led to shady places where they lie down and rest. When the sun begins to set the shepherd leads the sheep to the protection of a sheepfold.

Jesus continues His rebuke of these false shepherds in John 10:1,2, "Most assuredly, I say to you, he who does not enter the sheepfold by the door, but climbs up some other way, the same is a thief and a robber. But he who enters by the door is the shepherd of the sheep." Each village and city had a sheepfold which is a large walled in area where shepherds would bring their sheep at night. The walls of these public sheepfolds were made of loosely stacked stones and they enclosed an area large enough to hold several flocks of sheep. A hired doorkeeper would be stationed at the entrance of the sheepfold where he would watch over and guard the sheep while the shepherds slept. In the morning the shepherds would come to get their sheep. They didn't climb over the wall but rather went to the door of the sheepfold. Thieves and robbers, however, didn't go through the door but instead would climb over the wall in an effort to steal the sheep. Jesus is calling these Pharisees false shepherds who gained their power and authority over God's people in an illegitimate way and thus they are thieves and robbers.

Jesus is saying to these Pharisees that they are taking what doesn't belong to them. They have gained their position not out of a love for God and a desire to serve His people but rather out of their own self-interest. He says in vs. 3, "To him the doorkeeper opens, and the sheep hear his voice; and he calls his own sheep by name and leads them out." The doorkeeper would recognize the shepherd and let him in to the sheepfold to get his sheep. The sheep were mingled together with the sheep of other flocks but they knew the voice of their shepherd and came to him when he called. "And when he brings out his own sheep, he goes before them; and the sheep follow him, for they know his voice. Yet they will by no means follow a stranger, but will flee from him, for they do not know the voice of strangers" (vs. 4,5). The voices you're listening to are the shepherds of your life. Whose voice are you listening to? Don't listen to the voice of Hollywood or the evening news but instead listen to the voice of Jesus. There's a lot of noise in the world but still Jesus says, "My sheep hear My voice."

Most people when they talk to God only have a one-way conversation with Him. They do all the talking and expect Him to do all the listening. They're not interested in what He has to say as long as they can get off their chest what's bothering them. There is something selfish about all this. These people need to learn to be still long enough to know that He is God. They need to be quiet and take the time to listen for His still, small voice. It's not as important what you say to God as it is what He says to you. This is why Jesus said in Matt. 11:15, "He who has ears to hear, let him hear!" The Message Bible says, "Are you listening to Me? Really listening?" How can you walk with God and follow Him if you can't hear the instructions He's giving you? The problem is there is too much unnecessary noise in the world. There is gossip in the air and music that glorifies the devil and movies that promote lustful relationships. The biggest problem, however, is the sound of one's own voice. People are talking way too much. They talk so much, in fact, that it hinders their ability to hear from God.

How do you hear from God? The first step is learn to be quiet. That's a nice way of saying "Shut up!" You can't hear God if you're talking all the time. Put down that telephone and turn off the television and send the children outside to play. Then go off into a back bedroom by yourself, get still and be quiet, and then say to the Lord, "Speak, for Your servant hears" (1 Sam. 3:10). Say no more. Resist the temptation to unload on Him all your cares and concerns. There is a time to do that but this is not the time. He already knows what you're going through so you don't have to tell Him what He already knows. You, however, have to hear what you don't yet know and this is why you have to hold your tongue and open your ears. You have one mouth and two ears which means you should be doing twice as much listening as you do talking. In other words, be still and know He is God. You give God honor and respect when you get quiet long enough so that He can speak to you. He only speaks to listening ears and getting still shows God that you think what He's about to say is important.

As common as shepherding was, these Jewish leaders still did not understand what Jesus was saying (vs. 6). These Pharisees thought they were the doorkeepers of righteousness. It was through their intercession that others could be made right with God. Jesus rebuked them for this in Matt. 23:13, "But woe to you, scribes and Pharisees, hypocrites! For you shut up the kingdom of heaven against men; for you neither go in yourselves, nor do you allow those who are entering to go in." Jesus is saying that the blind can't lead the blind. The Message Bible says, "Frauds! Your lives are roadblocks to God's kingdom. You refuse to enter, and won't let anyone else in either." This healed blind man was one of their sheep and instead of celebrating his miracle they cast him out of the temple. These leaders cared about their own glory more than the glory of God. They failed to comprehend the King of glory who was standing there in front of them. He was full of love and compassion but still they hated everything about Him. They missed the opportunity being offered to them and continued to walk in spiritual darkness.

Jesus continued, "Most assuredly, I say to you, I am the door of the sheep. All who ever came before Me are thieves and robbers, but the sheep did not hear them. I am the door. If anyone enters by Me, he will be saved, and will go in and out and find pasture" (vs. 7-9). Every city had a public sheepfold but there were also private sheepfolds out in the countryside where the shepherd would bring the sheep at nightfall. Since there was no gate to close, the shepherd would keep the sheep in and the wild animals out by laying across the opening in the wall. Here he would sleep and literally became the door to the sheep. Jesus is saying that He is the door of salvation and only through Him is salvation possible. Any religious leader who offers salvation any other way is a thief and robber. When one believes the gospel and repents of their sin, they are assured of being in the sheepfold because they've entered through Jesus, the door of salvation. Jesus then says in vs. 10, "The thief comes not except to steal, and to kill, and to destroy. I have come that they may have life, and that they may have it more abundantly."

When you know who Jesus is, it changes who you are. Jesus is the door of salvation through which you can have abundant life. In Him you are guarded and protected. You have peace and nourishment and everything you need to live the life you were called to live. It is through this door that you'll find green pastures and still waters. A door or a gate is a dividing line that separates one area from another. Jesus came to bring division for He said in Luke 12:51, "Do you suppose that I came to give peace on earth? I tell you, not at all, but rather division." There are those on the inside and those on the outside. There are those who walk in the light and those who walk in darkness. He said in Matt. 12:30, "He who is not with Me is against me, and he who does not gather with Me scatters abroad." Jesus was always making bold statements where He was clearly drawing a line in the sand. Some believe, many don't. Without a doubt, Christianity is the most exclusive among faiths. Only those who believe in Jesus can enter the sheepfold. Some sheep recognize His voice, others don't.

Out in the field the sheep grazed under the constant care and ever watchful eye of the shepherd. They slept in peace because of the presence of Jesus watching over them. He is also watching over you (Ps. 121). Jesus is committed to your welfare and nothing can get to you unless it passes through Him first. The only trials Jesus will let come to you are those that in Him you can overcome (1 Cor. 10:13). He is calling you by name and this means you are His. Ps. 147:2 says, "The Lord builds up Jerusalem; He gathers the outcasts of Israel." You belong to Jesus and no longer are you on the outside looking in. You were bought with a price and are now a member of the household of God. It excites Him when you seek Him out and spend quality time with Him. Fellowship with the Almighty is the greatest thrill in life there is. He loves you and He cares for you. He is thinking about you all the time. Ps. 139:17,18 says, "How precious also are Your thoughts to me, O God! How great is the sum of them! If I could count them, they would be more in number than the sand; When I awake, I am still with You."

There is only one door that gives you protection and blessing and that is Jesus. You enter the sheepfold by having faith in Jesus and Him alone. He is the door of salvation. He is the only door but it will open for anybody and everybody. Christianity is the most inclusive of all faiths. There is no person who will be denied entrance to the sheepfold if their heart is in the right place. Nobody is excluded unless they exclude themselves. Open your ears and listen for His voice for He is certainly calling out to you. Heb. 3:15 says, "Today, if you will hear His voice, do not harden your hearts as in the rebellion." When you hear His voice, respond to it. Do not harden your heart and walk away. Don't put off coming to Jesus until tomorrow because, for you, tomorrow may never get here. It's true, those who wait until tomorrow usually die today. You need to realize that unbelief has killed its thousands but procrastination has killed its tens of thousands. So what should you do? Allow the words of Prov. 6:14 (NLT) to burn in your heart, "Don't put it off; do it now! Don't rest until you do."

-23-

"ONE FLOCK, ONE SHEPHERD"

The land of Israel was full of sheep and throughout the Bible is the imagery of a shepherd caring for his flock. David wrote in Ps. 23:1, "The Lord is my shepherd; I shall not want." Ps. 95:7 says, "He is our God, and we are the people of His pasture, and the sheep of His hand." Shepherding was serious business and it took a man's man to be one. Constant vigilance and fearless courage were necessary to be a good shepherd. It was a dirty job filled with high risk from the elements of nature, thieves and robbers, and the savage predators who stalked the flock. Danger was all around and the flock needed constant attention. Amos 3:12 tells of a shepherd who "takes from the mouth of a lion two legs or a piece of an ear." A shepherd was responsible for his sheep and if need be would confront wolves, bears, and lions who came to steal, kill, and destroy. Is. 31:4 tells how when a lion attacks it's the shepherds who were called upon to fight the lion. The Message Bible says, "Like a lion, king of the beasts, that gnaws and chews and worries its prey, not fazed in the least by a bunch of shepherds who arrive to chase it off."

In the central region of Judea is a rocky plateau about thirty-five miles long and fifteen miles wide. Crops cannot grow here so it became the place where sheep would graze. These feeding grounds were scarce but a good shepherd would know where to find them. On either side of this plateau the ground dropped down to the desert below and the sheep would sometimes get lost or fall into the deep crevices of the rocky terrain. To those sheep that kept wandering off to the danger zone a good shepherd would break its legs and carry it on his shoulders wherever it needed to go. This may appear to be a gruesome thing to do but it was necessary for the animal's survival. Jonah wandered off and spent three days in the belly of a whale. David said the Lord was his shepherd but when he wandered off he wrote in Ps. 51:8, "Make me to hear joy and gladness, that the bones which You have broken may rejoice." Afterward, when its leg healed, the sheep would stay by the shepherd's side for the rest of its life. Jesus came so that you might have life and have it more abundantly, but you'll never experience this type of life if you keep wandering off.

There are many shepherds listed in the Bible. Abel was a shepherd as was Abraham, Isaac, Jacob, Moses, and David. Of course, the greatest shepherd of all was Jesus Himself who said in John 10:11, "I am the good shepherd." This is a bold statement considering who He's talking to. These Pharisees know Ps. 23 as well as anybody. David said "The Lord is my shepherd" and here Jesus is saying He is the good shepherd. Jesus is saying He is the shepherd David talked about and this is a claim of deity. He is the door of salvation and He is the good shepherd who guards the door of the sheepfold. He is also the shepherd your heart is yearning for. He said, "I am the shepherd, the good one." Jesus is not just another shepherd for He continues in vs. 11, "The good shepherd gives His life for the sheep." Not only is He good, but the Greek word used here says He is 'beautiful, attractive, and excellent' on all levels. He is the great shepherd because He lays down His life for the sheep, He loves them and calls them by name, and He unites them into one big happy family. These are His sheep and the intimate relationship He has with them is like the relationship He has with the Father.

In ancient times it was a natural thing for a shepherd to risk his life for the sheep. They did this willingly for it's who they were and what they did. This was more than just a job for these shepherds. The sheep under their care was their life and they would do anything and everything to care for them and protect them from all predators. Without a doubt, sheep need a shepherd for they tend to be foolish and stubborn and are prone to wander off to their own peril. They are defenseless and don't know which way to turn in life. In order to thrive, sheep must depend on the shepherd for their very survival. It can be somewhat sentimental when one thinks about Jesus being their shepherd, but it's a different matter to live it out. In fact, most people don't enjoy the experience of this type of relationship with Jesus. Are you enjoying the abundant life Jesus came to give you? Are you surrounded by the goodness of God? Are you experiencing what it means to have Jesus as your shepherd? The sheep mean everything to the shepherd. Does the good shepherd mean everything to you?

You need to embrace this relationship with Jesus being your shepherd. He said in John 15:5, "Apart from Me you can do nothing." This means you have to obey Him completely in all areas of your life. He can't be Lord over some areas of your life and you be lord in those other areas. No, He must be Lord over every area of your life and this happens when you obey Him at all times, at all costs. If He is your shepherd, then there is nothing in your life that is off limits to Him. Prov. 3:6 says, "In all your ways acknowledge Him, and He shall direct your paths." If you're going to be led and protected by the good shepherd, you need to have a moment by moment dependency on Jesus. You need to trust Him completely in every detail of your life. When you live this way, there will be no limit as to what God can do in and through your life. And when you obey Him, do it joyfully. Being a Christian is supposed to be fun so why is it that so many believers walk around with a frown on their face? Where's the joy at? Where's the peace that passes all understanding?

Joy should be a characteristic of your obedience. It's a joy to obey and follow Jesus, not a burden. He said in Matt. 11:30, "For My yoke is easy and My burden is light." The Message Bible says, "Learn the unforced rhythms of grace. I won't lay anything heavy or ill-fitting on you. Keep company with Me and you'll learn to live freely and lightly." You serve a good God and Jesus is the good shepherd. The things He asks you to do are not burdensome but are expressions of His commitment to your joy. Don't murmur and complain when He tells you to do something. Put a smile on your face and obey Him joyfully. Be thankful because there are false shepherds in the world who won't care for you like Jesus does. He said in John 10:12,13, "But he who is a hireling and not the shepherd, one who does not own the sheep, sees the wolf coming and leaves the sheep and flees; and the wolf catches the sheep and scatters them. The hireling flees because he is a hireling and does not care about the sheep." A hireling can be compared to a selfish mercenary whose only interest is personal gain.

Hired hands don't love the sheep and all they want is a paycheck. They talk the talk but run away in a crisis because self-preservation is the only thing on their mind. Zech. 11:17 says, "Woe to the worthless shepherd, who leaves the flock! A sword shall be against his arm and against his right eye; His arm shall completely wither, and his right eye shall be totally blinded." What makes Jesus so different from these hired hands is found in Matt. 20:28, "Just as the Son of Man did not come to be served, but to serve, and to give His life a ransom for many." The word 'life' means 'soul' and refers to His innermost being. Jesus not only suffered and died physically but He also gave up His soul as a ransom for His sheep. His entire soul was tortured with the anguish of the sin He took upon Himself. 2 Cor. 5:21 says, "For He made Him who knew no sin to be sin for us, that we might become the righteousness of God in Him." In other words, He became what you were so that you might become what He is. He did this for the benefit of the sheep, those who were His and for those who would one day be a part of His flock.

Jesus said, "I am the good shepherd; and I know My sheep, and am known by My own" (vs. 14). There is a dual relationship here. Jesus knows the sheep and the sheep know Him. The word "know" speaks of intimacy. Jesus knows all about you. You don't even know yourself like Jesus knows you. He knows the type of person you truly are and still He lays down His life for you. "As the Father knows Me, even so I know the Father; and I lay down My life for the sheep" (vs. 15). Again Jesus says He came to give His life for the sheep. Is. 53:8 says, "For the transgressions of My people He was stricken." Matt. 1:21 says, "He will save His people from their sins." This does not say He would save the sinful world from their sins. It says He saves from sin those who are His, those people who belong to Him. Jesus then says something very shocking, "And other sheep I have which are not of this fold; them also I must bring, and they will hear My voice; and there will be one flock and one shepherd" (vs. 16). Jesus is revealing to this Jewish audience that Gentiles are to be a part of this flock also which means you were on His mind when He said this.

The idea that a non-Jew could be part of the universal church of God is stunning and unacceptable to the Pharisees. Who ever heard of such a thing? They resent Gentiles and believe they are permanently outside the covenant and promises of God. They cannot accept that the divine privilege they think belong only to them is in fact open to all men. They believed they were God's chosen people and He had no use for any other nation. Did these Pharisees not read Gen. 22:18 where God told Abraham, "In your seed all the nations of the earth shall be blessed, because you have obeyed My voice"? Or how about Is. 42:6 that said the coming Messiah would be "a light to the gentiles"? Did they consider Is. 49:6 that also says, "I will also give You as a light to the Gentiles, that You should be My salvation to the ends of the earth"? Jesus loves everybody and this is why He said in Mark 16:15, "Go into all the world and preach the gospel to every creature." Years later Paul wrote in Gal. 3:28, "There is neither Jew or Greek, there is neither slave nor free, there is neither male or female; for you are all one in Christ Jesus."

Jesus lived and died so everybody, Jew and Gentile alike, could have intimate unity with Himself and each other. When He walked the earth He met the needs of those Gentiles who came to Him. He healed the servant of the Roman centurion, the Samaritan leper, and the daughter of the Syrophenician woman. Regarding the woman at the well in Samaria, Jesus purposed to go out of His way and minister to the Gentiles who lived there. God loves the entire world and His ultimate plan from the very beginning was to have one flock, one shepherd. This plan began with one man, Abraham, and then a family which came through Jacob. Soon the nation of Israel was born and in time the blessing spread to the entire world. The Gentiles were aliens but Jesus came and made them part of the flock. Eph. 2:13 says, "But now in Christ Jesus you who once were far off have been made near by the blood of Christ." The Message Bible says, "Now because of Christ - dying that death, shedding that blood - you who were once out of it altogether are in on everything." The Pharisees were beside themselves and their only response was to say He was possessed by a demon and mad out of His mind (vs. 20).

"Therefore My Father loves Me, because I lay down My life that I may take it again. No one takes it from Me, but I lay it down of Myself. I have power to lay it down, and I have power to take it again. This command I have received from My Father" (vs. 17,18). In other words, Jesus is saying, "I'm in control, you're not!" Jesus was always talking about His relationship with the Father and here He is saying the Father loves Him because of His obedience. Jesus is not saying He needed to do something to earn the Father's love. On the contrary, the love between the Father and the Son existed long before man was created and needed redemption. There was a unity of purpose and trust between them and love always makes itself visible through obedience. Jesus loved the Father and voluntarily did what the Father commanded Him to do. Phil. 2:8 (MSG) says, "He lived a selfless, obedient life and then died a selfless, obedient death." For sure, love and obedience always go together. It was the Lord's obedience and His willingness to go to the cross that made salvation available to all mankind.

"Now it was the Feast of Dedication in Jerusalem, and it was winter. And Jesus walked in the temple, in Solomon's porch" (John 10:22,23). Two and a half months have passed and it is the cold and rainy season and snow fell in the mountains. Thousands of people are in Jerusalem for the last of the great Jewish feasts to be founded. This feast is not found in the Old Testament and its only mention in scripture is here in the gospel of John. It was sometimes called the Festival of Lights because this feast was celebrated by lighting candles and lamps in all their houses as a symbol of their celebration. The Jewish name for this feast is Hanukkah which means "to dedicate" and is celebrated on the 25th day of the Jewish month Chislew which corresponds to December on the modern calendar. It falls near Christmas time and is still observed today by Jews all over the world. Lights can be seen in the windows of every devout Jewish home as they celebrate the freedom represented by this feast. It is not without significance that Jesus said He was the light of the world.

The history of this feast began around 170 BC when a powerful Syrian monarch named Antiochus Epiphanes overtook Israel and became the first pagan king to persecute the Jews for their religion. It was said that 80,000 Jews were killed and just as many sold into slavery, This king passed a law forcing the people of Israel to accept the Greek culture and the false beliefs that went with it. To defy the God of Israel the temple chambers were turned into brothels. An altar to Zeus was erected in the temple and on it pigs were sacrificed to pagan gods. He profaned the Jewish temple and forced the Jews to abandon their sacrifices and adopt pagan rituals. He was brutal in his oppression of the Jews and this savage persecution caused a small band of faithful followers of God to rise up against this devilish tyranny. Against all odds they defeated one of the mightiest armies on earth and drove the Greeks from the land. They reclaimed the Holy Temple in Jerusalem and rededicated it to the service of God. Ever since then the eight day Feast of Dedication has been celebrated to commemorate this great event in Jewish history.

Jesus is here at this feast and is walking under the protective covering of Solomon's porch. Each time Jesus travels to Jerusalem there is a confrontation with the Jewish leaders and this day will be no different. The rulers of Israel see Jesus as the worst enemy they could ever imagine. He openly said their father was the devil and He called them hypocrites, thieves and robbers, liars and murderers. Never have they encountered anybody quite like Him. Soon multitudes of Jews surround Him and the leaders badger Him and ask questions that will justify their desire to arrest Him for blasphemy. They ask, "How long do You keep us in doubt? If You are the Christ, tell us plainly" (vs. 24). Are You the Messiah, the King who will reign forever? What is so strange about this question is these leaders know exactly who Jesus claimed to be. In fact, they had already tried to kill Him three times because He said He was the Christ. This question was asked with great sarcasm and hypocrisy. The dark motive for this question was they were trying to manipulate Him into signing His own death warrant.

Jesus has been gone for over two months but once He shows up the hatred of these Jews is instantly activated. They want Jesus to say He is the Christ because then the Romans would consider Him to be a political threat and would put Him to death. The Jewish people, being under Roman rule, were not allowed to conduct their own capital punishment so they were looking for a way to get the Romans to do the dirty work for them. Jesus answered in vs. 25,26, "I told you, and you do not believe. The works that I do in My Father's name, they bear witness of Me. But you do not believe, because you are not of My sheep, as I said to you." Jesus had already told them who He was and every one of His miracles was a claim that the Messiah had come. Still, the majority of the Jews would not accept who Jesus claimed to be. They explained His miracles by saying He did them by the power of Beelzebub, the ruler of the demons (Matt. 12:24). They said He was satanic and possessed by a demon. Jesus said they didn't believe because they were not His sheep.

Jesus then said there are three things His sheep have and do. "My sheep hear My voice, and I know them, and they follow Me" (vs. 27). Those who have a heart for God will stop what they're doing and take the time necessary to listen to the voice of God. They will hear Him speaking in the holy scriptures and in their own heart. When He speaks you will learn things you never knew before. He'll give you assurance and direction for your life. The sheep follow the shepherd and are known by Him. Those who are not His sheep close their eyes, plug their ears, and harden their hearts to the things of God. They cannot hear the voice of the shepherd and for this reason they do not believe. Jesus tells the benefit of being one of His sheep in vs. 28,29, "And I give them eternal life, and they shall never perish; neither shall anyone snatch them out of My hand. My Father, who has given them to Me, is greater than all; and no one is able to snatch them out of My Father's hand." Notice that Jesus said you are a love gift to Him given by the Father. How amazing is that?

Jesus promises His sheep eternal life, a life that knows no end. He also promised a life that was secure in Him. You are in both the hand of Jesus and the hand of the Father. You have double protection and this gives you eternal security. You are in the double-grip hold of God and Paul says in Rom. 8:38,39 (NLT), "And I am convinced that nothing can ever separate us from God's love, neither death nor life, neither angels or demons, neither our fears for today nor our worries about tomorrow - not even the powers of hell can separate us from God's love. No power in the sky above or in the earth below - indeed, nothing in all creation will ever be able to separate us from the love of God that is revealed in Christ Jesus our Lord." Jesus protects you from predators and thieves who come to steal, kill, and destroy. Never give up during times of difficulty. Ps. 21:3 says, "For You meet him with blessings of goodness; You set a crown of pure gold upon his head." Wherever you go, the goodness of God will be there waiting for you. That is something to shout about.

Jesus then says what everybody is waiting to hear. "I and My Father are one" (vs. 30). This is the clearest, most explicit statement of the deity of Christ. Jesus made Himself equal with God and this is a staggering claim coming from a Jewish carpenter. He was claiming to have the same nature of God, just as a natural son has the same essence as his physical father. Jesus said this after declaring that the Father and the Son are in perfect unity regarding the eternal salvation of those sheep that belong to Him. Jesus and the Father are one in purpose, one in power, and one in nature. They are equally sovereign, loving, and divine. The message that Jesus is God is the message of Christianity and this is why Paul said in Col. 2:9, "For in Him dwells all the fullness of the Godhead bodily." The Message Bible says, "Everything of God gets expressed in Him, so you can see and hear Him clearly." Heb. 1:3 (MSG) says, "This Son perfectly mirrors God, and is stamped with God's nature." The people don't know it yet but this is the final public declaration by Jesus of His deity and His final call to get people to believe.

This claim of deity infuriates the Pharisees as it did before and once again they pick up stones to kill Him (vs. 31). Like a mass of vigilantes they want to take the law into their own hands and end His life. As twisted as their motives were, they thought it was their religious duty to stone Him since Jewish law said in Lev. 24:16 that "whoever blasphemes the name of the Lord shall surely be put to death, and all the congregation shall certainly stone him." In their eyes He was a man only and not God when in truth He was both God and man (1 John 4:2,3). They were celebrating at this feast their human deliverer but here they want to stone their spiritual deliverer. As serious as this situation is, there is an unflinching, majestic calm about Jesus as He answers them in vs. 32, "Many good works I have shown you from My Father. For which of these works do you stone Me?" He is literally stopping them in their tracks. As out of control their anger was, He is stopping them not with physical force but with His words. He said the works He did was from the Father and even Nicodemus recognized this in John 3:2. For which good work do they want to stone Him?

No stones are yet thrown as they tell Jesus why they are stoning Him, "For a good work we do not stone You, but for blasphemy, and because You, being a Man, make Yourself God" (vs. 33). They're lying because in the past some of His good works were done on the Sabbath and for that they also wanted to kill Him. The truth is, they did want to kill Him because of His works. The problem is they can't deny the good works He did, whether they were done on the Sabbath or not. Instead, they now go after the words He has spoken. He is saying He is God and for that He must be stoned. These Jews accused Jesus of blasphemy when it was they who committed this sin by denying His deity. 1 John 2:22,23 says, "Who is a liar but he who denies that Jesus is the Christ? He is antichrist who denies the Father and the Son. Whoever denies the Son does not have the Father either; he who acknowledges the Son has the Father also." The Message Bible says, "No one who denies the Son has any part with the Father, but affirming the Son is an embrace of the Father as well." If justice was to be accurately carried out then these Pharisees should have been throwing stones at one another.

Thousands of people are gathered around and Jesus now turns the tables on the Jews and puts them on trial (vs. 34-36). He confronts them with their own law by quoting Ps. 82:6 where the Jewish judges are referred to as gods because they were commissioned by God to play a God-like role with the people. God said the same thing to Moses in Ex. 7:1, "See, I have made you as God to Pharaoh, and Aaron your brother shall be your prophet." Jesus is saying that Old Testament scripture calls mere men gods, so why are they struggling with who Jesus says He is? What's the problem? This is an amazing argument because He uses the words of the Old Testament to make His case, words the Pharisees cannot deny. Jesus said in vs. 35 that "the Scripture cannot be broken." It is an eternal chain where a single link cannot be removed or altered. Jesus is saying that scripture cannot be changed. This the Pharisees believe and understand. Scripture is the final word and they knew it. If corrupt rulers can be called gods, then why also can't the incorruptible, sinless Son of God be called God also?

Jesus continues, "If I do not do the works of My Father, do not believe Me; but if I do, though you do not believe Me, believe the works, that you may know and believe that the Father is in Me, and I in Him" (vs. 37,38). Having faith in miracles is better than having no faith at all. Jesus is encouraging these Jewish leaders to consider what His miracles say about Him. This is the final call for these Jews to believe. It was a gracious invitation but to these people it mattered not what He said. Their minds were already made up. This man must die and they screamed out for His blood all the way up to the point where He was nailed to a Roman cross. "Therefore they sought again to seize Him, but He escaped out of their hand. And He went away again beyond the Jordan to the place where John was baptizing at first, and there He stayed. Then many came to Him and said, 'John performed no sign, but all the things that John spoke about this Man were true.' And many believed in Him there" (vs. 39-42). Jesus went away to the place where He had been baptized to prepare for the storm that was soon to come.

Randall J. Brewer

-24-

"FOUR DAYS LATE"

A very important question is asked in Ps. 121:1. The good news is the answer is given in the very next verse. "I will lift up my eyes to the hills - from whence comes my help? My help comes from the Lord, Who made heaven and earth." The psalmist knew that when pain and afflictions come, with spiritual eyes one must look to the heavenly hill of Zion, the dwelling place of the Lord. Ps. 119:50 (ESV) says, "This is my comfort in my affliction, that Your promise gives me life." Like the psalmist, you also must be convinced that God is bigger than all your problems and that He will help you in your time of need. Ps. 46:1 says, "God is our refuge and strength, a very present help in trouble." Jesus is the good shepherd and the simple fact that you have a need will bring Him to your side in the twinkling of an eye. Then again, maybe not. John 11:1,2 says, "Now a certain man was sick, Lazarus of Bethany, the town of Mary and her sister Martha. It was that Mary who anointed the Lord with fragrant oil and wiped His feet with her hair, whose brother Lazarus was sick."

Martha, Mary, and Lazarus were beloved friends of Jesus and Luke 10:38 tells how they willingly received Him into their home. They were part of the Lord's inner circle of close friends and they worshiped Him with all their heart and soul. Here was a family that loved Jesus deeply but still they had a major problem. Yes, you can love Jesus with all your heart and make faith confessions from morning to night, and still you can be attacked by the enemy. Behind all those smiling faces at church are people with real problems they're afraid to admit they have. They believe worshipers of God aren't supposed to have problems forgetting that Jesus said in John 16:33, "In the world you will have tribulation."

The Message Bible says, "In this godless world you will continue to experience difficulties." These people act like everything is wonderful all the time and they don't have a care in the world. They hide the stone-cold reality that inside their hearts are crying out in anguish. The truth is, believers have problems just like everybody else, maybe more so because of the stand they've taken for Christ.

The devil is real and so are his attacks on the body of Christ. 1 Peter 5:8 says, "Be sober, be vigilant; because your adversary the devil walks around like a roaring lion, seeking whom he may devour." The Message Bible says, "Keep a cool head. Stay alert. The devil is poised to pounce, and would like nothing better than to catch you napping. Keep your guard up. You're not the only ones plunged into these hard times. It's the same with Christians all over the world" (vs. 8,9). While it's true you should never wear your problems on your sleeves for all the world to see, what about those problems you can't hide? It is hard to smile when your spouse tells you they're leaving you for another person. You can't hold back the tears when a loved one gets run over by a drunk driver. No, problems are real and they happen to the best of people. The thing to understand is that the problem is not an indictment against you as a worshiper of God. There is nothing wrong with you although the devil will make you think there is. He is a thief and a liar so don't allow him to use your problem to make you question your relationship with God.

Don't question your relationship with God, embrace it. It's your closeness to God that helps you stand strong in the midst of the storm. Be like Paul who said in 2 Cor. 4:8,9 (NLT), "We are pressed on every side by troubles, but we are not crushed. We are perplexed, but not driven to despair. We are hunted down, but never abandoned by God. We get knocked down, but we are not destroyed." Fortunately, Mary and Martha knew what to do in the face of calamity. Lazarus is sick and his sisters do something quite uncommon in today's world. "Therefore the sisters sent to Him, saying, 'Lord, behold, he whom You love is sick'" (vs. 3). Mary and Martha sent for Jesus before they got advise from their friends or went to the doctor. It is not a bad thing to go to a doctor but Jesus should always be the one Person you go to first. It is no wonder that the Hebrew word for "Lazarus" means 'God is my help.' It is also an amazing thing that these sisters knew where to find Jesus. Everybody needs to know how to get in touch with Jesus. Do you?

Jesus loved Lazarus as a friend. The Greek word used here is "phileo" which is an emotional love. It's when a person has a deep, personal affection for another. Mary and Martha made no specific request of Jesus only to remind Him of how much He loved their brother. By saying this they are hoping to stir up the emotions of Jesus that will cause Him to come quickly in their time of need. Jesus responded to this message by saying, "This sickness is not unto death, but for the glory of God, that the Son of God may be glorified through it" (vs. 4). Jesus is telling His friends and disciples what's going to happen at the end of this story. Just like with the man born blind, Jesus is saying that He will take this bad situation and use it so that God may be glorified. "Now Jesus loved Martha and her sister and Lazarus. So, when He heard that he was sick, He stayed two more days in the place where He was" (vs. 5,6). The love mentioned here is "agape," a divine love. Jesus loves with an emotional human love and a Godlike spiritual love but still He did not come when called upon. He was thirty miles away and still getting ready for what was about to happen to Him.

Mary and Martha sent for Jesus but He did not come when they wanted Him to. In desperation they must have cried out, "Where are You, Jesus?" Have you ever asked Him this question? Your bills are past due and your child is sick and tomorrow is the day your divorce becomes final. You ask, "Where are You, Jesus? I prayed and you didn't come." This is an emergency and Jesus is no where to be found. He expressed no concern over what was happening in the house of His dearly beloved friends. They needed Him right now but still He did not come. He got word that His friend was sick but He just kicked back and hung around for a couple of days. The scripture doesn't say specifically what Jesus was doing but if He was tired or busy couldn't He have spoken a few words and healed Lazarus from a distance like He did the others? This He did not do and finally, two days later, He told the disciples that it was time to go to Bethany where His friends lived (vs. 7). This city was only two miles from Jerusalem and the dangers that lurked there weighed heavily on the minds of the disciples.

The disciples said to Jesus, "Rabbi, lately the Jews sought to stone You, and are You going there again?" (vs. 8). They don't see the wisdom of going back to the danger zone and they are very much afraid. Jesus knows their faith needs a little stirring up so He says to them in vs. 9,10 (MSG), "Are there not twelve hours of daylight? Anyone who walks in daylight doesn't stumble because there's plenty of light from the sun. Walking at night, he might very well stumble because he can't see where he's going." Jesus is saying there is a period of time that is given for the work of the ministry. This time doesn't last forever so you must go out and make the most of the time you've been given. He then said, "Our friend Lazarus sleeps, but I go that I may wake him up" (vs. 11). This sounded like good news to the disciples for there is no better medicine than sleep. Clearly they did not understand what Jesus was saying so He told them plainly, "Lazarus is dead. And I am glad for your sakes that I was not there, that you may believe. Nevertheless, let us go to him" (vs.14,15).

Mary and Martha sent for Jesus and shortly thereafter Lazarus died. They did the right thing but still tragedy struck. They prayed the right prayers and confessed the right confessions but their brother died anyway. Notice that Lazarus did not die in the presence of Jesus. Death always flees from Him. At Calvary the two thieves did not die until Jesus had given up His spirit. Jesus does not view death the way most people do. The majority of people on this planet fear death and do everything they can to outrun it. They change their diet and try to exercise a little more in hopes of prolonging their days. Jesus does not fear death and it is no accident that He says His friend is sleeping. The idea of sleeping means it's a temporary thing as well as being very restful. If one is born again then death should be looked upon as a homecoming and nothing to be feared. 2 Cor. 5:8 says to be absent from the body is to be present with the Lord. The Message Bible says, "When the time comes, we'll be plenty ready to exchange exile for homecoming."

Death is a natural thing but yet it feels so unnatural. Why is that? Because it is unnatural. It wasn't God's original intention for man to die. Man was created to live forever. For all eternity was man to walk in the presence of God. That all changed when sin entered in and with it came death and pain and separation. This is why death is called an enemy to all mankind. The stark reality of life is that everybody will die unless the rapture of the church happens first. Death is unavoidable and inevitable should the Lord tarry His return to take His people home. No one is exempt from death and all people must face the fact that some day it will happen to them. Life's final finish line is out there yet most people don't want to think about it. They do believe that one day they're going to die, they just don't believe it's going to be today. The modern day culture wants to live and let live. They feel awkward talking about death so they deny it and go off and have plastic surgery so they can look and feel younger. They can ignore death all they want but for sure, one day it will happen.

Death is not a friend but an enemy (1 Cor. 15:26). For the born again believer, while still an enemy, death is a defeated enemy. Paul said in 1 Cor. 15:54,55 (NLT), "Then, when our dying bodies have been transformed into bodies that will never die, this scripture will be fulfilled: 'Death is swallowed up in victory. O death, where is your victory? O death, where is your sting?'" If Jesus is Lord of your life, you no longer have to fear death but instead embrace life for all it's worth. The Message Bible says, "In the resurrection scheme of things, this has to happen: everything perishable taken off the shelves and replaced by the imperishable, this mortal replaced by the immortal. Then the saying will come true: Death swallowed by triumphant Life! Who got the last word, oh, Death? Oh, Death, who's afraid of you now?" Jesus is telling the disciples that their faith will grow stronger as a result of what He is about to do. Afterward, Is. 55:13 will become a reality in their life, "Instead of the thorn shall come up the cypress tree, and instead of the brier shall come up the myrtle tree."

The man who would later be known as 'doubting Thomas" now says to his fellow disciples, "Let us also go, that we may die with Him" (vs. 16). This may not have been the wisest thing to say but in these words the loyalty and courage of Thomas stands out. Here he declares that he is willing to die alongside Jesus. Real courage is when you're aware that something bad could happen but you do the right thing anyway. It's when you don't allow fear to stop you from doing what you know deep in your heart needs to be done. That is the highest form of courage. Thomas didn't have to go to Bethany but he went anyway. "So when Jesus came, He found that he had already been in the tomb four days. Now Bethany was near Jerusalem, about two miles away. And many of the Jews had joined the women around Martha and Mary, to comfort them concerning their brother" (vs. 17-19). Because of the hot climate, it was Jewish custom to bury a body immediately, the same day as the death if possible. Being in the tomb four days meant that Lazarus was probably dead by the time the messengers arrived to tell the news of his illness to Jesus.

In Biblical times the Jews did not embalm dead bodies like the Egyptians did so by this time the body of Lazarus had begun to decompose and produce a foul-smelling odor. An ugly and disgusting thing is happening in that tomb and Mary and Martha both know it. They are a very prominent family and many of their friends and fellow Jews are there to comfort them in their grief. Hired mourners would stay seven days and the women would wail and scream loudly as a traditional way of showing sympathy. Lazarus died, they put him in a cave with a stone placed in front of it and now, four days later, Jesus shows up. Mary and Martha now have an attitude and are ready to speak their mind. "Then Martha, as soon as she heard that Jesus was coming, went out and met Him, but Mary was sitting in the house. Then Martha said to Jesus, 'Lord, if You had been here, my brother would not have died'" (vs. 20,21). In a round about way, Martha is saying it was the fault of Jesus that her brother died. He was four days late and had He been there, her brother would not have died. Here is a grieving human spirit dictating to God how things should have been.

In Gen. 3:5 the devil told Eve she could be like God, knowing good and evil. He was saying she could be judge over what is right and what is wrong. This theological belief is now operating in the life of Martha when she brought an accusation against the Son of God. She was saying to Him, "Where were You? You ate at our table and You had fellowship at our house. We loved You and we were kind to You. We know You love us but when we needed help You were nowhere to be found." Her brother is in the grave, the stone placed in front of it, finality has been declared and decay has set in. Martha was saying, "You had Your chance to help my brother but You didn't come. You were four days late." Martha accused Jesus but Mary sat still in the house. This was not a reverential stillness but a stillness wrapped in unbelief. Today people sit still in church and hide their disappointment in God. They think they know what's best for their lives and when God doesn't follow their plans they get still and no longer praise Him and seek Him out. Jesus is four days late so they no longer get excited about Him.

Martha partially recovers and says in vs. 22, "But even now I know that whatever You ask of God, God will give You." Was this real faith or merely mental assent? Thinking you believe when you really don't can be worse than open unbelief. Jesus said to her, "Your brother will rise again" (vs. 23). Jesus is saying that God has a better plan. He loves you enough to not give you what you ask for if He has something better planned for you. Eph. 3:20 (MSG) says, "God can do anything, you know - far more than you could ever imagine or guess or request in your wildest dreams!" It is love that delays the answer to your prayers. It was love that told Jesus to wait two more days. His timing is different than your timing. He doesn't set His clock according to your clock. Just because it's too late for you doesn't mean it's too late for God. Martha responds back to Jesus, "I know that he will rise again in the resurrection at the last day" (vs. 24). Martha believed for the eternal future but not for the present. She believed for victory in the sweet by-and-by but not for today. In her mind, hope was lost and victory dead.

Jesus said to her, "I am the resurrection and the life. He who believes in Me, though he may die, he shall live. And whoever lives and believes in Me shall never die. Do you believe this?" (vs. 25,26). These words were spoken to a grieving sister who was mourning the death of a loved one. Lazarus had been dead four days and this was an accurate picture of the condition of mankind at that time. When Jesus arrived on the earth, man had been spiritually dead four thousand years. He came to call man forth from death to life. In the face of pain and confusion, Jesus is telling Martha that He is the only hope for resurrection. It is only through Him that anybody gets raised from the dead. The resurrection isn't an event, it's a person and His name is Jesus. Christianity is all about Jesus and He is saying to look to Him in your darkest hour. He is the light of the world and He is the resurrection and the life. Jesus is the source of eternal life, the one who has power over life and death. He ends His proclamation with a very important question. He asks, "Do you believe this?"

Jesus is telling Martha that faith is needed to experience the miracles of God. In the kingdom of God, everything begins and ends in faith. Heb. 10:38 says, "The just shall live by faith." Faith stands strong and keeps on believing even when Jesus is four days late. Heb. 11:1 (TLB) says, "What is faith? It is the confident assurance that something we want is going to happen. It is the certainty that what we hope for is waiting for us, even though we cannot see it." Staying in the Word gives you the confident assurance that the promises of God will come to pass in your life. It may not happen today or tomorrow but surely it will come. Believing that is what faith is all about. 2 Cor. 5:7 says, "For we walk by faith, not by sight." The Message Bible says, "It's what we trust in but don't yet see that keeps us going. Do you suppose a few ruts in the road or rocks in the path are going to stop us?" Faith will transform your reaction to the trials that come your way. It gives you the strength to believe that no matter what happens, you have the resources and ability to overcome and rise above it all.

People who walk by faith never quit but keep on pressing forward no matter what. Jesus describes faith as "your trust and confidence in Me, springing forth from faith in God" (Mark 5:34 AMP). Do you have faith and confidence in Jesus? Will you trust Him not knowing when He'll arrive on the scene? If so, then be bold in your faith and aggressively go after what you're believing for. Stop moaning and groaning and feeling sorry for yourself. Pity parties get you no where except farther away from the miracle you so desperately need. Jesus said in Matt. 9:29, "According to your faith let it be to you." It's your faith that determines whether or not you receive the provisions of God. He also said in Mark 9:23, "If you can believe, all things are possible to him who believes." The Message Bible says, "If? There are no 'ifs' among believers. Anything can happen." You will never get anywhere with faith unless you trust God with all that is within you, even if He is four days late. Do not forget the words of Hab. 2:3 (MSG), "If it seems slow in coming, wait. It's on its way. It will come right on time."

The question people ask is if God is so loving and so powerful, then why does He take so long to perform His work? The answer is simple. Resurrection life is not for the living but for the dead. Rom. 6:7,8 says, "For he who has died has been freed from sin. Now if we died with Christ, we believe that we shall also live with Him." Jesus allowed a hopeless situation to turn into an impossible situation. God allows things that demand from you an unwavering faith. He wants you to find through the Holy Spirit a faith that will not be shaken when the rest of the world is overcome with fear and panic. He wants you to put your foot down and boldly declare that no matter what happens, you will believe God. Ps. 46:1-3 (MSG) says, "God is a safe place to hide, ready to help when we need Him. We stand fearless at the cliff-edge of doom, courageous in seastorm and earthquake, before the rush and roar of oceans, and tremors that shift mountains." Jesus already said He would come and raise Lazarus up. He was saying He was going to do a greater miracle than heal a sick man. All He wants is people to believe Him.

Martha said she believed Jesus was the Son of God (vs. 27) but there was no true conviction in her words. Vs. 28 then says "she went her way." She didn't understand what Jesus was saying to her and neither did she ask Him to explain or help her unbelief. She did what many people today do. She walked away. How do you think this made Jesus feel? Here is one of His closest friends and she is walking away from Him. This is how people wound Jesus. They walk away and go back to their unbelief. Jesus called for Mary to come and she also fell down at His feet and blamed Him for being four days late (vs. 32). He must have thought, "Oh, no. Not you too, Mary. I thought surely, of all people, you would understand and believe." Vs. 33 says, "Therefore, when Jesus saw her weeping, and the Jews who came with her weeping, He groaned in the spirit, and was troubled." The Message Bible says "a deep anger welled up within Him." This is the same Greek term used to describe the snorting of a horse. It means "to snort with anger, to be indignant." Jesus is upset because of the feeling of hopelessness in the people.

Jesus looks around and there is nobody believing Him. The Jews hate Him, His disciples don't understand what's going on, and His inner circle of close friends are blaming Him for their brother's death. Where's the faith? Luke 18:8 (NLT) asks, "But when the Son of Man returns, how many will He find on the earth who have faith?" If these people had believed they would not have put the body of Lazarus in the tomb. They would have waited for Jesus to arrive. In 2 Kings 4 the Shunammite woman's son died but she didn't bury him. She laid him on the bed and went out to search for the man of God who came and raised him back to life. She confessed that "all is well" (vs. 26) and eventually all was well. These weeping people need to remember the words of Is. 55:11 (MSG), "So will the words that come out of my mouth not come back empty-handed. They'll do the work I sent them to do, they'll complete the assignment I gave them." Jesus will do what He said He would do. It will be a work so profound and so amazing that nobody can deny it happened.

Jesus asked, "Where have you laid him?" They said to Him, "Lord, come and see" (vs. 34). Jesus wanted them to show Him the place where they had given up, the place where they stopped believing He could do the impossible. Vs. 35 then says, "Jesus wept." He isn't weeping because He misses His departed friend as the Jews think (vs. 36) nor are these tears of compassion and sorrow for the bereaved. Unbelief bothers Jesus and this is why He wept. The most hurtful wounds afflicted on Jesus is unbelief and hardness of heart from those in His inner circle. Mary and Martha were His friends and so are you. Please, don't make Jesus cry. Further unbelief is expressed in vs. 37 when some of them said, "Could not this Man, who opened the eyes of the blind, also keep this man from dying?" Faith always seemed to be in short supply and vs. 38 says Jesus groaned again. All those around Him are faithless, including those in His inner circle. He is about to leave soon and go back to heaven and here all around Him are people who don't believe.

Where are the people who will trust God no matter what happens? Where are those who believe He is a miracle-working God, the God of the impossible? Where are the people described in Heb. 10:39 (CSB), "But we are not of those who draw back and are destroyed, but those who have faith and are saved?" The Message Bible says, "But we're not quitters who lose out. Oh, no! We'll stay with it and survive, trusting all the way." Jesus came to the tomb which was a cave with a stone in front of it. He said to take the stone away but Martha said, "Lord, by this time there is a stench, for he has been dead four days" (vs. 39). She was trying to rationalize her lack of resurrection faith. She needs to stop making excuses and let God be God. She doesn't understand that in the darkness He is still God. In the stench of death He is the resurrection and the life. He is still God in bankruptcy, divorce, and death. He is God in your darkest hour, in the grief and confusion of life. Martha said, "But, Lord" when she should have said, "Yes, Lord."

Jesus then reminds her of a promise He made, "Did I not say to you that if you would believe you would see the glory of God?" (vs. 40). Martha doesn't realize it yet but what's about to happen is a sneak preview of what will one day happen to all who have made Jesus their Lord and Savior. There is coming a day when the graves will open and an eternal resurrection will take place (1 Thess. 4:16,17). They took the stone away and the first thing Jesus does is He looks up to heaven and prays to the Father (vs. 41,42). He thanks the Father for hearing Him. He wanted the people who were standing around to hear Him so that they would believe He is the Christ sent by God. This is the message of the entire gospel of John. Jesus then cried out with a loud voice, "Lazarus, come forth!" (vs. 43). "And he who had died came out bound hand and foot with graveclothes, and his face was wrapped with a cloth. Jesus said to them, 'Loose him, and let him go'" (vs. 44). Other than His own resurrection and the replacing of the soldier's ear which Peter had cut off with a sword, this is the final miracle Jesus does in His earthly ministry. Some may even consider this the most spectacular of them all.

-25-

"FRAGRANCE OF LOVE"

Why did Jesus wait for a man He deeply loved to die before He set out to help him? Why didn't He heal Lazarus from a distance when He first heard about His friend's sickness? He healed the nobleman's son from a distance (John 4:50), why not Lazarus? The answer is found in John 11:45, "Then many of the Jews who had come to Mary, and had seen the things Jesus did, believed in Him." The people were able to see the glory of God when Lazarus walked out of that tomb. Long ago, Jesus spoke the worlds into existence and here He spoke life into a dead man. To the amazement of all who were watching, Lazarus came forth. What is amazing about this story is that a great crowd was there but it was a dead man who heard Jesus speak and obeyed His voice. No longer are you to live in doubt and fear "but by every word that proceeds from the mouth of God" (Matt. 4:4). You don't live by your promises to God, you live by His promises to you. You live in the strength of the One who loved you and gave His life for you. He is the way, the truth, and the life (John 14:6). He has the Name that is above every name.

In Jesus, dead things are brought back to life. He can bring resurrection life to your dead marriage and to your barren bank account. Your sick body can be whole again and your troubled mind can have peace that passes all understanding (Phil. 4:7). Jesus will give you "beauty for ashes, the oil of joy for mourning, the garment of praise for the spirit of heaviness" (Is. 61:3). He is the resurrection and the life of all things that concern you. Jesus is saying that when you believe in Him, there is a spiritual resurrection that takes place inside of you. Paul said in Phil. 3:10 (NLT), "I want to know Christ and experience the mighty power that raised Him from the dead." You also can experience this resurrection power when you put your faith in Him. Ps. 30:11,12 (NLT) says, "I will exalt You, Lord, for You have rescued me. You refused to let my enemies triumph over me. O Lord my God, I cried to You for help, and You restored my health." You can face death and never fear. You can embrace life and have the confidence that if God be for you, nothing can be against you (Rom. 8:31).

There is one thing you must do if you want to receive this resurrection power in your life. You must choose to believe. If you believe in Jesus, you will never die (John 3:16). Eph. 2:1 says, "And you He made alive, who were dead in trespasses and sins." Jesus is calling you out of death and into life just like He loudly called out to Lazarus but you must believe. Believe that Jesus is on His way to fix your problem even if He is four days late. Believe even when you don't see anything happening in the natural. Believe anyway and then you will see the glory of God and His resurrection power. God is on your side so never give up. Don't get mad and bitter if He is late coming to your rescue. Trust Him anyway even when He seemingly delays answering a desperate cry for help. Many people get a hard heart if God doesn't do what they expect Him to do. They get resentful if He doesn't show up on time so they turn their back on Him and follow the ways of the world. They foolishly think their way is better than God's way. They don't understand that perfect timing is needed to do a perfect work.

Nobody can dispute this miracle but in the face of what happened many believed while others remained hardened in their unbelief. Many people saw this miracle but nothing changed in their hearts. The need to believe is paramount to your faith. Heb. 11:6 says without faith it is impossible to please God. It doesn't matter how good you are or how many rules you follow. If you don't believe, you won't please God and you won't make it into heaven. This miracle took place close to Jerusalem and the Jewish rulers there are worried that if Jesus continues doing good works they'll lose control of the people and their influence over them. They're even more concerned that they'll lose what little favor they have with Rome (John 11:47,48). They have a total disregard for who Jesus is and the miracle that just happened. All they care about is themselves. Likewise, people today like their sinful lifestyle and refuse to come to Jesus thinking they'll have to give up the wrong things they're currently doing. These people have to realize the wages of sin is death and getting your life changed is what coming to Jesus is all about.

The Jewish rulers didn't want Jesus to come and change the way things currently were. Jesus came to bring change and this they did not want. The Pharisees thought the people would start to follow Jesus and not them or else Rome might make Jesus the lone high priest. If that were to happen, the people might want to make Jesus their king which would then cause Rome to wipe out the entire city. The Romans didn't want a new king because Caesar was their king. What Jesus came to do is far more radical than what people in the world are willing to accept. Everybody wants to be loved, forgiven, and accepted but not everyone wants a lord to rule over their lives. The problem these people have is Jesus can't stop being Lord for that is who He is. Jesus is Lord! The reason Jesus is a threat to so many people is because there is no neutral ground with Him. He's either your Lord and King or He's not. These Jewish leaders certainly saw Jesus as a menace to their way of life. They exaggerated His threat to the temple and nation and moved to protect their own position of power and authority even if it meant killing Him.

Caiaphas, who was high priest at that time, said, "You don't know what you're talking about! You don't realize that it's better for you that one man should die for the people than for the whole nation to be destroyed" (John 11:49,50 NLT). Caiaphas was saying it was better for Jesus to die than to have the nation in trouble with Rome. Unbeknown to him, God had another purpose for the words he spoke. This high priest unwittingly gave a prophecy that was more true than he could possibly imagine. This shows that God can use any person He wants to get His message to the people. This priest is speaking of an important theological truth called "substitutional atonement." He is saying that one person can pay the price for all the wrong the people did. God was saying through Caiaphas that the people couldn't pay the price for sin themselves and that it had to be done by a substitute. This high priest probably doesn't realize he's saying it but he's telling the people that Jesus is to be that substitute. He would pay the price for sin for both the Jew and the Gentile (vs. 51,52).

Not only is God a God of love but He is also a God of justice. He is a holy God who says a price must be paid for sin. God loves you but He never stops being holy and just. For this reason He has chosen the death of a substitute to pave the way for salvation. This plan cannot violate who God is. He is the One who upholds the moral code of the universe so everything must be holy and just because He is holy and just. People are not this way and this is why Jesus went to the cross in your place. He became your substitute and the price was paid on Calvary's tree. Instead of you having to die, Jesus died for you and everyone else. Rom. 3:24,25 (MSG) says, "Out of sheer generosity He put us in right standing with Himself. A pure gift. He got us out of the mess we're in and restored us to where He always wanted us to be. And He did it by means of Jesus Christ. God sacrificed Jesus on the altar of the world to clear the world of sin. Having faith in Him sets us in the clear." The Amplified Bible says, "In His divine forbearance He has passed over and ignored former sins without punishment."

John 11:53 says, "Then from that day on they plotted to put Him to death." These chief priests and Pharisees didn't try to talk to Jesus because they didn't want to hear what He had to say. He was a threat to their control over the people and for that He must die. Jesus no longer walked openly among the Jews but traveled thirteen miles to the wild, uncultivated hill country northeast of Jerusalem. He went to a small village called Ephraim which is near the Judean desert and there He remained with His disciples (vs. 54). By this time Jerusalem was beginning to fill up with people because the feast of Passover was near. They came early to go through the necessary washings in order to ensure ceremonial cleanness. They knew that Jesus had been declared an outlaw and many wondered if He would even show up at the feast. If so, the Jewish leaders would arrest, try, and execute Him then and there. A command went out that if anyone knew where Jesus was, they were to report it so that they might seize Him (vs. 57). They don't realize it yet but Jesus is about to become the bravest outlaw of all time.

"Then, six days before the Passover, Jesus came to Bethany, where Lazarus was who had been dead, who He had raised from the dead" (John 12:1). Thousands upon thousands of people are pouring into Jerusalem and Bethany was one of the places outside the city limits where the overflow of people could find lodging during the feast. It is six days before Jesus goes to the cross and He returns to Bethany where He chooses to spend His closing hours with His beloved friends. "There they made Him a supper; and Martha served, but Lazarus was one of those who sat at the table with Him" (vs. 2). This evening meal was at the home of Simon the leper (Matt. 26:6). Since there was no cure for leprosy, it can rightly be assumed that this man had been healed by Jesus at some point in time. This had to have happened because if he was still a leper he wouldn't be allowed to come in contact with other people. This was a meal given to honor Jesus and noble service is needed to give Him the honor He is due.

Here at this gathering is seen the heartfelt service of Martha. She is a good woman with a heart of gold. Scripture speaks highly of those who serve and one day in heaven Jesus will say to those who do, "Well done, good and faithful servant" (Matt. 25:21). Martha was in the forefront of those serving for this is who she is and this is what she did. She is a practical, down to earth woman who showed her love for Jesus with the work of her hands. She always gave what she could showing that it's just as important to serve Jesus in the kitchen as it is behind a pulpit. The Bible gives honor to those who serve and even Jesus said in Matt. 20:26, "Whoever desires to become great among you, let him be your servant." Jesus came to be the example for all people to follow and He said in Luke 22:27, "I am among you as the One who serves." Martha is serving because she loves Jesus and those who are with Him. She needs to be thought of with reverence instead of being degraded because of the one time she complained because Mary wasn't helping her (Luke 10:41).

The nobility of serving is best expressed in Luke 12:37 (NLT) where Jesus said, "The servants who are ready and waiting for His return will be rewarded. I tell you the truth, He himself will seat them, put on an apron, and serve them as they sit and eat!" Jesus is saying if you'll serve Him here on earth, He'll serve you in heaven. That is a staggering thought. The Message Bible says, "Lucky the servants whom the Master finds on watch! He'll put on an apron, sit them at the table, and serve them a meal, sharing His wedding feast with them." If you love Jesus you will serve Him with all your heart and soul like Martha did. You will also give Him that which means the most to you. "Then Mary took a pound of very costly oil of spikenard, anointed the feet of Jesus, and wiped His feet with her hair. And the house was filled with the fragrance of the oil" (John 12:3). Mary took the most precious thing she possessed and gave it to Jesus. By doing this she expressed the lavish nature of her affection for Jesus, the sacrificial and unrestrained love she had for her Lord.

The spikenard plant is a very rare herb that grows in the high pasture lands of China, Tibet, and India. This eastern Himalayan plant produced an amazing fragrance that could be captured in oil. It came to Israel on the back of camels and because it was so pure and came so far, it was very expensive. This oil was used at funerals to lower the stench of a dead body since it was not embalmed. It was also used to fill a home with a sweet smelling fragrance. When poured on Jesus it became a fragrance of love. This was a lavish way to express overwhelming love and affection. This is love that knows no limits. This is love whose only regret is that it has not more to give. It is love and devotion without restraint. Ask yourself, how lavish is your sacrificial love for Jesus? Are you willing to give Him that which means the most to you? This special oil was a gift worthy of being given to a king and only such a gift would be a worthy expression of Mary's deep love and devotion for her Master. Mary's emotions are bursting out in deep reverence and her loving heart is beating faster and faster.

Abraham was willing to offer up to God that what was most precious to him, his son Isaac. David was also a strong believer in worship that was not cheap. Araunah the Jebusite was willing to give for free his threshing floor to David for a place to offer a sacrifice. David refused this offer and said, "No, but I will surely buy it from you for a price; nor will I offer burnt offerings to the Lord my God with that which costs me nothing" (2 Sam. 24:24). The wise men believed in extravagant worship as well. Matt. 2:11 says, "They bowed down and worshiped Him with gifts of gold and of incense and of myrrh." This expensive oil was in an alabaster jar which was a white stone carved out to hold the oil. Mary broke the alabaster flask and poured the oil on the head of Jesus where it ran all the way down to His feet (Mark 14:3). Suddenly, an overwhelming fragrance filled the room. The whole house was filled with the aroma of this oil. Not only did Jesus smell of this precious ointment but Mary did too. She smelled just like Jesus. Who do you smell like?

Mary then knelt down at the feet of Jesus and began to wipe His feet with her hair. At that time women didn't sit with men and respectable women didn't go out in public with their hair down. That was the mark of a loose woman but Mary had no concern about her image among the people who were there. She was fearless and willing to take their scorn as she took her hair and wiped the feet of Jesus. 1 Cor. 11:15 says a woman's long hair is a glory to her. Mary used her glory to bring glory to Jesus. It is interesting to note that whenever Mary is mentioned in scripture she is always found at the feet of Jesus. It brings to mind the words of Is. 52:7 (NLT), "How beautiful on the mountains are the feet of the messenger who brings good news, the good news of peace and salvation, the news that the God of Israel reigns!" Those who were there had probably never seen anything like this before. Silence may have filled the room over this humble sacrifice of Mary. If so, it was short-lived when they were interrupted by the hypocritical self-interest of Judas Iscariot.

"Then one of His disciples, Judas Iscariot, Simon's son, who would betray Him, said, 'Why was this fragrant oil not sold for three hundred denarii and given to the poor?' This he said, not that he cared for the poor, but because he was a thief, and had the money box; and he used to take what was put in it" (John 12:4-6). Judas seems to be concerned for the poor but he's only concerned about himself. He is offended and angry because in his mind Mary is exercising improper stewardship of this expensive oil which was worth a year's wages. He knew the price of everything but the value of nothing. He is so upset with her actions that he scolds her in front of everybody. These are the first recorded words of Judas in the gospels and Matt. 26:8 says the other disciples sided with him. Some people think the more offended they get, the more spiritual they are. This is a deception because Rom. 14:21 says those who get offended all the time stumble and are made weak. Along with that are the words of Prov. 18:19 (CEV), "Making up with a friend you have offended is harder than breaking through a city wall."

Jesus called this man a devil in John 6:70 and he is always referred to in scripture as the man who would betray Jesus. He was an embezzling thief and greed owned his heart. His life is the greatest tragedy in all human history. He rejected truth even when he had the knowledge of the truth. Sadly, this happens every day. The world is full of people who know about Jesus but reject Him anyway. This act of turning their back on Jesus is in the very fabric of every society and in all cultures around the world. The words of Judas contaminated the air that was filled with the fragrance of love and Jesus quickly responded, "Let her alone; she has kept this for the day of My burial. For the poor you have with you always, but Me you do not have always" (vs. 7,8). This false care for the poor did not impress Jesus so He rebuked Judas and those who sided with him. He then applauded Mary by saying, "Assuredly, I say to you, wherever this gospel is preached in the whole world, what this woman has done will also be told as a memorial to her" (Matt. 26:13). Jesus is saying you need to understand what she did and follow her example.

This is a story about worship and sacrifice and extravagance. If Jesus raised one of your loved ones from the dead, what would you give Him in gratitude? What's more, being born again means He raised you from the dead. What is that worth to you? Judas did not understand that things don't get wasted when you waste it on Jesus.

He gave His all to you, it's not a waste to give your all to Him. Mark 14:10,11 says Judas responded to this rebuke by going to the chief priests and offered to betray Jesus into their hands. For the Jewish leaders, things were getting out of hand. This Jesus, a man like no other, was threatening their lifestyle. A great crowd of people came to see Lazarus, the man who had been raised from the dead, and having seen him they believed in Jesus. The chief priests even wanted to kill Lazarus thus destroying the evidence that a miracle had taken place (vs. 9-11). Yes, many believed in Jesus but they were indifferent and hollow in their belief. In less than a week these same people would cry out, "Crucify Him! Crucify Him!"

"The next day a great multitude that had come to the feast, when they heard that Jesus was coming to Jerusalem, took branches of palm trees and went out to meet Him, and cried out: 'Hosanna! "Blessed is He who comes in the name of the Lord!" The King of Israel!'" (John 12:12,13). This was a monumental moment in the life of Jesus. On the surface, this time of praise and acclamation appears to have been a perfect conclusion to three years of public ministry. The hearts of the people are filled with hope and anticipation. The long-awaited Messiah is here and ready to set up His earthly throne, or so they thought. In ancient times, whenever a conquering king would return home from battle, the people would greet him by waving huge palm branches at him. He was their ruler and they were praising him as he came back into the city. The palm was a sign of one victorious in battle, the sign of a warrior and a conqueror. The people of Israel wanted a king who was a warrior so they took palm branches to wave at Him. This King, however, did not come to divide and conquer but to die on a sinner's cross.

The people cried out "Hosanna!" which means "save us now." This is a plea for deliverance. They want Jesus to restore their greatness as a nation, to remove the oppression of those who have them bound. Ps. 118:25 (ESV) says, "Save us, we pray, O Lord!" The word "Hosanna" literally means 'I beg you to save' or 'please deliver us.' The people are asking Jesus to step up and be a warrior king. They are not asking Him to save them from their sins, they're asking Him to save them from the Romans. They want Him to be a temporary solution to their current problem. Jesus is indeed the

King of Israel but He's not going to answer their request like they want Him to. How often does this happen today? People have an agenda for their lives and want God to fit in with their plans instead of them fitting in with His plan. Do you love Jesus for who He is or for what He can do for you? Mary worshiped Jesus because she loved Him for who He was. These people with the palm branches worshiped Him thinking He could do something for them.

The problem in the world today is that modern day millennials have a belief that God is backing off and giving them their own space to do whatever it is they want to do. If it feels good, do it. People like this for it gives them the freedom to seek the fulfillment of whatever fleshly desire they may have. The problem with this is that it is totally unbiblical. Eph. 2:10 says, "For we are His workmanship, created in Christ Jesus for good works, which God prepared beforehand that we should walk in them." This means you were created to fulfill God's plan for your life. The Message Bible says, "He creates each of us by Christ Jesus to join Him in the work He does, the good work He has gotten ready for us to do, work we had better be doing." Before the foundation of the world God had already decided that He wanted you to be His servant. That is God's agenda for your life and, if the truth be told, it matters not what your own personal agenda is if it doesn't line up with God's plan for your life. He came to give you life more abundantly and then He transforms you into His servant.

Then Jesus, when He had found a young donkey, sat on it; as it is written: 'Fear not, daughter of Zion; Behold, your King is coming, sitting on a donkey's colt'" (vs. 14,15). This event happened on the tenth day of the Jewish month Nisan. This was the day Jewish families would select a spotless lamb that would be sacrificed on the fourteenth day in honor of the Passover. It is interesting that on this very day Jesus is riding into Jerusalem on a donkey, presenting Himself to the nation as the spotless Lamb of God. What courage Jesus displayed! He knew the Jews were seeking to kill Him yet He rode before them all. Why didn't Jesus ride on a huge, white horse? The answer is that He's not your normal king. He is different from what the people were used to. He entered the city in a humble way, on a young colt that had never been ridden. A king who rode on a big horse came to bring war, Jesus rode on a small donkey because He wanted to bring peace between God and man. The people wanted a warrior king but Jesus came to be the Prince of Peace. For sure, the most important thing you can have on earth is peace between you and God.

The people found out that Jesus was coming into Jerusalem and they rushed out to meet Him. They are a religious crowd in town for a religious festival and they are hoping Jesus will be a breath of fresh air in a climate of stagnant religion. They wanted something that would go beyond their common, hollow religious experience. For many, the yearly rituals they had to go through may have become a little too monotonous so they were looking for something that would spark their interest in God once again. They wanted something more than what their religion was offering. Christianity is not a religion but is a relationship between you and God. People who act religious but don't have Jesus in their heart have a form of godliness but reject the power that can make them holy (2 Tim. 3:5). The Message Bible says, "They'll make a show of religion, but behind the scenes they're animals. Stay clear of these people." Religion without Jesus is so bad that the Bible warns in the last days much of the opposition to true Christianity will not come from outside the church but from within (Acts 20:29,30; 2 Peter 2:1,2).

There is a big difference between Jesus and the practice of stale religion. Religion boasts that it doesn't smoke or drink but yet it sits around and does nothing to advance the kingdom of God. Religious people always say "thou shall not" while Jesus invites you to come as you are and watch what He can do through your life. He is more concerned about what's in your heart than in the deeds you do. Religion puts up barriers, Jesus pulls down barriers. He said in Matt. 11:28, "Come to Me, all you who labor and are heavy laden, and I will give you rest." Religion says you work your way into heaven, Jesus says, "I am the way." The religion of human achievement is not what the gospel is all about. The true gospel is about divine achievement. It's about what Jesus did on the cross and His resurrection three days later. This day Jesus was riding on a donkey and the crowd cheered Him on, the same people who would soon cry out for His death. These people don't realize it yet but at the end of the age Jesus will return riding on a huge, white horse (Rev. 19:11-13). What will they say then?

-26-

"FOLLOW THE LEADER"

Everybody has their own opinion concerning who Jesus is. He once asked, "Who do men say that I am?" (Mark 8:29). Most opinions about Jesus at this time were wrong and for the first time in His ministry Jesus is presenting Himself as King of the people. He is coming into Jerusalem and with great enthusiasm the crowd greets Him with singing and rejoicing. Four groups of people observed the triumphal entry of Jesus into Jerusalem. The disciples were there (vs. 16) as well as those who witnessed Lazarus being raised from the dead (vs. 17). There were those who heard from these witnesses (vs. 18) and then there were the Pharisees (vs. 19). They feel frustrated and helpless. Nothing they can do will stop the crowd from cheering. They can't hold back their contempt for this Man and they call out to Him, "Teacher, rebuke Your disciples." Jesus answered and said to them, "I tell you that if these should keep quiet, the stones would immediately cry out" (Luke 19:39,40). Now is not the time to be quiet. Now is the time for Jesus to be recognized as the Messiah.

The crowd of people don't understand what's going on but Jesus is going to make it very clear why He's here and what He came to do. He said in John 12:23, "The hour has come that the Son of Man should be glorified." Throughout His ministry Jesus would say His hour had not yet come, but now it has. This is the final week before His death and the time has come for Jesus to fulfill what He came to do. The people thought being glorified meant an earthly kingdom was being set up but Jesus was referring to His death and resurrection. Is. 52:13 (NIV) says, "See, My servant will act wisely; He will be raised and lifted up and highly exalted." The Message Bible says, "Just watch My servant blossom! Exalted, tall, head and shoulders above the crowd!" Jesus then tells why He must die, "Most assuredly, I say to you, unless a grain of wheat falls into the ground and dies, it remains alone; but if it dies, it produces much grain" (vs. 24). He is saying that only by death does life come. Paul said the same thing in 1 Cor. 15:36, "What you sow is not made alive unless it dies." The NLT says, "When you put a seed into the ground, it doesn't grow into a plant unless it dies first."

Jesus continues, "He who loves his life will lose it, and he who hates his life in this world will keep it for eternal life" (vs. 25). Jesus is saying that he who loves his soulish life will lose his spiritual life. You must be willing to give up this earthly life for something greater. "If anyone serves Me, let him follow Me; and where I am, there My servant will be also. If anyone serves Me, him My Father will honor" (vs. 26). Christianity is not for the faint-hearted. If you want to serve Jesus, then follow the leader of the church even to the point of death. Do what He does and say what He says. Be a doer of the Word and not a hearer only (James 1:22). Giving your life to Jesus gives you what is needed to put someone else first. This is not a natural thing to do but is in fact quite spiritual. It's how Jesus told you to live. He lived a life of sacrifice and He wants you to do the same thing. He wants you to give your life away and be like a seed that falls into the ground and dies. If you'll do that, Jesus promises that you'll find eternal life and the Father will honor you for it.

"Now My soul is troubled, and what shall I say? 'Father, save Me from this hour'? But for this purpose I came to this hour. Father, glorify Your name" (vs. 27,28). Very rarely did Jesus say something this deep. Why is His soul troubled? He's about to take on the sin of the world which will separate Him from the Father He deeply loves. The gospel of John does not tell of the agony Jesus went through in the Garden of Gethsemane where "His sweat became like great drops of blood falling down to the ground" (Luke 22:44). It is here that John shows Jesus fighting His battle with His human desire to avoid the cross. He looks around and asks if He's supposed to ask the Father to change the plan. The answer, of course, is no because Jesus understands that going to the cross is exactly why He is here. He came to defeat a greater enemy than Rome. He came to defeat the power of sin that for four thousand years have held people in its deadly grasp. He knew that if He was obedient and went to the cross, a death blow would be struck to the ruler of this world, Satan himself.

Jesus understands His assignment. He was born to die and this has always been the message of the gospel. The trouble Jesus was experiencing would ultimately become your greatest blessing. The Father answered Jesus when a voice came from heaven saying, "I have both glorified it and will glorify it again" (vs. 28). The Father spoke to assure the people that He is with Jesus at this time (vs. 30). This is the third time the audible voice of the Father is heard in the ministry of Jesus and is the only one recorded in the gospel of John. The voice of God came to Jesus at great moments in His life. It was heard at His baptism (Matt. 3:17), His transfiguration (Matt. 17:5), and here when His human flesh had to be strengthened for what lay ahead. Some people thought this was thunder while others thought it was an angel speaking. People get distracted by thunder and this is how it is when people don't spend a lot of time in the presence of God. On the other hand, if you're in continual fellowship with Him, His voice comes as a gentle whisper, a still small voice. How you hear God reveals a lot about how close you are to Him.

Jesus said, "Now is the judgment of this world; now the ruler of this world will be cast out. And I, if I am lifted up from the earth, will draw peoples to Myself" (vs. 31,32). The people got it all wrong. They think they're passing judgment of Jesus but it's the cross that passes judgment on them. When they reject Jesus, they reject the Father who sent Him. A decision has to be made. Will they receive Jesus or will they not? What they don't understand is that by Jesus being lifted up on a cross, He's making it possible for people from every race and nation, Jew and gentile alike, to find entrance into the kingdom of God. Acts 4:12 says, "Nor is there salvation in any other, for there is no other name under heaven given among men by which we must be saved." The people are confused by what Jesus is saying (vs. 34). The Messiah is supposed to reign forever (Dan. 7:14) and here Jesus is saying He's going to be put on a cross. They don't realize it but He will reign forever at His second coming. At this His first coming He's going to hang on a cross. The good news is three days later He'll be lifted up again, this time from the grave.

"A little while longer the light is with you. Walk while you have the light, lest darkness overtake you; he who walks in darkness does not know where he is going. While you have the light, believe in the light, that you may become sons of light" (vs. 35,36). Jesus is saying to the crowd to trust in Him now while He's still here. He wants them to take advantage of His presence now before He goes to the cross and gets taken from them. 2 Cor. 6:2 says, "Behold, now is the accepted time; behold, now is the day of salvation." The Message Bible says, "Well, now is the right time to listen, the day to be helped. Don't put it off." Remember, those who wait until tomorrow to give their life to Jesus usually die today. Jesus told a parable about a rich fool who thought he had plenty of time to enjoy life (Luke 12:16-20). Little did he know that God had other plans. God said, "You fool! This night your soul will be required of you" (vs. 20). Today is all you have. Make the most of it because tomorrow may be too late.

It is a statistical fact that most conversions to Christianity happen before the age of seventeen with a steep decline afterward. The more a person gets engulfed in this sinful world and gets set in their ways, the harder it is to get free from sin's deadly hold on their lives. Yes, salvation is offered to everybody and it's never too late to ask Jesus into your heart. But why put it off? Why take a chance by saying you'll give your life to Jesus tomorrow? The truth is, tomorrow never gets here. You may be alive today when the sun comes up but not be alive when it goes down. Vs. 36,37 says, "These things Jesus spoke, and departed, and was hidden from them. But although He had done so many signs before them, they did not believe in Him." John is saying here that miracles don't always change hearts. How many people have said they would believe in God if only He would show them a sign? Here he is saying the people saw the signs Jesus did and still they didn't believe. The apostle must have been surprised by all this as he quotes two passages of scripture from Isaiah that foretold what was now happening (vs. 38-41).

"Nevertheless even among the rulers many believed in Him, but because of the Pharisees they did not confess Him, lest they should be put out of the synagogue; for they loved the praise of men more than the praise of God" (vs. 42,43). Here is described the faith of a coward. These rulers believe in Jesus but don't want anybody to know it. The same thing happens today. Peer pressure and the fear of persecution stop people from confessing their belief in Jesus. To say they trust in Jesus but are unwilling to acknowledge Him is one of the saddest things that could ever happen in a person's life. Jesus says to those who don't publicly honor and acknowledge Him, "But whoever denies Me before men, him I will also deny before My Father who is in heaven." The Message Bible says, "If you turn tail and run, do you think I'll cover for you?" It doesn't matter what other people think, it only matters what God thinks. Jesus is calling you to a life of faithfulness and if that means you'll get persecuted for what you believe in, then so be it. If you do get persecuted then rejoice because you're in good company. Jesus also was persecuted for who He claimed to be.

1 Peter 4:12-14 says, "Beloved, do not think it strange concerning the fiery trial which is to try you, as though some strange thing happened to you, but rejoice to the extent that you partake of Christ's sufferings, that when His glory is revealed, you may also be glad with exceeding joy. If you are reproached for the name of Christ, blessed are you, for the Spirit of glory and of God rests upon you. On their part He is blasphemed, but on your part He is glorified." The Message Bible says, "Be glad that you are in the very thick of what Christ experienced. This is a spiritual refining process, with glory just around the corner. If you're abused because of Christ, count yourself fortunate. It's the Spirit of God and His glory in you that brought you to the notice of others." In the last few verses of John 12 Jesus speaks encouragement to those who believe (vs. 44-46) and gives a warning to those who hear but do not follow the things He said (vs. 47-50). He says that the believer

will see the Father who sent Him and the unbeliever will be judged by the very words He is saying to them.

Jesus is all done dealing with the Jewish rulers and now His focus turns completely to His disciples. John spends the next five chapters of his gospel telling what happened in the upper room on the eve of the Lord's crucifixion. The most compact, condensed, and critically important teaching of Jesus is found here in His upper room talk with His disciples. Jesus is about to die and He knows this is His final opportunity to share with them what is on His heart. He is getting the disciples ready to carry on His mission once He is gone and His words to them are intense and powerful. Luke 22 also tells of the upper room encounter but describes things that happened that John does not mention. What happens immediately before John begins his narrative is found in Luke 22:24-27. The disciples are disputing among themselves as to which of them should be considered the greatest. This wasn't the first time this subject had come up. It is appalling that Jesus is about to die and here the disciples are arguing over matters of precedence and prestige.

Jesus hears this rivalry going on and proceeds to tell how in the world system the lowest of the low always serves those who are higher up on the social scale. In other words, the lesser always serves the greater. How bewildered these disciples must have been when Jesus goes on to say this is not how it is in the kingdom of God. Luke 22:26,27 (NLT) says, "Those who are the greatest among you should take the lowest rank, and the leader should be like a servant. Who is more important, the one who sits at the table or the one who serves? The one who sits at the table, of course. But not here! For I am among you as one who serves." Jesus then goes on in John 13:1-20 and uses a physical object lesson to teach them a spiritual reality. But first, John says in vs. 1, "Now before the feast of the Passover, when Jesus knew that His hour had come that He should depart from this world to the Father, having loved His own who were in the world, He loved them to the end." Jesus loved His disciples perfectly, completely, and forever. This is a radical love that is different and far more superior than the love that is in the world.

What Jesus says and does here in the upper room is an expression of that love. The next five chapters of John's gospel is dedicated to Jesus expressing His divine love to His own. Eph. 3:18,19 (NLT) says, "And may you have the power to understand, as all God's people should, how wide, how long, how high, and how deep His love is. May you experience the love of Christ, though it is too great to understand fully. Then you will be made complete with all the fullness of life and power that comes from God." Because of that love, Jesus is about to deposit into the hearts of the disciples, and all who will believe afterward, the great riches of the kingdom of God. Jesus will die the next day and what happens here is His going-away present to His disciples. He could have rebuked them at this time but this He does not do. Instead, He puts His love on display to these weak, self-centered disciples and gives them an example of how they are to show love to one another. Vs. 2 says Judas Iscariot is in the room with Jesus and the Lord is going to love on him knowing that this man would soon betray Him.

"Jesus, knowing that the Father had given all things into His hands, and that He had come from God and was going to God, rose from supper and laid aside His garment, took a towel and girded Himself" (vs. 3,4). What Jesus knew controlled His actions and the words He spoke. He knew His hour had come and He also knew that one day every knee will bow and every tongue confess that He is Lord to the glory of the Father. Jesus knew who He was and this is why He did what He did. He rose up and put on the apron of humility (1 Peter 5:5). "After that, He poured water into a basin and began to wash the disciple's feet, and to wipe them with the towel with which He was girded" (vs. 5). Jesus has all authority and He knows He is the King of kings and Lord of lords. He is a King but He is a servant King. In His heart is unprecedented love and deep humility. The only thing the disciples thought about was their own position of power not realizing that humility is the pathway to honor. Jesus is revealing what is deep down in His heart. He is showing you how far low He is willing to place Himself for your good.

God is calling you to this same supernatural level of humility. C.S. Lewis once said humility is not thinking less of yourself, but thinking of yourself less. To enforce this truth, Jesus took the place of a slave whose duty it was to wash the feet of those who entered the house. Jesus is the King of all creation and He has taken on the lowest task of the lowest servant slave. This task was too low even for the Jewish slave. For this reason it became the duty of the Gentile slave to do what no other Jew would do. If you don't grasp how low of a job this was, you'll miss the power that goes along with it. Jesus is showing you what your life will look like once He comes to live in your heart. Never think you're too good to clean the toilets at church or to take out the trash. Never think changing a messy diaper is below you or cleaning up a child's vomit in children's church. Don't think you're too distinguished to do humble things or too important to do some menial task. Look at Jesus and follow the Leader. He is the Lord of glory but still He washed the feet of the disciples.

Jesus is doing what no one else will do. 1 John 3:18 (NLT) says, "Dear children, let's not merely say that we love each other; let us show the truth by our actions." Being who Jesus was, He didn't deserve to become the lowest servant and serve those who by nature and choice deserve only judgment. But He did do it and He is telling you to do the same thing. Phil. 2:3,4 (NLT) says, "Don't be selfish; don't try to impress others. Be humble, thinking of others as better than yourselves. Don't look out only for your own interests, but take an interest in others, too." The Message Bible says, "Put yourself aside, and help others get ahead. Don't be obsessed with getting your own advantage. Forget yourselves long enough to lend a helping hand." Your capacity to love is in direct proportion to your ability to humble yourself. The less interest you have in yourself, the more you are able to love others and invest in their well-being. Biblical love in its purest form is totally unselfish and has no interest in personal gain or fulfillment. This is why 1 Cor. 13:5 says love "does not seek its own."

Paul said in 2 Cor. 12:15, "And I will very gladly spend and be spent for your souls." The Message Bible says, "I'd be most happy to empty my pockets, even mortgage my life, for your good." Loving one another in humility gives you the assurance that you've been born again (1 John 4:7,8). Beside the cross, this is the most intense lesson on the humility of Jesus you'll ever read. If He doesn't teach you this lesson, nobody else will. He is teaching by example and, if followed, this lesson will change and transform every area of your life. God is calling you to do things that are contrary to your human nature so you must continually crucify your flesh and reject what it's telling you to do. You can't do these things on your own but Jesus Christ in you can do all things. He would never tell you to do anything without first giving you the power to do it. The power comes through the Holy Spirit and is what enables you to follow the Leader and do the same things Jesus did. This is what it means to be made in His image.

How much does Jesus love you? He loves you enough to become your servant. He said in Mark 10:45, "For even the Son of Man did not come to be served, but to serve, and to give His life as a ransom for many." This is why He came. He came to serve people and to give His life for them. You also must make this your mission in life. Jesus wants you to embrace the life of a servant and He lived His life showing you how to do that. Here in the upper room Jesus is teaching His disciples by example. They think being close to Jesus means they'll have a special position in the kingdom. They believe the greater ones receive service but Jesus is saying the greater ones are those who serve. They did not understand His logic and you can imagine their amazement when Jesus knelt down and began to wash their feet. Jesus was doing the task of the lowest of all servants. This must have shocked the disciples but nobody said anything until Jesus got to Peter who said, "Lord, are You washing my feet?" (vs. 6). Jesus answered and said to him, "What I am doing you do not understand now, but you will know after this" (vs. 7).

Peter knew who Jesus was and he knew who he was as well. It was Peter who openly confessed, "You are the Christ, the Son of the living God" (Matt. 16:16). It was this same Peter who also said to Jesus in Luke 5:8, "Depart from me, for I am a sinful man, O Lord!" Jesus and Peter have been through a lot together. Jesus caught him when he started to sink in the water, He called him a friend, and He invited him along with James and John to witness His transfiguration and the raising of Jairus' daughter. Peter loves Jesus and he wants no part of what Jesus is now doing. With false humility he says, "You shall never wash my feet!" (vs. 8). The Greek language used here is extremely strong. It says Peter was offended to the point of anger. He reprimanded Jesus just like he did in Matt. 16:22. The Lord responds and says, "If I do not wash you, you have no part with Me." The NLT says, "Unless I wash you, you won't belong to Me." This got Peter's attention. He answered and said, "Lord, not my feet only, but also my hands and my head!" (vs. 9).

Peter is like a pendulum, going from one extreme to the other. This is what happens when you walk in the flesh. You choose whichever seems best at the moment. Both responses are in the flesh so Jesus has to explain what's taking place. Vs. 10 (NLT) says, "A person who has bathed all over does not need to wash, except for the feet, to be entirely clean." Jesus is talking about spiritual cleanliness. The person who has professed Jesus as their Lord and Savior and receives the forgiveness of their sins is completely clean. If you've been born again once, you don't have to be born again a second time. He is saying once is enough. However, as you journey down the road of life sometimes you'll slip and do things you shouldn't do. Because of this, your feet will get dirty with the muck of the world and this is what needs to be cleaned off. This is what Jesus is saying. If you've sinned you don't have to take a complete bath by getting born again over and over. You only have to wash your feet and get rid of whatever sin you may have committed. The road of worldly living is dirty and Jesus is talking about the necessity of walking in holiness.

Jesus is saying that if you don't ask to be forgiven of daily sins, if you don't allow Jesus to wash the dirt off you, then you'll not be able to have daily fellowship with Him. Sin will always separate you relationally from God. Is. 59:2 says, "But your iniquities have separated you from your God; And your sins have hidden His face from you, so that He will not hear." The Message Bible says,

"Your wrongheaded lives caused the split between you and God. Your sin got between you so that He doesn't hear." You need to continually be restored and cleansed of the sin that comes from walking in the world. 1 John 1:9 says, "If we confess our sins, He is faithful and just to forgive us our sins and to cleanse us from all unrighteousness." This is one of the greatest promises in all the Bible. Doing this will forever maintain your relationship with Christ. Jesus then assures Peter, "And you are clean, but not all of you" (vs. 10). This was the night in which He was betrayed and He informed His disciples that He knew it was Judas who was to betray Him (vs. 11).

"So when He had washed their feet, taken His garments, and sat down again, He said to them, 'Do you know what I have done to you?'" (vs. 12). They don't understand so Jesus explains it to them. "You call Me Teacher and Lord, and you say well, for so I am. If I then, your Lord and Teacher, have washed your feet, you also ought to wash one another's feet. For I have given you an example, that you should do as I have done to you" (vs. 13-15). Notice that this is not a public teaching. Jesus is talking to those who are closest to Him meaning that unbelievers are unable to do this. Only those who follow Jesus are able to put on the apron of humility and do the things He did. He is telling you to walk in extreme humility and daily holiness and to be a servant to all. He is telling you to follow the Leader. If Jesus can do it, so can you. He then says, "Most assuredly, I say to you, a servant is not greater than his master; nor is he who is sent greater than he who sent him. If you know these things, happy are you if you do them" (vs. 16,17). The Message Bible says, "If you understand what I'm telling you, act like it and live a blessed life."

-27-

"THE ONLY WAY"

The Lord's death is merely hours away and Jesus had previously implied that there was a traitor among them (John 6:70,71). Here in the upper room He quotes Ps. 41:9 and says, "He who eats bread with Me has lifted his heel against Me" (John 13:18). He said this to the disciples so that when it did happen they would further believe that Jesus was who He claimed to be (vs. 19). As the true Passover lamb, Jesus knew He had to be sacrificed prior to the Passover meal which will take place at sundown the following day. In order for this divine timetable to happen, Jesus knew the time had come to unmask the traitor for who he was and to send him out to do what he had to do. He said again in vs. 21, "Most assuredly, I say to you, one of you will betray Me." The disciples asked who it was and Jesus answered, "It is he to whom I shall give a piece of bread when I have dipped it" (vs. 26). He then dipped the bread and gave it to Judas Iscariot. At that moment Satan entered him and Jesus said, "What you do, do quickly" (vs. 27). Having received the piece of bread, he then went out immediately. And it was night (vs. 30).

It is no accident that Judas chose the darkness of the night to carry out his evil deeds. It is always dark when a person turns their back on Jesus and pursues their own purposes. The traitor is gone and Jesus now speaks to His true followers, "The time has come for the Son of Man to enter into His glory, and God will be glorified because of Him. And since God receives glory because of the Son, He will soon give glory to the Son" (vs. 31,32 NLT). God's plan of salvation is now coming to pass and Jesus is saying His death will result in Him being glorified. This will happen because He is accomplishing what the Father sent Him to do. By this time the Last Supper had already taken place where Jesus spoke of the breaking of His body and the shedding of His blood. The glory of Jesus has come and that glory is the cross. What Jesus wants the disciples to understand is that His death won't end in tragedy, but in glory. In the eyes of God, there is no greater glory than that which comes from sacrifice. In the life of a believer, it is those who make the greatest sacrifices that enter into the greatest glory.

"Little children, I shall be with you a little while longer. You will seek me; and as I said to the Jews, 'Where I am going, you cannot come,' so now I say to you" (vs. 33). Jesus is speaking passionately to His troubled disciples and He calls them "little children." This is a term of great affection and it's used in John's gospel only here. Jesus loves His disciples selflessly and His only desire is to give all of Himself to those He loved. If loving them meant going to the cross, then so be it. He would soon say in John 15:13, "Greater love has no one than this, than to lay down one's life for his friends." Jesus will soon be going away and He is speaking comfort and compassion into their souls. His words reveal the beauty and loveliness of who He is. They will set you free from all doubt and fear and will give you peace that passes all understanding. He then said, "A new commandment I give to you, that you love one another; as I have loved you, that you also love one another. By this all will know that you are My disciples, if you have love for one another" (vs. 34,35).

Why did Jesus call this a new commandment? Because He used Himself to set the example of how one should love others. This type of love had never been seen before. People didn't know what the love of God looked like until Jesus came on the scene. Jesus is saying that you are to be known by your love for others. People need to observe you doing nice things for other people. They need to know that you are always willing to give a helping hand in time of need. What are you known for? What comes to the minds of other people when your name is mentioned in a conversation? You can say you're a Christian all you want but if your actions don't back up what you say, then all your words are spoken in vain. It's true, actions speak louder than words (James 1:22). Nobody likes a hypocrite and non-believers curse the cross of Jesus when they see professed Christians acting and talking in an ungodly way. It is quite possible that the carnal actions of some believers may have driven people away from Christ rather than drawing them into the kingdom. Woe to them that causes this to happen.

Lam. 5:16 says, "The crown has fallen from our head; Woe to us, for we have sinned!" Jesus said in Luke 17:1 (NIV), "Things that cause people to stumble are bound to come, but woe to anyone through whom they come." The Message Bible says, "Hard trials and temptations are bound to come, but too bad for whoever brings them on!" Here in the upper room Jesus is laying down His farewell commandment to His disciples. He is saying to love "as I have loved you." It is no exaggeration to say that love is the theme of the entire New Testament. For sure, the mark of a true believer is love. It is a love so deep and so full of God Himself that one is able to love even those who persecute them for what they believe in. The world doesn't condemn other religions because of the fear of retaliation. On the other hand, they don't fear persecuting Christians because they know in return they'll receive love and forgiveness (Matt. 5:44). This is the difference between Christianity and all other religions in the world. Christianity is marked by unconditional love for this is the manifested evidence of a transformed life.

Peter, being who he was, seems to have let the words of Jesus go in one ear and out the other. He is more concerned about Jesus going away than he is about the love command Jesus had just given him. He asked, "Lord, where are you going?" Jesus answered him, "Where I am going you cannot follow Me now, but you shall follow Me afterward" (vs. 36). These words had to have brought tension to those who were listening to Him. One of the first commands Jesus said to some of them was "Follow Me." Here, He is saying they can't follow Him, at least not for a little while. Peter speaks up as he always does and says in vs. 37, "Lord, why can I not follow You now? I will lay down my life for Your sake." Once again Peter is more focused on what he wants than on the plan and will of God. Jesus appreciated the passion of Peter but He also wanted him to face the stark reality about himself. He answered Peter and said, "Will you lay down your life for My sake? Most assuredly, I say to you, the rooster shall not crow till you have denied Me three times. Let not your heart be troubled; you believe in God, believe also in Me" (John 13:38;14:1).

The Bible originally was not written by chapter and verse. These numbers were added much later for reference sake. This is all well and good but sometimes these chapter breaks can prevent a person from getting the full meaning of what's being said. This is what happens here at the end of John 13 and the beginning of John 14. To understand completely what Jesus is saying, you have to keep reading at the end of John 13 without stopping because it's the end of the chapter. Jesus is saying, "Peter, you'll deny me three times but let not your heart be troubled." Here is further evidence that Jesus is a man like no other. In just a matter of hours He will suffer the most excruciating pain and humiliation, yet here He is concerned about the hearts of the disciples. Jesus didn't give Peter a stern rebuke but rather a tender reassurance that He truly does care and understand. He knows their hearts are troubled and Jesus is telling Peter to put his entire trust in Him. He said, "You believe in God, believe also in Me." This is a claim of deity. These words of comfort were words the disciples could rely on in times of trouble.

For the past three years the disciples had wrapped their lives around Jesus. They left their family, their friends, and their jobs to follow Him and assist Him on His mission. They left everything and now He is leaving? They are confused and discouraged and don't know what to do or think. Words of comfort and assurance now pour out of the mouth of Jesus, "In My Father's house are many mansions; if it were not so, I would have told you. I go to prepare a place for you. And if I go and prepare a place for you, I will come again and receive you to Myself; that where I am, there you may be also. And where I go you know, and the way you know" (John 14:2-4). The Bible teaches that God always takes His people to prepared places. The garden of Eden was first planted and then God put Adam in it. The land of Canaan was filled with vineyards, wells, and houses before God brought His people in. Likewise, heaven is a prepared place for a prepared people. It is a place of extreme joy and ultimate life, a place where God will wipe away every tear (Rev. 7:17).

Jesus told the disciples "you know the way" but Thomas said to Him, "Lord, we do not know where You are going, and how can we know the way?" (vs. 5). Thomas gets a bad rap sometimes but the truth is he asks the very questions people the world over want to ask. Jesus answers him and says, "I am the way, the truth, and the life. No one comes to the Father except through Me" (vs. 6). Jesus is saying there is one way to heaven, not multiple ways. For this reason people struggle with Christianity. How can there be only one true faith? People ask this question all the time for this is the prevailing thought many wrestle with. They accuse Christians of being arrogant for thinking their faith is superior to all other religions. To the world, Christians are too narrow-minded. Certainly all religions are equal and it's up to each individual to accept whichever religion meets their needs. The world has a mindset of "anything goes" and don't like hearing that some things are right and some things are wrong. They don't want black and white, they want gray. Neither do they want hot or cold, they want lukewarm instead.

There is an exclusive truth you must understand and believe. Jesus is saying that being good and doing your best is not good enough to get you into heaven. He is saying that it is only through Him that one gets to go to heaven. Jesus is not "a" way, He is the only way, the only truth, the only life. He was a very humble person and had no modesty whatsoever. He touched the leper and conversed with prostitutes and sinners. He was always with the outcasts of society and He cared not what the religious rulers thought about it. Yes, He was very humble yet He held nothing back when He told the people who He was. He shows no modesty when He talks about Himself and His character and what He came to do. He wanted there to be no confusion as to who He was and where He came from. Without reservation He boldly claimed to be God. He healed the sick, raised the dead, and forgave sins, things that only God could do. It is no accident that He says, "I am the way, the truth, and the life." This is a radical claim and He knows it.

What Jesus is saying is very extreme because it demands a response. How you respond to what Jesus is saying is what determines your eternal destiny. You can't be lukewarm and you must decide if you're going to be hot or cold. You either crown Him as King of your life or else you nail Him to the cross. You accept Him or you don't. Jesus is drawing a line in the sand and you must decide whose side you're on. He is saying you're either in or out. There is no middle ground. God told Moses in Deut. 5:32,33, "Therefore you shall be careful to do as the Lord your God has commanded you; you shall not turn aside to the right hand or to the left. You shall walk in all the ways which the Lord your God has commanded you." Is. 30:21 says, "Your ears shall hear a word behind you, saying, 'This is the way, walk in it.'" All the Jews knew there was a way in which a man must walk. Jesus said, "I am the way." The only way to get to the Father is through Him. All other religions won't get you there. Being a good person won't get you there. No one comes to the Father except through Jesus. He is the only way.

When Jesus says "I am the way, the truth, and the life," He is eliminating all other possibilities. Most other religions don't have a problem believing in a historical Jesus. They know He existed and was truly a man like no other. What they do struggle with is His authority and His claim of deity. They don't believe He is the only way. Surely there is another way to reach God. No, there isn't. He's your only option. It is only through Him that you reach the Father. Indeed, He is the only way. What is also so amazing about this claim is that Jesus gives an open invitation to all people to become a member of His family. Nobody who comes to Jesus will be turned away. The reason you don't have to be good to go to heaven is because Jesus was good for you. Jesus lived the life you're supposed to live and, when you receive Him into your heart, in God's eyes you've lived the same life. His goodness becomes your goodness, His life becomes your life. He is the way, the truth, and the life. Believe in Him and trust in Him for He is the only way to the Father. It is only through Jesus that one enters heaven.

Christianity is not a set of rules that you have to follow. It's an announcement that the works you should have done were done by Jesus. All you have to do is trust Him and believe in Him. When you do that, He'll give you a new heart and will change you from the inside out. No other religion comes close to offering you what Jesus promises to give you. Religion says good people get in and bad people are left out. No, the Bible says all have sinned and fall short of the glory of God (Rom. 3:23). The only thing that keeps people out of the kingdom is pride, when they think their way is better than God's way. The proud are left out and it's the humble who are invited in, those who admit they can't make it on their own and are willing to believe that Jesus is the only way into the kingdom. Believing Jesus is the only way is what makes you humble. No more will you boast because of some good deed you did. No longer will you look down your nose at other people thinking you're better than they are. You know that you've been saved by grace through faith (Eph. 2:8) and that Jesus is the only way to the Father. He is the way, the truth, and the life.

Never far from the lips of Jesus were words about the Heavenly Father. Bringing people back to a personal relationship with the Father was the very reason Jesus came to the earth and walked among men. Jesus refers to the Father a hundred times in the gospel of John, over half of that amount here in the closing chapters. So well did Jesus mirror the words and actions of the Father that He was now able to say to the disciples, "From now on you know Him and have seen Him" (vs. 7). The word "know" means to personally and intimately know Him in a deep, meaningful relationship. To know Jesus is to know the Father. Philip didn't understand so he said, "Lord, show us the Father, and it is sufficient for us" (vs. 8). Jesus rebukes him and says, "Have I been with you so long, and yet you have not known Me, Philip? He who has seen Me has seen the Father" (vs. 9). To those in the ancient world, this may have been the most staggering thing Jesus ever said. Ex. 33:20 says no person shall see God and live but here Jesus says, "He who has seen Me has seen the Father."

Once again Jesus is declaring His deity as He tells of the close union He has with the Father (vs. 10,11). To see Jesus is to see what the Father is like. He had said this same thing over and over to the disciples (John 5:19; 8:28; 10:30,38; 12:49). He then said His works were proof of His deity and were signs that signified His identity (vs. 11). Jesus knew the disciples were still troubled and faint-hearted about being left alone in the world. To encourage them He gave three promises that were so tremendous one is reminded of Prov. 15:23, "A word spoken in due season, how good it is!" The first promise is found in vs. 12, "Most assuredly, I say to you, he who believes in Me, the works that I do he will do also; and greater works than these he will do, because I go to My Father." The works that Jesus did should be your works also. 1 John 3:8 says, "For this purpose the Son of God was manifested, that He might destroy the works of the devil." The Father used Jesus and He now wants to use you to do the same works. He wants you to be as Jesus in the world.

Jesus did the works of the Father, you do the works of Jesus. 1 John 4:17 says, "As He is, so are we in this world." For sure, Jesus performed many amazing and wonderful works. He raised the dead, He healed the sick, He walked on water, He fed thousands and thousands of people. Never let anybody tell you the working of miracles has ended. It hasn't so rise up in your faith and expect God to do miracles through you. Become an instrument of His miracle-working power. So what did Jesus mean when He said you could do greater works than He did? The works are greater because they're multiplied thousands of times over. The ministry of Jesus had been limited in part to Galilee and Judea but He later told His disciples to extend His ministry to the uttermost parts of the earth. Today, God manifests Himself through believers everywhere because they are indwelt by the same Holy Spirit who was in Jesus. Because the penalty of sin was paid on the cross, people can now get saved and cleansed of all unrighteousness. Forgiveness of sin is truly a greater work than getting a person healed or any other miracle Jesus did.

The next thing Jesus promises the disciples is that they would have a powerful prayer life. "And whatever you ask in My name, that I will do, that the Father may be glorified in the Son. If you ask anything in My name, I will do it" (vs. 13,14). Stop and think about what Jesus just said. If you want your life to bring glory to the Father, then let Him answer your prayers. Jesus has just been talking about His relationship with the Father. He is in the Father and the Father is in Him. Jesus is leaving soon and He wants His disciples to have the same type of relationship with the Heavenly Father. They need to trust the Father the same way they trusted in Him. Up until now they've walked by sight because Jesus was always there with them. Now, they must learn to walk by faith, to believe in what they cannot see. This is a radical change of epic proportions for the disciples. Jesus is saying that if they would pray in His name, distance would not be a barrier. He will answer as if He were right there with them. They believed in Him as a person, He is now telling them to trust in His name.

The phrase "in My name" occurs seven times in the gospel of John and they're all here in the Lord's final talk with the disciples. When you pray to the Father in the name of Jesus, it's the same thing as if Jesus is doing the praying. There are no limits to prayer, He said you could ask for anything, as long as it is in accordance with His will. Never ask for anything that is outside the will of God. The purpose of prayer is to see His will come to pass in your life. When you know what His will is, then boldly go to God in prayer as other saints in the Bible did. Don't be afraid to be bold when you go before God. He likes it when His children are bold for it's a sign that they're walking in faith. Heb. 4:16 says, "Let us therefore come boldly to the throne of grace, that we may obtain mercy and find grace to help in time of need." The NIV says you can "approach God's throne of grace with confidence." The mighty name of Jesus is full of God's authority and He's given it to you to use so that you may fulfill the will of the Father. This is why Jesus taught you to pray, "Your will be done, on earth, as it is in heaven" (Matt.6:10).

Jesus then said, "If you love Me, keep My commandments" (vs. 15). You need to stop and consider how much you truly love Jesus. The truth is, loving God is what these verses are all about. There is only one test of love and that is the test of obedience. Your love for God is based solely on the level of your obedience to Him. 1 John

5:3 (NLT) says, "Loving God means keeping His commandments, and His commandments are not burdensome." It was the obedience of Jesus that revealed His love for the Father, it's your obedience that reveals your love for Jesus. The way to become a great lover of Jesus is to appreciate the greatness of His love for you. 1 John 4:19 says, "We love Him because He first loved us." His love for you compels you to love Him back. You want to obey Him and will only be asking Him for that which is in accord with His divine will. The disciples are still concerned about being left alone and this is when Jesus gives them His third promise, "And I will pray the Father, and He will give you another Helper, that He may abide with you forever" (vs. 16).

Never are believers left alone to deal with the trials of living the Christian life. Jesus is saying that the Father is going to send another Helper to take His place once He is gone. Notice that the Father, the Son, and the Holy Spirit are all mentioned in this one verse. Some translations call the Holy Spirit a "Comforter" but in today's vernacular this is not a good rendering of what Jesus is saying. To the world, a comforter is someone who sympathizes with you when you are hurting and sad. Yes, God is always near to the broken-hearted but the role of the Holy Spirit goes way beyond that. The Greek word for "Helper" is 'parakletos' and refers to a person who is called in to help in time of trouble or need. He is there not to give pity but to encourage and enable a person to rise up and be brave in the midst of their adversity. The Holy Spirit puts power into your life (Acts 1:8) and helps you gain the victory in the battles you must fight. He will give you direction and guidance plus the power to be brave so you can do what needs to be done.

Jesus is saying the Holy Spirit will come and take His place. "He will teach you all things, and bring to your remembrance all things that I said to you" (vs. 26). The Holy Spirit is the "Spirit of truth" (vs. 17) and He gives you the life of Jesus to live. Jesus said, "You know Him for He dwells with you and will be in you" (vs. 17). No, the disciples were not going to be left alone. Jesus promised them in vs. 18, "I will not leave you orphans; I will come to you."

Through the Holy Spirit, the Father and the Son will make their home in the hearts of every believer. He said in vs. 23, "If anyone loves Me, he will keep My word; and My Father will love him, and We will come to him and make Our home with him." As a believer, God has chosen to make His home in you! How amazing is that? Wherever you go, you take God with you. God lives and abides in the very core of your being. Charles Spurgeon once said, "Little faith will take your soul to heaven, but great faith will take heaven to your soul." Your heart can become heaven on earth as you commune with God and worship Him continually.

-28-

"STAY CONNECTED"

Throughout His teachings, Jesus was always talking about change and transformation and personal growth. He made it known that He is the God who will bring the change you so desperately need and desire. A wretched sinner can now be a child of the living God. A dominating person can be transformed into a person who is tender and kind. An addict can now have self-control and a proud person can be humble. A selfish person will now care for others more than they care for themselves. Jesus says this change comes through Him. He can change a nobody into a somebody, a zero into a hero. Ezek. 36:26 says, "I will give you a new heart and put a new spirit within you; I will take the heart of stone out of your flesh and give you a heart of flesh." The Message Bible says, "I'll pour pure water over you and scrub you clean. I'll give you a new heart, put a new spirit in you. I'll remove the stone heart from your body and replace it with a heart that's God-willed, not self-willed." Jesus lived and died so you could be changed into the person you were predestined to become.

Change is coming! This is the message Jesus is giving His disciples here in the upper room. Change happened when Jesus was born, it happened while He lived, and it will happen when He leaves. He will be going back to the Father soon and from here on out the lives of the disciples will never be the same. But don't fear, He tells them. Let not your hearts be troubled. They'll soon be doing greater works than He did, God will give them whatever they ask for, and soon the Holy Spirit will come and be their constant Companion and Helper in time of need. He then says to them in John 14:27, "Peace I leave with you, My peace I give to you, not as the world gives do I give to you. Let not your heart be troubled, neither let it be afraid." Jesus makes it clear that His peace is different from the world's peace. The world thinks peace is the absence of conflict and comes from the avoidance of trouble. This is not the peace Jesus gives. He is giving you the peace of victory, the peace of conquest. No sorrow or trial can take away the peace of Jesus. You can bask in this peace no matter what your circumstances may be.

People wish for contentment and satisfaction in life but without "the peace of God which surpasses all understanding" (Phil. 4:7) they'll never have it. Job 5:7 (NIV) says, "Yet man is born to trouble as surely as sparks fly upward." Turmoil is all around and is what dominates this fallen world. This unrest manifests itself in horrible actions and is the reason prisons are over-crowded today. It is the reason people commit suicide and married couples get divorced and one nation goes to war against another nation. Everybody is seeking to be free from anxiety, fear, and depression. No longer do people want to live a life of conflict with those around them. They want peace but it is an almost impossible reality because they look for it in all the wrong places. They take drugs and go shopping and spend their weekends drinking and dancing at the local bar. They are trying to change their external circumstances not realizing that true peace, the peace of God, comes from within. The bottom line is that there is no peace without God in one's life.

Jesus is saying He will give you a peace the world does not have. It's a supernatural deposit that He's making in your heart and is the same peace He has. What is so amazing is that Jesus is saying this just hours before He will be tortured and crucified. He knows what's going to happen but here He is talking about having peace and not letting your heart be troubled. He said in John 16:33 (MSG), "I've told you all this so that trusting Me, you will be unshakable and assured, deeply at peace. In this godless world you will continue to experience difficulties. But take heart! I've conquered the world." It is through this peace that you have a sense of tranquility and well-being inside of you. You have a trusting confidence that everything is going to be all right. It's what prompts you to sing, "It is well with my soul." Rom. 15:13 says, "Now may the God of hope fill you with all joy and peace in believing, that you may abound in hope by the power of the Holy Spirit." The Message Bible says "your believing lives, filled with the life-giving energy of the Holy Spirit, will brim over with hope!"

Jesus was born so that He could bring peace to the earth. At His birth the angels praised God saying, "Glory to God in the highest, and on earth peace, good will toward men!" (Luke 2:14). In the midst of trial and confusion, you can have peace in your heart. Those who have asked God to put them on the front lines of battle will be in a spiritual war for the rest of their lives. You must face this reality because that's just the way it is for those who dedicate their lives to serving God. The devil never takes a break and he is forever roaming the earth seeking whom he may devour (1 Peter 5:8). The battle is real, there really is a devil, and it's a spiritual battle. The problem people have is they're always dealing with the physical manifestations that come as the result of this inward battle. It's not a physical problem nor is it a mental or emotional problem. Taking anti-depressant drugs won't make the devil go away nor will it give you the peace you so desperately need and crave. The good news is that Jesus promises to give you His peace in the midst of the storm.

Be encouraged knowing the devil can't devour everybody and it's the peace of God that prevents this from happening to you. Psalm 42 tells you what you must do to walk in this peace. Vs. 1,2 says, "As the deer pants for the water brooks, so pants my soul for You, O God. My soul thirsts for God, for the living God." The only time a deer ever pants is when it's being chased by an enemy. It doesn't go around panting all the time like a dog does. A deer can run very fast from an enemy and this causes it to use up its water resources very quickly. If it doesn't get to a stream soon after it's been chased, it will die. This is a thirst of desperation and the psalmist is saying you need God the same way a panting deer needs water. This is how peace comes to your life. Those who thirst for righteousness will be filled (Matt. 5:6). Ps. 62:5-7 says, "My soul, wait silently for God alone, for my expectation is from Him. He only is my rock and my salvation; He is my defense; I shall not be moved. In God is my salvation and my glory; The rock of my strength, and my refuge, is my God."

Jesus will soon be going back to the Father. He's being released from the limitations of this world and He says if the disciples loved Him, they should be glad this was happening (John 14:28). He then said, "I will no longer talk much with you, for the ruler of this world is coming, and he has nothing in Me. But that the world may know that I love the Father, and as the Father gave Me commandment, so I do. Arise, let us go from here" (vs. 30,31). Jesus knew He would soon suffer and the cross would be the final battle He would have with the forces of evil. He also knew that the devil had no hold on Him, no sin to accuse Him of. People become subject to blackmail when someone knows a dark secret from their past. But Satan can find nothing in Jesus to use as leverage. Because he can't, Jesus knew the victory would be His. Yes, He would hang on the cross in humility and shame but, because of His obedience to the Father, He also knew three days later He would rise again filled with glory and honor.

Jesus and the disciples are no longer in the upper room and are probably on the road to the Mount of Olives. He is still talking about change and surprisingly is not interrupted with questions from the disciples like He'd been so many times in the past. He has their attention as He talks not about the cross but the changes that will come in their lives because of the cross. What you need to understand is that God's idea of change may be different than your idea of change. Far too often a person's ambition for change is way too low. They can handle small changes but struggle with big changes, thus they lose out on the big things God has planned for their lives. Paul says in Eph. 3:20 that God "is able to do exceedingly, abundantly above all that we ask or think." Humble yourself and go to God saying you want the changes He'll bring into your life. Tell Him you want to become the person He wants you to be. The good news is that when Jesus changes you, He gives you a part of Himself. Without Him, no other change exists.

You can journey down the path of life with hope and expectation knowing that the Person who calmed the storm and raised the dead is committed to bringing positive change into your life. That's who He is and this is what He does. He'll transform you to the point that fruit is produced in your life. Honestly, isn't this what being a Christian is all about? He said in John 15:1, "I am the true vine, and My Father is the vinedresser." Jesus said He was the true vine because He knew there are other vines in the world you can tap into. The vine of man-made religion may have a form of godliness on the outside but inwardly its righteousness is as filthy rags. Religion says you give a part of your life and time and money to God, Jesus says He wants all of you, not just a portion. Is. 5:1-7 says the first vine was the house of Israel but it didn't produce like it was supposed to. Now Jesus comes along and says He is the true vine, the One who will produce the fruit through God's people according to the will of the Father. In other words, He's the real deal.

Jesus is the vine and the Father is the One who takes care of the vineyard. He is the vinedresser and the fruit that is produced is the fruit of the Spirit (Gal. 5:22,23). Jesus is saying that all three members of the Holy Trinity is involved in your personal growth. He next says something that at first appears to be quite shocking, "Every branch in Me that does not bear fruit He takes away; and every branch that bears fruit He prunes, that it may bear more fruit" (vs. 2). These are people who know Jesus, people who are connected to the vine, people who know and trust the Lord. Each branch receives special attention from the Father. He prunes the branches that bear fruit and takes away those that don't. Every believer is called to bear fruit and many preachers teach that harsh judgment comes to those who haven't reached a point in their lives where they can do that. They say God is an angry God who goes around with a machete chopping people away at will. They don't realize how wrong they are.

Vineyards are common in the land of Israel and everyone knows that a vine does not bear fruit if it's on the ground. For this reason a framework of wooden or metal bars, called a trellis, is set up and the vine climbs up off the ground and wraps itself around the trellis. This is where it bears fruit. The reason many believers don't bear fruit is because the devil cuts them down where they roll around and wallow in the dust of the ground. In the Old Testament the Philistines were the enemies of Israel and its name means "wallowing in the dust." Likewise, the devil is likened to a serpent whose lowest parts is in the dust of the earth. What people need to understand is that the Greek word for "takes away" is "airo" and means 'lifts up.' If a person is struggling in life to the point they can just barely hang on to their Christianity, let alone bear fruit, God is not going to come along and cast them into eternal judgment. No, He'll come alongside you and lift you up and set your feet on solid ground.

Everything is under the command of the Father and He is doing two things. He lifts up the lifeless and cultivates the living. He is working to improve your union with Jesus. He doesn't kick the branch when it's down and neither does He take it away and throw it into the fire. He doesn't abandon you, cast you off, and judge you harshly. No, He lifts you up so you can live a productive life. Never forget what Jesus said in John 6:37, "All that the Father gives Me will come to Me, and the one who comes to Me I will by no means cast out." Two verses later He says, "This is the will of the Father who sent Me, that of all He has given Me I should lose nothing, but should raise it up at the last day" (vs. 39). When you're down and out, go to Jesus and cling to Him with all your heart and soul. He'll feed you and nurture you until you get your strength back. He is a friend in need, a friend who sticks closed than a brother (Prov. 18:24). Then, when you're well and able to go on, you'll be able to bear fruit for the kingdom of God.

But wait! God's not done with you just yet. He'll lift you up but then He'll prune you so that you may bear more fruit. You need to submit to the cutting knife of God as He removes those dead things that prevent you from bearing fruit. You may be spending lots of time doing things that are fruitless. Maybe you're spending too much time with the wrong people. Perhaps you're struggling with "the sin which so easily ensnares us" (Heb. 12:1). Whatever is holding you back, submit to God and allow Him to cut those dead things from off your life. It may not be pleasant at the time but it is necessary if you are to bear fruit. Heb. 12:6 (NLT) says, "No discipline is enjoyable while it is happening - it's painful! But afterward there will be a peaceful harvest of right living for those who are trained in this way." Take comfort knowing everything God does in your life has meaning and purpose. God will never remove something that is necessary in your life. If He removed it, you didn't need it in the first place.

Pruning is the way God brings radical change and transformation into your life. You need to embrace this change and submit to what God is doing on your behalf. Everybody wants to change and the world offers you thousands of books and seminars on how to make that happen. The problem is nothing the world offers you works. It's a mechanical change. Do this and do that and change will happen. They try to bring change through outward behavioral patterns and rules you must follow but Jesus changes you from the inside out. It is a fact, in Jesus growth will come. You will bear fruit and, after that, you will bear more fruit. This is the purpose for which you have been called into the family of God. Rom. 8:29 says you were "predestined to be conformed to the image of His Son" and Eph. 2:10 (NLT) says, "For we are God's masterpiece. He has created us anew in Christ Jesus, so we can do the good things He planned for us long ago." The Message Bible says, "He creates each of us by Christ Jesus to join Him in the work He does, the good work He has gotten ready for us to do, work we had better be doing."

It will help to understand that a vine does not produce fruit right away. It takes three years for a vine to produce edible grapes. If you're starting out on a new adventure for Christ, give yourself some time. Rarely do results come forth right away. During these three years the roots are going deep into the ground and the branches are spreading out and connecting with other vine branches that are growing nearby. That way the vine will be strong enough to hold up the weight of the grapes as they grow. This is the nature of the church. Every person is connected to one another. Even though the grapes are growing and are ripe for consumption, it takes another five or six years of growth until they produce the quality with which a good wine is made. And then, when the wine is made, it has to sit and mature for a long period of time. The older a wine is, the better it gets. The same thing can be said about the children of God. Old age is to be your friend for it turns you into the best person you can possibly be. Remember, God is the God of time. To Him a day is as a thousand years, and a thousand years as one day (2 Peter 3:8).

Jesus tells the disciples they are already pruned and clean because of the message He spoke into their lives (vs. 3). They are worthy of being branches connected to Jesus because they believed in Him and the words He spoke. He then said, "Abide in Me, and I in you. As the branch cannot bear fruit of itself, unless it abides in the vine, neither can you, unless you abide in Me. I am the vine, you are the branches. He who abides in Me, and I in him, bears much fruit; for without Me you can do nothing" (vs. 4,5). The secret of the life of Jesus was His closeness to the Father. He now wants to have this same close relationship with you. For that to happen, you must abide in Jesus and remain in Him. Jesus says without this abiding presence you can never bear fruit. The word "abide" means 'to remain, to depend, to stay connected.' It means to stay in one place for a long time, even through times of trouble. Companies that produce good wine will tell you the grapes that make the best wine are the ones that stayed and remained through the struggles of a harsh growing season.

People who bear much fruit for the kingdom are those who stay in a committed relationship with God through the struggles of life. Those who stay connected to Jesus don't give up under pressure and neither is their fruit-bearing choked out by the weeds of carnal living. They abide in Jesus no matter what happens. It's because of Jesus that you get up in the morning and go to bed at night. He is everything to you. He is the vine, the source of the very life you live. Abiding in Jesus means there is nothing you can't ask of Him and nothing He can't ask of you. You're in Him and He's in you. You become a branch by believing and obeying the words of Jesus, you remain a branch and produce fruit by continuing to believe and obey. The more you believe and obey, the more fruit you will bear.

Jesus said in vs. 8, "By this My Father is glorified, that you bear much fruit; so you will be My disciples." You can't bear fruit by yourself but Phil. 4:13 says, "I can do all things through Christ who strengthens me."

God created the world so that everything would produce after its own kind. He created you in His image so that His divine life could flow through you. The best and most thrilling experience in all the universe is to be united to Christ. There is nothing greater than this, nothing more meaningful. When you abide in the vine, Jesus says you will bear much fruit. The word "bear" does not mean 'produce.' It means 'to carry' like a person would bear a burden. The vine produces the fruit, the branches carry it. You carry fruit in order to show the world how good God is. Fruit is an open display of the goodness of God and His love for all people. When people come in contact with you, they get a taste of what God is like. They're able to "taste and see that the Lord is good" (Ps. 34:8). Ps. 92:13,14 says, "Those who are planted in the house of the Lord shall flourish in the courts of our God. They shall still bear fruit in old age; They shall be fresh and flourishing."

There is no lack of power in Jesus and, when you stay connected to the vine, this same power will flow through you. Jesus says when you abide in Him and He in you, you will bear much fruit (vs. 5), you'll have an effective prayer life (vs. 7), the Father will be glorified (vs. 8), you'll abide in the Father's love (vs. 10), and your joy will be full (vs. 11). A warning is given in vs. 6, "If anyone does not abide in Me, he is cast out as a branch and is withered; and they gather them and throw them into the fire, and they are burned." Jesus is talking about branches that are not connected to the vine. These are unbelievers, those who have a form of godliness but deny the power thereof, those who are lukewarm. He said in Matt. 7:17-20, "Even so, every good tree bears good fruit, but a bad tree bears bad fruit. A good tree cannot bear bad fruit, nor can a bad tree bear good fruit. Every tree that does not bear good fruit is cut down and thrown into the fire. Therefore by their fruits you will know them." The Message Bible says, "These diseased trees with their bad apples are going to be chopped down and burned."

Abiding in the vine prepares you for action and makes you partners with Jesus in the work He was sent to do. Just as God so loved the world that He gave His only begotten Son, Jesus now says in vs. 12,13, "This is My commandment, that you love one another as I have loved you. Greater love has no one than this, than to lay down one's life for his friends." This is not necessarily a call to martyrdom, it's a call to put the needs of others above your own. If you'll do this and obey the words of Jesus, He says you will be His friend (vs. 14). The word "friend" means 'associate, partner, having a special interest in someone.' In ancient times, the friends of the king were those who had the closest and most intimate connection with him. So close were they that the king would talk to them before he talked to his generals. Before the destruction of Sodom and Gomorrah God said, "Shall I hide from Abraham what I am doing?" (Gen. 18:17). You cannot earn this friendship by being good. Jesus is saying that you doing what He commands is an indication that you love Him. Servants obey because they have to, friends obey because they want to.

"You did not choose Me, but I chose you and appointed you that you should go and bear fruit, and that your fruit should remain" (vs. 16). Jesus chose you in order to send you out into the world where you'll bear fruit that will stand the test of time. The way to bring others into the family of God is to show them the fruit of the Christian life. This is what you have been chosen to do and you must respond to your destiny. "These things I command you, that you love one another" (vs. 17). Jesus is still preparing the disciples for His departure. He is telling them what they must do once He is gone, plus He is telling them they will have to persevere in the work they've been called to do. "If the world hates you, you know that it hated Me before it hated you" (vs. 18). He is telling them to be prepared to be hated and rejected because this is how they treated Him. If the people didn't obey the word of the Lord when He was there among them, they also will not obey when the same word is preached by mere men. The world rejects those who are not like them and Jesus wants them to be ready for it.

Jesus goes on to say that there is no excuse for the people's rejection. He walked among them teaching and performing miracles for three years. They had undeniable proof that Jesus was the Messiah but still they intentionally rejected Him and chose not to believe. For this they will be held accountable. Jesus then said, "He who hates Me hates My Father also" (vs. 23). Jesus is telling the disciples that if He and the Father are hated, then they will be hated as well. This was the fulfillment of Ps. 69:4, "They hated Me without cause" (vs. 25). This warning may have disturbed the disciples but Jesus promises again that He will send the Holy Spirit to be with them (vs. 26,27). He'll be their constant Companion and Helper so that they can face all this opposition without falling. Yes, difficult times are ahead and all of them except John will die a martyr's death. Jesus is making them aware of what's coming but He is also encouraging them to abide in Him and continue to bear fruit, continue to love each other, and continue to serve in the ministry. He is saying to not pull back but to press forward at all costs.

Randall J. Brewer

-29-

"A HEAVENLY PRAYER"

Jesus had just told the disciples the world was going to hate them because of their relationship with Him. He wasn't trying to scare them but He did want them to know what was coming. He said in John 16:1, "These things I have spoken to you, that you should not be made to stumble." If they knew ahead of time what was going to happen, they'd be prepared and wouldn't fall down spiritually and be discouraged to the point of quitting. In the Parable of the Sower, Jesus warned that those who weren't deeply rooted in Him would only endure tribulations for a little while. "For when tribulation or persecution arises because of the word, immediately he stumbles" (Matt. 13:21). Jesus even went so far to say that those who did persecute them will think they're serving God by doing so. "They will put you out of the synagogues; yes, the time is coming that whoever kills you will think that he offers God service. And these things they will do to you because they have not known the Father nor Me" (vs. 2,3).

Jesus is saying that persecution is to be expected so don't be surprised when it happens (vs. 4). The truth is, if you're sold out for Jesus, you should expect nothing less. He never promised you a life filled with ease and comfort. He did promise, however, that you could live a victorious life if you would abide in Him and He in you. Rest assured that the road you're on is the way to glory. Yes, hard times are ahead but never fear, help is on the way. "But now I go away to Him who sent Me, and none of you asks Me, 'Where are You going?' But because I have said these things to you, sorrow has filled your heart" (vs. 5,6). Five times in this portion of scripture Jesus tells the disciples He is going away. They had followed Him closely for three years and it is understandable that sorrow would fill their heart. They're confused and bewildered and stricken with grief. Imagine your best friend moving to the other side of the world and being told you can't go where they're going. The good news is Jesus meets them where they're at.

"Nevertheless I tell you the truth. It is to your advantage that I go away; for if I do not go away, the Helper will not come to you; but if I depart, I will send Him to you" (vs. 7). Jesus is saying He's going away for their benefit. This is how He is. In times of need and sorrow He doesn't tell you what you want to hear, He tells you what you need to hear. Why is it to their advantage that He go away? Because now He can send the Holy Spirit to take His place and be with them forever. Eph. 1:13,14 (NLT) says, "And when you believed in Christ, He identified you as His own by giving you the Holy Spirit, whom He promised long ago. The Spirit is God's guarantee that He will give us the inheritance He promised and that He has purchased us to be His own people. He did this so we would praise and glorify Him." The Message Bible says, "This signet from God is the first installment in what's coming, a reminder that we'll get everything God has planned for us, a praising and glorious life." Jesus then tells of the work the Holy Spirit will do.

The Holy Spirit can only begin His mission after Jesus completes His. This is why it is to their advantage that He go back to the Father in heaven. Up until this point Jesus had told the disciples how the Holy Spirit would benefit them. He now explains how the Holy Spirit will affect the world. "And when He has come, He will convict the world of sin, and of righteousness, and of judgment" (vs. 8). It's the Holy Spirit who enables you to understand who Jesus is and all that He has done. It's the Holy Spirit who draws you into a relationship with Jesus. Sinful people have no ability to come to God on their own nor do they have the desire to do so. Their hearts are hard and their minds are darkened. Jer. 17:9 (NLT) says, "The human heart is the most deceitful of all things, and desperately wicked. Who really knows how bad it is?" The Message Bible says the heart is "a puzzle that no one can figure out." The world is guilty of the most grievous sin there is, the sin of unbelief. Jesus is saying if the Holy Spirit doesn't draw them in, they will never come.

God loves the world so much that He sent the Holy Spirit to convict the world that it needs Jesus. He will convict the world of sin not to make people feel guilty but to convince them that relief is found in the blood of Jesus. In Acts 2:37 the people "were cut to the heart" when they heard Peter preach. That is true, biblical conviction. The Holy Spirit convicts of sin but this is a gracious conviction. God wants nobody left out of His family and He wants the world to recognize their sin and turn to Jesus. 2 Peter 3:9 says God is "not willing that any should perish but that all should come to repentance." The Message Bible says, "He doesn't want anyone lost. He's giving everyone space and time to change." What this means is that every person who has ever been born has at one time or another been drawn to a relationship with God by the Holy Spirit. Sad to say, the majority of people don't respond to this call. Jesus said many times, "He who has ears to hear, let him hear" (Matt. 11:15). Everyone has ears but only a few are listening and responding.

The Holy Spirit also convicts concerning righteousness. Man's self-righteousness is not good enough to get him into heaven. Rom. 3:10 says, "There is none righteous, no, not one." The Holy Spirit will convict you of this and then He'll show you the righteousness of Jesus. It is in Him and Him alone that you can go to heaven. You get saved because of His righteousness and not your own. Phil. 3:9 (NLT) says, "I no longer count on my own righteousness through obeying the law; rather, I become righteous through faith in Christ. For God's way of making us right with Himself depends on faith." Finally, the Holy Spirit convicts of judgment. The ruler of this world is judged (vs. 11) and so are those who follow him. The wages of sin is death (Rom. 6:23) and the Holy Spirit lets people know that they will be held accountable for their deeds at the end of their life. The Message Bible says, "Work hard for sin your whole life and your pension is death." People know down in their heart that a day of reckoning is coming. This is what the Holy Spirit convicts them of, therefore, they are without excuse.

Jesus changes direction now and tells of the work of the Holy Spirit in the lives of all believers. He says, "When He, the Spirit of truth, has come, He will guide you into all truth; for He will not speak on His own authority, but whatever He hears He will speak; and He will tell you things to come" (vs. 13). The disciples are still confused and frightened and are not able to comprehend all Jesus is saying (vs. 12). Jesus is saying that in due time the Holy Spirit will explain everything to them. He will guide them into all truth and give them the direction they need. This will happen as the result of His power working in them. What's more, He'll even show them things that will come to pass in the future. Both Peter and John speak of future events and the end of the world in their epistles. "He will glorify Me, for He will take of what is Mine and declare it to you. All things that the Father has are Mine. Therefore I said that He will take of Mine and declare it to you" (vs. 14,15). The role of the Holy Spirit is to glorify Jesus and the work He does in your life is for the same purpose.

If you love Jesus and want to glorify Him, you'll need the Holy Spirit to help you do that. He is the Helper and His role is to glorify Jesus. What Jesus has came from the Father, and what the Holy Spirit has comes from Jesus. Again Jesus declares that the Holy Trinity is involved in spiritual growth. You can't live the Christian life on your own power and ability so don't hesitate to ask for help. Believe that God will produce in you the fruit of the Spirit (Gal. 5:23,24) that will help you walk in the way you should go. Ask the Holy Spirit to do what He came to do. Ask Him to convict you of sin, that problem you struggle with and can't seem to get the victory over it on your own. Ask Him to help you stop sinning. He'll give direction to your life and show you how to walk in love and self-control. Ask Him to help you glorify Jesus. The last thing Jesus said before ascending into heaven was about the Holy Spirit (Acts 1:8). He said you would receive power from Him and will be "witnesses to Me in Jerusalem, and in all Judea and Samaria, and to the end of the earth."

Jesus next begins to talk about His death and resurrection. By doing so, He is seeking to turn the sorrow of the disciples into great joy. He feels their pain for He knows the lack of hope is the ultimate agony in suffering. The passion of His heart is that the disciples will be filled with comfort, peace, and joy. Yes, great trauma is about to be released on Him but He knows what the outcome will be three days later. And it is this good news that Jesus uses in His attempt to turn their sorrow into joy. He said in vs. 20, "Most assuredly, I say to you that you will weep and lament, but the world will rejoice; and you will be sorrowful, but your sorrow will be turned into joy." People are able to endure great trials if they can see a light at the end of the tunnel. Without hope, life is not worth living. Prov. 13:12 says, "Hope deferred makes the heart sick, but when the desire comes, it is a tree of life." The Message Bible says, "Unrelenting disappointment leaves you heartsick, but a sudden good break can turn life around."

Jesus always seeks the joy of His people and, for this to become a reality, He gives His people hope. Jer. 29:11 says, "For I know the thoughts that I think toward you, says the Lord, thoughts of peace and not of evil, to give you a future and a hope." With all His heart, Jesus desires to give His disciples hope and joy in the midst of a horrific trial. He then tells how a woman in labor is filled with pain and sorrow but once the baby is born she remembers her anguish no more. This sorrow is replaced with an overwhelming joy that a human being has been born into the world (vs. 21). Jesus is saying their grief will be deep but coming soon is a joy that will never be taken away (vs. 22). Soon they will see Him raised from the dead in all His resurrection glory. They will then have a joy that is perfect and complete, a joy that is independent of what happens in the world around them. Because of this joy they will be unstoppable as they continue the work of Jesus across the face of the earth. Up until now Jesus has prayed for them. Now they can pray to the Father themselves in His Name and the Father will answer their requests (vs. 23-28).

Jesus is speaking to the disciples in words they can understand and this causes them to openly and loudly profess their belief in Him (vs. 30). This is the last time they will do this before His death. Jesus, however, was a realist. He knew the hour was soon coming when they would desert Him. He said, "Do you now believe?

Indeed the hour is coming, yes, has now come, that you will be scattered, each to his own, and will leave Me alone. And yet I am not alone, because the Father is with Me" (vs. 31,32). It is surprising that Jesus would say this at the same moment when they are confessing their faith in Him. He is using this failure as a way to build their faith in the future. Yes, they'll leave Him alone but His relationship with the Father is strong and deep. He knows the Father will never leave Him alone. "These things I have spoken to you, that in Me you may have peace. In the world you will have tribulation; but be of good cheer, I have overcome the world" (vs. 33). Jesus is telling the disciples that even in the darkest hour, remember that He has won the victory over sin and death.

The disciples don't have to overcome the world because Jesus did it for them. He has been having one long conversation with them that began in the upper room and now He takes one final opportunity to pray for them before He is arrested and crucified. This prayer was not prayed in the Garden of Gethsemane where His sweat became like drops of blood. This prayer was spoken just prior to His arrival there. As one studies the life of Jesus, it will be seen that He was continually praying to the Father. He was engaged in prayer at His baptism (Luke 3:21) and when He began His public ministry (Mark 1:35). He prayed on the eve of selecting the twelve disciples (Luke 6:12,13) and when He was transfigured (Luke 9:29). He even prayed when He took His last breath (Luke 23:46). This prayer in John 17 is the longest recorded prayer of Jesus in the four gospels. He prayed longer but those prayers were not written down and recorded. He had constant communication with the Father but very brief and very rare are recorded the words He prayed.

A question needs to be asked here. If Jesus is God, and He is, then why does He have to pray? When Jesus walked the earth, He was in submission to the Father. He had given up His heavenly glory (Phil. 2:5-11) and took upon Himself the form of a servant. His praying showed His dependence on the Father in His humanity to carry out the Father's plan of redemption. The Lord's continual submission to the Father was empowered through His prayer life.

His example is yours to follow. John 17:1 says, "Jesus spoke these words, lifted up His eyes to heaven, and said..." Lifting up your eyes to heaven is a symbolic posture you take when you pray, done in recognition that you're speaking to One who is above all, One who reigns over all, and One who has authority in heaven and on earth. Ps. 123:1 says, "Unto You I lift up my eyes, O You who dwell in the heavens." The Bible does not say you have to close your eyes, fold your hands, and bow your head when you pray. No, be bold when you pray. Look up and give recognition that He is Lord of all.

The Bible does speak of other postures you can take when you pray. It speaks of looking up and lifting holy hands while at other times it tells you to knell, to lay flat on the ground, and to dance before Him. Don't limit yourself to praying in just one posture but have the freedom to express yourself as you feel led in your heart to do so. John also says that Jesus lifted up His voice when He prayed. He prayed out loud showing that it is a good thing to pray verbally whenever possible. Many times when you pray silently you can be easily distracted so you pray out loud to prevent this from happening. Most prayers in the Bible are verbal prayers although Hannah spoke silently when she prayed (1 Sam. 1:13). Be sure to use wisdom and common sense when you pray for certainly there will be times when you don't want to pray out loud. Jesus is praying to the Father and the disciples there with Him are now treading on holy ground. This prayer takes you into the holy of holies, into the very presence of the heart of Jesus.

As Jesus prays the curtain is pulled back and what matters most to Him is seen as He pours out His heart to the Father in a heavenly prayer. He is about to reveal the things He truly cares about and He begins by saying, "Father, the hour has come. Glorify Your Son, that Your Son also may glorify You, as You have given Him authority over all flesh, that He should give eternal life to as many as You have given Him" (vs. 1,2). Jesus is operating in the divine timeline of the Heavenly Father and the time has come for all that He came to do to be fulfilled. He asks to be glorified so that He may glorify the Father. Jesus is asking the Father to give Him some of His glory yet Is. 42:8 says, "I am the Lord, that is My name; and My glory I will not give to another." Jesus can ask for this glory because He is just as much God as the Father is (John 1:1). The Message Bible says, "Father, it's time. Display the bright splendor of Your Son so the Son in turn may show Your bright splendor."

Jesus knows that the only way to glorify God is to obey Him. He glorified the Father by going to the cross in an act of perfect obedience. In turn, Jesus will also be glorified. The cross was not the end but it was the means that led to His glorification. For sure, the glory of the resurrection cancelled the shame of the cross. It is because of the resurrection that forgiveness is now available and with it the righteousness that produces eternal life for those who are forgiven. Jesus has all authority given to Him by the Father so He can give eternal life to those who the Father gives Him. Think about that for a moment. You are a gift to Jesus given to Him by the Heavenly Father. Eph. 1:4,5 (NLT) says, "Even before He made the world, God loved us and chose us in Christ to be holy and without fault in His eyes. God decided in advance to adopt us into His own family by bringing us to Himself through Jesus Christ." In Greek the word "chosen" means "Out, I say!" It means "to call out, to select, to elect, to personally choose." It conveys the great privilege and honor of being chosen.

In Greek, Eph. 1:4 says, "When God saw us, He said, 'Out, I say!'" In that moment, He separated you from a lost and dying world and He called you to be His own. You need to see yourself as being chosen, honored, esteemed, and respected. You are now a representative of the King of kings and Lord of lords. Being chosen speaks strongly of the responsibility placed on those who are chosen to walk, act, and live in a way that is honorable to their calling. God is saying to you, "Get up and jump in the race! I want you! I'm calling you to be a part of My team." He separated you from the rest of the world and enlisted you in His service. And He did all of this before He ever hurled the first layers of the earth's crust into existence. Jesus continued in vs. 3, "And this is eternal life, that they may know You, the only true God, and Jesus Christ whom You have sent." In a world of many false gods, Jesus is saying there is only one true God (1 Cor. 8:4-6).

There is more to eternal life than living forever. Even more so is Jesus referring to a quality of life, an "age abiding life" (John 10:10). It's about having a relationship with the living God through His Son, Jesus Christ. The Father and Son will be glorified and you will share in that glory because of your union with them. "I have glorified You on the earth. I have finished the work which You have given Me to do. And now, O Father, glorify Me together with Yourself, with the glory which I had with You before the world was" (vs. 4,5). Jesus repeats His request but this time He makes reference to His divine nature before He took on human flesh. He existed before the foundation of the world (John 1:2) and He was glorified then just as He was glorified through His death and resurrection. Jesus is glorified in heaven (Phil. 2:9-11) and He is glorified every time someone confesses their sins and repents. He is glorified in the way His people live and how they recognize that every good and perfect gift comes from Him (James 1:17). Indeed, your purpose for living is to glorify God and enjoy Him forever.

Jesus has been praying for Himself and He now begins to pray for His disciples (vs. 6-19). Jesus had revealed the Father to them and then He says "they have kept Your word" (vs. 6). This is a great summary of what a Christian does, they keep and obey the Word of God. You know that God's Word is the final authority in your life when you allow it to stop you from going in the wrong direction. The Bible will do you no good unless you're willing to do what it says. Vs. 8 says, "For I have given to them the words which You have given Me; and they have received them, and have known surely that I came forth from You; and they have believed that You sent Me." Notice the sequence here. The Word was given, it was heard, received, understood, and believed. This is what's supposed to be happening every day in the life of a born again believer. Rom. 10:17 says, "So then faith comes by hearing, and hearing by the Word of God." Jesus is praying for those who are His (vs. 9) and He says He is glorified in them (vs. 11). This should be the ultimate desire in your life (1 Cor. 6:19,20).

There are four major things that Jesus desires for those who believe in Him. His first prayer request to the Father is "that they may be one as We are" (vs. 11). Jesus is praying for unity among the brethren for He knows that oneness is a witness to a hostile world. It's sad but true that not all Christians get along. Division among believers is the primary goal of the devil in regards to the church. If he can divide, he can conquer. He knows there is strength in numbers (Deut. 32:30) and unity encourages believers to put their trust in Jesus and stand strong in the midst of trial (1 Cor. 1:10). The disciples are in the world but are not of the world (vs. 14), so Jesus prays that "they may have My joy fulfilled in themselves" (vs. 13). He is praying that you'll have a life that rises up and transcends the bad circumstances that happen in this cruel world. He is saying to not give up your joy, the joy He gives you, because of the hardship of life. He wants you to remember who you are, Who you belong to, and where you're going.

Jesus then prays for your protection (vs. 15,16). You're not of the world but you still have to live here. The fiery darts of the enemy are aimed at you and Jesus is praying for you to be protected in the midst of the trial. Jesus doesn't always take you out of the valley of the shadow of death, but He does stand by your side as He leads you through your trials. Finally, Jesus prays for your sanctification which means "to set apart for God's exclusive use." It's what happens from the time you get saved to the end of your life. It's when He transforms you into the image of Jesus (2 Cor. 3:18). He's not trying to make the path you're on easier, He is trying to turn you into a better person. Jesus is asking that this "setting apart" be done through the truth that is God's Word (vs. 17). When you read the Bible, your thoughts begin to conform to God's thoughts. In His Word is the power to change your heart and mind thus making you like Jesus and well able to adopt His mission into your own.

Jesus closes out His prayer by praying for those who will believe in Him through the word of the disciples. In other words, He's praying for you right now and this is why with faith and confidence you can say, "The Lord is on my side; I will not fear. What can man do to me?" (Ps. 118:6). Jesus is burdened with the perfect unity of His people and this is what He once again prays for (vs. 21). He knows that the growth and unity of the church will be an ongoing witness to an unbelieving world (John 13:35). This is why you need to humble yourself and do what you can to be at peace with other believers. Your oneness of heart with every follower of Jesus on the face of the earth is what He is praying for. Don't let Him down. Don't carry offences toward other people but forgive them and move on. "Love bears all things, believes all things, hopes all things, endures all things" (1 Cor. 13:7). The greatest failure in life is the failure to love. The Lord's final request is "that the love with which You loved Me may be in them, and I in them" (vs. 26). It is this love, God's love, that will be the strongest bond that produces unity in the body of Christ.

Randall J. Brewer

-30-

"BETRAYED AND DENIED"

The hour has now come for Jesus to fulfill the purpose for which He was born and He spends His final moments with the disciples teaching them and giving them words of exhortation. He expresses His love for them because of their faith and prays that they will be one as He and the Father are one. "When Jesus had spoken these words, He went out with His disciples over the Brook Kidron, where there was a garden, which He and the disciples entered" (John 18:1). Going to the Garden of Gethsemane was no accident. According to Old Testament law, the sin offering was killed and sacrificed outside the camp (Lev. 16:27). This garden was on the slopes of the Mount of Olives and was located outside the city boundaries of Jerusalem. This is where Jesus offered Himself as a sacrifice for the sins of man. Heb. 13:11,12 says, "For the bodies of those beasts, whose blood is brought into the sanctuary by the high priest for sin, are burned outside the city. Therefore Jesus also, that He might sanctify the people with His own blood, suffered outside the gate."

To get to the garden, Jesus and His disciples had to walk down a steep valley and cross over the Brook Kidron. This valley was about a mile and a half long and at this time of year very little water was flowing in the brook. The word "Kidron" means 'dark waters' and is symbolic of the horrendous events that are about to take place. The feast of Passover was at hand and hundreds of thousands of animals were being sacrificed in the temple area. The temple was on a hillside above the valley where the Brook Kidron flowed. Built into the temple wall were channels where the blood of all the sacrificed animals left the temple and ran downhill into the Brook Kidron. Jesus and the disciples had to cross over this brook that was filled with the blood of all these animals. Jesus is the true Passover lamb and the thought of His own sacrifice was vivid in His mind. The Hebrew word for "Gethsemane" means 'olive press' and in just a matter of hours the very life of Jesus would be pressed out of Him.

The Garden of Gethsemane was on the road that led to Bethany where Mary, Martha, and Lazarus lived. You could see the holy city from the garden and many times Jesus and His disciples would stop and rest at this halfway point between Jerusalem and Bethany. Jerusalem is built on top of a hill and there is little space for private gardens within its borders. Wealthy people would go to the Mount of Olives and plant their gardens alongside the olives that grew on the hill. In times past, Jesus and the disciples would go there for some peace and quiet. Not this time. Matt. 26:37,38 says Jesus is exceedingly sorrowful and deeply distressed, even to death. He is about to be separated from the Father as He hangs on the cross. That is spiritual death, the worst kind of death there is. He took Peter, James, and John with Him and went off to pray. He "fell on the ground, and prayed that if it were possible, the hour might pass from Him. And He said, 'Abba, Father, all things are possible for You. Take this cup away from Me; nevertheless, not what I will, but what You will'" (Mark 14:35,36).

The word "Abba" was the Aramaic word for 'daddy.' It's a very personal and intimate term for one's father and, prior to Pentecost in Acts 2, only Jesus had used this title for God. He is calling the Father "Daddy" and He's asking for the cup of wrath to be taken from Him. He is speaking as a human being and never in all eternity has He been separated from the Father. The wages of sin is death and death is separation from God. Not only will Jesus die physically on the cross, He'll also die spiritually and this is why Jesus pleas that if it is possible, let this cup, this separation, be taken from Him. He then says, "Nevertheless, not what I will, but what You will." He is in complete submission to the Father whose will is that the Son become the substitute for all mankind. "Then He came and found them sleeping, and said to Peter, 'Simon, are you sleeping? Could you not watch one hour? Watch and pray, lest you enter into temptation. The spirit truly is ready, but the flesh is weak'" (Mark 14:37,38).

Notice that Jesus called him "Simon" after He changed His name to "Peter" (Matt. 16:18). He is saying that if your heart has not been changed, then you will be overcome with the temptation to run away and deny Him. This is why Paul says in 1 Cor. 10:12 to "take heed lest he fall." You need to realize the importance of prayer in your life for this is how you maintain your relationship with God. For some people, it's easier to read their Bible or set up chairs at church than it is to pray. The truth is, most people are too busy to pray. They do a lot of things but accomplish very little. Jesus asked, "Could you not watch one hour?" No, you don't have to pray for an hour at a time. However, you should never go an hour without praying. Mark 14:39 says, "Again He went away and prayed, and spoke the same words." Heb. 5:7 gives further insight into this prayer. It says Jesus, "who, in the days of His flesh, when He had offered up prayers and supplication, with vehement cries and tears to Him who was able to save Him from death, and was heard because of His godly fear."

The writer of Hebrews says the Father heard what Jesus was praying. The Message Bible says, "While He lived on earth, anticipating death, Jesus cried out in pain and wept in sorrow as He offered up priestly prayers to God. Because He honored God, God answered Him." The Father answered His prayer but still Jesus went to the cross. This may seem confusing until you realize in Greek the words "save Him from death" literally means "save Him from out of death." Jesus is not praying to escape the cross but that the Father would raise Him up three days later. The Father heard this prayer and in three days the entire universe would know that death could not keep Him down. "And when He returned, He found them asleep again, for their eyes were heavy; and they did not know what to answer Him. Then He came the third time and said to them, 'Are you still sleeping and resting? It is enough! The hour has come; behold, the Son of Man is being betrayed into the hands of sinners. Rise up, let us go. See, My betrayer is at hand" (Mark 14:40-42).

Because of the Lord's many visits to this garden, Judas knew where to find Him. He brought with him six hundred Roman soldiers, the temple police, and the chief priests and Pharisees. Not knowing what to expect, they came armed with lanterns, torches, and weapons (John 18:3). Jesus is in complete control in spite of the small army that came to arrest Him. Instead of slipping away as He had done on previous occasions because His time had not yet come, Jesus takes them all by surprise by stepping forward and initiating contact with His accusers. He asks them, "Whom are you seeking?" (vs. 4) and they answer, "Jesus of Nazareth" (vs. 5). This is the most earthly, human name that you can give to the Son of God. They give Him no respect as a teacher and prophet and they give Him no divine recognition because, in their eyes, nothing good comes out of Nazareth. To them, He is just a man. Most translations of the Bible say Jesus answered and said, "I am He." The word "He," however, is not in the original text and what Jesus actually said was "I am." This is the title and name of God (Ex. 3:14).

When Jesus made this divine claim, those who came to arrest Him "drew back and fell to the ground" (vs. 6). In the Old Testament, whenever someone came in the presence of God they fell to the ground (Ezek. 1:28). The Greek word for "fell" refers to 'one overcome in battle by a superior.' Jesus declared He is God and everybody fell down from the power and majesty that radiated out of Him. He had no weapons and used no force but the authority in the words He spoke made Him stronger than the might of His enemies. This same power is in the Word of God for you to use. Jesus asks again whom they are seeking and, when they tell Him, He confirms a second time that He is the One they're looking for. He then says, "Therefore, if you seek Me, let these go their way" (vs. 8). Jesus wants His disciples to be safe. He is the Savior (John 14:6) and the Protector (John 10:28). He is the Good Shepherd and He always protects His sheep, even to the point of death. He said this so that the saying may be fulfilled, "Of those whom You gave Me I have lost none" (vs. 9).

At this point Judas, who earlier had worked out an identifying sign with the soldiers, walked up to Jesus and said, "Greetings, Rabbi!" and kissed Him (Matt. 26:48,49). The Greek word for "kiss" implies that he kissed Jesus warmly and fervently. Jesus said to him, "Friend, why have you come?" He did not address His betrayer as an enemy but as a friend. This shows the heart and compassion of Jesus. At this time the soldiers laid hands on Jesus and took Him (vs. 50). The plan of God was rapidly unfolding but Peter had other plans. In the upper room Jesus told the disciples to provide themselves with weapons because of the approaching danger (Luke 22:36). The disciples told Jesus they had two swords which were ceremonial daggers used to kill a lamb for the Passover meal. Peter carried one of these small weapons and he drew it and cut off the right ear of the servant of the high priest. Peter was not aiming for his ear but for the top of his head. He was trying to kill the man but the servant leaned away so that the sword struck his ear instead. Peter was trying to keep Jesus safe and in doing so was going against the divine will of God.

Peter missed the plan and so do millions of people all over the world today. They want to earn their way to heaven by trying to be good and to do good works. Paul explained that you cannot do anything to save yourself, but salvation comes only as the result of God's grace (Eph. 2:8,9). Jesus looked at Peter and commanded him, "Put your sword into the sheath. Shall I not drink the cup which My Father has given Me?" (John 18:11). Jesus is saying that He's supposed to die for this is the cup the Father gave Him to drink. It was the cup of wrath and judgment for He came to suffer and die for the sin of man. Jesus then went over to the servant "and He touched his ear and healed him" (Luke 22:51). Everybody witnessed a miracle but still they continued in their plot to arrest Jesus and put Him on trial. They hated Him and treated Him like a common criminal. They thought Him worthy of death and the disciples all forsook Him and fled. "Then the detachment of troops and the captain and the officers of the Jews arrested Jesus and bound Him (John 18:12).

Jesus was willing to go with them willingly but they bound Him anyway. In Gen. 22:9, Abraham bound his son Isaac and laid him on the altar to be sacrificed. It was also the first thing done when animals were sacrificed. Ps. 118:27 says, "Bind the festival sacrifice with cords to the horns of the altar." Each animal that was sacrificed was led first to the priest (Lev. 17:5) and John 18:13 says, "And they led Him away to Annas first, for he was the father-in-law of Caiaphas who was high priest that year." Jesus was willingly submissive. They didn't drag Him nor did they carry Him. They led Him and Is. 53:7 says, "He was led as a lamb to the slaughter." Annas was no longer the high priest but he was the patriarch of the family and commanded great influence among the rulers of Israel. Caiaphas held the title of high priest but it was Annas who had the real power of this priestly office. He was a very wealthy man and was allowed to do what he wanted as long as he didn't get out of line and cause trouble for the Roman government.

Aaron, the brother of Moses, was the first high priest. His oldest son became the next high priest, and his son's son would follow after him. This was how the role of high priest was passed on from generation to generation. Each high priest was a descendant of Aaron but by the time when Jesus came this pattern was no longer being followed. The Romans had taken over the country and they chose whoever they wanted to be high priest with no regards to what bloodline they were from. Also, they didn't stay high priest for life as was originally God's plan. Annas was only high priest from 7 AD to 14 AD and his son-in-law Caiaphas was high priest from 15 AD to 37 AD. The family of Annas was cold-hearted and they were always grasping for power and wealth. The Romans would auction off the office of high priest and the position went to the highest bidder and to the man most likely to cooperate with the Roman government. Annas was wealthy because of the profits made from the money changers in the temple. When Jesus drove them out of the temple, the heart of Annas was filled with anger and rage.

The soldiers bound Jesus and brought Him to Annas with Peter and John following from a distance. A wall surrounded the property of the high priest and between the wall and the house was the courtyard. They led Jesus through this gate into the courtyard and

John followed Him in. John and his family had a successful fishing business and because of their financial well-being they were well known to the wealthy high priest. Peter, on the other hand, was not known by the high priest so he kept his distance and stood at the door outside. Learn from this. John remained close to Jesus while Peter kept his distance. Jesus wants a close relationship with you and this won't happen if you follow Him from a distance (Luke 22:54). John then went and spoke to the servant girl who kept the door and received permission to bring Peter into the courtyard. The girl looked at Peter and asked, "You are not also one of this Man's disciples, are you?" Peter answered, "I am not" (John 18:17). In Greek this question was asked in anticipation of a negative response. The doorkeeper was expecting Peter to say he was not a disciple of Jesus. Sad to say, she was not disappointed.

"And the servants and officers who had made a fire of coals stood there, for it was cold, and they warmed themselves. And Peter stood with them and warmed himself" (John 18:18). Notice the movements of Peter. In the garden he's next to Jesus. When Jesus is arrested he's following from a distance. When he denies Jesus he removes himself even further away and now he's warming himself around a fire with the very people who arrested Jesus. He's trying to blend in with the world proving that the values of some believers are no different than those of unbelievers. Be careful who you associate with. Inside the house, Annas is interrogating Jesus as he asks Him about His disciples and His doctrine (vs. 19). This trial is a mockery for it is being done illegally. According to Jewish law, witnesses would be brought in to testify against the accused and then the person on trial would be called upon to defend himself. That's not happening here and Annas is asking Jesus to incriminate Himself. He is searching for a charge so that Caiaphas can have something to work with when judgment is passed.

Jesus knows what's going on. He knows this trial is illegal and unjust. He does not answer the question about the disciples for He will always protect His sheep. He did respond that what He has taught has been done openly and anyone who heard Him can give Annas the information he wants (vs. 20,21). In other words, provide witnesses like they should have done in the first place. The high priest doesn't want justice, he only wants Jesus to be found guilty and he'll do whatever it takes to make it happen. The hands of Jesus are bound and an officer strikes Jesus with the palm of his hand saying, "Do You answer the high priest like that?" (vs. 22). This also was an illegal act. You could not strike or punish a prisoner until the trial was over and the person was found guilty. The Jews have violated every one of their own laws. It was illegal for a trial to take place at night and they're not calling any witnesses. Seeing that his questioning is getting him nowhere, Annas sent Jesus bound to Caiaphas for a more official hearing.

As this interrogation was coming to a close, Peter is still outside warming himself by the fire. He's concealing his true identity and pretending he was one of the enemy. Those standing with Peter looked at him and said, "You are not also one of His disciples, are you?" Peter denied it and said, "I am not!" (John 18:25). When you do something wrong, it's easier to do it again the second and third time. This is what happened to Peter. He acted in fear and got caught in the snare of the enemy (Prov. 29:25). A relative of the man whose ear Peter cut off was also there by the fire and he said, "Did I not see you in the garden with Him?" (vs. 26). Matt. 26:74 says "he began to curse and swear, saying, 'I do not know the Man!'" Peter was saying, "May God put a curse on me if I'm not telling the truth." And immediately, while he was still speaking, a rooster crowed. Luke 22:61,62 says, "And the Lord turned and looked at Peter. And Peter remembered the word of the Lord, how He had said to him, 'Before the rooster crows, you will deny Me three times.' Then Peter went out and wept bitterly."

Never should sin be taken lightly. When you sin, it should break your heart. Because of this denial, Peter has been unfairly treated down through the centuries. Those who criticize him don't realize that any person, at any time, is capable of any sin. Like Peter, if you're at the wrong place at the wrong time, in truth, you may do the same thing. Paul said in 1 Cor. 10:12, "Therefore let him who thinks he stands take heed lest he fall." The Message Bible says, "We are just as capable of messing up as they were. Don't be so naive and self-confident. You're not exempt. You could fall flat on your face as easily as anyone else. Forget about self-confidence; it's useless. Cultivate God-confidence." Believers every day deny Jesus and don't even realize they're doing it. They keep quiet when others speak against Him or take His name in vain. They say nothing when others say there is no God. They can choose to not live for Him, to ignore Him, to disown Him. When they live for themselves, when they choose to do their own will and not His will, they're in fact denying the One who saved them from eternal judgment.

The four gospels record that Jesus had three trials before the Jewish authorities. John only describes His session with Annas and a brief mention of Caiaphas. Jesus was found guilty in all three trials even though each one was done illegally. It was now time to get the Romans involved because they couldn't execute Jesus without Roman approval. John 18:28 (NLT) says, "Jesus' trial before Caiaphas ended in the early hours of the morning. Then He was taken to the headquarters of the Roman governor. His accusers didn't go inside because it would defile them, and they wouldn't be allowed to celebrate the Passover." These Jewish leaders are really acting religious. They don't want to defile themselves but they want to execute an innocent Man, the Son of God. What is interesting about their behavior is nowhere in Old Testament law does it say a Jew is defiled by going into a Gentile's house. This was a man-made law later put in place by rabbis and was based on tradition and not on the actual Word of God.

Pontius Pilate was the Roman governor and he ruled over Judea from 26 AD to 36 AD. Pilate was a weak man but he was an evil man. His job was to keep the Jews and their religious leaders under control. They could worship any way they wanted to as long as they understood the Romans were in control over the nation. Pilate did not have a good relationship with the Jewish leaders for they opposed his atheistic ways and his heathen attempts to portray the Roman rulers as gods. Oftentimes they complained to Rome about his actions and tried to make him look bad. Each time the Jews complained, Pilate backed down. And now here these Jewish leaders are, early in the morning at the break of dawn, asking Pilate to quickly carry out their judgment on Jesus. They want him to approve their mockery with a form of legality. Pilate's main job was to keep these Jews under control so he goes out to them instead of making them come in to him. He asks, "What accusation do you bring against this Man?" (John 18:29).

As a judge and governor, this was the proper question to be asked but notice their self-righteous response, "If He were not an evildoer, we would not have delivered Him to you" (vs. 30). They weren't coming for a trial but for Pilate to confirm their sentence. They were telling Pilate to stop asking questions and trust that He is a bad person. They want him to confirm their decision or they'll make trouble for him, possibly by complaining to Rome once again. Pilate knew they had no evidence against Jesus but, to keep the peace, he gave them permission to do whatever they wanted. He wanted nothing to do with their evil scheme so he told them to judge Jesus by their own Jewish law. He was hoping this would make the problem go away. People think that ignoring a problem will make it go away. It doesn't and most times the problem only gets worse. The Jews want Jesus dead but they don't have the right under Roman law to kill Him. Instead, they want Pilate to do the dirty work for them.

Pilate decides to question Jesus himself. He called Jesus to be brought to him and he asked mockingly, "Are You the King of the Jews?" (John 18:33). Why would Pilate ask Jesus this question? Being called a god would not bother the Romans for there were many gods. In fact, some of the Roman leaders thought they were gods themselves. But to call Jesus a King got their attention because there is only one king and that is Caesar. Jesus turns the situation around and asks Pilate a question, "Are you speaking for yourself on this, or did others tell you about Me?" (vs. 34). Pilate gets mad and answers, "Am I a Jew? Your own nation and the chief priests have delivered You to me. What have You done?" Everybody knows what Jesus did. He healed the sick, raised the dead, forgave sins, calmed the storm, walked on water, fed the multitudes, taught the Word of God. Still, the religious leaders hate Him because they think He's going to take their authority away from them. This is why they want Him killed. Jesus has done nothing wrong and He proceeds to tell Pilate what kind of King He is.

Jesus answered, "My kingdom is not of this world. If My kingdom were of this world, My servants would fight, so that I should not be delivered to the Jews; but now My kingdom is not from here" (vs. 36). Jesus' kingdom is different from any other kingdom for it is established by God and not man. In a worldly kingdom, the king rules and then he dies. In a heavenly kingdom, the King dies and then rules forever. Pilate doesn't understand what Jesus is saying so he asks Him again, "Are You a king then?" (vs. 37). He asks this knowing that if Jesus said He was a king, He'd be in direct opposition to Caesar. Jesus answers, "You say rightly that I am a king. For this cause I was born, and for this cause I have come into the world, that I should bear witness to the truth. Everyone who is of the truth hears My voice." When people listen to Jesus and believe in Him, they'll understand what He's saying. Pilate then asked, 'What is truth?" (vs. 38). This is the same question the world is asking today. Pilate then walks away without giving Jesus a chance to answer.

In today's world, there is no foundation for what truth is. Things change and what's true today won't be true tomorrow. There is no right and wrong and ethics can vary from one situation to another. People believe there is no absolute truth and each person should decide for themselves what truth is. There is very little integrity in the world and rarely do people say what they mean and mean what they say. No longer are people held accountable for the words they speak because the world has taken on the belief that all views are equal. They say Allah is just as much God as Jesus is and you will be condemned if you say otherwise. Pilate asked, "What is truth?" The Bible says that truth is found in three places. John 14:6 says Jesus is the way, the truth, and the life. The Word of God is truth (John 17:17) and the Holy Spirit is called the Spirit of Truth (John 15:26). Do you want to know truth? Go to the Bible for it never changes. Pilate then went to the people and said, "I find no fault in Him at all" (vs. 38). The Jews say He's guilty, Pilate says He's not. Who will prevail?

-31-

"ABSORBING THE WRATH"

Pontius Pilate has a dilemma on his hands. He wants to let Jesus go and keep the Jews happy all at the same time. He doesn't want another uproar from the people, fearing the Roman government would remove him from his position of power. He doesn't know what to do but he knows the crowd wants Jesus dead. A few days earlier these very same people were shouting to Jesus, "Hosanna! 'Blessed is He who comes in the name of the Lord!' The King of Israel!" (John 12:13). Then an idea comes to him and Pilate thinks he has a solution to his problem. He says to the people, "But you have a custom that I should release someone to you at the Passover. Do you therefore want me to release to you the King of the Jews?" (John 18:39). This was a custom to win over the favor of the Jewish people. He expected the people to say they want Jesus released but instead they all cried out, "Not this man, but Barabbas!" (vs. 40). Barabbas was a robber, a notorious prisoner (Matt. 27:16) who had committed murder in a government upheaval (Mark 15:7).

The name "Barabbas" comes from the Greek words "bar" which means 'son' and "abba" meaning 'father.' The name "Barabbas" means 'son of the father.' The people have a choice. They can choose Jesus, the righteous Son of the Father, or they can choose Barabbas, the unrighteous son of the father. Jesus did good things throughout His life while Barabbas was a murderous rebel. He was guilty of his crimes and was condemned to die. To the surprise of Pilate, the people chose this heathen criminal to be released instead of Jesus. On this fateful day, Jesus took the place of Barabbas. He also took your place when He went to the cross. You also deserved to die for your sins, but Jesus died for you. 1 Peter 3:18 says, "For

Christ also suffered once for sins, the just for the unjust, that He might bring us to God, being put to death in the flesh but made alive by the Spirit." The Message Bible says, "He went through it all - was put to death and then made alive - to bring us to God."

Barabbas was an enemy to Rome and the Jewish people were trying to flaunt their power over Pilate in demanding his release. They now want to force Pilate to execute Jesus. As a Roman governor, Pilate is committed to justice which would require him to release Jesus. He really believes Jesus is innocent but neither does he release Him. The Jewish leaders are pressing Pilate to do something and in the back of his mind he knows that Rome is expecting him to keep his territory peaceful. He does not want to execute a man who is clearly innocent so he decides to punish Jesus severely to satisfy the crowd and then let Him go in the interests of justice. John 19:1 says, "So then Pilate took Jesus and scourged Him." As soon as a man was condemned, he was turned over to four soldiers whose job it was to carry out the punishment. These soldiers took Jesus and stripped Him of all His clothes. They tied His hands to a post above His head to stretch His skin thus making His wounds much worse. They then did what they were ordered to do.

So horrific and painful was this scourging that many died right there at the whipping post. Few remained conscious and many went raving mad. This ordeal was so dreadful and gruesome that Roman law would not allow their own citizens to undergo it (Acts 22:24-29). In a satanic frenzy, the Roman soldiers took a whip with cattle bone and sharp metal attached to the end of it and began to beat this innocent Man. He was beaten by two soldiers whose alternating blows would ensure the beating was continuous. Jesus stood there absorbing the wrath of these Roman soldiers and He opened not His mouth (Is. 53:7). Huge strips of skin were hanging from His body and His muscles, vital organs, and His spine were seen openly. According to Jewish law, this beating had to be stopped after forty lashes (Deut. 25:1-3). The Romans, however, had no such law and may have exceeded this limit. They scourged their victims until an inch of their life, even checking their pulse to see if they could inflict more damage.

Driven by the devil himself, these soldiers inflicted as much pain on Jesus as they possibly could. Because of this beating, Jesus was dehydrated from profuse sweating, extremely weak from extensive blood loss, and in a near state of shock. "And the soldiers twisted a crown of thorns and put it on His head, and they put on Him a purple robe. Then they said, 'Hail, King of the Jews!' And they struck Him with their hands" (John 19:2,3). First came the scourging, then came the mocking. This crown of thorns was put on Jesus both to cause Him pain and to mock His claim of authority. The Greek word for "crown" is "stephanos" which means 'victor's crown.' It was the word used for the crown put on the head of the winner of an athletic contest such as the Greek Olympics. It was a crown of victory and the soldiers used these thorns as a symbol of their complete contempt for Jesus and what He stood for. These thorns were about two inches long and very sharp. Historians say the Roman soldiers used a wooden mallet to pound this crown of thorns onto the head of Jesus.

Because of the sin of Adam and Eve, Gen. 3:17,18 says, "Cursed is the ground for your sake; In toil you shall eat of it all the days of your life. Both thorns and thistles it shall bring forth for you." The Roman soldiers unknowingly took an object of the curse and fashioned it into a crown for the One who would deliver man from that curse. What was intended to be a symbol of mockery was, in fact, a true symbol of who Jesus is and what He came to accomplish. These thorns crashed into His skull and tore nerves that caused explosive and indescribable pain. The soldiers struck Him repeatedly and His head and face was badly swollen and in a state of inflamed sensitivity. So painful was this beating that talking and swallowing would cause even more excruciating pain. His beard was pulled out and He is so bloody and beaten He does not look human. Is. 50:6 says, "I gave My back to those who struck Me, and My cheeks to those who plucked out the beard; I did not hide My face from shame and spitting." Here is the suffering Servant willingly enduring this horrific pain, the insults, and the shame on behalf of all mankind.

Is. 52:14,15 says He was beaten beyond recognition. The Message Bible says, "He didn't even look human - a ruined face, disfigured beyond recognition. Nations all over the world will be in awe, taken aback, kings shocked into silence when they see Him. For what was unheard of they'll see with their own eyes, what was unthinkable they'll have right before them." Jesus was mocked and suffered great physical abuse. This happened to a Man whom Pilate said was innocent of any wrong doing. The Jews in times past had complained that they were beaten too harshly by the Romans but they don't complain here as Jesus is severely beaten. Pilate still intends to release Jesus (Luke 23:16) so he brings Him before the people and says to them, "Behold the Man!" (John 19:5). Pilate is making fun of the Jews. He's saying, "Here's your King but He don't look like a King to me." The people cried out, "Crucify Him, crucify Him!" (vs. 6). Pilate said, "You crucify Him" even though he knew they didn't have the authority to do it. No person could be put to death without Roman approval.

Jesus is standing there in a purple robe with a reed in His right hand to indicate a scepter (Matt. 27:29). Both are symbols of royalty. The Jews tell Pilate that Jesus broke their law by saying He was the Son of God (John 19:7). This was the wrong thing to say because the Romans don't care if He's a god or not. There are many gods so what difference is one more going to make? Besides, Pilate does not care about Jewish law. He is saying that Jesus broke no Roman law. Still, the charges against Jesus alarm him. "Therefore, when Pilate heard that saying, he was the more afraid, and went again into the Praetorium, and said to Jesus, 'Where are You from?' But Jesus gave him no answer" (vs. 8,9). Why is Pilate afraid? His wife had a dream about Jesus and she came to him and said, "Have nothing to do with that just Man, for I have suffered many things today because of Him" (Matt. 27:19). Pilate is becoming afraid of Jesus and even more afraid of the crowd. He knows that if he does not handle this uprising properly he'll get on the wrong side of Caesar.

Self-preservation is the motive for everything Pilate is doing. He's getting irritated for he's not used to Jewish prisoners not answering him or not doing what he tells them to do. He is mystified. Why isn't this Man pleading for mercy? He then tells Jesus that it is he who has the power to kill Him or let Him go. Jesus responds and says the only power Pilate has came from above (vs. 10,11). Jesus is saying that He may be Pilate's prisoner but he has no control over Him. What's happening is not outside the will of Jesus for He is in total control of what's going on. Pilate again tries to release Jesus but the Jews cried out, "If you let this Man go, you are not Caesar's friend. Whoever makes himself a king speaks against Caesar" (vs. 12). The Jews are threatening to report Pilate to the Emperor and by doing so they are manipulating him into crucifying Jesus. This is so hypocritical because the Jews hate Caesar and everything he stands for. They also know there is power in manipulation and they use Caesar as a leverage to get Pilate to give them what they want.

Pilate does not know what to do. He thinks Jesus is innocent but he's getting caught up in the unruly and out of control ramblings of the Jewish people. What will he do? He went and sat down on the judgment seat which was a raised platform where decisions were made and rewards given out. Pilate is going to tell the people what he's going to do. "Now it was the Preparation Day of the Passover, and about the sixth hour. And he said to the Jews, 'Behold your King!'" (vs. 14). Preparation Day was when all the lambs would be brought out and prepared for slaughter in order to be sacrificed for the sins of the people. Jesus is the Lamb of God and He's being prepared for sacrifice at the same time the lambs are. The Jews cried out for Jesus to be crucified and Pilate asks, "Shall I crucify your King?" The chief priests answered, "We have no king but Caesar!" (vs. 15). How could these Jews say such a despicable thing? The truth is, they'd say anything to get Jesus killed. They hated the Romans but were willing to pledge allegiance to Caesar in order to get what they wanted.

Pilate's in trouble. The Jews are getting out of hand and if he doesn't do something soon he'll be reported to Rome. When under pressure, people do what's best for them and not necessarily what's right. "So he delivered Him to them to be crucified. So they took Jesus and led Him away" (vs. 16). Pilate conceded to the demands of the people. He gives the order for Jesus to be crucified and the Roman soldiers took over from there. "And He, bearing His cross, went out to a place called the Place of a Skull, which in called in Hebrew, Golgotha, where they crucified Him, and two others with Him, one on either side, and Jesus in the center" (vs. 17,18). The Romans learned crucifixion from the Carthaginians and rapidly perfected its means to bring its victims maximum pain and suffering. Its purpose was to drain out a person's life in a slow, tortuous way. If a victim was beaten too severely beforehand, he would sometimes die after a few hours. More times than not, they would live for several days, sometimes for even a week or more.

There was no more terrible death than to be crucified on a Roman cross. It was considered the most disgraceful form of execution and was used on the most evil of all criminals, traitors, and murderers. Some of these criminals hung there until they starved to death while others died at the hands of hungry vultures and crows. Once convicted, a heavy cross was put on the bloody back of Jesus and He was forced to drag this beam to the place of His execution. He is weak and He staggers and falls, unable to continue. Simon of Cyrene is taken from the crowd and forced to carry the cross the rest of the way (Luke 23:26). Jesus is taken to a hill outside Jerusalem called Golgotha, the Place of the Skull. The Latin word for "skull" is "Calvary" and this place of execution is a cliff face whose rock protrusions and indentations give it the distinct appearance of a human skull. It is also believed that this was the place where David buried the head of Goliath of Gath. The word "Golgotha" is a term made up of the words "Goliath Gath." Just as David crushed the head of the giant with a smooth stone, so will Jesus crush the head of Satan on this very hill (Gen. 3:15).

Once they arrived, the soldiers stripped Jesus of all His clothes and threw Him on top of the cross. Huge spikes that were eight inches long were hammered into His wrists and feet. Tendons and nerves began to tear and break and Jesus cried out in excruciating pain. The word "excruciating" comes from the Latin word "excruciatus" which means 'to crucify.' When people were crucified, the list of charges against them was put above their head for all to see. Pilate wrote a title and put it on the cross. The sign above Jesus said, "Jesus of Nazareth, the King of the Jews" (vs. 19). In the eyes of Rome, Jesus was being killed because He said He was the King of the Jews. Pilate put this sign up on purpose for he's making fun of the Jewish people. This sign was written in three languages: in Hebrew for the Jewish people, in Greek for the nations, and in Latin which was the official language of the Romans (vs. 20). This sign was an embarrassment to the Jewish leaders. If Jesus truly was their King, then why would they want Him dead? They want Pilate to change the sign but he said, "What I have written, I have written" (vs. 22).

With ropes the soldiers lifted Jesus and the cross off the ground and placed it in a hole that had already been dug. The heavy impact of the cross falling into this hole caused the bones of Jesus to be shaken and come out of joint. This was the fulfillment of Ps. 22:14, "I am poured out like water, and all My bones are out of joint; My heart is like wax; It has melted within Me." Jesus is hanging there, crucified alongside common criminals, and the first thing He says is, "Father, forgive them, for they do not know what they do" (Luke 23:34). Even in death, Jesus is seeking redemption for those who hate Him most. The soldiers were allowed to keep the clothes of the victims and, as Jesus was suffering before their very eyes, they divided His clothes among themselves. Every Jew wore five articles of apparel. They had a covering for their head, a shirt, a girdle, and sandals for their feet. A tunic was an undergarment that was worn beneath their outer clothing. This tunic was seamless and woven all in one piece. Each soldier received one piece of clothing and cast lots to see which one of them would get the tunic.

Another prophecy is being fulfilled. Ps. 22:16-18 says, "For dogs have surrounded Me; The assembly of the wicked has enclosed Me. They pierced My hands and My feet; I can count all My bones. They look and stare at Me. They divide My garments among them, and for My clothing they cast lots." John is listing these Old Testament prophecies because he wants his readers to know that what happened to Jesus was not some random act but was, in fact, the fulfillment of scripture. "Now there stood by the cross of Jesus His mother, and His mother's sister, Mary the wife of Clopas, and Mary Magdalene" (John 19:25). It is interesting that, except for John, all the men ran off but the women didn't. Jesus says to His mother, "Woman, behold your son!" He was referring to John and He then says to him, "Behold your mother!" (vs. 26,27). Even while hanging on a cross, Jesus cares about the well-being of His mother. He is telling John to take care of her proving that by this time her husband Joseph has passed away. If he were still alive, Jesus would not have told John to take care of her.

Mark 15:25 says Jesus was put on the cross at nine in the morning. At twelve noon a strange phenomenon occurred, "Now when the sixth hour had come, there was darkness over the whole land until the ninth hour" (vs. 33). Darkness is symbolic of sin and fellowship with the Father is now broken. Jesus is hanging on the cross drinking the cup the Father gave Him to drink. In this cup was the guilt of every person past, present, and future. Is. 53:3-6 (NLT) says, "He was despised and rejected - a man of sorrows, acquainted with deepest grief. We turned our backs on Him and looked the other way. He was despised, and we did not care. Yet it was our weaknesses He carried; it was our sorrows that weighed Him down. And we thought His troubles were a punishment from God, a punishment for His own sin! But He was pierced for our rebellion, crushed for our sins. He was beaten so we could be whole. He was whipped so we could be healed. All of us, like sheep, have strayed away. We have left God's paths to follow our own. Yet the Lord laid on Him the sins of us all."

Like the ferocious blows of a heavyweight fighter, Jesus is hit with the penalty of every sin ever committed. There on that cross He absorbed the wrath of God like no other person before or since. This is the darkest moment in all eternity. "For He made Him who knew no sin to be sin for us, that we might become the righteousness of God in Him" (2 Cor. 5:21). So dreadful is the weight of sin that His soul is exceeding sorrowful, even unto death. In pain and sorrow, the Father removed His life-sustaining and hope-filled hand of protection from off His beloved Son. Immediately a violent torrent of demons are released upon Him.

"Herds of bulls come at Me, the raging bulls stampede, horns lowered, nostrils flaring, like a herd of buffalo on the move. I'm a bucket kicked over and spilled, every joint in My body has been pulled apart. My heart is a blob of melted wax in My gut. I'm dry as a bone, My tongue black and swollen. They have laid Me out for burial in the dirt. Now packs of wild dogs come at Me; thugs gang up on Me. They pin Me down hand and foot, and lock Me in a cage" (Ps. 22:12-16 MSG).

An avalanche of demons overwhelm Jesus as He absorbs the wrath of God. The Father is a God of love but He is also a God of justice. He is holy and His wrath against sin is fierce because it is the cause of all the pain and suffering and death in the world. Since Jesus has become the substitute for all mankind, it is on Him that all this wrath is released. Ps. 88:15-17 says, "I suffer Your terrors; I am distraught. Your fierce wrath has gone over me; Your terrors have cut me off. They come around me all day long like water; They engulfed me altogether." On that cross Jesus was absorbing the wrath of God. Nahum 1:6 says, "Who can stand before His indignation? And who can endure the fierceness of His anger? His fury is poured out like fire, and the rocks are thrown down by Him." Jesus was experiencing something that no other human being would ever experience. As the Father withdrew His hand from the Son, the heart of Jesus was pierced with an anguish unknown to man. He cried out, "My God, My God, why have You forsaken Me?" (Matt. 27:46).

Jesus and the Father had been united together since eternity past and now that bond of oneness is no more. So great was this pain of separation that His physical sufferings were hardly felt. His anguish of heart was far greater than His physical pain. Jesus actually started to die the night before in the Garden of Gethsemane. Luke 22:44 says, "And being in agony, He prayed more earnestly, and His sweat became like great drops of blood falling down to the ground." The Message Bible says, "Sweat wrung from Him like drops of blood, poured off His face." Jesus had been forsaken by the nation, by His own disciples, and now by the Father. This separation, this spiritual death, is the payment for sin. Physical death was not the payment, separation from the

Father was. He was separated so you wouldn't have to be. Ps. 69:2 gives a moving insight into the suffering of Jesus, "I sink in deep mire, where there is no standing; I have come into deep waters, where the floods overflow me." Like a person who is about to drown, Jesus is grasping for the Father with everything that is in Him.

Jonah 2:5 (ESV) says, "The water closed in over me to take my life; the deep surrounded me; weeds were wrapped about my head." The Message Bible says, "Ocean gripped me by the throat. The ancient Abyss grabbed me and held tight." The Father is the air Jesus so desperately needs. Yes, He had the power to save Himself. He was still God as He hung on the cross but He didn't use His divine power to come down from that cross of suffering. The temptation to do so was fierce as the crowd mocked Him to do this very thing (Mark 15:29,30). He didn't come down from that cross because to hang there and die was the reason He came. He came to save these people even though they despised and rejected Him. "After this, Jesus, knowing that all things were now accomplished, that the Scripture might be fulfilled, said, 'I thirst!'" (John 19:28). Jesus can hardly breathe. He must pull Himself up each time He takes a breath. He is exhausted yet there are a few final words He has to say. He asks for something to drink to wet His lips for this final effort.

"Now a vessel full of sour wine was sitting there; and they filled a sponge with sour wine, put it on a hyssop, and put it to His mouth" (John 19:29). Jesus had earlier been offered wine mingled with myrrh to help dull the pain but He did not take it (Mark 15:23). Here, He was given sour wine vinegar which was the fulfillment of Ps. 69:21, "They also gave me gall for my food, and for my thirst they gave me vinegar to drink." Wine vinegar doesn't have any alcohol left, but is sour wine that has turned to vinegar. After taking the wine, Jesus is able to speak again. He wants to tell the world that He has completed the work the Father sent Him to do. He said, "It is finished!" (John 19:30). Only John records these words of Jesus. This is the Greek word "tetelestai" and is an accounting term meaning "paid in full." As Jesus was about to breathe His last breath, He was saying that His works as a human being was finished. He had finished living a sinless life, He had finished the work the Father gave Him to do (John 4:34).

"And when Jesus had cried out with a loud voice, He said, 'Father, into Your hands I commend My spirit!' And having said this He breathed His last" (Luke 23:46). John 19:30 says, "And bowing His head, He gave up His spirit." The Romans didn't take His life, He gave it up. He decided when He was going to die. "And behold, the veil of the temple was torn in two from top to bottom; and the earth quaked, and the rocks were split" (Matt. 27:51). This veil was forty feet wide, twenty feet tall, and four inches thick. It stood in front of the Holy of Holies preventing everyone except the High priest from going into the presence of God. When Jesus died the penalty of sin was paid and now all have the freedom to enter into God's glorious presence. The splitting of the veil was divine confirmation that Jesus was indeed the true Lamb of God sacrificed for the sins of man. "Now when the centurion and those with him, who were guarding Jesus, saw the earthquake and the things that happened, they feared greatly, saying, 'Truly this was the Son of God!'" (Matt. 27:54). Jesus was now dead. The Jews got what they wanted. So did the Father.

Randall J. Brewer

-32-

"FOLLOW ME"

The greatest enemy of man is death because people don't know how to deal with it. Nothing makes you feel more helpless than the thought of taking your last breath. In the world two people die every second. That's over one million people a week. Death treats everybody the same way, whether you're young or old, male or female, rich or poor. It brings everybody to a common end. Ps. 49:10 says, "For he sees that wise men die; Likewise the fool and the senseless person perish, and leave their wealth to others." Don't be jealous of movie stars, professional athletes, or rich millionaires. They will all die for death is the most common denominator in all of life. "Their inner thought is that their houses will continue forever, and their dwelling places to all generations; They call their lands their own names. Nevertheless man, though in honor, does not remain; He is like the beasts that perish" (vs. 11,12). People exercise and eat right and take vitamins because they fear death. Young people think they're going to live forever but they may not be here next week. Indeed, death is an appointment that every person must keep.

Jesus also had an appointment with death. It is a fact that He was born to die. Death entered the earth when Adam sinned and God had to deal with it Himself. John 3:16 says, "For God so loved the world that He gave His only begotten Son." The death of Jesus was a gift to you from the Heavenly Father. This same verse says "that whoever believes in Him should not perish but have everlasting life." You must do more that acknowledge Him. You must believe in Him to receive eternal life. Most people believe in their doctor more than they believe in Jesus. They want proof before they'll believe in Him but never want proof that a doctor knows what he's doing. Death equalizes everybody and those who don't trust in Jesus will die a senseless death. Ps. 49:14 says, "Like sheep they are laid in the grave; Death shall feed on them; The upright shall have dominion over them in the morning; And their beauty shall be consumed in the grave, far from their dwelling." The Message Bible says, "They waste away to nothing - nothing left but a marker in a cemetery." The good news is that the kingdom of God has a vision that cannot be killed by death.

Death is so diabolical that God did something about it. He sent His Son to the cross and there He hung, forsaken by both God and man. It was the day before the Sabbath and Jewish law required that those who had been executed needed to be removed before sundown so as not to defile and pollute the land (Deut. 21:22,23). Normally, the Romans left their victims on the cross to rot as a warning to others. The Jews wanted to remove the bodies before sundown so they asked Pilate to speed up the death process by breaking the legs of the victims (John 19:31). Those who hung on a cross died not from the pain but from suffocation. In order to breathe, the person would have to lift up on their feet in order to do so. If their legs were broken, however, they wouldn't be able to lift themselves up. Their windpipe would then be cut off and they would suffocate. Pilate wants the matter to be over with and he quickly agrees to their request. The soldiers then broke the legs of the two criminals on either side of Jesus. By this time Jesus had already given up His spirit so His legs were not broken (vs. 33).

"But one of the soldiers pierced His side with a spear, and immediately blood and water came out" (John 19:34). This spear was five inches long at its base and the soldiers pierced Jesus to be assured that He was actually dead. John was an eye-witness to all this and he writes and tells how what happened to Jesus was a fulfillment of prophecy concerning the Messiah and His treatment at the hands of others (vs. 35-37). After this, a man named Joseph of Arimathea asked Pilate if he could take away the body of Jesus (vs. 38). Pilate gave his permission and it is surprising that he would let them do this. Normally, criminals would stay on the cross for several days and when taken down they'd be buried in a graveyard for criminals south of the city. There is no reason that Pilate would allow this to happen other than that prophesy might be fulfilled. Is. 53:9 says that Jesus would be buried with the rich. Joseph was a wealthy leader in Israel, a disciple of Jesus. By placing Jesus in his own tomb, the Son of God was buried in a rich man's grave and not the poor criminal's common grave.

John 19:41 says this tomb was in a garden. It was in a garden where sin entered the world, it was in another garden where the body of Jesus was laid to rest. This was a clean tomb where no one had yet been laid. Num. 19:9 tells how the ashes of a sacrificial heifer were also to be laid in a clean place. The body of Jesus was saturated with a hundred pounds of myrrh and aloes and was then wrapped with strips of linen. A huge round stone was rolled in front of the entrance to the tomb and here the Son of Man lay. Yes, His body was there but His spirit was long gone. Very little is said about what happened next and newer translations of the Bible tend to lead people to a different conclusion to what actually happened. The fact remains, Jesus died as a sinner separated from God and He went to the place where unforgiven sinners go. In Ex. 12:8 the sacrificed Passover lamb was to be "roasted in fire." Jesus is the Lamb of God and when He died He suffered the same fate as that original Passover lamb. He became a burnt offering in the fires of hell.

In Matt. 12:40 Jesus compared His death to Jonah being in the belly of a great fish for three days and three nights. Jonah 2:5,6 tells what happened, "The waters encompassed me, even to my soul; The deep closed around me; Weeds were wrapped around my head. I went down to the moorings of the mountains; The earth with its bars closed behind me forever." The Message Bible says, "Ocean gripped me and held tight. My head was all tangled in seaweed at the bottom of the sea where the mountains take root. I was as far down as a body can go, and the gates were slamming shut behind me forever." Jesus was not in Abraham's bosom for three days having a preaching party with the Old Testament saints who were there. That would come afterward but first Jesus had to suffer everything there is to suffer. Ps. 16:10 says the soul of Jesus went to Sheol and the Bible clearly teaches that this is a place of dread and torment. God said in Deut. 32:22 (NAS), "For a fire is kindled in My anger, and burns to the lowest part of Sheol."

The devil did not torment Jesus in hell because the devil isn't there. In hell Jesus absorbed the wrath of God the Father just like He did on the cross before He died. Ps. 88:3-7 (ESV) says, "For my soul is full of troubles, and my life draws near to Sheol. I am counted among those who go down to the pit; I am a man who has no strength. They have left me among the dead, and I lie like a corpse in a grave. I am forgotten, cut off from Your care. You have put me in the depths of the pit, in the regions dark and deep. Your wrath lies heavy upon me, and You overwhelm me with all your waves." The Message Bible says, "I'm battered senseless by Your rage, relentlessly pounded by Your waves of anger." People don't like to think about this so they make attempts to change the meaning of scripture saying Jesus never went to hell and suffered. What they fail to realize is that if it didn't happen to Jesus, then eventually it would happen to them. Theologians will argue that Jesus did not die spiritually. They think the price of sin was paid solely on the cross. If that were the case, the two thieves who hung next to Jesus could have paid the price for sin. No, Jesus died physically and then He died spiritually. He then suffered in hell separated from God.

Jesus tasted spiritual death for every man, woman, and child. Many people don't want to believe that but Jesus Himself said in Rev. 1:18, "I am He who lives, and was dead, and behold, I am alive forevermore." When you breathe your last breath physically, if you're saved you don't die but continue living on the other side. Jesus said in John 11:26, "Whoever lives and believes in Me shall never die." When Jesus said He was once dead, He was saying that He was once spiritually dead, separated from the Father. Thankfully, this spiritual death only lasted three days. Luke 16:19-31 tells how across from hell there was a place called "Abraham's bosom." Since the penalty for sin had not yet been paid, this place called "paradise" was where the Old Testament saints went when they died. After spending three days in the torments of hell, Jesus crossed over this great gulf and preached salvation to the Old

Testament saints. Eph. 4:8 says He then "led captivity captive." This means He led them up to heaven where He would sprinkle His blood on the heavenly mercy seat (Heb. 9:12-14). But first, on the way there, He stopped for a moment to have a conversation with Mary Magdalene.

"On the first day of the week Mary Magdalene came to the tomb early, while it was still dark, and saw that the stone had been taken away from the tomb" (John 20:1). Mary was from the city of Magdala which was on the western shore of the Sea of Galilee. She loved Jesus deeply for it was He who had cast seven demons out of her (Luke 8:13). History has portrayed Mary Magdalene as a prostitute and loose woman but nowhere in scripture does it say she was a sinful woman involved in sexual immorality. The Bible does say in this passage in Luke that she and a handful of other women traveled with Jesus and His disciples for two and a half years and provided for Him out of their own substance. It has been three days since Jesus had died and Mary could not stay away from the tomb any longer. She arrived in the dark, somewhere between 3 A.M. and 6 A.M., and to her shock and surprise she saw that the stone had been rolled away. She is not thinking Jesus was resurrected, she is thinking somebody stole His body and laid it somewhere else. Immediately she goes to tell Peter and John what happened.

Jesus had told all of them that He would rise again in three days. Why weren't they at the tomb waiting for Him to come out on His own? It still had not registered in their minds that this was going to happen. Their faith had been shaken by the arrest of Jesus and His ultimate death on the cross. If Jesus had been killed, they assumed they would be killed also. When tragedy strikes, people don't think, they react. The first person Mary went to was the man who had denied Jesus three days earlier. Peter had wept and repented of what he did and now he's back in the company of the other disciples. Peter and John both run to the tomb and John makes it clear that he arrived at the tomb first (John 20:4). Male competition didn't start in the present day culture. John outran Peter but stopped at the entrance to the tomb. Peter then arrived and in his typical impulsiveness went into the tomb. There he saw the grave clothes lying undisturbed and the facecloth folded nice and neat (vs. 6,7). Grave robbers would not have done this. The grave clothes looked as if Jesus had just disappeared out of them.

John then went into the tomb and took a long, careful look. He began to perceive and discern what had happened and vs. 8 says he believed. He didn't fully understand everything that had happened but he believed anyway, proving that faith is of the heart and not the mind. So what did they do? They went home. "For as yet they did not know the Scriptures that He must rise again from the dead. Then the disciples went away again to their own homes" (vs. 9,10). They should have stayed at the tomb because shortly thereafter Jesus shows up. Mary didn't leave but she stood outside the tomb weeping. This was a death wail, sobbing that comes from the depth of a broken heart. She then stooped down and looked into the tomb. "And she saw two angels in white sitting, one at the head and the other at the feet, where the body of Jesus had laid" (vs. 12). This is a spiritual analogy of the ark of the covenant. Ex. 25:19 says two angels were on top of the ark, one at each end, with the mercy seat between them. Today, Jesus is the ark of the covenant and there are two angels sitting where He had been laid.

Peter and John did not see these angels although they were probably there the entire time. Matt. 28:2 says the angel who rolled away the stone was outside sitting on it. Neither did they see this angel. Mary is weeping so hard that she doesn't recognize that these are angels. They ask why she's weeping and she says, "Because they have taken away my Lord, and I do not know where they have laid Him" (vs. 13). When she said this, she turned around and saw Jesus standing there. Remarkably, she did not know it was Him. How many times have people been so preoccupied with their sorrow that they don't know that Jesus is standing right there beside them? He asked her, "Woman, why are you weeping? Whom are you seeking?" (vs. 15). He asks the same question as the angels and she gives the same response. She thinks He's the gardener and she wants the body of Jesus back. Jesus breaks through her grief by calling her name. He said "Mary!" She now knows who He is. She recognized His voice for Jesus had once said, "My sheep hear My voice" (John 10:27). She turned and called Him "Rabboni!" which means "Teacher!" (vs. 16).

Jesus calls Mary by her name, she calls Him by His position in her life. What do you call Jesus? Master? Lord? Teacher? Savior? If you don't call Him by these names, you need to do it now before it's too late. Jesus said to her, "Do not cling to Me, for I have not yet ascended to My Father; but go to My brethren and say to them, 'I am ascending to My Father and your Father, and to My God and your God.'" This is the first time in scripture that Jesus called the disciples "My brethren." They are now joint-heirs with Jesus and so are you (Rom. 8:17). His Father is now your Father, His God is now your God. A question needs to be asked, "Where were all the Old Testament saints while this conversation was taking place?" As Jesus was talking to Mary Magdalene, they decided to take a walk around Jerusalem. Matt. 27:52,53 says, "And the graves were opened; and many bodies of the saints who had fallen asleep were raised; and coming out of the graves after His resurrection, they went into the holy city and appeared to many." Abraham, Joseph, Moses, David, and Daniel were among those walking around in the city. How amazing is that? Mary then obeyed Jesus and went and told the disciples what He had said to her (vs. 18).

Dan. 7:13,14 tells what happened when Jesus left Mary Magdalene and ascended into heaven, "I was watching in the night visions, and behold, One like the Son of Man, coming with the clouds of heaven! He came to the Ancient of Days, and they brought Him near before Him. Then to Him was given dominion and glory and a kingdom, that all peoples, nations, and languages should serve Him. His dominion is an everlasting dominion, which shall not pass away, and His kingdom the one that shall not be destroyed." The "clouds of heaven" are the Old Testament saints and the "Ancient of Days" is the Heavenly Father (vs. 9). The devil no longer has any dominion over you. It was taken away by Jesus two thousand years ago. Rom. 6:14 says, "For sin shall not have dominion over you, for you are not under law but under grace." Adam lost this authority but Jesus got it back. Paul said in Col. 2:15, "Having disarmed principalities and powers, He made a public spectacle of them, triumphing over them in it." The

Message Bible says, "He stripped all the spiritual tyrants in the universe of their sham authority at the Cross and marched them naked through the streets."

The resurrection is absolutely central to the entire gospel message. It is central to your faith in Christ because, without the resurrection, there would be no Christianity. 1 Cor. 15:14 (MSG) says, "If there's no resurrection, there's no living Christ." Jesus is the resurrection and the life (John 11:25). Because of the resurrection, you are now a fully adopted child of God. His resurrection becomes your resurrection. His victory over sin is your victory over sin. His victory over death and the grave is your victory over death and the grave. The darkness of Calvary lifted at the moment of the Lord's resurrection. The disciples, however, were still engulfed in that dark cloud of fear and unbelief and did not grasp what Jesus told them would happen. They are overwhelmed by an incorrect view of their circumstances and are in a state of despair and depression. Prov. 13:12 says, "Hope deferred makes the heart sick." The Message Bible says, "Unrelenting disappointment leaves you heartsick." Fortunately for them, Jesus steps into this mass of confusion.

That same evening the disciples were gathered together behind closed doors. Jesus had appeared to Mary Magdalene that morning and in between these times He led captivity captive and talked to the disciples on the road to Emmaus (Luke 24:13-32). The disciples are in hiding for they are in fear of the Jews, thinking they'll be killed just like Jesus was. It's a scary time when suddenly Jesus appears in their midst even though the doors were closed and locked (John 20:19). Something was different. Something had changed. A mere man can't walk through walls and closed doors. The fact that Jesus was there proves that He can go in your life where nobody else can go. He can go where your doctor can't go or your marriage counselor. There is not a part of your life where Jesus can't penetrate. Things unknown to you are known to Him. He understands you even during those times when you don't understand yourself. Everything about you is familiar territory to the risen Christ. The disciples are in danger and they are greatly afraid. It is into this fear that Jesus comes.

Jesus is standing in their midst. He didn't stand outside the door calling them to come out. No, He went where they were, proving that He is not a distant entity. He is a friend who sticks closer than a brother (Prov. 18:24). The disciples are startled and the first thing Jesus does is tell them to calm down. He says, "Peace be with you" (vs. 19). He then showed them His hands and His side to prove that it was really Him and not some ghost. He said to them again, "Peace to you! As the Father has sent Me, I also send you" (vs. 21). He then breathed on them and said, "Receive the Holy Spirit" (vs. 22). Jesus came to give His disciples three gifts. He gave them peace, purpose, and power. You can build your life on these three things knowing that lives are destroyed by conflict, weakness, and pointless living. You can build your life on peace with God, peace with yourself, and peace with others. You can have a purpose that satisfies your inner man from beginning to end. You can also have the power to do what you need to do in life. These three things will take you into eternity knowing you lived your life well.

Before you think about accomplishing anything with purpose or doing anything with power, you've got to first have peace with God. Before these frightened disciples were given purpose and power, Jesus first gave them peace. Rom. 5:1 says, "Therefore, having been justified by faith, we have peace with God through our Lord Jesus Christ." Jesus breathed on them to show that His life would come to them through the Holy Spirit. They didn't receive this power right then but this action was a living parable telling what would happen in Acts 2:2-4. Jesus then said, "If you forgive the sins of any, they are forgiven them; if you retain the sins of any, they are retained" (vs. 23). This is not the best translation of what Jesus was saying because, in truth, only God can forgive sin (Mark 2:7). What's happening here is the disciples are being given the authority to tell people their sins are forgiven when they accept Jesus. If the people reject Jesus, the disciples have the authority to tell them their sins are not forgiven. As an ambassador of Christ, you have this same commission, this same power, this same authority.

For some reason Thomas, called "the twin," was not with the other disciples when Jesus appeared to them. He's told that Jesus is alive but refused to believe unless he can first see the nail prints in His hands and put his hand into His side (vs. 24,25). So many people want proof that God exists before they'll believe in Him. How much proof do they need? All they have to do is go see the sun rise and set, the flower when it blossoms, and the stars at night (Heb. 11:3). Thomas does not believe but neither did the others at one time and, to be honest, neither did you. Thomas should not be continually condemned for this because a little humanity needs to be injected into this moment. He's afraid, confused, and disoriented and is in hiding like all the others. Eight days later the disciples are again behind locked doors. Jesus appears in their midst like He did last time and again says to them, "Peace to you!" (vs. 26). He tells Thomas to put his finger in the nail prints and in His side. Jesus knew what Thomas had said for He always hears what you say in secret. Thomas' fears melt away and he says to Jesus, "My Lord and my God!"

Have you ever seen Jesus with your own eyes? If not, do you believe in Him anyway? If so, Jesus says you are blessed. Jesus said, "Thomas, because you have seen Me, you have believed. Blessed are those who have not seen and yet have believed." This is the definition of faith. Surprisingly, John stops his narrative and tells the reason why he wrote his gospel message. He says Jesus did many more signs than what was recorded "but these were written that you may believe that Jesus is the Christ, the Son of God, and that believing you may have life in His name" (vs. 30,31). Matthew was written to show Jesus as the King of the Jews. Mark reveals Jesus as the Servant, the One who came to do the will of the Father. Luke describes Jesus as the perfect Man, and John presents Jesus as the Son of God. He is the Christ, the Anointed One. He was the Prophet who taught the Word of God and represented God to man. He was the Priest who offered Himself as a sacrifice and represented man to God. He is the great King, God's ruler over all the earth. He is the King of kings and Lord of lords.

John's gospel closes with an encounter between Jesus and seven of His disciples at the Sea of Galilee. This was the place where Peter lived and fished for a living. They went home instead of going to the mountain Jesus told them to go to (Matt. 28:10,16). They're not where they should be and they're not doing what they should be doing. They went fishing but Jesus called them to be fishers of men (Matt. 4:18,19). Peter said, "I am going fishing" and the other disciples joined him (John 21:3). In reality, he's saying he's going back to his old life, back to his comfort zone, back to what he's familiar with. He does this even though he knows Jesus is alive. They fished all night and caught nothing. They're failing at what they're trying to do and then Jesus shows up. He's on the shore and He calls out to them, "Children, have you any food?" (vs. 5). These are grown men who are rugged fishermen but Jesus calls them a Greek word that means, "lads; little boys up to seven years of age." They said no fish were caught and Jesus told them to cast the net on the right side of the boat and they would catch some. They didn't know it was Jesus but they did it anyway.

"So they cast, and now they were not able to draw it in because of the multitude of fish" (vs. 6). John said to Peter, "It is the Lord!" Peter put on his outer garment and plunged into the sea followed by the others in the boat. "Then, as soon as they had come to land, they saw a fire of coals there, and fish laid on it, and bread" (vs. 9). There are only two places in scripture where a charcoal fire is mentioned, here and when Peter stood in front of a charcoal fire warming himself the night he denied Jesus. Jesus then told them to bring some of the fish they had caught. Peter pulls the net to land and John points out specifically that there were one hundred and fifty-three fish caught in the net. In the Hebrew alphabet the numerical value of the word "Elohim" is one hundred fifty-three. Also, Jesus ministered personally to one hundred fifty-three people as recorded in scripture. There were also one hundred fifty-three known nations in the world at the time Jesus walked the earth. John also points out that the net was not broken and that was a miracle in itself. Jesus then said, "Come and eat breakfast" (vs. 12).

When they had finished eating, Jesus took Peter aside and began to privately talk to him. He said, "Simon, son of Jonah, do you love Me more than these?" (vs. 15). Jesus changed his name to Peter but here He calls him Simon. The word for "love" that Jesus used is "agape," a God-kind of love. Jesus asked, "Do you love Me with the highest form of love? Do you think you demonstrate love for Me more than all the others?" Peter responded and said, "Yes, Lord; You know that I love you." This love that Peter answered with is the Greek word "phileo" which is a brotherly love. It's a lot of love but not the love Jesus is asking for. Are you guilty of not loving Jesus the way He asks you to love Him? Jesus didn't criticize Peter's response but He answers with a command, "Feed My lambs." Jesus asks again, "Do you agape Me?" Peter responds a second time, "I phileo you." Jesus said, "Feed My sheep." He is telling Peter to take care of, feed, protect, and provide for young believers. Jesus then changed His question. He asks, "Do you phileo Me?" (vs. 17). Peter is now grieved and he answers, "Lord, you know all things; You know that I phileo You."

For the third time Jesus says, "Feed My sheep." Jesus is trying to restore Peter so He takes His finger and pokes it into the wound in Peter's heart. He's not trying to hurt Peter. He's trying to heal him. Jesus then tells Peter that in the future he will indeed follow his Lord and will ultimately hang on a cross just like He did. Jesus looks at him and said, "Follow Me" (vs. 19). Peter had failed Jesus but his failure was not final. God uses failures all the time. Abraham was a liar, Moses was a murderer, David was an adulterer, and Paul persecuted the church. Peter turns around and asks, "What about John?" (vs. 21). Jesus said don't worry about it. Focus on what God tells you to do and not on others. All believers have the responsibility to follow Jesus and use the spiritual gifts God gives them, gifts to lead, feed, and protect. John closes by saying Jesus did more things that if written down all the books in the world could not contain them all (vs. 24,25). John is saying that Jesus is so glorious, so majestic, so indescribable. He is truly a Man like no other.

Jesus: A Man Like No Other

Randall J. Brewer

www.ingramcontent.com/pod-product-compliance
Lightning Source LLC
Chambersburg PA
CBHW071258110526
44591CB00010B/710